Basic Legal Research

How to use your Connected Casebook

Step 1: Go to **www.CasebookConnect.com** and redeem your access code to get started.

Access Code: 

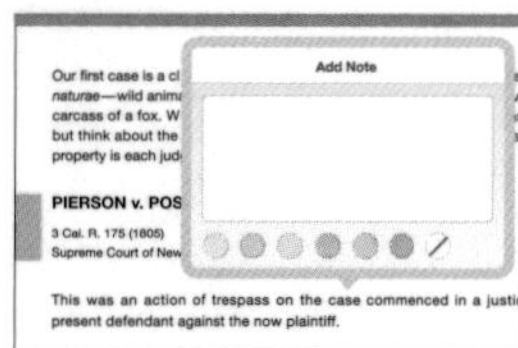

Step 2: Go to your **BOOKSHELF** and select your Connected Casebook to start reading, highlighting, and taking notes in the margins of your e-book.

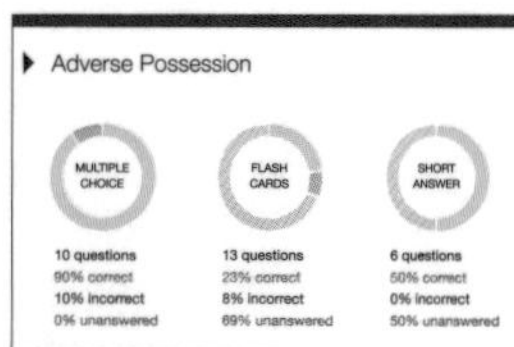

Step 3: Select the **STUDY** tab in your toolbar to access a variety of practice materials designed to help you master the course material. These materials may include explanations, videos, multiple-choice questions, flashcards, short answer, essays, and issue spotting.

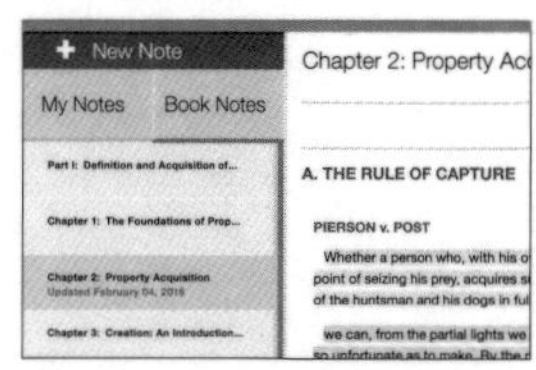

Step 4: Select the **OUTLINE** tab in your toolbar to access chapter outlines that automatically incorporate your highlights and annotations from the e-book. Use the My Notes area for copying, pasting, and editing your book notes or creating new notes.

Step 5: If your professor has enrolled your class, you can select the **CLASS INSIGHTS** tab and compare your own study center results against the average of your classmates.

Is this a used casebook? Access code already scratched off?

You can purchase the Digital Version and still access all of the powerful tools listed above.
Please visit CasebookConnect.com and select Catalog to learn more.

PLEASE NOTE: Each access code can only be used once. This access code will expire one year after the discontinuation of the corresponding print title and must be redeemed before then. CCH reserves the right to discontinue this program at any time for any business reason. For further details, please see the Casebook Connect End User Agreement.

PIN: 9111149709

66692

EDITORIAL ADVISORS

ASPEN COURSEBOOK SERIES

Basic Legal Research

TOOLS AND STRATEGIES

SEVENTH EDITION

Amy E. Sloan

Professor of Law
University of Baltimore School of Law

Published by Wolters Kluwer in New York.

Wolters Kluwer Legal & Regulatory U.S. serves customers worldwide with CCH, Aspen Publishers, and Kluwer Law International products. (www.WKLegaledu.com)

To contact Customer Service, e-mail customer.service@wolterskluwer.com, call 1-800-234-1660, fax 1-800-901-9075, or mail correspondence to:

Wolters Kluwer
Attn: Order Department
PO Box 990
Frederick, MD 21705

Printed in the United States of America.

1 2 3 4 5 6 7 8 9 0

ISBN 978-1-4548-9401-8

Library of Congress Cataloging-in-Publication Data

Names: Sloan, Amy E., 1964- author.
Title: Basic legal research : tools and strategies / Amy E. Sloan, Professor of Law, University of Baltimore School of Law.
Description: Seventh edition. | New York City : Wolters Kluwer, [2018] | Series: Aspen coursebook series | Includes bibliographical references and index.
Identifiers: LCCN 2018000453 | ISBN 9781454894018
Subjects: LCSH: Legal research--United States.
Classification: LCC KF240 .S585 2018 | DDC 340.072/073--dc23
LC record available at https://lccn.loc.gov/2018000453

About Wolters Kluwer Legal & Regulatory U.S.

Wolters Kluwer Legal & Regulatory U.S. delivers expert content and solutions in the areas of law, corporate compliance, health compliance, reimbursement, and legal education. Its practical solutions help customers successfully navigate the demands of a changing environment to drive their daily activities, enhance decision quality and inspire confident outcomes.

Serving customers worldwide, its legal and regulatory portfolio includes products under the Aspen Publishers, CCH Incorporated, Kluwer Law International, ftwilliam.com and MediRegs names. They are regarded as exceptional and trusted resources for general legal and practice-specific knowledge, compliance and risk management, dynamic workflow solutions, and expert commentary.

For Bebe

Summary of Contents

Contents

Preface

The seventh edition of *Basic Legal Research: Tools and Strategies* is fully updated and contains the following new material:

- **Updated sample pages and screen shots**—The annotated examples, screen shots, and sample pages have all been updated.
- **Updated coverage of online sources**—The text covers the latest releases of Lexis Advance, Westlaw, and Bloomberg Law, including Bloomberg Law's natural language searching, BCite citator, and Points of Law function. It also discusses other services such as Fastcase, Casetext, and govinfo.gov (the successor to the Federal Digital System as the official digital repository of federal documents).
- **Updated coverage of citation**—The text has been updated to cover both the ALWD Guide to Legal Citation (6th ed.) and the Bluebook (20th ed.).
- **Coverage that reflects both teaching needs and actual practice**—Several chapters have been reorganized to better align the text's coverage with the holdings in most law libraries. Many libraries have significantly reduced their print collections, making online sources the predominant focus of instruction. Chapter 4 (Secondary Source Research), Chapter 5 (Case Research), and Chapter 7 (Statutory Research) have been revised so that professors can skip print materials in classes that emphasize online research. For those who teach print research, the text retains thorough print coverage to give students a strong foundation in print research, as well as the information about print material necessary to understand legal citations.

The philosophy and the format of the seventh edition remain the same as those of earlier editions. The genesis of this book was a conversation I had with Todd Petit, a student in my Lawyering Skills class at Catholic University, in the fall of 1994. Todd was working on a research project, and he came to me in frustration and bewilderment over the research process. Over the course of the year, Todd ultimately mastered the skill of legal research. Nevertheless, our conversation that fall caused me to start thinking about how I could teach research more effectively, a process that ultimately culminated in this book.

I do not believe Todd's experience was unique. Mastering a skill is a form of experiential learning—learning that can be done only by doing. And the "doing" aspect necessarily involves periods of trial and error until a person grasps the skill. It is not surprising that this can be frustrating and even bewildering at times.

Having said that, however, even experiential learning has to be built on a base of information. My goal with this book is to provide two kinds of information necessary for students to learn the process of legal research: basic information about a range of research sources and a framework for approaching research projects.

This text provides instruction for using a variety of legal research sources, including secondary sources, cases and digests, citators, statutes, federal legislative history, and federal administrative regulations. Each of these sources is described in a separate chapter that includes the following components:

- introductory information about the source
- step-by-step instructions for print research
- an explanation of online research tools available for the source
- an explanation of citation rules for the source
- an annotated set of sample pages and screen shots illustrating the research process for the source
- a checklist summarizing both the research process and the key features of the source.

The range of material in each of these chapters is intended to accommodate a variety of teaching and learning styles. These chapters contain textual explanations, charts, and checklists that can be used for in-class discussions and for out-of-class reference as students are conducting research. In addition, the sample pages and screen shots illustrating the research process provide both instructional material and a useful summary synthesizing the information on the source from the rest of the chapter.

This text does more, however, than simply explain the bibliographic features of various research sources. It also provides instruction in research as a process, and it does this in two ways. First, Chapters 1–3 provide an overview of research sources and the research process. These chapters provide a framework for understanding the relationships among different types of legal authority, a method for generating and prioritizing search terms, and an overview of different approaches to searching. Through this material, these chapters set the stage for a process-oriented introduction to research instruction. Second, Chapter 11 provides a framework for creating a research plan. By setting out a process based on a series of questions students can ask to define the contours of any type of research project, it provides a flexible approach that can be adapted to a variety of assignments. Although Chapter 11 is the last chapter in the text, it can be used whenever students are required to develop a strategy for approaching a research project.

Most legal research is now accomplished online. The coverage of online research within each chapter devoted to an individual research source covers online search techniques specifically suited to that source. General techniques for conducting online research, however, appear in a separate chapter, Chapter 10. This chapter can be used in conjunction with other chapters at any point in the research course.

Moreover, the text provides instruction in a wide range of online research sources. It discusses research using commercial services such as Westlaw, Lexis Advance, and Bloomberg Law. But it also covers a range of other online research options, including subscription services and publicly available websites. As part of this instruction, the text discusses cost considerations so that students can learn to make informed decisions about when to use online sources and how to select the best online source for any research project.

This text seeks to provide students with not only the bibliographic skills to locate the legal authorities necessary to resolve a research issue, but also an understanding of research process that is an integral component of students' training in problem-solving skills. I hope this text will prove to be a useful guide to students as they undertake this intellectual challenge.

Amy E. Sloan
February 2018

Acknowledgments

Many people contributed to the seventh edition of this book. My thanks here will not be adequate for the assistance they provided. I want to thank the reference librarians at the University of Baltimore Law Library, especially Adeen Postar and Joanne Colvin. I am grateful to Shavaun O'Brien for her administrative support. A number of my colleagues at other schools contributed to this project by sharing their experiences in teaching with earlier editions, both by communicating with me directly and through anonymous reviews.

The people at Wolters Kluwer have been incredibly generous with their time and talents. Donna Gridley and her colleagues provided everything from moral support to editorial advice to production assistance. Their guidance and expertise contributed greatly to the content, organization, and layout of the text, and I am grateful for their assistance. I very much appreciate the assistance of everyone at The Froebe Group, my partners on this and many other projects, especially Maxwell Donnewald and Kathy Langone for their patience, skill, and good humor in the production process.

I want to thank my family and friends for their support, especially Peggy Metzger and Jack and Andrew Metzger-Sloan.

I would be remiss if I limited my acknowledgments to those who assisted with the seventh edition of the text because much of what appears here originated in the earlier editions. In particular, I would like to acknowledge Diana Donahoe, Susan Dunham, Lauren Dunnock, Lynn Farnan, Melanie Oberlin Knapp, Susan B. Koonin, Jan Levine, Carli Masia, Jaquetta Oram, Katie Rolfes, Herb Somers, Jessica Thompson, Robert Walkowiak III, and Michelle Wu for their work on earlier editions of the text.

I would also like to acknowledge the publishers who permitted me to reprint copyrighted material in this text:

Figure 4.1 Index to Am. Jur. 2d. Reprinted with permission from Thomson Reuters/West, *American Jurisprudence*, 2d Series, General Index (2017 Edition), p. 394 © Thomson Reuters/West.

Figure 4.2 Am. Jur. 2d main volume entry under "False Imprisonment." Reprinted with permission from Thomson Reuters/West, *American Jurisprudence*, 2d Ed., Vol. 32 (2007), p. 46. © 2007 Thomson Reuters/West.

Figure 4.3 Am. Jur. 2d pocket part entry for False Imprisonment. Reprinted with permission from Thomson Reuters/West, *American Jurisprudence*, 2d Series, Vol. 32 Cumulative Supplement (2017), p. 2. © 2017 Thomson Reuters/West.

Figure 4.4 ILP citation list. Reprinted with permission from H.W. Wilson. © 2017 H.W. Wilson. Reproduced with permission.

Figure 4.5 LegalTrac citation list from Gale. LegalTrac ©, a part of Cengage Learning, Inc. Reproduced by permission. www.cengage.com/permissions.

Figure 4.6 HeinOnline display of a legal periodical article from HeinOnline. © 2017 HeinOnline. Reproduced with permission.

Figure 4.8 A.L.R. annotation. Reprinted with permission from Thomson Reuters/West, *American Law Reports,* 4th Ser., Vol. 20 (1983), pp. 823-825 & 831. © 1983 Thomson Reuters/West.

Figure 4.9 Section of Am. Jur. 2d in Lexis Advance. © 2017 LexisNexis, a division of Reed Elsevier Inc. All rights reserved. LexisNexis and the Knowledge Burst logo are registered trademarks of Reed Elsevier Properties Inc. and are used with the permission of LexisNexis.

Figure 4.10 Portion of an A.L.R. annotation in Westlaw. A.L.R. annotation in Westlaw © 2017 Thomson Reuters/West. Reproduced with permission.

Figure 4.11 Restatement search options in Bloomberg Law. Reprinted with permission from Bloomberg Law. © 2017 by the Bureau of National Affairs, Inc. (800) 372-1033, www.bna.com.

Figure 4.12 Section 35 of the Restatement (Second) of Torts, Rules and Appendix Volumes. Reprinted with permission from Bloomberg Law. © 2017 by the Bureau of National Affairs, Inc. (800) 372-1033, www.bna.com.

Figure 5.2 *Padilla-Mangual v. Pavia Hosp.*, 516 F.3d 29-30 (1st Cir. 2008). Reprinted with permission from Google Scholar. © 2008 Google Scholar.

Figure 5.3 *Padilla-Mangual v. Pavia Hosp.*, 516 F.3d 29 (1st Cir. 2008). Reprinted with permission from Thomson Reuters/West, *West's Federal Reporter*, 3d Ser., Vol. 516 (2008), Pp. 29-34. © 2008 Thomson Reuters/West.

Figure 5.4 Beginning of the West topic for "Domicile". Reprinted with permission from Thomson Reuters/West, *West's Federal Practice Digest*, 5th Ser., Vol. 160 (2015), p. 1121. © 2015 Thomson Reuters/West.

Figure 5.5 Case Summary under the "Domicile" topic, Key Number 1. Reprinted with permission from Thomson Reuters/West, *West's Federal Practice Digest*, 4th & 5th Ser., February 2017 Pamphlet, p. 1238. © 2017 Thomson Reuters/West.

Figure 5.9 Example of a case in Westlaw. Reprinted with permission of Thomson Reuters/West, from Westlaw, 516 F.3d 29-30. © 2017 Thomson Reuters/West.

Figure 5.10 Example of a case in Lexis Advance. © 2017 LexisNexis, a division of Reed Elsevier Inc. All rights reserved. LexisNexis and the Knowledge Burst logo are registered trademarks of Reed Elsevier Properties Inc. and are used with the permission of LexisNexis. Lexis Advance, 516 F.3d 29.

Figure 5.11 Example of a case in Bloomberg Law, 516 F.3d 29. Reprinted with permission from Bloomberg Law, © 2017 by the Bureau of National Affairs, Inc. (800) 372-1033, www.bna.com.

Figure 5.12 Search results in Fastcase. Reprinted with permission of Fastcase. © 2017 Fastcase, Inc.

Figure 5.13 Search results in Casetext. Reprinted with permission of Casetext. © 2017 Casetext, Inc.

Figure 5.15 Descriptive-word index. Reprinted with permission from Thomson Reuters/West, *West's Federal Practice Digest*, 4th Ser., Vol. 97A (2002), p. 550. © 2002 Thomson Reuters/West.

Figure 5.16 Key Number Outline, "Domicile" topic. Reprinted with permission from Thomson Reuters/West, *West's Federal Practice Digest*, 5th Ser., Vol. 160 (2015), p. 1121. © 2015 Thomson Reuters/West.

Figure 5.17 Case summaries under "Domicile" topic. Reprinted with permission from Thomson Reuters/West, *West's Federal Practice Digest*, 5th Ser., Vol. 160 (2015), p. 1122. © 2015 Thomson Reuters/West.

Figure 5.18 Digest volume, pocket part. Reprinted with permission from Thomson Reuters/West, *West's Federal Practice Digest*, 5th Ser., Pocket Part, Vol. 160 (2016), p. 190. © 2016 Thomson Reuters/ West.

Figure 5.19 West Key Number search options and results. Westlaw search results © 2017 Thomson Reuters/West. Reproduced with permission.

Figure 5.20 Results of a word search in Lexis Advance. © 2017 LexisNexis, a division of Reed Elsevier Inc. All rights reserved. LexisNexis and the Knowledge Burst logo are registered trademarks of Reed Elsevier Properties Inc. and are used with the permission of LexisNexis.

Figure 5.21 Results of a word search in Bloomberg Law. Reprinted with permission from Bloomberg Law, © 2017 by the Bureau of National Affairs, Inc. (800) 372-1033, www.bna.com.

Figure 5.22 *Padilla-Mangual v. Pavia Hosp.*, 516 F.3d 29 (1st Cir. 2008). Reprinted with permission from Thomson Reuters/West, *West's Federal Reporter*, 3d Ser., Vol. 516 (2008), Pp. 29-34. © 2008 Thomson Reuters/West.

Figure 6.1 Case with Shepard's® summary. © 2017 LexisNexis, a division of Reed Elsevier Inc. All rights reserved. LexisNexis and the Knowledge Burst logo are registered trademarks of Reed Elsevier Properties Inc. and are used with the permission of LexisNexis.

Figure 6.3 Shepard's® entry excerpt for 165 Ohio App. 3d 699. © 2017 LexisNexis, a division of Reed Elsevier Inc. All rights reserved. LexisNexis and the Knowledge Burst logo are registered trademarks of Reed Elsevier Properties Inc. and are used with the permission of LexisNexis.

Figure 6.4 Shepard's® entry for 165 Ohio App. 3d 699, citing decisions grid view. © 2017 LexisNexis, a division of Reed Elsevier Inc. All rights reserved. LexisNexis and the Knowledge Burst logo are registered trademarks of Reed Elsevier Properties Inc. and are used with the permission of LexisNexis.

Figure 6.5 Headnote 9 from the original case, *Uddin v. Embassy Suites Hotel.* © 2017 LexisNexis, a division of Reed Elsevier Inc. All rights reserved. LexisNexis and the Knowledge Burst logo are registered trademarks of Reed Elsevier Properties Inc. and are used with the permission of LexisNexis.

Figure 6.6 Shepard's® entry excerpt for *Uddin v. Embassy Suites Hotel.* © 2017 LexisNexis, a division of Reed Elsevier Inc. All rights reserved. LexisNexis and the Knowledge Burst logo are registered trademarks of Reed Elsevier Properties Inc. and are used with the permission of LexisNexis. LexisNexis, 165 Ohio App. 3d 699, Headnote 9; Shepard 's entry for 165 Ohio App. 3d 699.

Figure 6.7 *Davis v. Accor North America, Inc.*, citing *Uddin v. Embassy Suites Hotel.* © 2017 LexisNexis, a division of Reed Elsevier Inc. All rights reserved. LexisNexis and the Knowledge Burst logo are registered trademarks of Reed Elsevier Properties Inc. and are used with the permission of LexisNexis. *Davis v. Accor N. Am., Inc.*, 2010 U.S. Dist. Lexis 40057.

Figure 6.8 KeyCite tabs and status flag. Reprinted with permission from Thomson Reuters/West, From Westlaw, 165 Ohio App. 3d 699. © 2017 Thomson Reuters/West.

Figure 6.10 KeyCite "Negative treatment" tab. Reprinted with permission from Thomson Reuters/West, From Westlaw, 165 Ohio App. 3d 699. © 2017 Thomson Reuters/West.

Figure 6.11 KeyCite "History" Tab. Reprinted with permission from Thomson Reuters/West, from Westlaw, KeyCite entry for 165 Ohio App. 3d 699. © 2017 Thomson Reuters/West.

Figure 6.12 KeyCite "Citing references" tab. Reprinted with permission from Thomson Reuters/West, From Westlaw, KeyCite Entry for 165 Ohio App. 3d 699. © 2017 Thomson Reuters/West.

Figure 6.14 KeyCite filtering options. Reprinted with permission from Thomson Reuters/West, from Westlaw, KeyCite Entry for 165 Ohio App. 3d 699. © 2017 Thomson Reuters/West.

Figure 6.16 BCite display. Reprinted with permission from Bloomberg Law. © 2017 by the Bureau of National Affairs, Inc. (800) 372-1033, www.bna.com.

Figure 6.17 Shepard's® display. © 2017 LexisNexis, a division of Reed Elsevier Inc. All rights reserved. LexisNexis and the Knowledge Burst logo are registered trademarks of Reed Elsevier Properties Inc. and are used with the permission of LexisNexis. Shepard's® Entry for 165 Ohio App. 3d. 699.

Figure 6.18 KeyCite display. Reprinted with permission from Thomson Reuters/West, from Westlaw, KeyCite Entry for 165 Ohio App. 3d 699. © 2017 Thomson Reuters/West.

Figure 6.19 BCite display. Reprinted with permission from Bloomberg Law, BCite entry for 165 Ohio App. 3d 699. © 2017 by the Bureau of National Affairs, Inc. (800) 372-1033, www.bna.com.

Figure 7.4 18 U.S.C.A. § 915. Reprinted with permission from Thomson Reuters/West, United States Code Annotated, Title 18 (2015), pp. 723-724. © 2015 Thomson Reuters/West.

Figure 7.6 Chapter outline in Title 18. Reprinted with permission from Thomson Reuters/West, United States Code Annotated, Title 18 (2015), p. 683. © 2015 Thomson Reuters/West.

Figure 7.7 Pocket part update for 18 U.S.C.A. § 915. Reprinted with permission from Thomson Reuters/West, United States Code Annotated, 2017 Supplement, Title 18, p. 34. © 2017 Thomson Reuters/West.

Figure 7.8 Excerpt from 18 U.S.C.A. § 915 in Westlaw. Reprinted with permission from Thomson Reuters/West, from Westlaw, 18 U.S.C.A. § 915. © 2017 Thomson Reuters/West.

Figure 7.9 Westlaw U.S.C.A. Table of contents and search options. Reprinted with permission from Thomson Reuters/West, From Westlaw, U.S.C.A. table of contents screen. © 2017 Thomson Reuters/West.

Figure 7.10 Excerpt from 18 U.S.C.S. § 915 in Lexis Advance. © 2017 LexisNexis, a division of Reed Elsevier Inc. All rights reserved. LexisNexis and the Knowledge Burst logo are registered trademarks of Reed Elsevier Properties Inc. and are used with the permission of LexisNexis. From Lexis Advance, 18 U.S.C.S. § 915.

Figure 7.11 Lexis Advance U.S.C.S. table of contents. © 2017 LexisNexis, a division of Reed Elsevier Inc. All rights reserved. LexisNexis and the Knowledge Burst logo are registered trademarks of Reed Elsevier Properties Inc. and are used with the permission of LexisNexis, U.S.C.S table of contents.

Figure 7.12 18 U.S.C. § 915 in Bloomberg Law. Reprinted with permission from Bloomberg Law. © 2017 by the Bureau of National Affairs, Inc. (800) 372-1033, www.bna.com.

Figure 7.13 Excerpt from Maryland Code Annotated General Index. Reprinted with permission from Thomson Reuters/West, *West's Annotated Code of Maryland*, 2017 General Index M-Z, p. 1154. © 2017 Thomson Reuters/West.

Figure 7.14 Code section. Reprinted with permission from Thomson Reuters/West, *West's Annotated Code of Maryland*, Transportation Volume, pp. 270-71. © 2010 Thomson Reuters/West.

Figure 7.15 Chapter outline and code section. Reprinted with permission from Thomson Reuters/West, *West's Annotated Code of Maryland*, Transportation Volume, p. 269. © 2010 Thomson Reuters/West.

Figure 7.16 Pocket part entry for Maryland Transportation Code § 20-102. Reprinted with permission from Thomson Reuters/West, *West's Annotated Code of Maryland*, Transportation Volume, 2017 Cumulative Annual Pocket Part, p. 137-138. © 2017 Thomson Reuters/West.

Figure 7.17 *West's Annotated Code of Maryland* index. Reprinted with permission from Thomson Reuters/West, from Westlaw, statutory index for *West's Annotated Code of Maryland*. © 2017 Thomson Reuters/West.

Figure 7.18 Maryland Transportation Code § 20-102. Reprinted with permission from Thomson Reuters/West, From Westlaw, *West's Annotated Code of Maryland*, Transportation Code § 20-102. © 2017 Thomson Reuters/West.

Figure 7.19 Outline of Title 20, Maryland Transportation Code. Reprinted with permission from Thomson Reuters/West, From Westlaw, *West's Annotated Code of Maryland*, Transportation Code Title 20 Outline. © 2017 Thomson Reuters/West.

Figure 7.20 Related code section. Reprinted with permission from Thomson Reuters/West, From Westlaw, *West's Annotated Code of Maryland*, Transportation Code Title 20 § 20-102. © 2017 Thomson Reuters/West.

Figure 7.21 Lexis Advance search results. © 2017 LexisNexis, a division of Reed Elsevier Inc. All rights reserved. LexisNexis and the Knowledge Burst logo are registered trademarks of Reed Elsevier Properties Inc. and are used with the permission of LexisNexis. From Lexis Advance, statutory search results.

Figure 7.22 Maryland Transportation Code § 20-102. © 2017 LexisNexis, a division of Reed Elsevier Inc. All rights reserved. LexisNexis and the Knowledge Burst logo are registered trademarks of Reed Elsevier Properties Inc. and are used with the permission of LexisNexis. From Lexis Advance, *Maryland Code Annotated*, Transportation Code § 20-102.

Figure 7.23 Bloomberg Law search results. Reprinted with permission from Bloomberg Law. © 2017 by the Bureau of National Affairs, Inc. (800) 372-1033, www.bna.com.

Figure 8.1 "How a Bill Becomes a Law." Reprinted with permission from *Guide to Congress*, CQ Press, 7th Ed. (2013), P. 1364. © 2013 CQ Press, an imprint of Sage Publications, Inc.

Figure 8.2 Excerpt from annotations accompanying 18 U.S.C.A. § 2441. Reprinted with permission from Thomson Reuters/West, *United States Code Annotated*, Vol. 18 (2015), p. 202. © 2015 Thomson Reuters/West.

Figure 8.3 Starting page, House Judiciary Committee Report on the War Crimes Act of 1996. Reprinted with permission from Thomson Reuters/West, *United States Code Congressional and Administrative News*, 104th Congress—Second Session 1996, Vol. 5 (1997), p. 2166. © 1997 Thomson Reuters/West.

Figure 8.7 HeinOnline *Sources of Compiled Legislative Histories* entry. Reproduced with permission of HeinOnline. © 2017 HeinOnline.

Figure 8.8 Search options for congressional publications in ProQuest Legislative Insight. Reprinted with permission of Proquest © 2017 ProQuest Congressional.

Figure 9.2 Annotations to 42 U.S.C.S. § 300v-1. © 2017 LexisNexis, a division of Reed Elsevier Inc. All rights reserved. LexisNexis and the Knowledge Burst logo are registered trademarks of Reed Elsevier Properties Inc. and are used with the permission of LexisNexis. United States Code Service, Title 42 Public Health and Welfare (2011) §§ 300f-300aa-34, p. 337.

Basic Legal Research

CHAPTER 1

Introduction to Legal Research

A. Introduction to the legal system

B. Introduction to the process of legal research

C. Introduction to research planning

D. Introduction to legal citation

E. Overview of this text

What is legal research and why do you need to learn about it? Researching the law means finding the rules that govern conduct in our society. To be a successful lawyer, you need to know how to research the law. Lawyers are often called upon to solve problems and give advice, and to do that accurately, you must know the rules applicable to the different situations you and your clients will face. Clients may come to you after an event has occurred and ask you to pursue a remedy for a bad outcome, or perhaps defend them against charges that they have acted wrongfully. You may be asked to help a client accomplish a goal like starting a business or buying a piece of property. In these situations and many others, you will need to know your clients' rights and responsibilities, as defined by legal rules. Consequently, being proficient in legal research is essential to your success in legal practice.

As a starting point for learning about how to research the law, it is important to understand some of the different sources of legal rules. This chapter discusses what these sources are and where they originate within our legal system. It also provides an introduction to the process of legal research, an overview of some of the research tools you will learn to use, and an introduction to legal citation. Later chapters explain how to locate legal rules using a variety of resources.

A. INTRODUCTION TO THE LEGAL SYSTEM

1. SOURCES OF LAW

There are four main sources of law, which exist at both state and federal levels:

- constitutions;
- statutes;
- court opinions (also called cases);
- administrative regulations.

A constitution establishes a system of government and defines the boundaries of authority granted to the government. The United States Constitution is the preeminent source of law in our legal system, and all other rules, whether promulgated by a state or the federal government, must comply with its requirements. Each state also has its own constitution. A state's constitution may grant greater rights than those secured by the federal constitution, but because a state constitution is subordinate to the federal constitution, it cannot provide lesser rights than the federal constitution does. All of a state's legal rules must comport with both the state and federal constitutions.

Since grade school, you have been taught that the U.S. Constitution created three branches of government: the legislative branch, which makes the laws; the judicial branch, which interprets the laws; and the executive branch, which enforces the laws. State governments are also divided into these three branches. Although this is elementary civics, this structure truly does define the way government authority is divided in our system of government.

The legislative branch of government creates statutes, which must be approved by the executive branch (the president, for federal statutes; the governor, for state statutes) to go into effect. The executive branch also makes rules. Administrative agencies, such as the federal Food and Drug Administration or a state's department of motor vehicles, are part of the executive branch. They execute the laws passed by the legislature and create their own regulations to carry out the mandates established by statute.

The judicial branch is the source of court opinions. Courts interpret rules created by the legislative and executive branches of government. If a court determines that a rule does not meet constitutional requirements, it can invalidate the rule. Otherwise, however, the court must apply the rule to the case before it. Court opinions can also be an independent source of legal rules. Legal rules made by courts are called "common-law" rules. Although courts are empowered to make these rules, legislatures can adopt legislation that changes or abolishes a common-law rule, as long as the legislation is constitutional.

Figure 1.1 shows the relationships among the branches of government and the types of legal rules they create.

An example may be useful to illustrate the relationships among the rules created by the three branches of the federal government. As you know, the U.S. Constitution, through the First Amendment, guarantees the right to free expression. Congress could pass legislation requiring television stations to provide educational programming for children. The Federal Communications Commission (FCC) is the administrative agency within the executive branch that would have responsibility for carrying out Congress's will. If the statute were not specific about what constitutes educational programming or how much educational programming must be provided, the FCC would have to create administrative regulations to execute the law. The regulations would provide the information not detailed in the statute, such as the definition of educational programming. A television station could challenge the statute and regulations by arguing to a court that prescribing the content of material the station must broadcast violates the First Amendment. The court would then have to interpret the statute and regulations to decide whether they comport with the Constitution.

Another example illustrates the relationship between courts and legislatures in the area of common-law rules. The rules of negligence have largely been created by the courts. Therefore, liability for negligence is usually determined by common-law rules. A state's highest court could decide that a plaintiff who sues a defendant for negligence cannot recover any damages if the plaintiff herself was negligent and contributed to her

FIGURE 1.1 BRANCHES OF GOVERNMENT AND LEGAL RULES

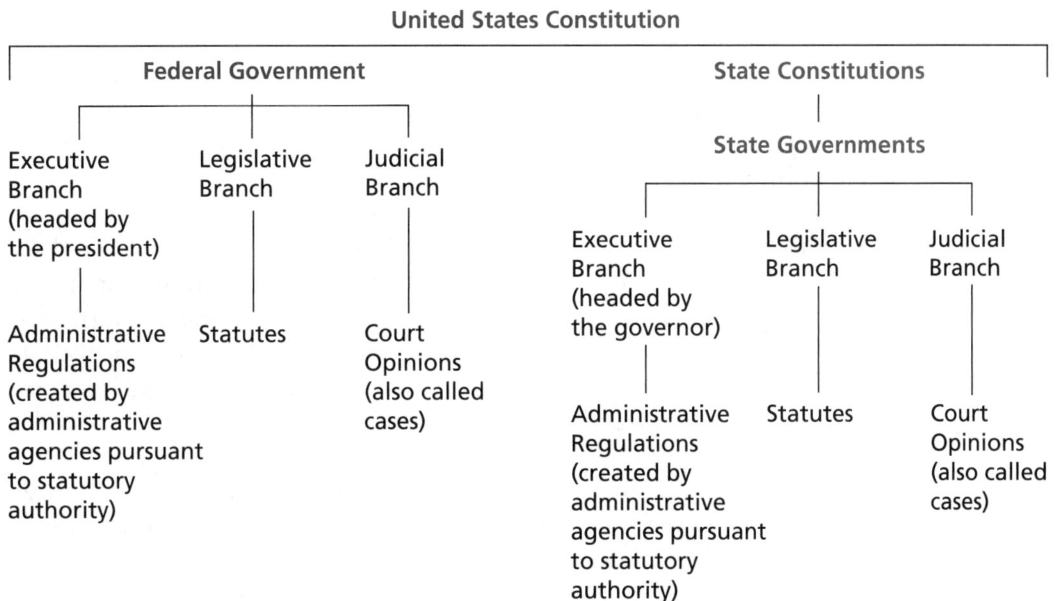

own injuries. This decision would create a common-law rule governing future cases of negligence within that state. The state legislature could step in and pass a statute that changes the rule. For example, the legislature could enact a statute providing that juries are to determine the percentage of negligence attributable to each party and to apportion damages accordingly, instead of completely denying recovery to the plaintiff. Courts in that state would then be obligated to apply the rule from the statute, not the former common-law rule.

Although these examples are simplified, they demonstrate the basic roles of each of the branches of government in enunciating the legal rules governing the conduct of society. They also demonstrate that researching a legal issue may require you to research several different types of legal authority. The answer to a research question may not be found exclusively in statutes or court opinions or administrative regulations. Often, these sources must be researched together to determine all the rules applicable to a research issue.

2. TYPES AND WEIGHT OF AUTHORITY

a. Types of authority

One term used to describe the rules that govern conduct in society is "authority." "Authority," however, is a broad term that can describe both legal rules that must be followed and other types of information that are not legal rules. To understand the weight, or authoritative value, an authority carries, you must learn to differentiate "primary" authority from "secondary" authority and "binding" authority from "nonbinding" authority.

Primary authority is a term used to describe a source of a rule of law. All of the sources of rules discussed so far in this chapter are primary authorities. Constitutional provisions, statutes, cases, and administrative regulations contain legal rules, and as a consequence, are primary authorities. Because "the law" consists of legal rules, primary authority is sometimes described as "the law."

Secondary authority, by contrast, refers to commentary on the law or analysis of the law, but not "the law" itself. An opinion from the U.S. Supreme Court is a primary authority, but an article written by a private party explaining and analyzing the opinion is a secondary authority. Secondary authorities are often quite useful in legal research because their analysis can help you understand complex legal issues and refer you to primary authorities. Nevertheless, a secondary authority is not "the law" and therefore is distinguished from a primary authority.

Binding and nonbinding authority are terms courts use to categorize the different sources of law they use in making their decisions. Binding authority, which can also be called mandatory authority, refers to an authority that the court is obligated to follow. A binding authority contains one or more rules that you must apply to determine the correct answer to your research question. Nonbinding authority, which can also be called persuasive authority, refers to an authority that the court may follow if it is persuaded to do so, but is not required to follow. A nonbinding authority, therefore, will not dictate the answer to your research question, although it may help you figure out the answer. Whether an authority is binding or nonbinding depends on several factors, as discussed in the next section.

b. Weight of authority

The degree to which an authority controls the answer to a legal question is called the weight of the authority. Not all authorities have the same weight. The weight of an authority depends on its status as primary or secondary, as well as its status as binding or nonbinding.

An authority's status as a primary or secondary authority is fixed. An authority is either part of "the law," or it is not. Anything that does not fit into one of the categories of primary authority is secondary authority. Distinguishing primary authority from secondary authority is the first step in determining how much weight a particular authority has in the resolution of your research question. Then you can determine whether the authority is binding or nonbinding.

(1) Secondary authority: always nonbinding

Once you identify an authority as secondary, you can be certain that it will not control the outcome of the question you are researching because all secondary authorities are nonbinding. Nevertheless, some are more persuasive than others. Some are so respected that a court, while not technically bound by them, would need a good reason to depart from or reject their statements of legal rules. Others do not enjoy the same degree of respect, leaving a court free to ignore or reject such authorities if it is not persuaded to follow them. Further discussion of the persuasive value of various secondary authorities appears in Chapter 4. The important thing to remember for now is that secondary authorities are always categorized as persuasive or nonbinding.

(2) Primary authority: sometimes binding, sometimes nonbinding

Sometimes a primary authority is a binding, or mandatory, authority, and sometimes it is not. You must be able to evaluate the authority to determine whether it is binding on the question you are researching.

One factor affecting whether a primary authority is binding is jurisdiction. A rule contained in a primary authority applies only to conduct occurring within the jurisdiction in which the authority is in force. For example, all laws in the United States must comport with the federal Constitution because it is a primary authority that is binding, or mandatory, in all United States jurisdictions. The New Jersey constitution is also a primary authority because it contains legal rules establishing the scope of state government authority, but it is binding authority only in New Jersey. The New Jersey constitution's rules do not apply in Illinois or Michigan.

Determining the weight of a case is a little more complex. All cases are primary authorities. Whether a particular case is binding or non-binding is a function not only of jurisdiction, but also level of court. To understand how these factors work together, it is easiest to consider level of court first and jurisdiction second.

(i) *Determining the weight of a case: level of court*

The judicial branches of government in all states and in the federal system have multiple levels of courts. Trial courts are at the bottom of the judicial hierarchy. In the federal system, the United States District Courts are trial-level courts, and each state has at least one federal district court. Intermediate appellate courts hear appeals of trial court cases. Most, but not all, states have intermediate appellate courts. In the federal system, the intermediate appellate courts are called United States Courts of Appeals, and they are divided into 13 separate circuits: 11 numbered circuits (First through Eleventh), the District of Columbia Circuit, and the Federal Circuit. The highest court or court of last resort is often called the supreme court. It hears appeals of cases from the intermediate appellate courts or directly from trial courts in states that do not have intermediate appellate courts. In the federal system, of course, the court of last resort is the U.S. Supreme Court.

Trial court opinions, including those from federal district courts, bind the parties to the cases but do not bind other trial courts considering similar cases, nor do they bind courts above them in the court structure. They are usually nonbinding, or persuasive, authority.

The opinions of intermediate appellate courts bind the courts below them. In other words, intermediate appellate cases are binding authorities for the trial courts subordinate to them in the court structure. The weight of intermediate appellate cases on the intermediate appellate courts themselves varies. In jurisdictions with multiple appellate divisions, the opinions of one division may or may not be binding on other divisions. In addition, in some circumstances, intermediate appellate courts can overrule their own prior opinions. Intermediate appellate cases are nonbinding authorities for the court of last resort.

The court of last resort may, but is not required to, follow the opinions of the courts below it. Its opinions, however, are binding authorities for both intermediate appellate courts and trial courts subordinate to the court of last resort in the court structure. The court of last resort is not bound by its own prior opinions but will be reluctant to change an earlier ruling without a compelling justification.

Figure 1.2 illustrates the structures of federal and state court systems and shows how the level of court affects the weight of cases.

FIGURE 1.2 **STRUCTURE OF THE FEDERAL COURT SYSTEM AND MOST STATE COURT SYSTEMS**

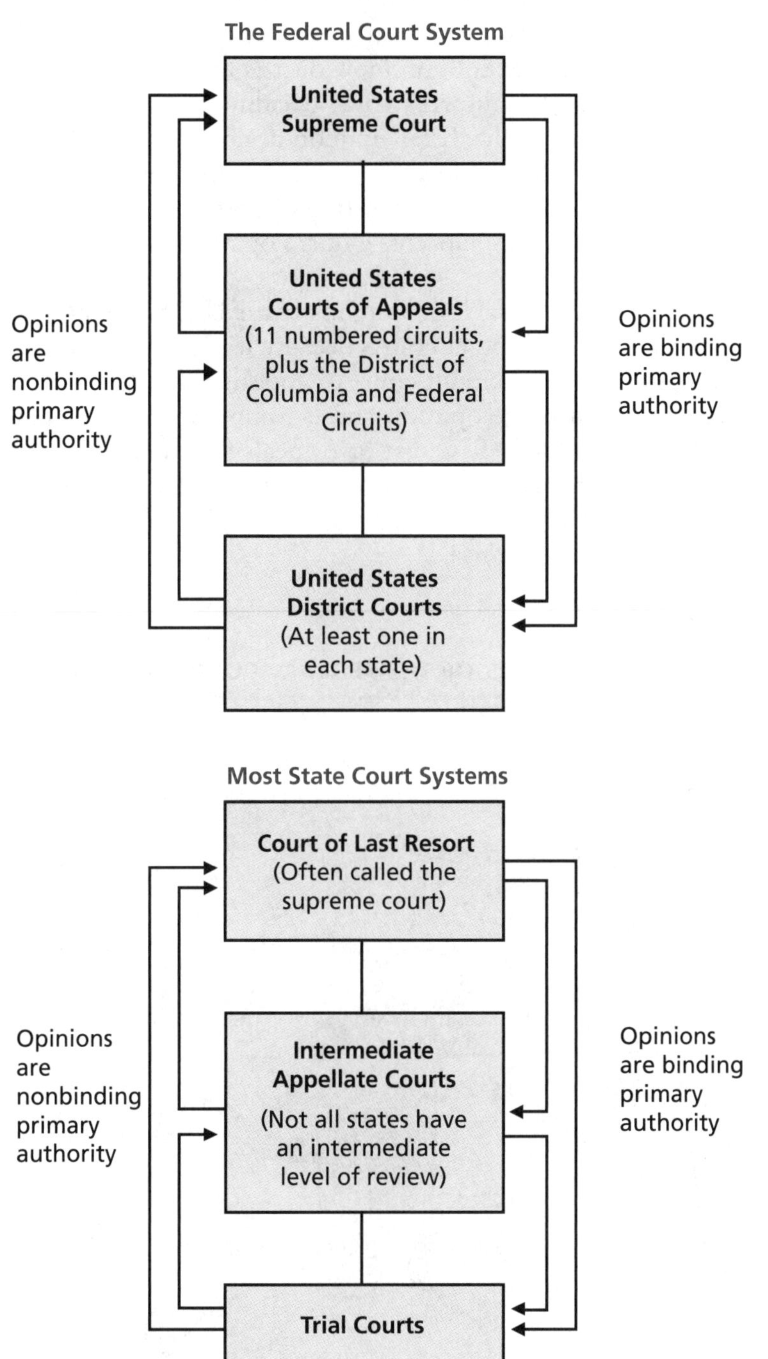

(ii) *Determining the weight of court opinions: jurisdiction*

The second factor affecting the weight of court opinions is jurisdiction. As with other forms of primary authority, rules stated in court opinions are binding authority only within the court's jurisdiction. An opinion from the Texas Supreme Court is binding only on a court applying Texas law. A California court deciding a question of California law would consider the Texas opinion nonbinding authority. If the California court had to decide a new issue not previously addressed by binding California authority (a "question of first impression"), it might choose to follow the Texas Supreme Court's opinion if it found the opinion persuasive.

On questions of federal law, opinions of the U.S. Supreme Court are binding authority for all other courts because it has nationwide jurisdiction. An opinion from a circuit court of appeals is binding only within the circuit that issued the opinion and is nonbinding everywhere else. Thus, a decision of the U.S. Court of Appeals for the Eleventh Circuit would be binding within the Eleventh Circuit, but not within the Seventh Circuit. **Figure 1.3** shows the geographic boundaries of the federal circuit courts of appeals.

FIGURE 1.3 GEOGRAPHICAL BOUNDARIES OF THE FEDERAL COURTS OF APPEALS

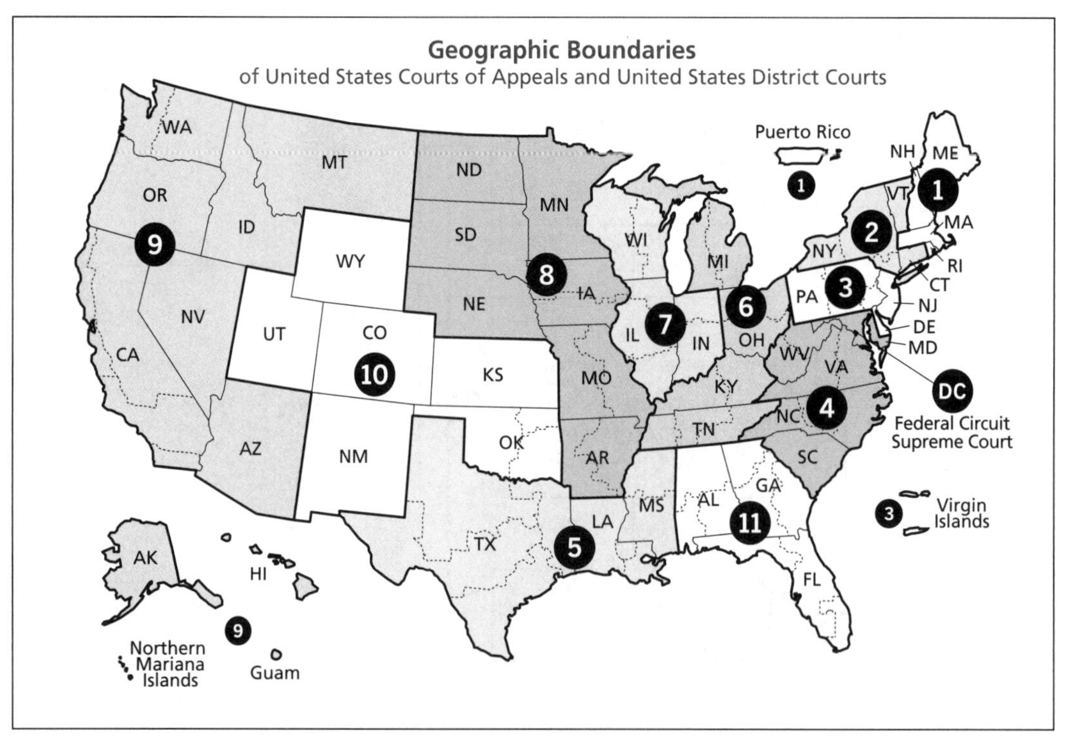

In considering the weight of a court opinion, it is important to remember that the federal government and each state constitute different jurisdictions. On questions of state law, each state's courts get the last word, and on questions of federal law, the federal courts get the last word. For an issue governed by state law, the opinions of the courts within the relevant state are mandatory authority. For an issue governed by federal law, the opinions of the relevant federal courts are binding authority.

Ordinarily, understanding how jurisdiction affects the weight of authority is fairly intuitive. When a Massachusetts trial court resolves a case arising out of conduct that took place in Massachusetts, it will treat the opinions of the Massachusetts Supreme Judicial Court as binding authority. Sometimes, however, a court has to resolve a case governed by the law of another jurisdiction. State courts sometimes decide cases governed by the law of another state or by federal law. Federal courts sometimes decide cases governed by state law. When that happens, the court deciding the case will treat the law of the controlling jurisdiction as binding authority.

For example, assume that the U.S. District Court for the Western District of Texas, a federal trial court, has to decide a case concerning breach of a contract to build a house in El Paso, Texas. Contract law is, for the most part, established by the states. To resolve this case, the federal court will apply the contract law of the state where the dispute arose, in this case, Texas. The Texas Supreme Court's opinions on contract law are binding authority for resolving the case. Now assume that the same court has to decide a case concerning immigration law. Immigration law is established by the federal government. To resolve the case, the court will apply federal law. The opinions of the U.S. Supreme Court and the U.S. Court of Appeals for the Fifth Circuit are binding authority for resolving the case.

This discussion provides an overview of some common principles governing the weight of authority. These principles are subject to exceptions and nuances not addressed here. Entire fields of study are devoted to resolving questions of jurisdiction, procedure, and conflicts regarding which legal rules apply to various types of disputes. As you begin learning about research, however, these general principles will be sufficient to help you determine the weight of the authority you locate to resolve a research issue.

Figure 1.4 illustrates the relationships among the different types of authority.

FIGURE 1.4 **TYPES OF AUTHORITY**

TYPE OF AUTHORITY	BINDING (MANDATORY)	NONBINDING (PERSUASIVE)
PRIMARY (legal rules)	Constitutional provisions, statutes, and regulations in force within a jurisdiction are binding authority for courts within the same jurisdiction.	Decisions from courts within one jurisdiction are nonbinding authority for courts in other jurisdictions.
	Decisions from higher courts within a jurisdiction are binding authority for lower courts within the same jurisdiction.	Decisions from lower courts within a jurisdiction are nonbinding authority for higher courts within the same jurisdiction.
SECONDARY (anything that is not primary authority; usually commentary on the law)	Secondary authority is *not* binding authority.	Secondary authority is nonbinding authority.

B. INTRODUCTION TO THE PROCESS OF LEGAL RESEARCH

Imagine that you are standing in the parking lot at Disney World. You have a key in your hand, but you have no idea which car it starts. The key is not much use to you unless you have some way of figuring out which car it starts. The more information you can gather about the car, the easier the car will be to find. Knowing the make, model, or color would narrow the options. Knowing the license plate number would allow you to identify the individual vehicle.

Understanding the mechanics of using various legal research tools is like having that key in your hand. You have to know the features of the research tools available to you to conduct research, just as you must have the key to start the car. But that is not enough to make you an effective researcher. Effective legal research combines mastery of the mechanics of research with legal problem-solving skills. The research process is part of the reasoning process. It is not a rote task you complete before you begin to evaluate an issue. Rather, it is an analytical task in which you narrow the field of all legal information available to the subset of information necessary to assess an issue. As you locate and evaluate information, you will learn about the issue you are researching, and that knowledge will help you determine both whether you have located useful information and what else you should be looking for to complete your understanding of the issue.

To understand the process of research, you must first understand how legal information is organized. Most, if not all, of the authorities you will learn to research are available from a variety of sources. They may be published in print, online, or in both formats. Online research services that provide access to legal publications include commercial databases that charge a fee for access and websites freely available to anyone. Of course, you can obtain legal information from a general search engine like Google or a general source of information like Wikipedia, but lawyers often conduct legal research with more specialized tools.

Most legal information is organized by type of authority and jurisdiction. In print, this means individual types of authority from individual jurisdictions are published in separate sets of books. Court opinions from Maryland will be in one set of books (called "reporters"), and those from Massachusetts will be in another set of reporters. The same holds true for print collections of statutes and other types of legal authority.

Online research tools are organized similarly. Some are like print sets of books in that they provide access to one type of authority from one jurisdiction. The website for the Arizona Supreme Court, for example, contains only Arizona Supreme Court opinions. Others provide access to multiple types of authority from many different jurisdictions. Although these services aggregate a wide range of legal authority, they generally subdivide their contents much like print sources into individual databases organized by jurisdiction and type of authority. There are many commercial and government sources that provide online access to legal authority.

Westlaw and Lexis Advance are the best known online legal research services. Bloomberg Law is another online provider. All three are commercial databases that allow you to access all of the types of legal authority discussed in this chapter. They charge subscribers for use of their services, although your law school undoubtedly subsidizes the cost of student research while you are in school. Other commercial and free research services you may encounter in law school include Fastcase, Casemaker, Findlaw, and Cornell Law School's Legal Information Institute, among others. They provide access to many of the same types of authorities you can find in Lexis Advance and Westlaw. You will also learn about federal, state, and local government websites you can use for legal research.

The organization of legal information by jurisdiction and type of authority affects the way individual legal authorities are identified. All legal authorities have citations assigned to them. The citation is the identifying information you can use to retrieve a document from a book or database. Thus, if you have the citation to an authority, you can locate it using that identifying information. To return to the key analogy, this is like knowing the state and license plate number of the car you are trying to locate in the parking lot.

Citations were originally formulated so that researchers could find authorities in print. Although most authorities are now available online, they are still primarily identified by their print citations. In print research, the citation generally includes the name of the book in which the source is published, the volume of the book containing the specific item, and the page or section number where the item begins. For example, each court opinion is identified by a citation containing the volume number of the reporter in which it is published, the name of the reporter, and the starting page of the opinion. If you had the citation for a case, you could go to the library or get online and locate it easily. Statutes, secondary sources, and other forms of authority also have citations you can use to retrieve specific documents.

Of course, with most research projects, you will not know the citations to the authorities you need to find. You will have been assigned the project to find out which legal authorities, if any, pertain to the subject of your research issue. Moreover, although occasionally you will need to locate only one specific item, such as a specific case, more often you will need to collect a range of authorities that pertain to the issue, such as a statute and cases that have interpreted the statute. Therefore, you will need to narrow the field of all legal information to that subset of information necessary to analyze your research issue.

You will generally narrow the field of information using two types of criteria: general document characteristics and specific content. General document characteristics include the jurisdiction and type of authority (e.g., cases, statutes, secondary sources). By narrowing the field of information to documents with particular characteristics, you can identify binding authority relevant to your research issue. Focusing on documents that contain specific content is another way to narrow the field to information relevant to your research question. Although you will usually use both types of criteria in conducting research, the order in which you use them affects your research process.

With some research tools, you must determine jurisdiction and type of authority before you begin to look for content related to your research issue because the information available is organized into separate books or databases according to jurisdiction and type of authority. In other words, you filter the available information by source first and then identify relevant content within each source. When you filter first by source, you use a source-driven approach to research.

FIGURE 1.5 **SOURCE-DRIVEN AND CONTENT-DRIVEN APPROACHES TO RESEARCH**

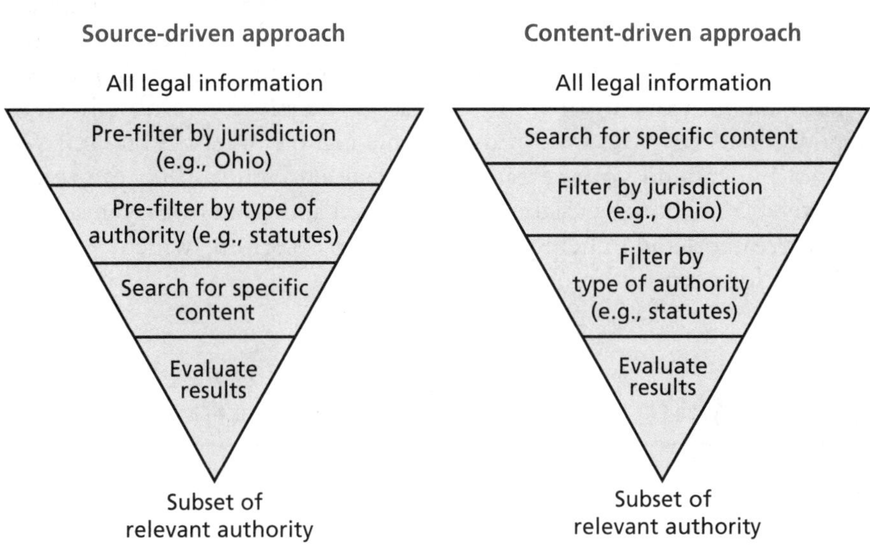

With some online services, including Westlaw, Lexis Advance, and Bloomberg Law, you can, but do not have to, filter by jurisdiction or type of authority before you execute a search. You have the option of searching for content related to your research issue first and then filtering the results by jurisdiction, type of authority, or both. When you filter first by content, you use a content-driven approach to research.

With either approach, once you locate information, you must evaluate the results of your research to determine whether the information you have found is useful. The source-driven and content-driven approaches are illustrated in **Figure 1.5**.

One question you may have is whether it is better to use a source- or content-driven approach. The answer depends on the nature of your research project and your level of expertise about the subject matter. With a source-driven approach, you have to think carefully about a research issue to figure out which type(s) of authority are most likely to contain relevant information. Although selecting a type of authority can be challenging, choosing specific types of authority to research can make it easier to analyze the results because they are confined to the particular type of authority you selected. In addition, a savvy researcher may know exactly what type of authority governs—such as a state statute—and may not want to bother filtering through other types of authority included in the results. Conversely, if you are not sure which type(s) of authority to use, you may miss some relevant material altogether if it is in a source you did not consider using.

Because the content-driven approach allows you to search without first selecting a source, it shifts much of the analytical work involved in research to filtering the search results. This can be an advantage because the search results can include sources you might not have considered using. On the other hand, this approach frequently retrieves a large amount of information that has to be sifted carefully. Retrieving hundreds or thousands of documents can feel overwhelming if you do not understand your research issue well enough to filter the results effectively. Chapter 3 explains source-driven and content-driven searching in greater detail to help you learn how to determine which approach is better for your research project.

C. INTRODUCTION TO RESEARCH PLANNING

The chapters that follow explain how to use a range of research tools to locate various types of legal authority. As noted above, however, knowing the mechanics of the research tools available to you is only part of learning to be an effective researcher. To research effectively, you must incorporate your technical knowledge into a research plan so that you can find the information you need to analyze your research issue. To do this, you will want to proceed in an organized manner to make sure your research is accurate and complete. Chapter 11, Developing a Research Plan, explores research planning in depth. This introduction to the planning process will help provide context as you learn the features of various research tools.

When you have a research task to complete, you will ordinarily proceed as follows:

- Define the scope of your research project and the issue(s) you need to research.
- Generate a list of search terms specific to your research issue(s).
- Plan your research path for each issue.
- Execute your research plan to search for relevant information.
- Assess the information you find and update your research to ensure that all the information is current.
- Revise your search terms and research plan as necessary and repeat the search process to complete your understanding of your research issue(s).

It is always a good idea to define the scope of your project before searching for information. Think about what you are being asked to do. Are you being asked to spend three weeks locating all information from every jurisdiction on a particular subject, or do you have a day to find out how courts in one state have ruled on an issue? Will you write an extensive analysis of your research, or will you summarize the results orally to the person who made the assignment? Evaluating the type of work product you are expected to produce, the amount of time you have, and the scope of the project will help you determine the best way to proceed.

You should also think carefully about the issue(s) you are being asked to research. Sometimes you will be asked to research a specific issue. Sometimes you will be presented with a research scenario and asked to determine the issue(s) it presents. It sounds almost silly to say this, but knowing what you are looking for will make it easier to find what you need.

Once you have defined your research task, you will need to generate search terms to use to search for information. Chapter 2 discusses different ways to do this. In general, however, you will need to construct a list of words or concepts to use to search for relevant content.

You will then want to plan your research path. The more you know about your research issue going in, the easier it will be to plan your research process. The less you know, the more flexible you will need to be in your approach. One of the goals of this text is to help you learn to plan your research path and assess the appropriate starting, middle, and ending points for your research.

Your ultimate goal in most research projects will be to locate binding primary authority, if it exists, on your research issue. Thus, regardless of whether you use a source- or content-driven approach, at some point you must consider type of authority and jurisdiction because these two factors determine whether the information you have located is binding primary authority. If binding primary authority is not available or does not directly answer your research question, nonbinding authority (either primary or secondary) may help you analyze the issue. Therefore, in planning your research path, it may be helpful for you to think about three categories of authority: binding primary authority, nonbinding primary authority, and secondary authority.

Because your goal will usually be to locate binding primary authority, you might think that that should be the starting point for all your research. In fact, if you know a lot about the issue you are researching, you might begin with binding primary authority, but that is not always the case. Secondary authorities that cite, analyze, and explain the law can provide a very efficient way to obtain background information and references to primary authority. Although secondary authorities are not controlling in your analysis, they are invaluable research tools and can be a good starting point for your project. Nonbinding primary authority will rarely provide a good starting place because it provides neither the controlling rules nor analysis explaining the law. **Figure 1.6** shows the relationships among these three categories of authority.

FIGURE 1.6 **WHERE TO BEGIN YOUR RESEARCH PROJECT**

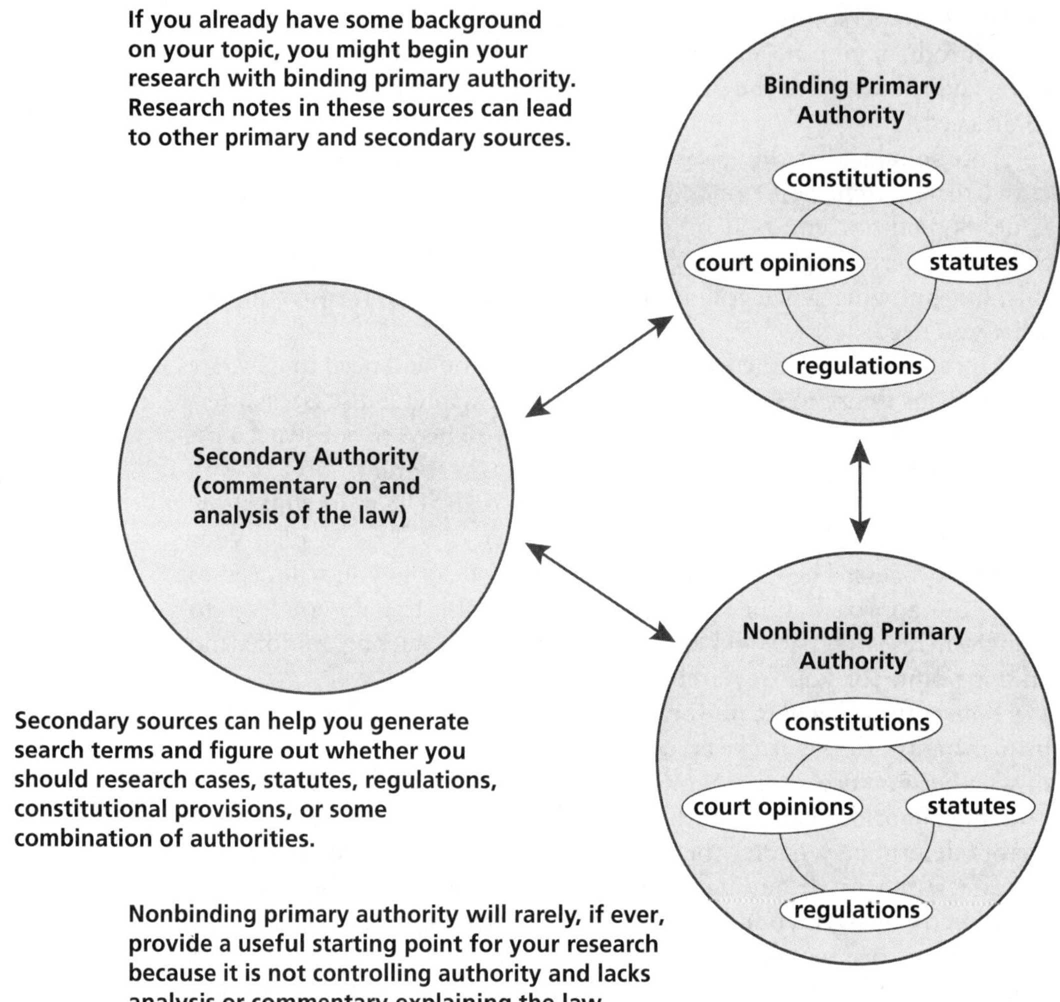

Many research sources contain notes that refer to other sources, so once you locate one relevant source, you may be able to use the research notes to find additional useful information. Thus, there may be more than one appropriate starting point for your research. This text explains the features of a wide range of research sources so you can learn to make this assessment for different types of research projects.

Once you have planned your research path, you will execute your plan to search for information. As you locate information, you will need to evaluate its relevance to your research issue. One important aspect of assessing the information you find is making sure it is up to date. The law can change at any time. New cases are decided; older cases may be overruled; statutes can be enacted, amended, or repealed. Therefore, keeping your research current is essential. One way to update your research is with a specialized research tool called a citator, which is explained in Chapter 6. In addition, most sources of legal information will indicate how recently they have been updated to help you assess whether the information is current.

Most print research sources consist of hardcover books that can be difficult to update when the law changes. Some print resources are published in chronological order. For those resources, new books are published periodically as new material is compiled. Many, however, are organized by subject. For those resources, publishers cannot print new books every time the law changes. This would be prohibitively expensive, and because the law can change at any time, the new books would likely be out of date as soon as they were printed. To keep the books current, therefore, many print sources are updated with softcover pamphlets containing new information that becomes available after the hardcover book is published. These supplementary pamphlets are often called "pocket parts" because many of them fit into a "pocket" in the inside back cover of the hardcover book. The hardcover book and the pocket part will each indicate the period of time it covers. You will see pocket parts mentioned throughout this text in reference to print research tools.

Online sources also usually contain publication or revision date information that you can use to assess how current it is. Online sources can be updated easily in the sense that new information can be added and older information revised at any time and as frequently as necessary. Westlaw, Lexis Advance, and Bloomberg Law update at least some of their content on a daily basis. Providers other than major commercial vendors may not update their content as frequently. In addition, updates for some content may only become available when the print version of the source is updated, which means the online version may only be as current as the latest print version. No matter how you locate information, you must pay careful attention to the date of any information you find.

Because research is not a linear process, you may find that you have to revise your search terms or your research plan to complete your work. If you do not find any information, or find too much information, you may need to backtrack or rethink your approach. Even if you find relevant information from the start, what you learn when you assess that information may take you in new directions. The process of searching, reading, and assessing will continue until you have narrowed the field of all legal information to the subset of information necessary to evaluate your research issue. This text explains a variety of search strategies you can use to tailor your research process to the specific issue you are researching.

D. INTRODUCTION TO LEGAL CITATION

When you present the results of your research in written form, you will need to include citations to the legal authorities you have found. Rules for formatting legal citations appear in *The Bluebook: A Uniform System of Citation* (20th ed. 2015) and the *ALWD Guide to Legal Citation* (6th ed. 2017). Citation formats are the same using either source. Any minor differences are typically addressed in online updates to maintain consistency between both manuals. You should use whichever citation manual your professor directs you to use.

This section provides a brief overview of the organization of both citation manuals and will make the most sense if you have your citation manual in front of you as you read. Later chapters contain instructions for citing individual sources of legal authority.

1. THE *BLUEBOOK*

The *Bluebook* is available in print and online. Both versions contain the same citation rules. The online version offers search options unavailable in the print version. Additionally, it allows you to bookmark commonly used rules and add your own annotations to the rules, tasks you would otherwise need to do manually with a print *Bluebook.* The online version also requires an annual subscription fee, whereas a print *Bluebook* requires only a single purchase. Most of the discussion in this section applies equally to the print and online versions of the *Bluebook,* but a few variations are noted.

The first part of the *Bluebook* that you should review is the Introduction. This section explains how the *Bluebook* is organized. As you will see when you review the Introduction, the *Bluebook* contains two sets of instructions for citing authority: "basic" citation rules used in legal practice and more complex rules used for citations in scholarly publications such as law journals, a type of secondary source discussed in more detail in Chapter 4. The "basic" citation rules apply to the types of documents most students write in their first year of law school, such as briefs, memoranda, and other documents used in legal practice. The remainder of the citation rules apply primarily to law journals, although some aspects of these rules also apply to practice documents. You are unlikely to write documents in law journal format at the beginning of your legal studies; therefore, you will want to focus your attention on the format for citations in briefs, memoranda, and other similar legal documents.

Learning to cite authority using the *Bluebook* requires you to become familiar with five items:

- the Bluepages and corresponding Bluepages Tables;
- the citation rules in the Rules section of the *Bluebook;*

- the Tables;
- the finding tools for locating individual citation rules (i.e., Table of Contents and Index; Quick Reference guides in print; Quick Style Guide and search features online);
- *Bluebook* updates.

THE BLUEPAGES AND CORRESPONDING BLUEPAGES TABLES

The Bluepages section contains the rules for citing legal authority in briefs, memoranda, and legal documents other than law journals. This section contains general information applicable to any type of citation, such as the placement of citations in legal documents. It also contains specific instructions for citing cases, statutes, secondary sources, and other forms of authority, as well as examples of many types of citations. The Bluepages Table BT1 contains the abbreviations for words commonly found in the titles of court documents. In addition, some courts require special citation formats for authorities cited in documents filed with those courts. Table BT2 refers you to sources for local citation rules. In print, the Bluepages appear at the beginning of the *Bluebook.* Online, use the **Bluepages** link to review the outline of the Bluepages rules.

THE TEXT OF THE CITATION RULES

Most of the *Bluebook* is devoted to explaining the rules for citing different types of authority. In print, the Rules section appears in the white pages in the middle of the *Bluebook.* Online, use the **Rules** link. These rules can be divided into five categories:

1. Rules 1 through 9 are general rules applicable to a citation to any type of authority. For example, Rule 5 discusses the proper format for quotations.
2. Rules 10 through 17 contain rules for citing various primary and secondary authorities published in print. For example, Rule 10 explains how to cite a court opinion, and Rule 12 explains how to cite a statute.
3. Rule 18 contains rules for citing authorities published online.
4. Rule 19 contains rules for citing authorities published in services for researching law related to specific subject areas.
5. Rules 20 and 21 contain rules for citing foreign and international materials.

Some of the material contained in the Rules section also appears in the Bluepages. If the information you need for the authority you are citing is contained in the Bluepages, you may not need to consult the individual rules in the Rules section. If you face a citation question not addressed in the Bluepages, however, you should consult the individual rules for more detailed guidance. Most of the rules for citing specific types of legal authority begin with a description of the elements necessary for a full citation. The remainder of the rule will explain each component in greater detail.

Most rules are accompanied by example citations showing the format for citing various authorities. These examples are not always in the same typeface required for a citation used in a memorandum or other practice document. The examples in the Rules section are in the typefaces required for law journals, which are not always used in other types of legal documents. Therefore, although the examples in the Rules section will be somewhat useful to you in understanding how to cite legal authority, you cannot rely on them exclusively. The instructions in Bluepages B2 explain the differences between typeface conventions for citations in law journals and other documents.

THE TABLES

In print, the Tables appear in the white pages with blue edges at the back of the *Bluebook*. Use the **Tables** link online. The citation rules in the Bluepages and Rules sections of the *Bluebook* explain the general requirements for different types of citations. Often they require that certain words be abbreviated. The Tables contain abbreviations necessary for proper citations. For example, Table T1 lists each jurisdiction in the United States, and under each jurisdiction, it shows the proper abbreviations for citations to that jurisdiction's cases and statutes. Whenever you have a citation that includes an abbreviation, you will need to check the appropriate Table to find the precise abbreviation required for a proper citation. You should note, however, that the type styles of some of the abbreviations in the Tables are in law journal format and may need to be modified according to Bluepages B2 for the work you will produce in your first year of law school.

THE FINDING TOOLS FOR LOCATING INDIVIDUAL RULES

As noted above, the Bluepages should be your starting point for determining how to construct a citation in *Bluebook* format. If you cannot find what you need in the Bluepages, you can find individual citation rules in the Rules section using the Table of Contents or the Index. In print, the Index references in black type refer to the pages with relevant rules. Those in blue type refer to examples of citations. The online Index refers only to rule and table numbers, not page numbers.

In the print version, you can also refer to the Quick Reference examples of different types of citations on the inside front and back covers. The examples on the inside front cover are in the format for law review and journal footnotes and will be of little or no use to you in your first year of law school. The examples on the inside back cover are in the proper format for the types of documents you are likely to draft in your first year.

The online version does not contain the Quick Reference examples. It has a Quick Style Guide with limited citation examples formatted for law review and journal footnotes. Although these examples may be of limited use to you in your first year, they are different from those in the print Quick Reference and are available to view without a subscription. Additionally, the search box at the top of the screen allows you to do a basic search of *Bluebook* content. You can, as noted above, bookmark frequently used rules and add annotations to the rules. With an Advanced Search, you can tailor a search more specifically to target rules, examples, and tables, as well as your bookmarked rules and annotations.

■ ***BLUEBOOK* UPDATES**

You will find updates to the *Bluebook* on the *Bluebook* website. Updates (as well as the online Table of Contents, Index, and Quick Style Guide) are available without a subscription, so you will want to look for updates whether you use the *Bluebook* in print or online. The URL for the *Bluebook's* online resources appears in Appendix A at the end of this text.

All of the pieces of the *Bluebook* work together to help you determine the proper citation format for a legal authority:

1. Use the Bluepages to find citation instructions governing the authority you want to cite.
2. If the Bluepages do not contain all the information you need for the citation, use the Index, Table of Contents, Quick Reference guides (in print) or search functions (online) to find the relevant rule in the Rules section.
3. Use the Tables to find abbreviations and other information necessary for a complete citation.
4. If necessary, convert the typefaces in the examples and Tables into the proper format for briefs and memoranda according to Bluepages B2.

As you read the remaining chapters in this text, you will find more specific information about citing individual legal authorities. In general, however, you will be able to use the *Bluebook* to figure out how to cite almost any type of authority by following these four steps.

2. THE *ALWD GUIDE*

The *ALWD Guide* is a print publication. Although it is available as a Kindle e-book, it is not published online through a dedicated website the way the *Bluebook* is. The first part of the *ALWD Guide* that you should review is Part 1, Introductory Material. This section explains what citations are and how to use them, how to use the *ALWD Guide,* how local citation rules can affect citation format, and how your word processing settings may affect citations. It explains the *ALWD Guide's* organization, so it would be redundant to repeat all of that information here. Nevertheless, a few comments on the *ALWD Guide* may be useful as you begin learning about it.

The *ALWD Guide* is organized differently than the *Bluebook* in that the *ALWD Guide* incorporates information on citations for practice documents and scholarly publications together within each citation rule. The *Bluebook,* by contrast, largely separates rules for practice documents into the Bluepages, as explained above. When you are using the *ALWD Guide,* you do not need to refer to a separate set of rules for different types of documents.

As you will see when you review Part 1, learning to cite authority using the *ALWD Guide* requires you to become familiar with five items:

- the finding tools for locating individual citation rules (Table of Contents and Index);
- the text of the citation rules;
- the Appendices;
- the "Fast Formats" and "Snapshots";
- the *ALWD Guide* website.

■ THE TABLE OF CONTENTS AND INDEX

To locate individual citation rules, you can use the Table of Contents at the beginning of the *ALWD Guide* or the Index at the end. Unless otherwise indicated, the references in the Index are to rule numbers, not page numbers or specific examples.

■ THE TEXT OF THE CITATION RULES

Most of the *ALWD Guide* is devoted to explaining the rules for citing different types of authority. The rules are divided into the following Parts:

1. Part 2 (Rules 1 through 11) contains general rules applicable to a citation to any type of authority. For example, Rule 3 discusses spelling and capitalization.
2. Part 3 (Rules 12 through 29) contains rules for citing various primary and secondary authorities. For example, Rule 12 explains how to cite a court opinion, and Rule 14 explains how to cite a statute.
3. Part 4 (Rules 30 through 33) contains rules for citing online sources.
4. Part 5 (Rules 34 through 37) contains rules for incorporating citations into documents.
5. Part 6 (Rules 38 through 40) contains rules regarding quotations.

In each citation rule in Parts 3 and 4, you will find a description of the elements necessary for a full citation to an authority, followed by an annotated example showing how all of the elements fit together to create a complete citation. You should read this part of the rule first. The remainder of the rule will explain each component in greater detail.

Within the text of each rule in the *ALWD Guide,* you will find cross-references to other citation rules and to Appendices containing additional information that you may need for a complete citation. An explanation of the Appendices appears below.

You will also find "Sidebars" in some rules. The "Sidebars" are literally asides on citation. They provide information about sources of legal authority, help you avoid common citation errors, and offer citation tips.

■ THE APPENDICES

The *ALWD Guide* contains seven Appendices that follow the Parts containing the citation rules. The citation rules in Parts 3 and 4 explain the general requirements for citations to different types of authority. Most of these rules require that certain words be abbreviated. Appendices 1, 3, 4, and 5 contain abbreviations necessary for proper citations. For example, Appendix 1 lists Primary Sources by Jurisdiction. It lists each jurisdiction in the United States, and under each jurisdiction, it shows the proper abbreviations for citations to that jurisdiction's cases, statutes, and other primary authorities. Whenever you have a citation that includes an abbreviation, you will need to check the appropriate Appendix to find the precise abbreviation required for a proper citation.

Appendix 2 contains references to local court citation rules. As noted above, some courts require special citation formats for authorities cited in documents filed with those courts. The *ALWD Guide* provides information on these local rules in Appendix 2.

Appendix 6 contains information on citations to federal taxation materials, and Appendix 7 contains information on selected federal administrative publications.

■ THE "FAST FORMATS" AND "SNAPSHOTS"

Before the text of each rule for citing an individual type of authority in Parts 3 and 4, you will find a section called "Fast Formats." The "Fast Formats" provide citation examples for each rule, in addition to the examples interwoven with the text of the rule. A "Fast Formats Locator" appears on the inside front cover of the *ALWD Guide.* You can use this alphabetical list to find "Fast Formats" pages without going to the Table of Contents or Index.

"Snapshots" also accompany the citation rules for some of the most commonly cited types of legal authority. "Snapshots" are annotated sample pages from sources of law that show you where to find the components of a full citation within the document.

■ THE *ALWD GUIDE* WEBSITE

Updates to the *ALWD Guide* are posted online (and updates to the Kindle e-book are made automatically). The URL for the *ALWD Guide* website is listed in Appendix A at the end of this text.

All of the pieces of the *ALWD Guide* work together to help you determine the proper citation format for a legal authority:

1. Use the Table of Contents or Index to find the rule governing the authority you want to cite.
2. Read the rule, beginning with the components of a full citation at the beginning of the rule.
3. Use the Appendices to find additional information necessary for a correct citation.
4. Use the "Fast Formats" and "Snapshots" preceding the rule for additional examples and information.
5. If necessary, check the website for any updates.

As you read the remaining chapters in this text, you will find more specific information about citing individual legal authorities. In general, however, you will be able to use the *ALWD Guide* to figure out how to cite almost any type of authority by following these five steps.

E. OVERVIEW OF THIS TEXT

Because different research projects have different starting and ending points, it is not necessary for you to follow all of the chapters in this text in order. The sequence of assignments in your legal research class will determine the order in which you need to cover the material.

Although you may not cover the chapters in order, a brief overview of the organization of this text may provide useful context for the material that follows. As noted earlier, Chapter 2 discusses how to generate search terms, one of the first steps in any research project, and Chapter 3 describes source- and content-driven search strategies. Chapters 4 through 9 explain how to research different types of authority. Chapter 10 discusses online search techniques, and Chapter 11 covers how to create a research plan.

Chapters 4 through 9 are each organized in a similar way. They all begin with an overview of the type of authority discussed. Then you will find an explanation of the process of researching the authority. After the discussion of the research process, you will find information on citation format. The next item in each of these chapters is a section of sample pages. The sample pages contain step-by-step illustrations of the research process described earlier in the chapter. As you read through the text, you may find it helpful to review both the excerpts within the chapter and the sample pages section to get a sense of the research process for each type of authority. These chapters conclude with research checklists that summarize the research process and may be helpful as you conduct research.

Chapter 10 discusses general techniques for online research. The process of using print research sources varies according to the type of authority you are researching. With online research, however, there are certain common search techniques that can be used to research many types of authority. As a consequence, the discussion of online research in Chapters 4 through 9 focuses on search techniques specific to individual sources, and Chapter 10 focuses on more general online search techniques and strategies. As you learn about online research, you may also want to review Appendix A at the end of the text, which lists a number of research websites.

The final chapter, Chapter 11, discusses research strategy and explains how to create a research plan. You do not need to read all of the preceding chapters before reading Chapter 11, although you may find Chapter 11 easier to follow after you have some background on a few research sources. Learning about research involves more than simply learning how to locate individual types of authority. You must also be able to plan a research strategy that will lead to accurate research results, and you must be able to execute your research strategy efficiently and economically. Chapter 11 sets out a process that will help you achieve these goals in any research project, whether in your legal research class or in legal practice.

CHAPTER 2

Generating Search Terms

A. Generating search terms based on categories of information

B. Expanding the initial search

C. Prioritizing search terms

As Chapter 1 explains, generating search terms is part of the research planning process. Developing a list of words or concepts that are likely to lead you to useful information is a preliminary step necessary for almost any type of research, whether source-driven or content-driven. This chapter explains techniques you can use to generate search terms for virtually any research project.

A. GENERATING SEARCH TERMS BASED ON CATEGORIES OF INFORMATION

When presented with a set of facts, you could generate a list of search terms by constructing a random list of words that seem relevant to the issue. But a more structured approach—working from a set of categories—will help ensure that you are covering all of your bases in conducting your research.

There are a number of ways that you could categorize the information in your research issue to create a list of search terms. Some people prefer to use the six questions journalists ask when covering a story: who, what, when, where, why, and how. Another way to generate search terms is to categorize the information presented by the facts as follows.

■ THE *PARTIES* INVOLVED IN THE PROBLEM, DESCRIBED ACCORDING TO THEIR RELATIONSHIPS TO EACH OTHER

Here, you might be concerned not only with parties who are in direct conflict with each other, but also any other individuals, entities, or groups involved. These might include fact witnesses who can testify as to what happened, expert witnesses if appropriate to the situation, other potential plaintiffs (in civil cases), or other potential defendants (in criminal or civil cases).

In describing the parties, proper names will not ordinarily be useful search terms, although if one party is a public entity or corporation, you might be able to locate other cases in which the entity or corporation was a party. Instead, you will usually want to describe the parties in terms of their legal status or relationships to each other, such as landlords and tenants, parents and children, employers and employees, or doctors and patients.

■ THE *PLACES AND THINGS* INVOLVED IN THE PROBLEM

In thinking about place, both geographical locale and type of location can be important. For example, the conduct at issue might have taken place in Pennsylvania, which would help you determine which jurisdiction's law applies. It might also have taken place at a school or in an office, which could be important for determining which legal rules apply to the situation.

"Things" can involve tangible objects or intangible concepts. In a problem involving a car accident, tangible things could include automobiles or stop signs. In other types of situations, intangible "things," such as a vacation or someone's reputation, could be useful search terms.

■ THE *POTENTIAL CLAIMS AND DEFENSES* THAT COULD BE RAISED

As you become more familiar with the law, you may be able to identify claims or defenses that a research problem potentially raises. The facts could indicate to you that the problem potentially involves particular claims (such as breach of contract, defamation, or bribery) or particular defenses (such as consent, assumption of the risk, or self-defense).

Lawyers use their accumulated knowledge, including both specialized knowledge gained in practice and foundational legal principles that all lawyers learn in law school, to identify legal doctrines that may apply to a client's situation. Even as a beginning law student, you are being introduced to a body of information common to all lawyers that you can use to brainstorm potential legal theories. When that is the case, you can often use claims and defenses effectively as search terms to help you identify applicable rules of law.

If you are dealing with an unfamiliar area of law, however, you might not know of any claims or defenses potentially at issue. In that situation, you can generate search terms by thinking about the conduct and mental states of the parties, as well as the injury suffered by the complaining party. Claims and defenses often flow from these considerations, and as a result, these types of terms can be used to locate useful information. When considering conduct, consider what was not done, as well as what was done. The failure to do an act might also give rise to a claim or defense.

For example, you could be asked to research a situation in which one person published an article falsely asserting that another person was guilty of tax evasion, knowing that the accusation was not true. You might recognize this as a potential claim for the tort of defamation, which occurs when one person publishes false information that is damaging to another person's reputation. Even if you were unfamiliar with this tort, however, you could still generate search terms relevant to the claim by considering the defendant's conduct (publication) or mental state (intentional actions), or the plaintiff's injury (to reputation). These search terms would likely lead you to authority on defamation.

■ THE *RELIEF* SOUGHT BY THE COMPLAINING PARTY

The relief a party is seeking is another way to categorize information. Damages, injunction, specific performance, restitution, attorneys' fees, and other terms relating to the relief sought can lead you to pertinent information.

As an example of how you might go about using these categories to generate search terms, assume you have been asked to research the following situation:

> Your client recently ended a long-term relationship with her partner. She and her partner never participated in a formal marriage ceremony, but they had always planned to get married "someday." They lived together for five years and referred to each other as husband and wife. Your client and her former partner orally agreed to provide support for each other, and your client's former partner repeatedly made statements like, "What's mine is yours." Your client wants to know if she is entitled to part of the value of the assets her former partner acquired during their relationship or to any support payments.

- PARTIES: husband, wife, spouse, unmarried couple, unmarried cohabitants.
- PLACES AND THINGS: property, assets, ownership, support, non-marital relationship.
- POTENTIAL CLAIMS AND DEFENSES: common-law marriage, breach of contract, detrimental reliance.

These terms might not have occurred to you if were not already familiar with the relevant legal principles. Additional terms could be generated according to conduct ("reliance" on "promises" of support) or mental state (intentional conduct if the client's former partner purposely misled her into believing the parties shared ownership of the assets).

- RELIEF: damages, division or disposition of assets, support.

This is not an exhaustive list of search terms for this problem, but it illustrates how you can use these categories of information to develop useful search terms.

B. EXPANDING THE INITIAL SEARCH

Once you have developed an initial set of search terms for your issue, the next task is to try to expand that list. The terms you originally generated may not appear in an index or a database. Therefore, once you have developed your initial set of search terms, you should try to increase both the breadth and the depth of the list. You can increase the breadth of the list by identifying synonyms and terms related to the initial search terms, and you can increase the depth by expressing the concepts in your search terms both more abstractly and more concretely.

Increasing the breadth of your list with synonyms and related terms is essential to your research strategy. This is especially true for word searches. As **Chapter 3** explains in more detail, some research tools can cross-reference content related to your search terms. A literal word search, however, searches only for the specific terms you identify. Therefore, to make sure you locate all of the pertinent information on your issue, you need to have a number of synonyms for the words and concepts in your search. In the research scenario described above, there are several synonyms and related terms for one of the initial search terms: ownership. As **Figure 2.1** illustrates, you might also search for terms such as title or possession.

FIGURE 2.1 EXPANDING THE BREADTH OF SEARCH TERMS

Increasing breadth with synonyms and related terms:

title ⟷ ownership ⟷ possession

FIGURE 2.2 INCREASING THE DEPTH OF SEARCH TERMS

Increasing depth with varying levels of abstraction:

intimate partners
↕
unmarried cohabitants
↕
boyfriend, girlfriend

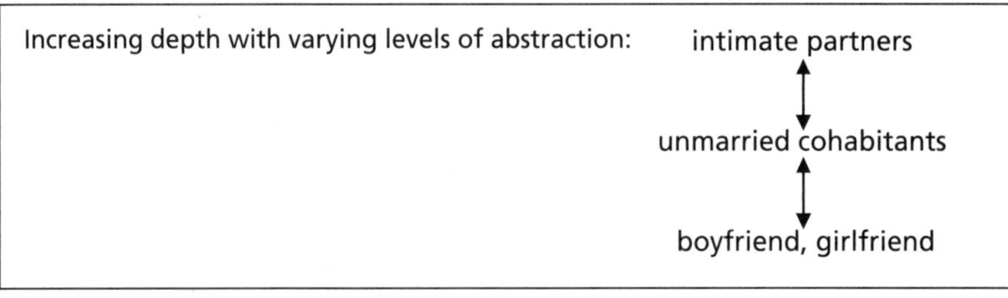

You are also more likely to find useful research material if you increase the depth of your list by varying the level of abstraction. In the research scenario described above, the client and her former partner were unmarried cohabitants. You might find relevant information if you described the relationship more abstractly as "intimate partners" or more concretely as "boyfriend" or "girlfriend." See **Figure 2.2**.

C. PRIORITIZING SEARCH TERMS

Once you have generated and expanded a list of search terms, you must prioritize them. Recall the key analogy from Chapter 1: If you had the key to a car parked at Disney World, how would you figure out which car it starts? Three relevant criteria would be make, model, and color, and ideally you would narrow the field by all three together. If that were not possible, which criterion would you use first? When you generate an extensive list of search terms for legal research, you will often use some combination of terms together, but you usually will not use all of them simultaneously. You can only look up one term or concept at a time in a print index. You can combine terms together in a word search, but putting too many in one search may limit the search's effectiveness. Consequently, you must decide where to focus your attention first.

You may find it helpful to think about two goals when you prioritize your search terms: identifying the legal rules that apply to your client's situation, and determining how the facts of the situation fit with the requirements of the rules. Of course, this is a bit of a chicken-or-egg problem in that the facts of the situation determine which rules apply and the application of the rules depends on the facts of the situation. Nevertheless, one element of your search strategy will be deciding whether to prioritize terms describing legal doctrines or terms describing the specific facts of your client's situation. This does not mean that you will ignore or discard other terms; it simply means that you must decide which terms to emphasize initially and which to use in fine-tuning the search results.

Prioritizing terms relating to legal doctrines makes sense when you know the theory or theories most likely to apply to your client's situation. To return to the key analogy, using the make and model to narrow the field of options would make sense. Prioritizing search terms related to the legal doctrine that applies to your research issue can similarly be an effective way to narrow the field of legal information.

As you begin learning about legal research, your professor may specify the legal doctrines you are to research. In the research scenario in Section A, above, regarding the dissolution of a long-term relationship, your professor might direct you to research whether the parties formed a common-law marriage. You would certainly prioritize "common-law marriage" as a search term based on your professor's instructions.

In real life, clients bring the facts of their problems to you, not instructions to research particular legal theories, and as you become a more experienced researcher, your professor is less likely is to identify the legal doctrines or rules that apply to your research scenario. As you gain experience in the law, you will learn to identify the legal issues a situation presents and will be able to prioritize terms related to those issues in your research.

Sometimes, however, you will not begin your research with a sense of the applicable legal doctrines and will need to prioritize the facts of your client's situation instead. You can then use the search results to determine the legal doctrines that govern situations involving those types of facts. To return to the key analogy again, prioritizing facts is like trying to find the parked car by searching by color. This will narrow the field, but the remaining choices will reflect substantial diversity of makes and models. Similarly, prioritizing terms relating to the specific facts of the client's situation can lead to diffuse search results involving many different legal rules. The search results will also be affected by the level of abstraction of your terms. Search terms that are too concrete may yield little information, or little relevant information. More abstract factual terms may better steer you toward authority that describes applicable legal doctrines.

In the example involving dissolution of a client's long-term relationship, prioritizing factual terms relating to the parties' relationship could lead to rules about common-law marriage but would also likely lead to information about a variety of other legal doctrines. This is especially true for concrete terms like "boyfriend" or "girlfriend," which can occur in virtually any legal context. Although prioritizing factual terms may not be a useful approach when you need to locate information about a particular legal doctrine (such as common-law marriage), it can be useful when you need to identify all possible avenues of recovery for a client or do not have a sense of the legal doctrines that may apply to the situation.

Neither the list nor the priority of your search terms should remain static. Reading the information you find early in your research may reveal new search terms you can use to locate better information. The terminology of applicable legal rules that you did not consider at first might appear in the documents you locate in your initial research efforts, and they can then become useful terms for additional research (unless you have been instructed to limit your research to a particular legal doctrine). Facts that did not seem important at first could turn out to be critical to your analysis. As you work through your research path, therefore, you should revise both the content and priority of your search terms.

CHAPTER 3

Evaluating Search Options

A. INTRODUCTION TO SEARCH APPROACHES

Recall the research scenario introduced in Chapter 2:

> Your client recently ended a long-term relationship with her partner. She and her partner never participated in a formal marriage ceremony, but they had always planned to get married "someday." They lived together for five years and referred to each other as husband and wife. Your client and her former partner orally agreed to provide support for each other, and your client's former partner repeatedly made statements like, "What's mine is yours." Your client wants to know if she is entitled to part of the value of the assets her former partner acquired during their relationship or to any support payments.

Assume that your supervisor asked you to find out whether the parties' relationship qualified as a common-law or "informal" marriage under the state's family law statutes and to submit a summary of your research by the end of the day. How would you approach the task?

Assume instead that your supervisor gave you a week to research the law and submit a memorandum analyzing any legal theories that might apply to your client's situation. How would you approach that task?

Neither of these assignments requires you to explain how you conducted your research. Your supervisor and the client will be focused on the substantive results of your research, not on the process. But each of these research tasks is different in terms of the complexity of the research required, the work to be produced, and the deadline for completion. Accordingly, you would use a different research process for each one. Knowing how to vary your research process to suit the task you need to accomplish is vital for performing complete, accurate, and efficient research.

Chapter 1 gave you a brief introduction to the source-driven and content-driven approaches to research and summarized the research planning process. This chapter will explain these search approaches in more detail so you can learn how to assess which approach is best for the specific research tasks you will be asked to do as a student and in legal practice. This assessment is important for effective research planning. As you read this chapter, consider how you might approach the research tasks described above. The last section of this chapter sets out possible approaches to these assignments. You can compare your approaches with those outlined in Section D.

As a starting point, Sections B and C, below, contrast source- and content-driven research strategies and are organized around two questions:

- What source(s) will be included in my search?
- What content will my search strategy identify?

B. SOURCE-DRIVEN SEARCH PROCESS

The source-driven approach can be used with virtually any source of information: print, Lexis Advance, Westlaw, Bloomberg Law, and other providers of legal information. When you use the source-driven approach, you will select a source to search, search for content within the source, and read and evaluate the information you find.

1. WHAT SOURCE(S) WILL BE INCLUDED IN MY SEARCH?

With the source-driven approach, only the publication(s) you select will be included in the search. In print, each publication is a separate book or set of books, and, as explained in Chapter 1, the publication will often be organized by jurisdiction and type of authority. For example, each set of statutes for each jurisdiction is in a separate set of books. The California state code is in one set of books, and the Illinois state code is in another. Therefore, the source you would select to research California statutes is the California state code.

Online services typically divide individual sources of information into separate databases organized by jurisdiction and type of authority, although some databases will combine related information. For example, in Westlaw, Lexis Advance, and Bloomberg Law, you could research California statutes by selecting the California code database and Illinois statutes by selecting the Illinois code database, but a database containing all state codes is also available in each of those services.

To research effectively with the source-driven approach, you need to know two things: the range of publications or databases available to you and the type of source you want to research. You have to know that a publication or database exists to select it as a source. You also have to have at least a general idea about the type of information you need so you can select a source that contains that information. If you do not realize that an issue is likely one of federal law instead of state law or statutory law instead of common law, you may have trouble finding relevant information because you will not be looking in the right source or sources. Conversely, however, when you know the source of the information you need, researching only that source is efficient because all the information you find will be from the appropriate source.

2. WHAT CONTENT WILL MY SEARCH STRATEGY IDENTIFY?

Once you have selected a source, you are ready to search for information within that source. In print or online, you can search by subject. Online providers also allow you to execute word searches. Both of these methods of searching are discussed below.

a. Subject Searching

You can search for information within a specific publication by subject using the publication's table of contents or index. The index will usually contain more detail than the table of contents, and because it is organized by subject, will contain cross-references to related material. Online providers also often offer specialized subject-searching tools, such as a directory of subject area topics.

One advantage to subject searching is that if the concept you are searching is described with commonly used words, an index or other subject compilation will reference only significant discussions of the concept, not every occurrence of commonly used words. For example, virtually every civil law suit is initiated by the filing of a document called a complaint. "Complaint," however, is both a legal term of art and a common, everyday word. If you wanted to research "complaints," you would want references to the document used to initiate a civil suit, not to the everyday use of the term. Subject-searching tools like an index prioritize the information within a source to help direct you to the most important information even when the topic you are researching is described with commonly used words.

Another advantage of subject searching is that index cross-references will point you in the right direction if you look up terms that are close to, but perhaps not exactly on point with, the topic you are researching. For example, a concept in contract law called the "mailbox" rule is also known as the "deposit acceptance" rule and the "postal acceptance" rule. If you knew one of those terms but not the others, index cross-references could direct you to an alternative entry containing relevant information under a different heading.

On the other hand, if you want to search for terms or topics that the publisher did not include in the index or subject compilation, you have no way to find the information you need. And if the publisher has compiled the material using topic names that are completely unfamiliar to you, you may not be able to find index or subject entries that are helpful.

b. Word Searching

Word searching is a search option when you research online. You have probably executed thousands of word searches in search engines like Google. Different services offer different options for word searching that may include terms and connectors searching, natural language searching, or plain language searching. The various types of word searches are discussed in Chapter 10.

Because word searches look for specific terms, you can establish your own search criteria without regard for whether the publisher included those words in the index. This can be helpful for fact-specific research, such as when you are searching for cases with specific facts similar to the facts of your research issue, or when the applicable legal concepts are expressed with relatively unique phrasing, such as "negligence per se," a well-known tort doctrine.

But because a word search focuses on individual words in a document instead of general concepts, it can retrieve irrelevant documents or miss important documents. For example, executing a word search for a commonly used term such as "complaint" can retrieve many documents that use the term in an everyday sense instead of as a term of art. Although all concepts must ultimately be expressed in words, a literal search for the individual terms that express a general concept may not be focused enough to be as effective as a subject search. Conversely, a word search for the "mailbox" rule in a source that uses the alternative label "deposit acceptance" rule to characterize the concept may miss important documents because the search term "mailbox" will not appear in that source.

C. CONTENT-DRIVEN SEARCH PROCESS

The content-driven approach uses the same steps as the source-driven approach, but it modifies the order of the steps. With content-driven research, you can execute a word search for specific content before you select a source.

1. WHAT SOURCE(S) WILL BE INCLUDED IN MY SEARCH?

With services such as Lexis Advance, Westlaw, and Bloomberg Law, you can do a true general search for information from all jurisdictions and all types of authority, much as you search for content without regard to source in Google. Although this sort of broad search is possible, it is not likely to be a strategy you will use often. What you are more likely to do is pre-filter or narrow the scope of your research before you execute a search for specific content. For example, if you pre-filter by selecting a specific jurisdiction, the search results will be limited to sources from that jurisdiction but will include many types of information, including cases, statutes, secondary sources, court filings, and the like.

When you search this way, you may retrieve hundreds or thousands of documents. Your task then becomes one of narrowing the results to target the information you need. You can narrow or filter the results by general document characteristics, such as type of authority or level of court. You can also filter by specific content by searching for terms within the results.

The advantage of this approach is that it may prompt you to review sources you would not otherwise have considered. For example, if you thought an issue was governed by common law, but in fact, a statute applied to the issue, the general search may retrieve the relevant statute. The disadvantage is that a search that retrieves a large number of documents may be overwhelming, especially if you do not know enough about the issue to filter the results effectively. Another caution is the need to pay close attention to differences among sources of information. Regulations issued by agencies may look very similar to statutes. Briefs and other court filings may look very similar to a court's opinion, but only the opinion constitutes legal authority. When all sources of information are combined in a single search result, it is easy to lose track of the authoritative value of an individual document.

2. WHAT CONTENT WILL MY SEARCH STRATEGY IDENTIFY?

When you execute a word search, the search engine searches a database of documents and retrieves those that meet the criteria you set for the search. To do this, the search engine uses an algorithm, or set of rules, to evaluate the search criteria and the documents in the database. Legal research services use three types of search algorithms: terms and connectors (also called Boolean), natural language, and plain language.

The type of search you execute will affect the content of the results. A terms and connectors or natural language search will retrieve documents that include one or more of your search terms. A plain language search retrieves not only documents that contain your search term(s), but also other content that the search algorithm has identified as relevant to your search term(s). The differences among search algorithms means the same search executed in multiple services can retrieve somewhat different content.

The default option for searching in Lexis Advance and Bloomberg Law is natural language searching, and the default option in Westlaw is plain language searching. All three services allow you to choose terms and connectors searching. Other services may use natural language or terms and connectors and may let you choose which type of search to execute.

Terms and connectors, natural language, and plain language search techniques are discussed in Chapter 10.

D. EVALUATING SEARCH OPTIONS

Now that you have read about the source-driven and content-driven approaches to research, consider how you might approach the research tasks described at the beginning of this chapter. Compare your approach with the potential research strategies outlined below.

The scenario involved disposition of assets upon dissolution of a non-marital relationship:

> Your client recently ended a long-term relationship with her partner. She and her partner never participated in a formal marriage ceremony, but they had always planned to get married "someday." They lived together for five years and referred to each other as husband and wife. Your client and her former partner orally agreed to provide support for each other, and your client's former partner repeatedly made statements like, "What's mine is yours." Your client wants to know if she is entitled to part of the value of the assets her former partner acquired during their relationship or to any support payments.

The first task was to determine whether the parties' relationship qualified as a common-law or "informal" marriage under the state's family law statutes and summarize your research by the end of the day.

For this task, your supervisor has given you some direction about the type of authority you need to locate: family law statutes. The statutes will likely set out the requirements for establishing a common-law marriage. The statutory language alone, however, may not fully answer the question. For example, if the statutory language does not say how long people must hold themselves out as married to establish a common-law marriage, cases interpreting the statute may provide some guidance.

After you generate your search terms, using a source-driven approach would be a good way to accomplish your research task. You know the jurisdiction and type of authority you need, so you can limit your search to the state code. This will reduce the number of documents you locate and make it easier to evaluate what you have found. Your search terms would relate to the legal theory you have been instructed to research. Looking up index entries or executing word searches for terms such as "common-law marriage" or "informal marriage" would likely lead you in the right direction.

Once you locate the relevant provision(s) of the code, you can read the language to determine the requirements for this type of marriage. Research notes accompanying the statute will likely summarize cases interpreting the statute, making it easy for you to locate and read pertinent cases. Given the short deadline for reporting the results of your research, this would be a good approach for making a preliminary assessment of the law so that you and your supervisor can decide whether further research is appropriate.

Now consider the second task: to research any legal theories that might apply to your client's situation. This is a more complex research task because you have not been instructed to research any specific legal theory or type of authority. Your job is to identify the theories that potentially provide a remedy. Unless you are already familiar with applicable legal rules, you will need to begin in a more general way by learning about potential theories of recovery and then evaluating the potential success of those theories under your state's law. This work could be accomplished with either a source-driven or content-driven approach.

Again, you would begin by generating search terms. Terms relating to property rights of unmarried cohabitants or boyfriend and girlfriend living together would likely be relevant. From there, you could use a source-driven approach for your research. You know that your state is the controlling jurisdiction, but you may not know which type(s) of binding primary authority will apply to your client's situation. Recall from Chapter 1, however, that secondary authorities can be a good starting point for research when you need background information because they cite, analyze, and explain the law. You could begin your research by selecting a secondary source. Chapter 4, on secondary source research, describes a range of secondary sources you could use to obtain background information. One that might be useful is *American Jurisprudence*, Second Edition, a legal encyclopedia with general information about a wide range of legal issues. You could use *American Jurisprudence* in print or online to search for content related to property rights of unmarried cohabitants. The results of your search would reveal that legal rules relating to detrimental reliance on a promise, common-law marriage, and breach of contract (among other theories) may apply to your client's situation. You could then use this information to search for relevant cases and statutes to determine whether your client might be able to prevail under these or other theories.

Another option would be to use a content-driven approach in Lexis Advance, Westlaw, or Bloomberg Law. You would likely pre-filter the search by selecting your state as the jurisdiction. By searching for content related to property rights of unmarried cohabitants, you could retrieve secondary sources, cases, statutes, and other material that may be germane to your client's situation. After executing a search, you could filter this information according to any number of criteria and read what you found to identify rules that might apply to your client's situation. For example, you might retrieve secondary sources describing detrimental reliance on a promise, a statute regarding the status of common-law marriage in your state, and a case analyzing a breach of contract claim by an unmarried person against a former partner. The search might also retrieve documents relating to domestic violence, wills and estates, same-sex marriage, or any number of other legal matters that could arise between unmarried partners but that do not apply to your client's situation. With no limitation on the type of authority, the search would likely retrieve several hundred to several thousand documents, making the post-search filtering process critical to identifying relevant information.

The differences between the source- and content-driven approaches can seem abstract when you read a textual description of the research process. When you start doing research, the differences will become readily apparent. You might try searching for information about the property rights of unmarried cohabitants in your state using the source- and content-driven approaches to see how the results differ and which you think is most effective. More detailed information on research planning appears in Chapter 11.

As you begin conducting research independently, you may find yourself gravitating toward the content-driven process. It will likely feel familiar because it strives to replicate the types of online searching everyone does on a regular basis, and it has appealing features that make it a good choice for many types of research. It is worthwhile for you to learn effective content-driven searching.

Nevertheless, it is important for you to gain facility with source-driven searching as well. Source-driven searching is often the most effective way to conduct research, which is why it remains an option in services that also offer content-driven searching. Many employers continue to rely on providers of legal information that offer only source-driven searching. And some employers have invested thousands of dollars in print collections and see more benefit in having their attorneys use those resources than in investing in new online services.

Incentives such as reward points that can be redeemed for products may also provide inducements unrelated to your research goals to use particular research services. There is nothing wrong with these incentives as long as you understand that they are marketing efforts by commercial entities directed toward you as a consumer of information products. You do not rely exclusively on sellers' marketing messages when making purchases in your daily life. You should not do so when you select research services, either. As a consumer, you should make your own assessment of the resources available to you so that you can employ search processes most in line with your professional goals and needs.

CHAPTER 4

Secondary Source Research

A. INTRODUCTION TO SECONDARY SOURCES

As you read in Chapter 1, primary authority refers to sources of legal rules, such as cases, statutes, and administrative regulations. Secondary sources, by contrast, provide commentary on the law. Although they are not binding on courts and are not cited as frequently as primary sources, secondary sources are excellent research tools. Because they often summarize or collect authorities from a variety of jurisdictions, they can help you find binding or nonbinding primary authority on a subject. They also often provide narrative explanations of complex concepts that would be difficult for a beginning researcher to grasp thoroughly simply from reading primary sources. Equipped with a solid understanding of the background of an area of law, you will be better able to locate and evaluate primary authority on your research issue.

1. WHEN SECONDARY SOURCES WILL BE MOST USEFUL

Secondary sources will be most useful to you in the following situations:

(1) WHEN YOU ARE RESEARCHING AN AREA OF LAW WITH WHICH YOU ARE UNFAMILIAR. Secondary sources can give you the necessary background to generate search terms. They can also lead you directly to primary authorities.

(2) WHEN YOU ARE LOOKING FOR NONBINDING PRIMARY AUTHORITY BUT DO NOT KNOW HOW TO NARROW THE JURISDICTIONS THAT ARE LIKELY TO HAVE USEFUL INFORMATION. If you need to find nonbinding primary authority on a subject, conducting a nationwide survey of the law on the topic is not likely to be an efficient research strategy. Secondary sources can help you locate nonbinding authority relevant to your research issue.

(3) WHEN YOU ARE RESEARCHING AN UNDEVELOPED AREA OF THE LAW. When you are researching a question of first impression, commentators may have analyzed how courts should rule on the issue.

(4) WHEN AN INITIAL SEARCH OF PRIMARY SOURCES YIELDS EITHER NO AUTHORITY OR TOO MUCH AUTHORITY. If you are unable to find any authority at all on a topic, you may not be looking in the right places. Secondary sources can educate you on the subject in a way that may allow you to expand or refocus your research efforts. When your search yields an unmanageable amount of information, secondary sources can do two things. First, their citations to primary authority can help you identify the most important authorities pertaining to the research issue. Second, they can provide you with information that may help you narrow your search or weed out irrelevant sources.

2. LIMITS ON THE APPROPRIATE USE OF SECONDARY SOURCES

Knowing when *not* to use secondary sources is also important. As noted above, secondary sources are not binding on courts. Therefore, you will not ordinarily cite them in briefs or memoranda. This is especially true if you use secondary sources to lead you to primary authority. It is important never to rely exclusively on a discussion of a primary authority that appears in a secondary source. If you are discussing a primary authority in a legal analysis, you must read that authority yourself and update your research to make sure it is current.

This is true for two reasons. First, a summary of a primary authority might not include all of the information necessary to your analysis. It is important to read the primary authority for yourself to make sure you represent it correctly and thoroughly in your analysis.

Second, the information in the secondary source might not be completely current. Although most secondary sources are updated on a regular basis, the law can change at any time. The source may contain incomplete information simply because of the inevitable time lag between changes to the law and the publication of a supplement. One mistake some beginning researchers make is citing a secondary source for the text of a case or statute without checking to make sure that the case has not been overturned or that the statute has not been changed. Another potential error is citing a secondary source for a proposition about the state of the law generally, such as, "Forty-two states now recognize a cause of action for invasion of privacy based on disclosure of private facts." While statements of that nature were probably true when the secondary source was written, other states may have acted, or some of those noted may have changed their law, in the intervening time period. Accordingly, secondary sources should only be used as a starting point for locating primary authority, not an ending point.

3. COMMONLY USED SECONDARY SOURCES

This section describes the following commonly used secondary sources: legal encyclopedias, treatises, legal periodicals, *American Law Reports*, Restatements of the law, and uniform laws and model acts.

a. Legal Encyclopedias

Legal encyclopedias are just like the general subject encyclopedias you have used in the past, except they are limited in scope to legal subjects. Legal encyclopedias provide a general overview of the law on a variety of topics. They do not provide analysis or suggest solutions to conflicts in the law. Instead, they simply report on the general state of the law. Because encyclopedias cover the law in such a general way, you will usually use them to get background information on your research topic and, to a lesser extent, to locate citations to primary authority. You will rarely, if ever, cite a legal encyclopedia.

There are two general legal encyclopedias, *American Jurisprudence*, Second Edition (Am. Jur. 2d) and *Corpus Juris Secundum* (C.J.S.). In addition, encyclopedias are published for many individual states (e.g., *California Jurisprudence*, *Maryland Law Encyclopedia*, and *Michigan Law and Practice*). When you are researching a question of state law, state encyclopedias are often more helpful than general encyclopedias for two reasons. First, the summary of the law will be tailored to the law of that state, and therefore is likely to be more helpful. Second, the citations to primary authority will be from the controlling jurisdiction. Consequently, state encyclopedias can be more useful for leading you to primary sources.

b. Treatises

Treatises have a narrower focus than legal encyclopedias. Where legal encyclopedias provide a general overview of a broad range of topics, treatises generally provide in-depth treatment of a single subject, such as torts or constitutional law. The goal of a treatise is to address in a systematic fashion all of the major topics within a subject area. Treatises often trace the history of the development of an area of law and explain the relationship of the treatise's subject to other areas of the law. To provide a comprehensive treatment of the subject's major topics, a treatise will explain the legal rules in the subject area, analyze major cases and statutes, and address policy issues underlying the rules. In addition to providing textual explanations, treatises also usually contain citations to many primary and secondary authorities.

Some treatises are widely respected and considered definitive sources in their subject areas. These treatises have often existed for a number of years and may be identified by the names of their original authors, even though other scholars now update and revise them. These well-known treatises may address broad areas of the law (Prosser on torts, Corbin on contracts, Wright & Miller on federal civil procedure) or more specialized subjects (Nimmer on copyright, White & Summers on the Uniform Commercial Code, Sutherland on statutory interpretation). These are not, however, the only treatises. Any book that provides comprehensive treatment of a single subject in a systematic fashion is a treatise, and many treatises exist on both broad areas of the law and narrower subjects. If you use a definitive treatise in your research, you might cite it in a brief or memorandum. Ordinarily, however, you will use treatises for research purposes and will not cite them in your written analysis.

Using a treatise, once you have located it, ordinarily is not difficult. The more difficult aspect of using treatises is finding one on your research topic. Because treatises do not usually have titles identifying them as treatises, sometimes it can be difficult figuring out which sources constitute treatises. The reference librarians in your library are a great asset in this area; they should be able to recommend treatises on your subject. Further, although many treatises are accessible online, some are still only available in print. Your library may keep important treatises on reserve.

c. Legal Periodicals

Articles in legal periodicals can be very useful research tools. Many law schools publish periodicals known as law reviews or journals that collect articles on a wide range of topics. Many other types of legal periodicals also exist, however, including commercially published journals, legal newspapers, and magazines.

The commercial legal press includes magazines such as the *ABA Journal* and local bar journals, as well as newspapers such as *The National Law Journal*. These publications are good for keeping abreast of newsworthy developments in the law. Because they are news sources, their articles are generally short and focused more on describing legal developments than on analysis. These types of articles can provide limited background information, but they usually do not focus on the kinds of issues first-year law students research.

Articles published in law reviews or journals, by contrast, are thorough, thoughtful treatments of legal issues by law professors, judges, practitioners, and even students. The articles are usually focused fairly narrowly on specific issues, although they often include background or introductory sections that provide a general overview of the topic. They are generally well researched and contain citations to many primary and secondary authorities. In addition, they often address undeveloped areas in the law and propose solutions for resolving problems in the law. As a result, periodical articles can be useful for obtaining an overview of an area of law, finding references to primary and secondary authority, and developing ideas for analyzing a question of first impression or resolving a conflict in the law.

Law review or journal articles fall into the following general categories:

■ ARTICLES WRITTEN BY LEGAL SCHOLARS

These are articles written by law professors and other scholars. They frequently address problems or conflicts in the law. They may propose solutions to legal problems, advocate for changes to the law, identify new legal theories, or explore the relationship between the law and some other discipline. Articles by leading or established scholars may be helpful in your research, especially if they explain doctrines or developments in a useful way. The weight of an individual article will depend on a number of factors, including the author's expertise, the reputation of the journal in which it is published, the article's age, and the depth of the article's research and analysis.

■ ARTICLES WRITTEN BY JUDGES AND PRACTITIONERS

These are articles written by people who work with the law on a daily basis in very practical ways. Judges often write about their judicial philosophies or offer advice or insights to practitioners. Practitioners may write about areas of law in which they practice. These articles may help you understand a legal issue and provide an overview of important authorities, but practitioner articles in particular may not have the depth of other types of articles.

■ STUDENT NOTES OR COMMENTS

These are articles written by law students. Often, they describe a significant new case or statute. They may analyze a problem in the law and propose a solution. Because these articles are written by students, they carry less weight than other periodical articles and are useful primarily for background information and citations to primary authorities.

These are, of course, generalizations that may not hold true in every instance. For the most part, however, law review and journal articles will be useful to you as research tools, rather than as support for written analysis. You will not ordinarily cite an article if you can support your analysis with primary authority. If you cannot find primary support, however, you might cite a persuasive article. Additionally, if you incorporate an argument or analysis from an article in your written work, it is important to cite the source to avoid plagiarism.

Periodical articles are unique among legal authorities in that there is no way to update an individual article, short of locating later articles that add to or criticize an earlier article. As a consequence, it is important to note the date of any periodical article you use. If the article is more than a few years old, you may want to supplement your research with more current material. In addition, if you use the article to lead you to primary authority, you will need to update your research using the updating tools available for those primary sources to make sure your research is completely current.

d. *American Law Reports*

American Law Reports, or A.L.R., contains articles called "Annotations." Annotations collect summaries of cases from a variety of jurisdictions to provide an overview of the law on a topic. A.L.R. combines the breadth of topic coverage found in an encyclopedia with the depth of discussion in a treatise or legal periodical. Nevertheless, A.L.R. is different from these other secondary sources in significant ways. Because A.L.R. Annotations provide summaries of individual cases, they are more detailed than encyclopedias. Unlike treatises or legal periodicals, however, they mostly report the results of the cases without much analysis or commentary.

A.L.R. Annotations are especially helpful at the beginning of your research to give you an overview of a topic. Because Annotations collect summaries of cases from many jurisdictions, they can also be helpful in directing you toward binding or nonbinding primary authority. More recent Annotations also contain references to other research sources, such as other secondary sources and tools for conducting additional case research. Although A.L.R. is a useful research tool, you will rarely, if ever, cite an A.L.R. Annotation.

There are ten series of A.L.R. that address United States law: A.L.R. first through seventh series and A.L.R. Fed. first through third series. Each series contains multiple volumes organized by volume number. A.L.R. Fed. covers issues of federal law. The remaining series cover issues of state law, although they do bring in federal law as appropriate to the topic. One additional series, A.L.R. International, addresses issues of international law.

e. Restatements

The American Law Institute publishes what are called Restatements of the law in a variety of fields. You may already be familiar with the Restatements for contracts or torts from your other classes. Restatements essentially "restate" the common-law rules on a subject. Restatements have been published in the following fields:

- Agency
- Conflicts of Laws
- Contracts
- Employment Law
- Foreign Relations Law of the United States
- Judgments
- Law Governing Lawyers
- Property
- Restitution and Unjust Enrichment
- Security
- Suretyship and Guaranty
- Torts
- Trusts
- Unfair Competition.

In determining what the common-law rules are, the Restatements often look to the rules in the majority of United States jurisdictions. Sometimes, however, the Restatements will also state emerging rules where the rules seem to be changing or proposed rules in areas where the authors believe a change in the law would be appropriate. Although the Restatements are limited to common-law doctrines, the rules in the Restatements are set out almost like statutes, breaking different doctrines down into their component parts. In addition to setting out the common-law rules for a subject, the Restatements also provide commentary on the proper interpretations of the rules, illustrations demonstrating how the rules should apply in certain situations, and summaries of cases applying and interpreting the Restatement.

Although a Restatement is a secondary source, it is one with substantial weight. Courts can adopt a Restatement's view of an issue, which then makes the comments and illustrations especially persuasive in that jurisdiction. If you are researching the law of a jurisdiction that has adopted a Restatement, you can use the Restatement effectively to locate persuasive authority from other Restatement jurisdictions. As a result, a Restatement is an especially valuable secondary source.

f. Uniform Laws and Model Acts

Uniform laws and model acts are proposed statutes that can be adopted by legislatures. Two examples with which you may already be familiar are the Uniform Commercial Code (U.C.C.) and the Model Penal Code. Uniform laws and model acts are similar to Restatements in that they set out proposed rules, followed by commentary, research notes, and summaries of cases interpreting the rules. Unlike Restatements, which are limited to common-law doctrines, uniform laws and model acts exist in areas governed by statutory law.

Although uniform laws and model acts look like statutes, they are secondary sources. Their provisions do not take on the force of law unless they are adopted by a legislature. When that happens, however, the commentary, research references, and case summaries become very useful research tools. They can help you interpret the law and direct you to nonbinding authority from other jurisdictions that have adopted the law.

You are most likely to research uniform laws and model acts when your project involves research into state statutes. If you decide to use this resource, you may also want to review Chapter 7, which discusses statutory research.

4. METHODS OF LOCATING SECONDARY SOURCES

You can locate secondary sources using either a source-driven or content-driven approach. If you use a source-driven approach, the first step will be deciding which type(s) of source(s) to use.

Once you know which types of secondary sources are likely to meet your research needs, you will need to locate relevant information within each source. Three common search techniques are retrieving a document from its citation, searching by subject, and executing a word search. Some secondary sources are only published in print. Few of the ones published online are available from publicly available websites. Therefore, you will use these search techniques most often either in print or in a commercial database such as Westlaw or Lexis Advance.

If you are just beginning your research, searching by subject is often a good strategy. Most secondary sources, other than legal periodicals, have subject indexes (in print) and tables of contents (in print and online). To locate legal periodicals, you can use a separate periodical index that organizes periodical citations by subject. Word searching is another search option for locating secondary sources in a full-text database and may be an option in a periodical index as well.

If you choose content-driven searching in Westlaw, Lexis Advance, or Bloomberg Law, your search results will include secondary sources. When you view the secondary sources your search retrieves, you can filter the results according to a number of criteria to focus on specific publications or types of content.

Many secondary sources cross reference other secondary sources. Therefore, once you have located one secondary source on your research issue, it may provide links or citations to other secondary sources.

Sections B and C, below, explain how to research secondary sources in print and online. Not all law libraries maintain print collections of all of the secondary sources discussed in this chapter. Even if you will be accessing these sources primarily (or exclusively) online, you may want to read the section on print research because the citation rules for these sources flow from their print formats and may make more sense to you if you understand how secondary sources are organized in print.

B. RESEARCHING SECONDARY SOURCES IN PRINT

Researching secondary sources in print generally involves three steps: (1) using an index or table of contents to find references to material on the topic you are researching; (2) locating the material in the main text of the source; and (3) updating your research.

The first step is using an index or table of contents to find out where information on a topic is located within the secondary source. As with the index or table of contents in any other book, those in a secondary source will refer you to volumes, chapters, pages, or sections where you will find text explaining the topic you are researching. Some secondary sources consist only of a single volume. In those situations, you need simply to look up the table of contents or index references within the text. Often, however, the information in a secondary source is too comprehensive to fit within a single volume. In those cases, the source will consist of a multivolume set of books, which may be organized alphabetically by topic or numerically by volume number. The references in the index or table of contents will contain sufficient information for you to identify the appropriate book within the set, as well as the page or section number specifically relating to the topic you are researching. Locating material in the main text of the source is the second step in the process.

The final step in your research is updating the information you have located. Most secondary sources are updated with pocket parts, as described in Chapter 1. The pocket part will be organized the same way as the main volume of the source. Thus, to update your research, you need to look up the same provisions in the pocket part that you read in the main text to find any additional information on the topic. If you do not find any reference to your topic in the pocket part, there is no new information to supplement the main text.

You can research legal encyclopedias, treatises, and A.L.R. Annotations using this three-step process. **Figures 4.1** through **4.3** on the following pages illustrate this process with Am. Jur. 2d, a legal encyclopedia.

FIGURE 4.1 INDEX TO AM. JUR. 2D

Reference to an individual section

AMERICAN JURISPRUDENCE 2D

FALLING OBJECTS—Cont'd
Premises Liability (this index)
Wires and Poles (this index)

FALLS
Attractive Nuisances (this index)
Automobiles and Highway Traffic (this index)
Boats and boating, falling overboard, **Boats § 48**
Carriers (this index)
Federal Tort Claims Act (FTCA) (this index)
Highways, Streets, and Bridges (this index)
Hotels and Motels (this index)
Laundries, dyers, and dry cleaners, self-service laundries, **Laundries § 19**
Premises Liability (this index)
Shipping (this index)
(this index)
onditions (this index)
Water, falls into
  boats and boating, **Boats § 48**
Workers' compensation, **Workers § 338**

Cross-reference

FALSE AND FALSITY
Advertising (this index)
Aviation, furnishing false information, **Aviation § 219**
Conflict of laws, **ConflictLw § 4, 118**
Contempt (this index)
Credibility of Witnesses (this index)
Credit Reporting Agencies (this index)
Estoppel and Waiver (this index)
Fair Housing Act (this index)
Fictitious Matters (this index)
Honesty or Dishonesty (this index)
Housing discrimination. **Fair Housing Act** (this index)
Impersonation (this index)
Injunctions (this index)
Insurance (this index)
Libel and Slander (this index)
Passports (this index)
ecords § 11 to 16
rding, **Records § 11 to 16**
tions (this index)
rge (this index)

Index entry for False Imprisonment

FALSE CLAIMS ACT
False Pretenses (this index)

FALSE IMPERSONATION
Impersonation (this index)

FALSE IMPRISONMENT
Generally, **FalseImp § 1 to 163**
Abduction and kidnapping, **Abduction § 2**
Abuse of process, **Abuse § 4**
Acquittal or discharge, subsequent, **FalseImp § 23**
Actual malice, punitive damages, **FalseImp § 147**

FALSE IMPRISONMENT—Cont'd
Advice of counsel, acting on, **FalseImp § 61**
Affidavits, acting without sufficient affidavit or complaint, **FalseImp § 93**
Agency. Vicarious liability, below
Answers, **FalseImp § 117**
Apportionment of damages, **FalseImp § 136**
Apprehension, necessity of, **FalseImp § 17**
Arraignment, damages, **FalseImp § 138**
Arrests
  false arrests, below
  legal process, below
Assisting officer on request, private persons, **FalseImp § 42**
Attorneys
  civil litigation, liability of attorneys or parties in, **FalseImp § 46**
  justification, acting on advice of counsel, **FalseImp § 61**
Attorney's fees, **FalseImp § 145**
Awareness of confinement, **FalseImp § 12**
Bail, denial of opportunity to post, **FalseImp § 31**
Carriers (this index)
Character or reputation, evidence as to, **FalseImp § 126**
Children, confinement of, **FalseImp § 161**
Circumstantial evidence, **FalseImp § 126**
Clerks of court, immunity, **FalseImp § 99**
Commitment of mentally ill persons
  generally, **FalseImp § 33**
  immunity of judicial officers, **FalseImp § 96**
  improper commitment, **FalseImp § 34**
  persons initiating commitment proceedings, **FalseImp § 44**
  warrant of commitment, **FalseImp § 79**
Common law, shoplifters, **FalseImp § 64, 65**
Complainant
  legal process, protection of complainant, **FalseImp § 77**
  liability of complainant, **FalseImp § 43**
Conditional restraint, **FalseImp § 14**
Conduct of officer in seeking warrant, **FalseImp § 82**
Confinement. Detention or restraint, below
Conflict of laws, **ConflictLw § 121**
Consent
  defense of consent, **FalseImp § 53**
  ratification. Vicarious liability, below
Contempt proceedings, immunity of judicial officers, **FalseImp § 95**
Continuing offense, **FalseImp § 157**
Contributory negligence, defense of, **FalseImp § 54**
Conviction of plaintiff, evidence as to
  generally, **FalseImp § 125**
  weight and sufficiency of evidence, **FalseImp § 127**

FALSE IMPRISONMENT—Cont'd
Court of Federal Claims (this index)
Criminal liability
  generally, **FalseImp § 154 to 163**
  acceptance of criminal disposition, **FalseImp § 57**
  children, confinement of, **FalseImp § 161**
  continuing offense, **FalseImp § 157**
  defenses, **FalseImp § 160**
  degree of offense, **FalseImp § 159**
  elements of offense, **FalseImp § 155**
  evidence, **FalseImp § 162**
  guilty plea, below
  nature of restraint, **FalseImp § 156**
  other offenses, relation to, **FalseImp § 158**
  penalties, **FalseImp § 163**
  relation to other offenses, **FalseImp § 158**
  sentence and punishment, **FalseImp § 163**
  sufficiency of evidence, **FalseImp § 162**
Damages
  generally, **FalseImp § 135 to 153**
  amount of compensatory damages, **FalseImp § 142 to 145**
  apportionment of damages, **FalseImp § 136**
  arraignment, **FalseImp § 138**
  attorney's fees, **FalseImp § 145**
  emotional distress, **FalseImp § 143**
  evidence
    enhancement of damages, **FalseImp § 121**
    mitigation of damages, **FalseImp § 122**
  excessive damages, **FalseImp § 140**
  foreseeable consequences, **FalseImp § 137**
  future damages, **FalseImp § 144**
  inadequate damages, **FalseImp § 140**
  legal process, **FalseImp § 138**
  mental suffering, **FalseImp § 143**
  natural consequences, **FalseImp § 137**
  nominal damages, **FalseImp § 139**
  pleadings, **FalseImp § 116**
  punitive damages, below
  remittitur, **FalseImp § 141**
Defamation, **FalseImp § 5**
Defective on its face, process, **FalseImp § 81**
Defenses
  generally, **FalseImp § 52 to 107**
  consent, **FalseImp § 53**
  contributory negligence, **FalseImp § 54**
  criminal liability, **FalseImp § 160**
  immunity, below
  justification, below
  legal process, below
  release from liability, **FalseImp § 55**
  res judicata, **FalseImp § 59**

For assistance using this Index, call 1-800-328-4880

394

Reference to multiple sections

FIGURE 4.2 **AM. JUR. 2d MAIN VOLUME ENTRY UNDER FALSE IMPRISONMENT**

Sections on false imprisonment

AMERICAN JURISPRUDENCE 2D

interference with that person's personal liberty.[6]

§ 2 False arrest

Research References

West's Key Number Digest, False Imprisonment ⚷2
Am. Jur. Pleading and Practice Forms, Instructions to jury defining false imprisonment, False Imprisonment § 7

False arrest, a name sometimes given to the tort more generally known as false imprisonment,[1] has been defined as the unlawful restraint by one person of the physical liberty of another by acting to cause a false arrest, that is, an arrest made without legal authority,[2] or without sufficient legal authority,[3] resulting in an injury.[4] The claim usually arises from being unlawfully imprisoned through some extrajudicial act that does not amount to legal process, such as an unlawful detention by the police.[5] However, the tort of false arrest does not require a formal arrest, but a manifest intent to take someone into custody and subject that person to the defendant's control.[6] For false arrest to give rise to a cause of action, there is no requirement that the arrest be formal, that the detention be for the purpose of arraignment, or that the detention continue until [...] judicial officer.[7]

References to primary authority from multiple jurisdictions

§ 3 Distinction between false imprisonment an[...]

Research References

West's Key Number Digest, False Imprisonment ⚷2

Some courts have stated that false arrest and false imprisonment are distinguishable only in terminology.[1] The two have been called

[6]Phillips v. District of Columbia, 458 A.2d 722 (D.C. 1983).

[Section 2]

[1]Headrick v. Wal-Mart Stores, Inc., 293 Ark. 433, 738 S.W.2d 418 (1987); Highfill v. Hale, 186 S.W.3d 277 (Mo. 2006).

[2]Stern v. Thompson & Coates, Ltd., 185 Wis. 2d 220, 517 N.W.2d 658 (1994).

[3]Limited Stores, Inc. v. Wilson-Robinson, 317 Ark. 80, 876 S.W.2d 248 (1994).

[4]Landry v. Duncan, 902 So. 2d 1098 (La. Ct. App. 5th Cir. 2005).

[5]Snodderly v. R.U.F.F. Drug Enforcement Task Force, 239 F.3d 892 (7th Cir. 2001); Dumas v. City of New Orleans, 803 So. 2d 1001, 161 Ed. Law Rep. 713 (La. Ct. App. 4th Cir. 2001), writ denied, 811 So. 2d 912 (La. 2002).

[6]Cooper v. Dyke, 814 F.2d 941 (4th Cir. 1987).

[7]Day v. Wells Fargo Guard Service Co., 711 S.W.2d 503 (Mo. 1986).

[Section 3]

[1]Johnson v. Weiner, 155 Fla. 169, 19 So. 2d 699 (1944); Fox v. McCurnin, 205 Iowa 752, 218 N.W. 499 (1928); Holland v. Lutz, 194 Kan. 712, 401 P.2d 1015 (1965).

46

FIGURE 4.3 **AM. JUR. 2D POCKET PART ENTRY FOR FALSE IMPRISONMENT**

FALSE IMPRISONMENT

KeyCite®: Cases and other legal materials listed in KeyCite Scope can be researched through the KeyCite service on Westlaw®. Use KeyCite to check citations for form, parallel references, prior and later history, and comprehensive citator information, including citations to other decisions and secondary materials.

I. CIVIL ACTIONS

A. DEFINITIONS AND DISTINCTIONS

1. *In General*

§ 1 False imprisonment

Cases

False imprisonment is the unlawful violation of the personal liberty of another, where the restraint required may be effectuated by means of physical force, threat of force, confinement by physical barriers, or by means of any other form of unreasonable duress. Jon Davler, Inc. v. Arch Insurance Company, 229 Cal. App. 4th 1025, 2014 WL 4628477 (2d Dist. 2014), as modified, (Sept. 15, 2014).

New research reference is listed for § 2.

§ 2 False arrest

Cases

Under Ohio law, false arrest, rather than malicious prosecution, was proper claim for arrestee to pursue against township police officers, since he was arrested pursuant to void legal process. U.S.C.A. Const.Amend. 4. Ruble v. Escola, 898 F. Supp. 2d 956 (N.D. Ohio 2012).

§ 3 Distinction between false imprisonment and false arrest

Cases

Courts analyze false arrest and false imprisonment claims brought pursuant to California law under the same rubric as § 1983 claims based on false arrest under the Fourth Amendment. U.S. Const. Amend. 4; 42 U.S.C.A. § 1983. Jaramillo v. City of San Mateo, 76 F. Supp. 3d 905 (N.D. Cal. 2014).

Under District of Columbia law, false arrest is indistinguishable as practical matter from common law tort of false imprisonment. Dormu v. District of Columbia, 795 F. Supp. 2d 7 (D.D.C. 2011).

Under Michigan law, a false imprisonment is broader than, but includes, a false arrest involving law enforcement. Valdez v. U.S., 58 F. Supp. 3d 795 (W.D. Mich. 2014).

Under Minnesota law, an arrest made without proper legal authority is a false arrest, and any subsequent restraint ; false imprisonment. Strei v. Blaine, 996 F. Supp. 2d 763 (D. Minn. 2014).

In New York, claim colloquially known as false arrest is variant of tort of false imprisonment, and that tort is used to analyze an alleged Fourth Amendment violation in the § 1983 context. U.S.C.A. Const.Amend. 4; 42 U.S.C.A. § 1983. Slack v. County of Suffolk, 50 F. Supp. 3d 254 (E.D. N.Y. 2014).

In New York, the claim colloquially known as "false arrest" is a variant of the tort of false imprisonment, and that tort is used to analyze an alleged Fourth Amendment violation in the § 1983 context. U.S.C.A. Const.Amend. 4; 42 U.S.C.A. § 1983. Pittman v. Incorporated Village of Hempstead, 49 F. Supp. 3d 307 (E.D. N.Y. 2014).

B. ELEMENTS

1. *In General*

§ 7 Generally

Cases

A plaintiff bringing a claim for false arrest under Louisiana law must prove: (1) detention of the person, and (2) the unlawfulness of the detention. Harvey v. Caesars Entertainment Operating Co., Inc., 55 F. Supp. 3d 901 (N.D. Miss. 2014).

2. *Detention or Restraint*

§ 10 Generally

Cases

Supervisor of employee, who sought to leave work due to severe chest pain and headache, did not engage in willful detention, as element of false-imprisonment claim against employer, when supervisor allegedly told employee that employee could not leave work without accumulating "double points" under point system governing employee absences, where there was no indication that supervisor or employer would have fired employee if employee had left. Service Companies, Inc. v. Estate of Mautrice Vaughn, 169 So. 3d 875 (Miss. 2015).

2

Reprinted with permission from Thomson Reuters/West, *American Jurisprudence*, 2d Series, Vol. 32 Cumulative Supplement (2017), p. 2.

The print research process is slightly different for legal periodicals, Restatements, and uniform laws and model acts.

For legal periodicals, you need to use a periodical index to research articles by subject. The *Index to Legal Periodicals and Books* and *Legal-Trac* are online periodical indexes discussed in Section C, below.

Print research with Restatements requires you to understand the unique organization of this publication. Restatements have two components: the Restatement Rules volumes, which contain the Restatement rules, comments, and illustrations; and the Appendix volumes, which contain case summaries. To research a Restatement, you must follow two steps: (1) find relevant sections of the Restatement in the Rules volumes using the index or table of contents; and (2) find case summaries interpreting the Restatement in the Appendix volumes. The Appendix volumes are not cumulative; each covers only a specific period of time. The latest Appendix volume is updated with a pocket part.

For print research into uniform laws and model acts, one of the best resources to use is a publication entitled *Uniform Laws Annotated, Master Edition* (ULA). This is a multivolume set of books containing the text of a number of uniform laws and model acts. You can locate it through the online catalog in your library.

Once you have located the ULA set, you have several research options. To determine the best research option for your project, you should review the *Directory of Uniform Acts and Codes: Tables and Index*. This softcover booklet is published annually and explains the finding tools available in this resource. You can research uniform laws and model acts by subject, by the name of the law, or by adopting jurisdiction. Once you have located relevant information in the main volumes of the ULA set, use the pocket part to update your research.

C. RESEARCHING SECONDARY SOURCES ONLINE

1. WESTLAW

Westlaw provides access to a wide range of secondary sources, including both Am. Jur. 2d and C.J.S. Westlaw also provides comprehensive coverage of A.L.R. Annotations. Many legal periodicals and selected treatises are available, as are Restatements of the law, uniform laws and model acts, and the *Uniform Laws Annotated* (ULA) set described in Section B, above.

Westlaw allows you to retrieve a secondary source by entering the citation in the search box. Source-driven searching is another option. You can search across secondary sources or within individual publications.

Once you select a publication, you have several search options. One option is executing a word search. Another option is searching by subject by browsing the table of contents for a secondary source. This will allow you to retrieve sections of the publication by selecting them from the table of contents without having to execute a word search. Table of contents searching is available for legal encyclopedias, treatises, Restatement rules, and many uniform laws but not for A.L.R. Annotations or legal periodicals. Westlaw also provides access to the indexes to selected secondary sources, including A.L.R.

To select a specific secondary source, browse the menu options on the home page until you locate the publication you want to research. You can choose **Secondary Sources** under the **All Content** tab to select a publication. You can also use the options under the **State Materials** tab for state-specific secondary sources or under the **Practice Areas** tab for subject-specific secondary sources. On the page for an individual publication you will see the table of contents. If the index is available, a link to the index will appear under **Tools & Resources** on the right side of the screen.

To research Restatements, remember that each Restatement consists of two components: rules (including comments and illustrations) and annotations summarizing cases interpreting the rules. Westlaw combines all of the components for individual Restatements together. When you view a Restatement section, the case annotations will follow the comments and illustrations in a single document. This means that any word search you execute that includes a Restatement will search for the terms in both the rules and the case annotations (unless you specifically limit the search).

To research uniform laws in *Uniform Laws Annotated* (ULA), you must select the database for that publication. One way to access that database is by selecting **Statutes and Court Rules** under the **All Content** tab on the home page. A link to *Uniform Laws Annotated* appears on the right under **Tools & Resources.**

You can also locate secondary sources using a content-driven search. After you execute a search, the **Secondary Sources** section of the search results will include secondary sources such as legal encyclopedias, A.L.R. Annotations, treatises, Restatements, and uniform laws. You can filter the results as you would other search results by publication type, words in the documents, and other criteria. If you pre-filter your search by jurisdiction, Westlaw will include secondary sources from that jurisdiction in the search results, as well as resources that are not jurisdiction-specific such as Am. Jur. 2d and A.L.R.

More information on researching in Westlaw appears in Chapter 10. An example of a secondary source from Westlaw appears in the sample pages in Section E, below.

2. LEXIS ADVANCE

Lexis Advance is another useful source for secondary material. It provides access to Am. Jur. 2d but not C.J.S. Lexis Advance also provides access to most A.L.R. Annotations; only the first series of A.L.R. and A.L.R. International are excluded from its coverage. Restatements of the law and a number of uniform laws and model acts are available in Lexis Advance, as are many legal periodicals and selected treatises.

Lexis Advance allows you to retrieve a secondary source by entering the citation in the search box. Source-driven searching is another option. You can search across secondary sources or within individual publications.

In general, if you know which type of secondary authority you want to research, you will begin a source-driven search by selecting **Secondary Materials** as the content type from the **Explore Content** menu and choosing a publication. You can also select the source you want to search from the **Browse** menu. Choose the option to browse by **Source** and enter the publication name. If you search by **Category**, most secondary sources appear under the category for **Secondary Materials**, but uniform laws and model acts appear under **Statutes and Legislation**. Within each category, you can select one or more publications. Once you select a publication, you can add it as a search filter to execute a word search within the publication. You may also have the option to view the publication's table of contents. If so, selecting that option will allow you to search within the table of contents or expand the outline to view the publication's content.

To research Restatements, remember that each Restatement consists of rules (including comments and illustrations) and annotations summarizing cases interpreting the rules. Lexis Advance separates these two components of Restatements. You can execute word searches or browse the table of contents for the rules component of an individual Restatement. When you view an individual Restatement section, the link to **Citators** in the **About this Document** section retrieves case annotations.

You can execute a word search for secondary sources generally by selecting **Secondary Material** under the **Explore Content** tab or executing a content-driven search and viewing the results in the **Secondary Materials** section. The results for either type of search will include secondary sources such as legal encyclopedias, A.L.R. Annotations, treatises, and Restatements. Uniform laws and model acts are listed under **Statutes and Legislation.** You can filter the results as you would other search results by publication type, words in the documents, and other criteria.

Pre-filtering by jurisdiction can affect your secondary source search results in Lexis Advance. If you pre-filter by jurisdiction from **State** tab in the **Explore Content** menu, Lexis Advance will only include jurisdiction-specific secondary sources in the results. If you pre-filter by jurisdiction using the drop-down menu on the right side of the search bar, you will have the option to include non-jurisdictional content such as Am. Jur. 2d and A.L.R.

To search for secondary sources by topic, use the topic choices under the **Explore Content** and **Browse** menus.

More information on researching in Lexis Advance appears in Chapter 10. An example of a secondary source from Lexis Advance appears in the sample pages in Section E, below.

3. BLOOMBERG LAW

Bloomberg Law provides access to a different universe of secondary sources than Lexis Advance and Westlaw. It has commentary and analysis created by the Bureau of National Affairs (BNA), a commercial publisher that Bloomberg Law acquired. It also contains treatises and practice manuals on various subject areas and from a variety of jurisdictions. It provides access to selected law reviews and journals. Additionally, Bloomberg Law includes uniform laws with commentary but not the *Uniform Laws Annotated* set available through Westlaw. Bloomberg Law does not provide access to Am. Jur. 2d, C.J.S., or A.L.R.

You can use source- or content-driven searching in Bloomberg Law. For source-driven searching, select secondary sources by choosing the option to **Browse All Content** or using the **Select Sources** drop-down menu in the search bar. Once you select one or more secondary sources, you can execute a word search or browse a publication's table of contents.

If you use a content-driven search approach, secondary sources will be listed with other search results in the left-hand menu. You can filter the results as you would other search results in Bloomberg Law. If you pre-filter your search by jurisdiction, the search results may or may not include secondary sources, depending on the jurisdictional filter.

When you research Restatements, note that Bloomberg Law organizes the material the same way print Restatements are organized. Rules are separated from case summaries. You can select a Restatement as a source to search under **U.S. Secondary Sources**. Restatements are categorized by content type under **Books and Treatises** in the sub-category for the American Law Institute. When you select a specific Restatement, you can search the Rules, Appendix volumes, or both. If you execute a content-driven search, Restatements are included in the search results, but entries from the Rules volumes will be listed separately from those from the Appendix volumes.

More information on researching in Bloomberg Law appears in Chapter 10. An example of a secondary source from Bloomberg Law appears in the sample pages in Section E, below.

4. SUBSCRIPTION SERVICES FOR LEGAL PERIODICALS

As noted in Section B, above, you can locate legal periodicals by subject using a periodical index. Two popular indexes are the *Index to Legal Periodicals & Books* (ILP) and LegalTrac. Both of these services index a wide range of periodicals and provide full text access to many articles. You can access one or both through your law library portal.

ILP is divided into two separate databases: *Index to Legal Periodicals Retrospective*, which indexes articles from 1908 to 1980, and *Index to Legal Periodicals Full Text*, which covers articles from 1980 to the present and includes the full text of selected articles. LegalTrac indexes articles from 1980 to present and also provides access to the full text of some articles. Both services allow you to search for legal periodicals in a variety of ways, including by author, subject, or keyword. When you execute the search, you will retrieve a list of citations to articles that fit the specifications of your search. If the document is available in full text, you can access it from the appropriate link. If the search results include articles that are not available in these services, you can use the citations to access the articles from other sources.

Figure 4.4 shows partial results of a search in ILP for articles on false imprisonment, and **Figure 4.5** shows search results from LegalTrac. LegalTrac also has a Topic Finder function that visually displays the words and subjects found most often within the text of your search results. This feature can help refine your search results.

FIGURE 4.4 **ILP CITATION LIST**

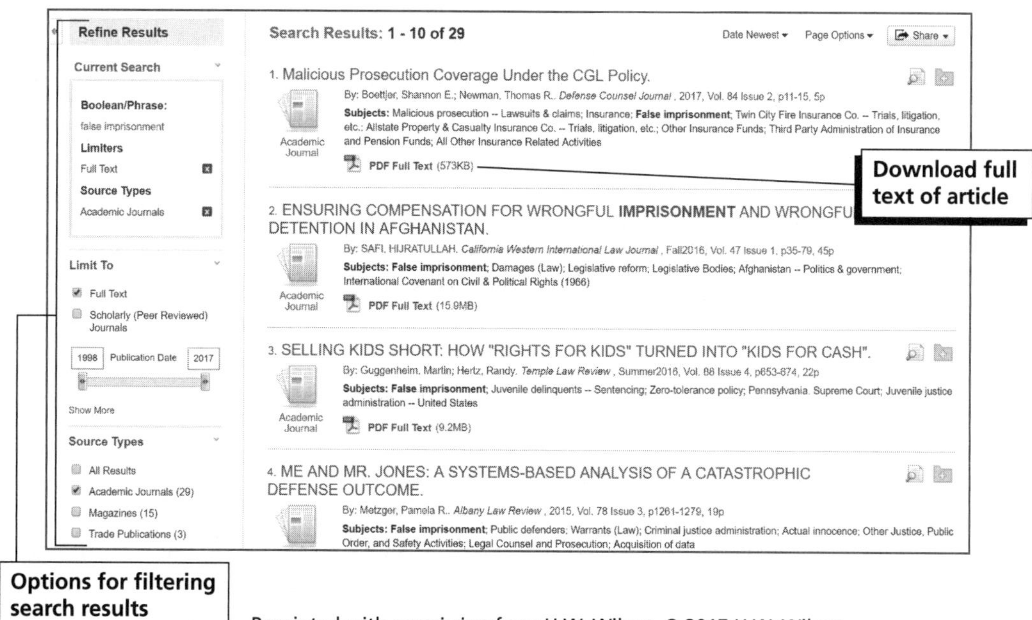

FIGURE 4.5 **LEGALTRAC CITATION LIST**

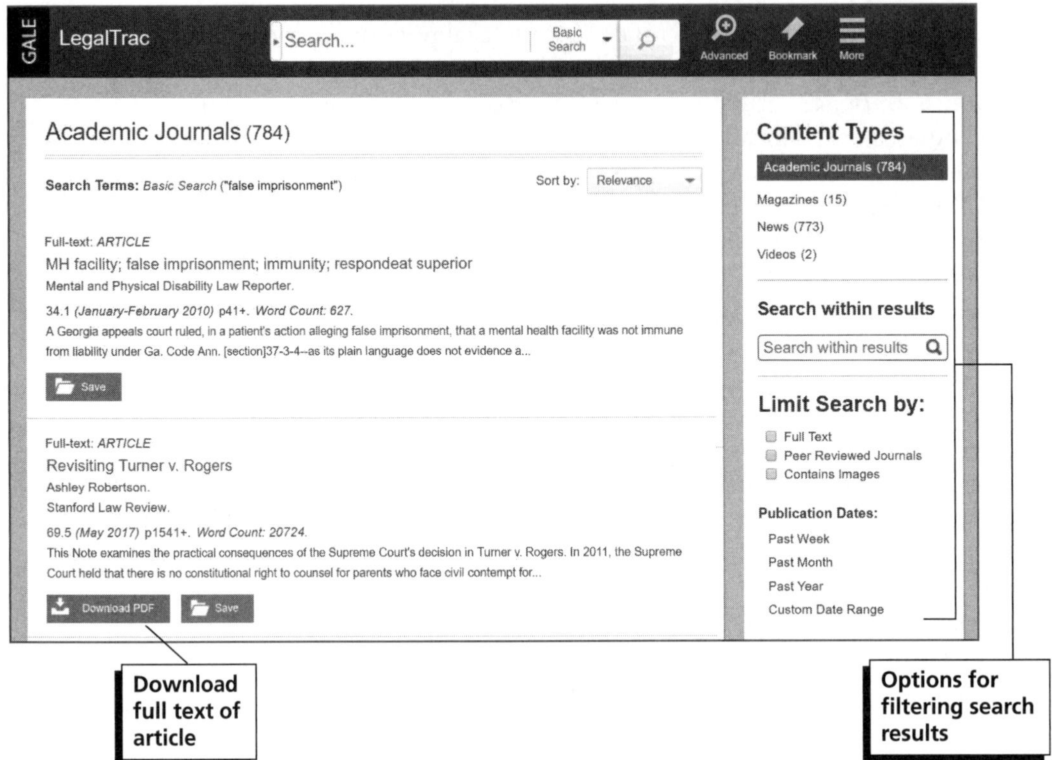

Reprinted Gale. LegalTrac ©, a part of Cengage Learning, Inc. Reproduced by permission. www.cengage.com/permissions.

HeinOnline is another service that provides online access to legal periodicals, among other types of authority. Many law libraries subscribe to this service; users generally access it through the library portal. HeinOnline's holdings go back further in time than those of ILP, LegalTrac, Lexis Advance, or Westlaw, often dating back to the inception of the periodicals in its database. You can search for legal periodical articles in HeinOnline in several ways. You can retrieve an article from its citation, search by title or author, or conduct word searches in the full text of the articles in HeinOnline's database. You can also browse the table of contents of individual publications. HeinOnline displays articles in .pdf format.

Figure 4.6 shows the HeinOnline display of a legal periodical article.

5. PUBLICLY ACCESSIBLE SOURCES

You use publicly accessible websites on a daily basis for news, entertainment, shopping, and many other purposes. It is natural, therefore, to

FIGURE 4.6 HEINONLINE DISPLAY OF A LEGAL PERIODICAL ARTICLE

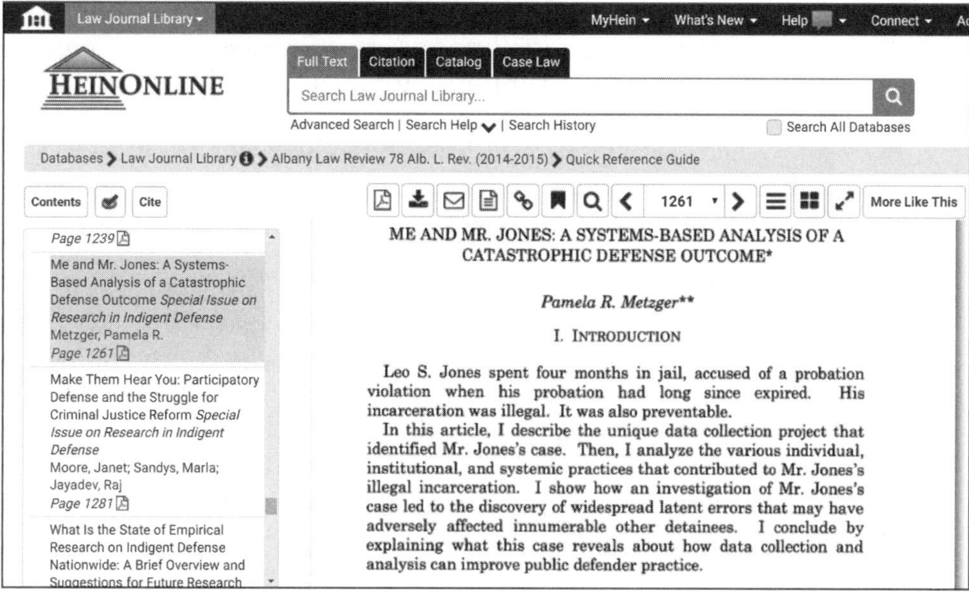

think of using the Internet for legal research as well. You may decide to use general Internet sources as one component of your research strategy, but you would not want that to be your sole approach for locating secondary material on an issue.

Legal encyclopedias, treatises, and A.L.R. Annotations are not available via publicly accessible Internet sites. You may be able to find some uniform laws or model acts and selected sections of Restatements on the Internet, but you will not generally find complete compilations of these sources, nor will you find the comments, illustrations, or annotations.

A significant amount of recent legal scholarship in law reviews and journals is available on the Internet through two additional sources: Social Science Research Network (SSRN) and Digital Commons Network. The URLs for both of these sources appear in Appendix A.

SSRN provides free access to scholarly articles in a number of fields, including law. Authors make their published work and ongoing research available by posting it on SSRN. Because SSRN largely relies on authors to post their own work, its coverage is somewhat idiosyncratic, but many legal academics have posted their entire publishing histories. You can research articles on SSRN in a number of ways, including by keyword or author.

The Digital Commons Network is another resource that provides free access to law review articles, as well as scholarship in other fields.

It is an institutional repository, meaning that an institution, like a law school, uses Digital Commons for digital storage of its publications. Some journals now publish exclusively through Digital Commons and no longer produce physical print copies. Because Digital Commons is a publicly accessible repository, articles published here will appear in Google search results.

General legal research websites may also contain links to legal periodicals. Google Scholar, a specialty version of Google's search engine described in more detail in Chapter 5, allows you to search for law journal articles. Sometimes, however, access to the full text requires a subscription to the service (such as HeinOnline) that hosts the article. A few law schools publish special online versions of their law journals. Virtually all make at least their current volume, and often prior volumes, available on their websites. If you have the citation or title of an article that is available online, this can be a quick and economical way to obtain it.

The secondary sources discussed so far in this chapter are the traditional sources used for legal research, but many non-traditional secondary sources are available online. Sources such as Wikipedia contain information about the law. Free legal research sites like FindLaw often include articles written by lawyers or legal, and websites located through a Google search can provide useful information. These non-traditional Internet sources are secondary sources, and all of the caveats regarding appropriate uses of traditional legal secondary sources apply to them with equal force. Lawyers do not consider these sources authoritative, and it is difficult to imagine circumstances under which you would cite one.

Using publicly available Internet sites can be both easier and harder than using more traditional legal research tools. It can be easier in the sense that Internet sources are cost-effective to use and can provide easy access to information relevant to your research. It can be harder in the sense that you cannot assume that a non-traditional secondary source is reliable. It is important to remember that any person with a message and the appropriate equipment can publish material online. Because online sources can be updated at any time, they may be perceived as providing current information even if they have not been updated for a long period of time. Therefore, you must take special care to evaluate any secondary information you find on the Internet. Chapter 10, on online legal research, discusses publicly available websites, blogs, and other Internet-based research sources. You may want to review that chapter before using the Internet to locate non-traditional secondary sources. In addition, Appendix A lists websites that may be useful for secondary source research.

FIGURE 4.7 **RULES FOR CITING SECONDARY SOURCES**

SECONDARY SOURCE	*ALWD GUIDE* (6th ed.)	*BLUEBOOK* (20th ed.)
Legal encyclopedias	Rule 22.3	Bluepages B15
Treatises	Rule 20	Bluepages B15
Legal periodicals	Rule 21	Bluepages B16
A.L.R. Annotations	Rule 22.5	Rule 16.7.6
Restatements	Rule 23.1	Bluepages B12.1.3
Uniform laws	Rule 23.5	Bluepages B12.1.3; see also Rule 12.9.4
Model acts	Rule 23.3	Rule 12.9.4

D. CITING SECONDARY SOURCES

The chart in **Figure** 4.7 lists the rules in the *ALWD Guide* (6th ed.) and the *Bluebook* (20th ed.) governing citations to secondary sources. Citations to each of these sources are discussed in turn.

1. LEGAL ENCYCLOPEDIAS

Citations to legal encyclopedias are covered in *ALWD Guide* Rule 22.3 and *Bluebook* Bluepages B15. The citation consists of five elements: (1) the volume number; (2) the abbreviated name of the encyclopedia; (3) the name of the topic, underlined or italicized; (4) the section cited (with a space between the section symbol (§) and the section number); and (5) a parenthetical containing the date of the book, including, if appropriate, the date of the pocket part or supplement. Here is an example:

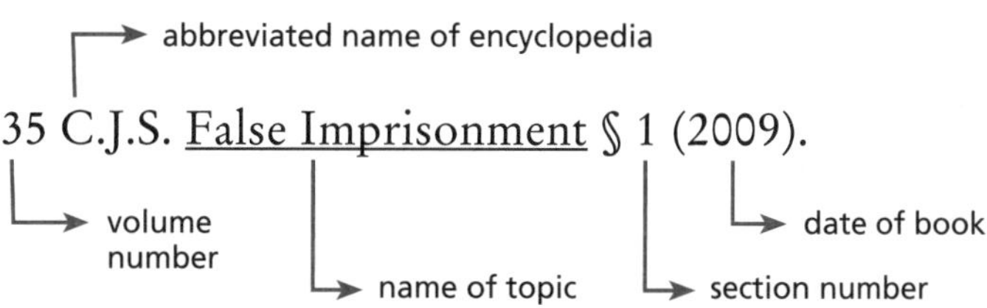

Sometimes determining which date or dates to include in the parenthetical can be confusing. The answer is always a function of where a reader would have to look to find all of the text and footnote information on the section you are citing. If all of the information appears in the main volume of the encyclopedia, the date in the parenthetical should refer only to the main volume. If the section is a new section that appears only in the pocket part, the date should refer only to the pocket part. If the reader must refer both to the main volume and to the pocket part, the parenthetical should list both dates. Here are several examples:

35 C.J.S. False Imprisonment § 1 (2009).

In this example, the reference is only to the main volume.

35 C.J.S. False Imprisonment § 1 (2009 & Supp. 2018).

In this example, the reference is both to the main volume and to the pocket part.

32 Am. Jur. 2d False Imprisonment § 1 (Supp. 2018).

In this example, the reference is only to the pocket part.

2. TREATISES

Citations to treatises are covered in *ALWD Guide* Rule 20 and *Bluebook* Bluepages B15. The citation consists of five elements: (1) the volume number of the treatise (in a multivolume set); (2) the author's full name (if the treatise has more than two authors, you can list the first, followed by et al.); (3) the title of the treatise, underlined or italicized; (4) a pinpoint reference to the material cited; and (5) a parenthetical containing the edition (if more than one edition has been published) and the date, including, if appropriate, the date of the pocket part. Here is an example:

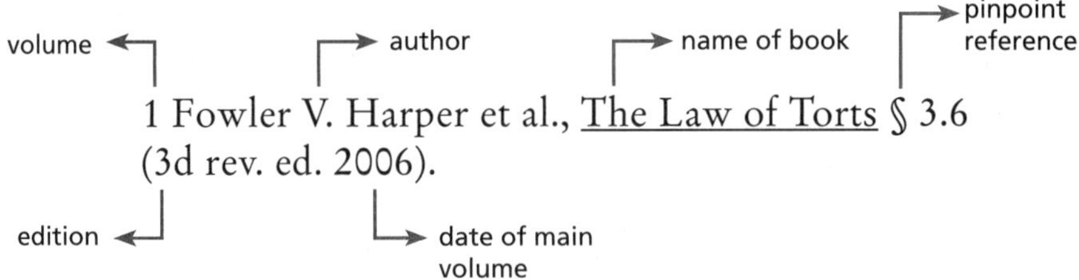

Note that a comma separates the part of the citation identifying the author from the title of the treatise. No other commas appear in the citation. Additional rules apply to citations to books with editors, translators, or multiple authors.

3. LEGAL PERIODICALS

Legal periodicals are published in two formats. Some publications begin the first issue within each volume with page one and continue numbering the pages of subsequent issues within that volume consecutively. These are called consecutively paginated publications. Most law reviews and journals are consecutively paginated. Other publications, such as monthly magazines, begin each new issue with page one, regardless of where the issue falls within the volume. These are called nonconsecutively paginated publications.

There are some differences in the citations to articles published in consecutively and nonconsecutively paginated periodicals. The explanation in this section focuses on citations to articles published in consecutively paginated law reviews, which are covered in *ALWD Guide* Rule 21 and *Bluebook* Bluepages B16.

A citation to a law review article consists of seven elements: (1) the author's full name; (2) the title of the article, underlined or italicized; (3) the volume number of the publication; (4) the abbreviated name of the publication; (5) the starting page of the article; (6) the pinpoint citation to the specific page or pages cited; and (7) a parenthetical containing the date of the publication. Here is an example:

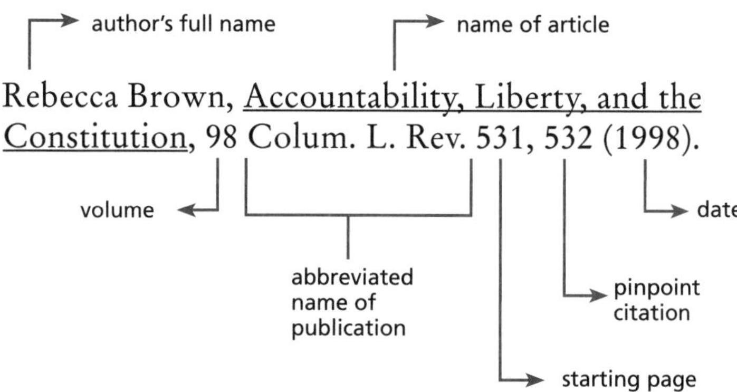

Note that the author's name, the name of the article, and the starting page of the article are followed by commas. The comma following the name of the article is not underlined or italicized.

Publication abbreviations can be found in *ALWD Guide* Appendix 5 and *Bluebook* Table T13. Notice that the abbreviations in *Bluebook* Table T13 appear in large and small capital letters. According to Bluepages B2, large and small capitals are permissible, but not required, when citing authority in a brief or memorandum. You may use ordinary roman type for the publication's name. Additional rules apply to citations to articles appearing in nonconsecutively paginated publications, articles written by students, and articles with more than one author.

4. A.L.R. ANNOTATIONS

Citations to A.L.R. Annotations are covered in *ALWD Guide* Rule 22.5 and *Bluebook* Rule 16.7.6. A citation to an A.L.R. Annotation consists of seven elements: (1) the author's full name followed by the notation "Annotation"; (2) the title of the Annotation, underlined or italicized; (3) the volume number; (4) the A.L.R. series; (5) the starting page of the Annotation; (6) the pinpoint citation to the specific page or pages cited; and (7) a parenthetical containing the date, including, if appropriate, the date of the pocket part. Here is an example:

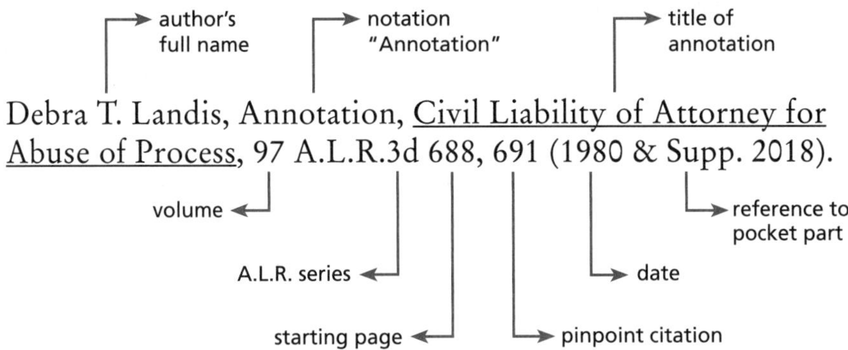

Although the example in *Bluebook* Rule 16.7.6 shows A.L.R. FED. in large and small capital letters, you may use ordinary roman type pursuant to Bluepages B2 for a citation in a memorandum or brief.

5. RESTATEMENTS

Citations to Restatements are covered in *ALWD Guide* Rule 23.1 and *Bluebook* Bluepages B12.1.3. They contain three elements: (1) the name of the Restatement; (2) the section cited (with a space between the section symbol (§) and the section number); and (3) a parenthetical with the abbreviation for the American Law Institute and the year of publication. Here is an example:

name of the Restatement — section — parenthetical

Restatement (Second) of Torts § 35 (Am. Law Inst. 1965).

6. UNIFORM LAWS AND MODEL ACTS

The citation format for a uniform law depends on whether the law has been adopted by a jurisdiction. If a jurisdiction adopts a uniform law, the law will be published with all of the other statutes for that jurisdiction. In that situation, cite directly to the jurisdiction's statute. The requirements for statutory citations are explained in Chapter 7.

Citations to uniform laws published in the ULA set are governed by *ALWD Guide* Rule 23.5. In the *Bluebook*, Bluepages B12.1.3 gives an example of a citation to a uniform law; additional information on citing laws published in the ULA set appears in Rule 12.9.4. The citation consists of six elements: (1) the abbreviated title of the act; (2) the section cited (with a space between the section symbol (§) and section number); (3) the ULA volume number; (4) the abbreviation U.L.A.; (5) the page of the ULA on which the section appears; and (6) a parenthetical containing the date of the ULA volume, including, if appropriate, the date of the pocket part. Here is an example:

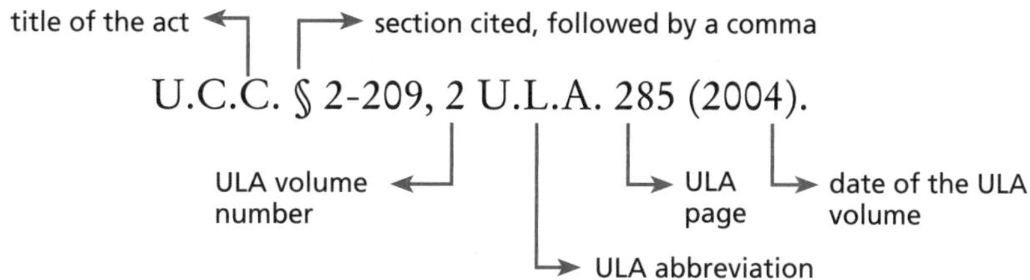

Citations to model acts are covered in *ALWD Guide* Rule 23.3 and *Bluebook* Rule 12.9.4. The citation consists of three elements: (1) the name of the act; (2) the section cited (with a space between the section symbol (§) and the section number); and (3) a parenthetical with the publisher and date. Here is an example:

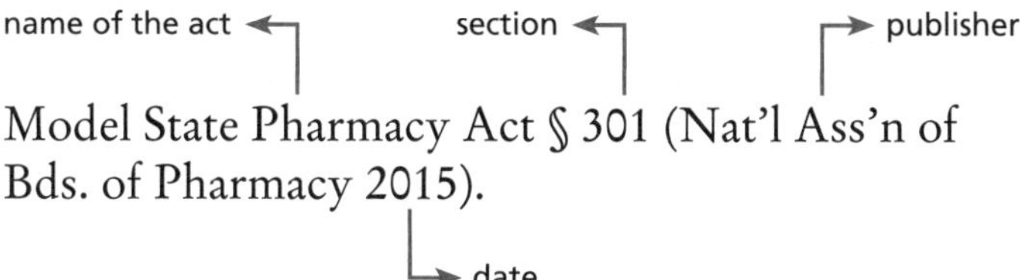

The examples of citations to uniform laws and model acts in *Bluebook* Rule 12.9.4 show the names of the laws in large and small capital letters. According to Bluepages B2, however, you may use ordinary roman type to cite these authorities in a memorandum or brief.

E. SAMPLE PAGES FOR SECONDARY SOURCE RESEARCH

Beginning on the following page, **Figure 4.8** contains sample pages from a print A.L.R. Annotation. **Figures 4.9** through **4.12** show documents in Lexis Advance, Westlaw, and Bloomberg Law.

To locate an A.L.R. Annotation, begin by looking up your subject in the A.L.R. Index. The A.L.R. index will refer you to Annotations. The reference will tell you the volume number, series, and starting page of the Annotation. The A.L.R. Index includes a reference to this Annotation about whether a parent who takes a child without permission commits false imprisonment.

The Annotation will begin with a list of research references, an outline of the Annotation, and an alphabetical index of topics within the Annotation.

FIGURE 4.8 **A.L.R. ANNOTATION**

ANNOTATION

KIDNAPPING OR RELATED OFFENSE BY TAKING OR REMOVING OF CHILD BY OR UNDER AUTHORITY OF PARENT OR ONE IN LOCO PARENTIS

by

William B. Johnson, J.D.

References to other research sources, including Am. Jur. 2d

TOTAL CLIENT-SERVICE LIBRARY® REFERENCES

1 Am Jur 2d, Abduction and Kidnapping § 19; 24 Am Jur 2d, Divorce and Separation §§ 801–804, 811 59 Am Jur 2d, Parent and Child §§ 108–110

Annotations: See the related matters listed in the annotation, infra.

19 Am Jur Pl & Pr Forms (Rev), Parent and Child, Forms 62–65

13 Am Jur Legal Forms 2d, Parent and Child § 191:53

15 Am Jur Proof of Facts 1, Child Custody; 1 Am Jur Proof of Facts 2d, 41 Change in Circumstances Justifying Modification of Child Support Order; 2 Am Jur Proof of Facts 2d 791, Denial of Child Visitation Rights

2 Am Jur Trials 171, Investigating Particular Crimes; 22 Am Jur Trials 347, Child Custody Litigation

18 USCS § 1201

US L Ed Digest, Abduction and Kidnapping § 1

L Ed Index to Annos, Abduction; Children and Minors; False Imprisonment; Kidnapping

ALR Quick Index, Abduction and Kidnapping; Children; Custody and Support of Children; False Imprisonment or Arrest; Uniform Child Custody Jurisdiction Act

Federal Quick Index, Abduction and Kidnapping; Children and Minors; Custody of Children; Divorce and Separation; False Imprisonment and Arrest

Consult POCKET PART in this volume for later cases

FIGURE 4.8 A.L.R. ANNOTATION *(Continued)*

Outline of the Annotation

Note that cases coming to different conclusions are summarized in the Annotation.

KIDNAPPING—TAKING OF OWN CHILD 20 ALR4th
20 ALR4th 823

Kidnapping or related offense by taking or removing of child by or under authority of parent or one in loco parentis

I. PRELIMINARY MATTERS

§ 1. Introduction:
[a] Scope
[b] Related matters
§ 2. Summary and comment:
[a] Generally
[b] Practice pointers

II. EFFECT ON CRIMINAL LIABILITY OF COURT ORDER AWARDING CUSTODY

§ 3. Absence of decree awarding custody—liability of parent or person in loco parentis
§ 4. —Liability of agent:
[a] View that agent may be held liable
[b] View that agent may not be held liable
[c] View that liability of agent depends on circumstances
§ 5. Presence of decree—generally:
[a] Parent or agent held liable or subject to liability
[b] Parent or agent held not liable or subject to liability
§ 6. —Where parent or agent lacked actual knowledge of custody decree

III. ASSERTED DEFENSES

§ 7. Consent of custodian
§ 8. Consent of child
§ 9. Unconstitutional vagueness of criminal statute

After the outline, each Annotation has its own subject index to help you locate information within the Annotation.

INDEX

824

Following the index, you will see a list of the jurisdictions from which authority is cited within the Annotation. The first part of the Annotation will set out the scope of coverage, list Annotations on related subjects, and summarize the law on the topic.

FIGURE 4.8 **A.L.R. ANNOTATION *(Continued)***

20 ALR4th KIDNAPPING—TAKING OF OWN CHILD § 1[a]
20 ALR4th 823

Jurisdictions from which authority is cited

TABLE OF JURISDICTIONS REPRESENTED
Consult POCKET PART in this volume for later cases

US: §§ 3
Ariz: §§ 2[b], 5[a]
Cal: §§ 2[b], 3, 4[a], 5[a]
Colo: §§ 5[a]
DC: §§ 3
Ga: §§ 3
Idaho: §§ 3, 4[b]
Ill: §§ 2[b], 5[a]
Ind: §§ 5[a], 9
Iowa: §§ 3, 4[b]
Kan: §§ 3, 4[a, b], 5[a], 6
La: §§ 3, 4[b]
Me: §§ 5[b]
Mass: §§ 5[a, b], 6, 8
Mich: §§ 3, 4[b, c], 5[b], 8
Minn: §§ 5[b]
Miss: §§ 3
Mo: §§ 3, 4[a]
NH: §§ 5[a], 7, 8
NJ: §§ 3, 4[c]
NM: §§ 3
NY: §§ 3, 4[b], 5[a, b], 6, 9
NC: §§ 3, 4[b], 7
Ohio: §§ 2[b], 5[a, b]
Or: §§ 3, 4[b]
Pa: §§ 3, 4[b]
Tenn: §§ 5[a], 6, 9
Wash: §§ 5[a], 8
Wyo: §§ 3, 7, 8

I. Preliminary matters

§ 1. Introduction

[a] Scope

This annotation[1] collects and analyzes the state and federal criminal cases in which the courts have discussed or decided whether, or under what circumstances, a parent or or

1. This annotation supersedes the annotation at 77 ALR 317.

Introduction to the Annotation

After the introductory material, the Annotation will explain the law on the topic in greater detail, summarize key cases, and provide citations to additional cases on the topic. To update, you would need to check the pocket part for summaries of more recent cases.

FIGURE 4.8 **A.L.R. ANNOTATION *(Continued)***

20 ALR4th KIDNAPPING—TAKING OF OWN CHILD §
20 ALR4th 823

of a parent would be greater where the child passes into the hands of one having no parental obligations towards it.

For Kansas cases, see § 4[b].

In State v Brandenburg (1911) 232 **Mo** 531, 134 SW 529, the court, sustaining the conviction of one acting as agent of the mother, said that, under the applicable statute, the right of one parent to invade the possession of another parent, to take or decoy away their mutual offspring, if such a right exists, cannot be delegated to an agent. Under a different construction of the statute, the court reasoned, before a person could be arrested for taking a child from a parent, the parent would be required to first ascertain whether the person who took the child acted as an agent for the other parent, or was a mere kidnapper. In this case the child's mother had left the father, taking the child with her, and apparently obtained a foreign divorce. Thereafter she married the defendant. After experiencing some financial difficulties, she returned the child to the father, allegedly in return for a promise that the child would be returned to her when her situation improved. But the father instituted his own action for divorce and sought sole custody of the child. Then the defendant decoyed the child away, at a time when the father was not home, by telling the child that he was going to take it to its mother. Instead of going directly to the mother, he took the child to San Francisco where, he claimed, the mother had agreed to meet him later.

[b] View that agent may not be held liable

In the following cases the courts held or recognized that one who acts as an agent of a parent or assists a parent in taking exclusive possession of a child is not criminally liable for kidnapping or a similar crime, where there has been no court order establishing custody of the child.

Idaho—State v Beslin (1911) 19 Idaho 185, 112 P 1053.

Iowa—State v Dewey (1912) 155 Iowa 469, 136 NW 533.

Kan—State v Angel (1889) 42 Kan 216, 21 P 1075.

La—State v Elliott (1930) 171 La 306, 131 So 28.

Mich—People v Nelson (1948) 322 Mich 262, 33 NW2d 786.

NC—State v Walker (1978) 35 NC App 182, 241 SE2d 89.

NY—People v Workman (1916) 94 Misc 374, 157 NYS 594.

Or—State v Edmiston (1979) 43 Or App 13, 602 P2d 282.

Pa—Burns v Commonwealth (1889) 129 Pa 138, 18 A 756; Commonwealth v Myers (1892) 146 Pa 24, 23 A 164.

In State v Angel (1889) 42 **Kan** 216, 21 P 1075, the court reversed the conviction of a man who had merely assisted a woman in leaving her husband and, in doing so, had assisted her in taking her child. The woman had wanted to leave her husband, and the man assisted by going to her house at her request and falsely saying that she was needed to help a sick child at a nearby home. The woman bundled her child and the man drove them away. After leaving, the mother had lawful charge of the child all of the time. Since there had been no judicial decree as to custody of the child, the court stated that the mother had an equal right with her husband to the actual care and control of the child; and she could not be punished under applicable kidnapping statutes. The court

831

Citations to cases from multiple jurisdictions

Discussion of the law with a more detailed case summary

Am. Jur. 2d is available in Lexis Advance and Westlaw. To locate information in Am. Jur. 2d, you can execute a content-driven search and filter the results for secondary sources. You can also execute a source-driven search by browsing sources and selecting Am. Jur. 2d as a source to search.

When you view an individual section of Am. Jur. 2d, the text of the section appears at the beginning and contains links to footnotes with supporting citations. In Lexis Advance, use Previous and Next to browse preceding or subsequent sections and the Table of Contents tab to view the table of contents of the entry on False Imprisonment.

FIGURE 4.9 **SECTION OF AM. JUR. 2D IN LEXIS ADVANCE**

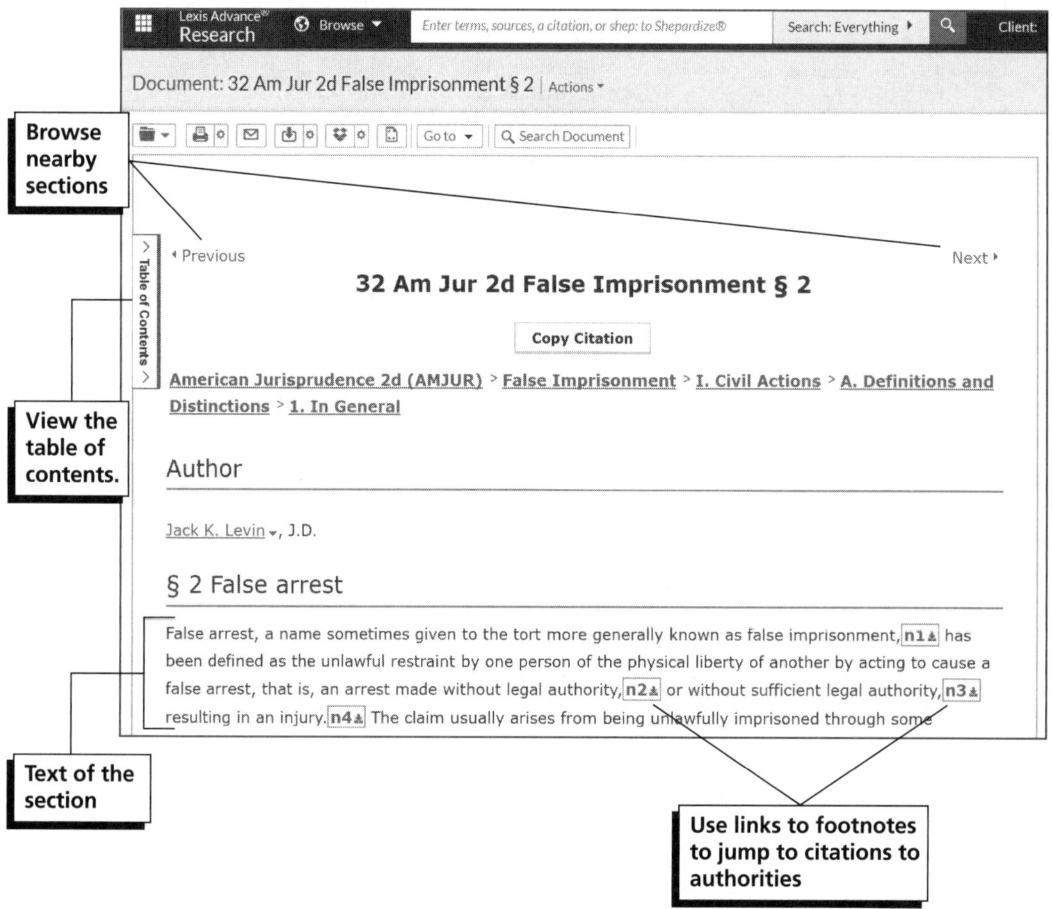

Following the text is a Supplement section. This section contains updated information from the pocket part in the print version of Am. Jur. 2d. The footnotes appear at the end of the document and contain links to the cited sources.

FIGURE 4.9 SECTION OF AM. JUR. 2D IN LEXIS ADVANCE *(Continued)*

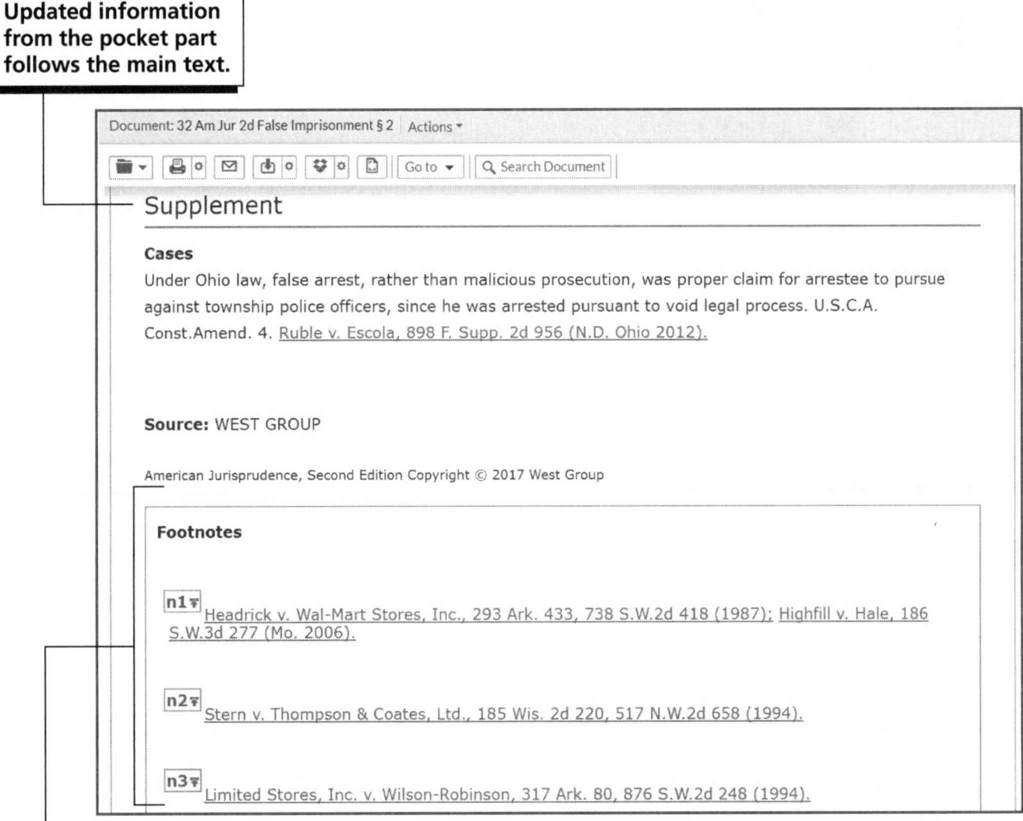

A.L.R. Annotations are available in Lexis Advance and Westlaw. Figure 4.10 shows part of an A.L.R. Annotation in Westlaw. When you view an A.L.R. Annotation in Westlaw, the updated material from the pocket part follows the text of each individual section from the main volume.

FIGURE 4.10 PORTION OF AN A.L.R. ANNOTATION IN WESTLAW

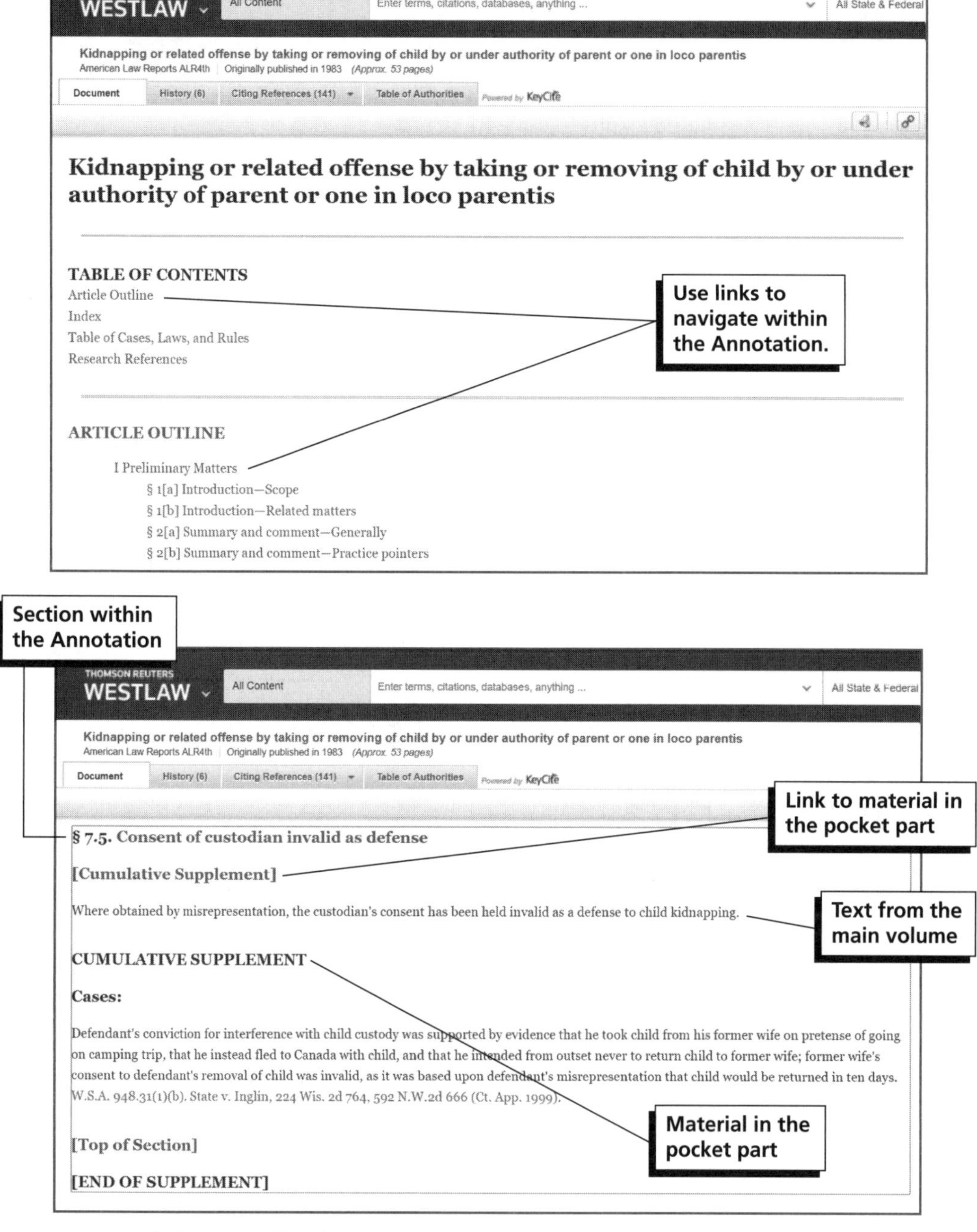

Restatements are available in Lexis Advance, Westlaw, and Bloomberg Law. If you execute a content-driven search, Restatement provisions will be included in the search results. Bloomberg Law organizes its Restatement content the same way the print version is organized. When you select a Restatement as a source to search, you can browse the table of contents, search within the entire Restatement (Rules and Appendix volumes), or select specific volumes to search.

FIGURE 4.11 **RESTATEMENT SEARCH OPTIONS IN BLOOMBERG LAW**

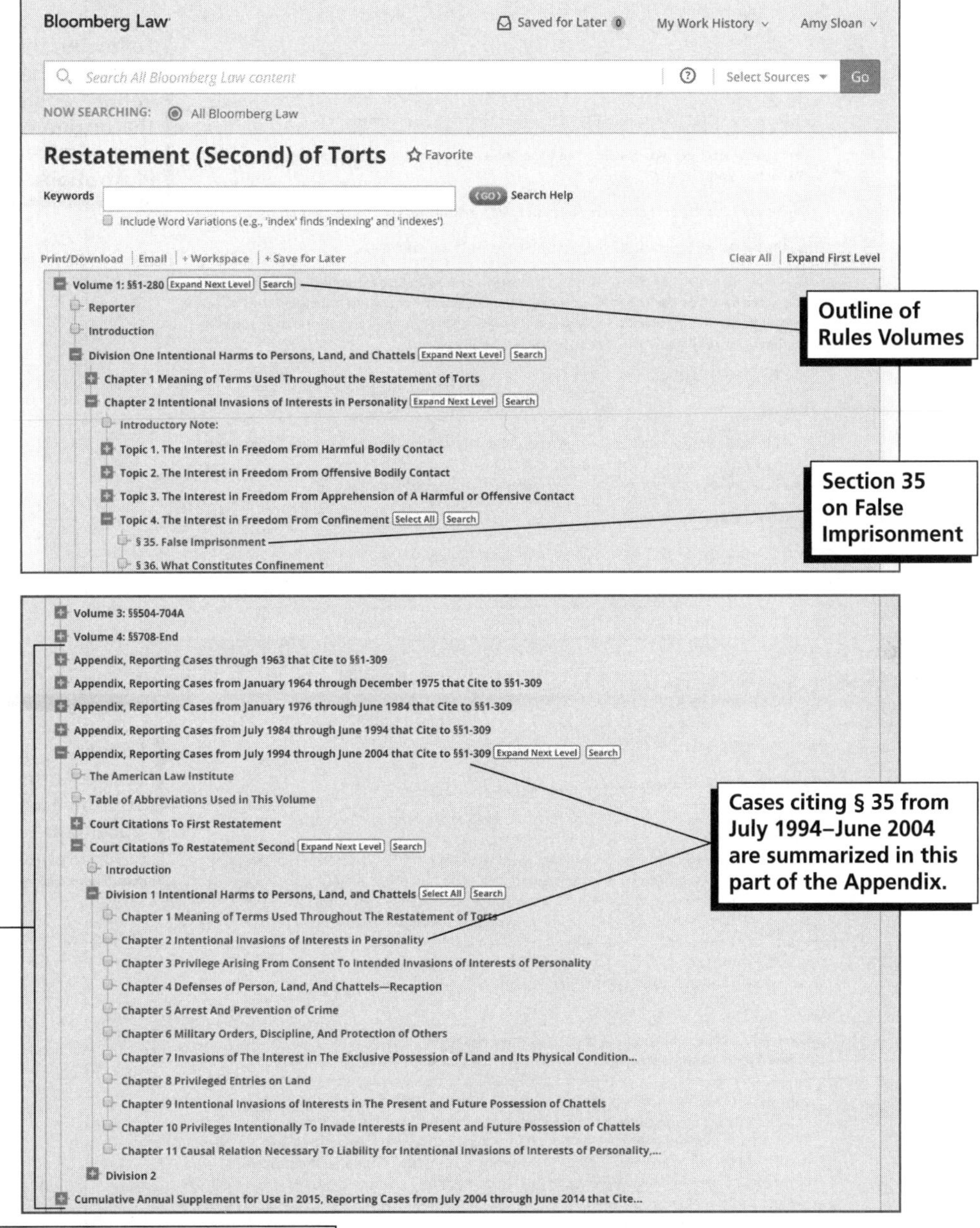

The Restatement rule includes comments and illustrations. The Appendix volume includes summaries of cases that have cited the Restatement rule.

FIGURE 4.12 **SECTION 35 OF *THE RESTATEMENT (SECOND) OF TORTS*, RULES AND APPENDIX VOLUMES**

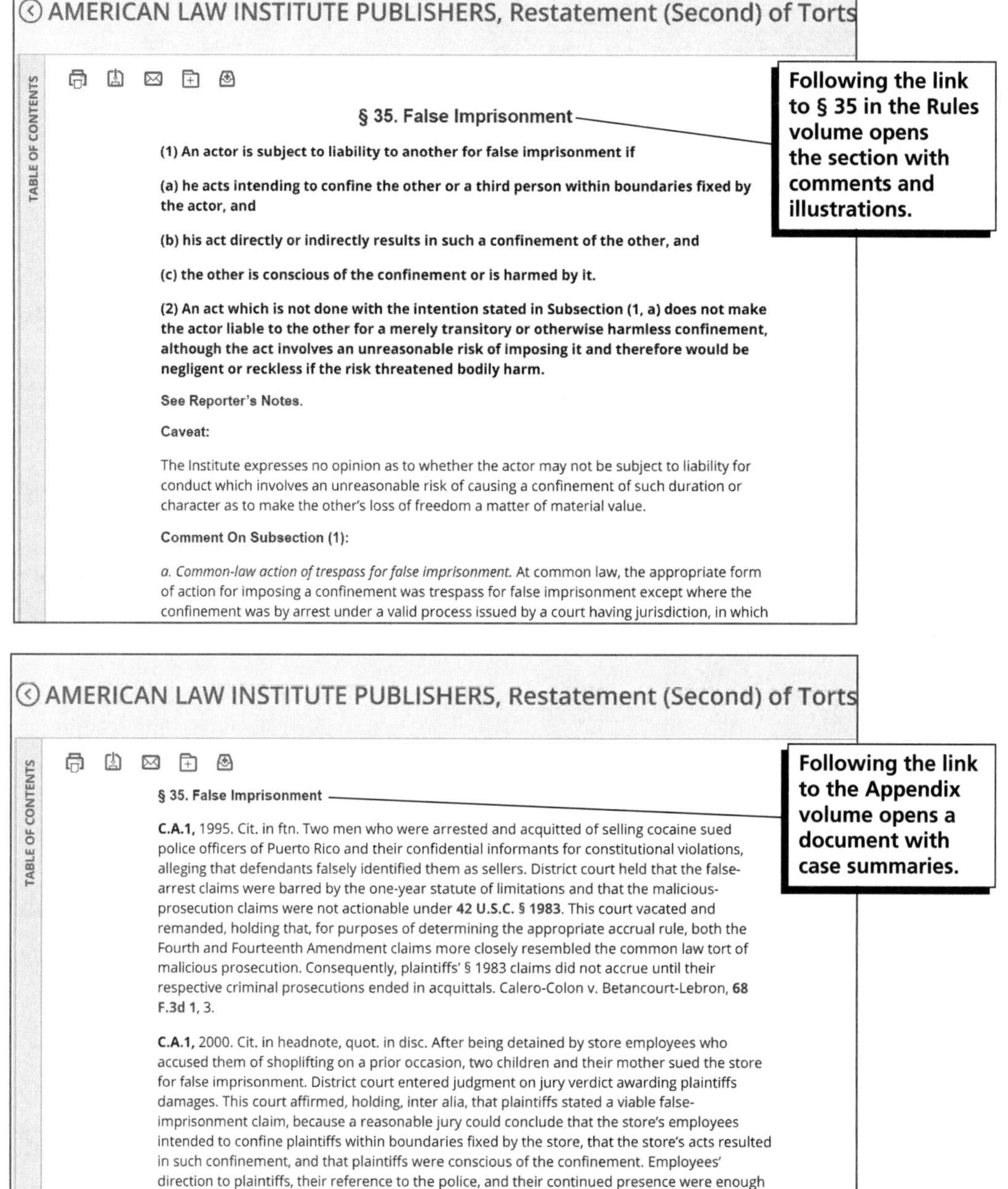

AMERICAN LAW INSTITUTE PUBLISHERS, Restatement (Second) of Torts

TABLE OF CONTENTS

§ 35. False Imprisonment

(1) An actor is subject to liability to another for false imprisonment if

(a) he acts intending to confine the other or a third person within boundaries fixed by the actor, and

(b) his act directly or indirectly results in such a confinement of the other, and

(c) the other is conscious of the confinement or is harmed by it.

(2) An act which is not done with the intention stated in Subsection (1, a) does not make the actor liable to the other for a merely transitory or otherwise harmless confinement, although the act involves an unreasonable risk of imposing it and therefore would be negligent or reckless if the risk threatened bodily harm.

See Reporter's Notes.

Caveat:

The Institute expresses no opinion as to whether the actor may not be subject to liability for conduct which involves an unreasonable risk of causing a confinement of such duration or character as to make the other's loss of freedom a matter of material value.

Comment On Subsection (1):

a. Common-law action of trespass for false imprisonment. At common law, the appropriate form of action for imposing a confinement was trespass for false imprisonment except where the confinement was by arrest under a valid process issued by a court having jurisdiction, in which

AMERICAN LAW INSTITUTE PUBLISHERS, Restatement (Second) of Torts

TABLE OF CONTENTS

§ 35. False Imprisonment

C.A.1, 1995. Cit. in ftn. Two men who were arrested and acquitted of selling cocaine sued police officers of Puerto Rico and their confidential informants for constitutional violations, alleging that defendants falsely identified them as sellers. District court held that the false-arrest claims were barred by the one-year statute of limitations and that the malicious-prosecution claims were not actionable under **42 U.S.C. § 1983**. This court vacated and remanded, holding that, for purposes of determining the appropriate accrual rule, both the Fourth and Fourteenth Amendment claims more closely resembled the common law tort of malicious prosecution. Consequently, plaintiffs' § 1983 claims did not accrue until their respective criminal prosecutions ended in acquittals. Calero-Colon v. Betancourt-Lebron, **68 F.3d 1**, 3.

C.A.1, 2000. Cit. in headnote, quot. in disc. After being detained by store employees who accused them of shoplifting on a prior occasion, two children and their mother sued the store for false imprisonment. District court entered judgment on jury verdict awarding plaintiffs damages. This court affirmed, holding, inter alia, that plaintiffs stated a viable false-imprisonment claim, because a reasonable jury could conclude that the store's employees intended to confine plaintiffs within boundaries fixed by the store, that the store's acts resulted in such confinement, and that plaintiffs were conscious of the confinement. Employees' direction to plaintiffs, their reference to the police, and their continued presence were enough to induce reasonable people to believe either that they would be restrained physically if they sought to leave, or that the store was claiming lawful authority to confine them until the police

F. CHECKLIST FOR SECONDARY SOURCE RESEARCH

1. LEGAL ENCYCLOPEDIAS

☐ Use legal encyclopedias for very general background information and limited citations to primary authority, but not for in-depth analysis of a topic.
☐ Use Am. Jur. 2d or C.J.S. for a general overview; look for a state encyclopedia for an overview of the law in an individual state.
☐ Locate material in a print encyclopedia by (1) using the subject index or table of contents; (2) locating relevant sections in the main subject volumes; and (3) updating with the pocket part.
☐ Locate material in legal encyclopedias in Westlaw and Lexis Advance by:
- Executing word searches in the databases for individual publications or by viewing an encyclopedia's table of contents.
- Executing a content-driven search, reviewing results for secondary sources, and filtering the content by source or other appropriate criteria.

2. TREATISES

☐ Use treatises for an in-depth discussion and some analysis of an area of law and for citations to primary authority.
☐ Locate treatises in print through the online catalog or by asking a reference librarian for a recommendation; locate material within a treatise by (1) using the subject index or table of contents; (2) locating relevant sections within the main text; and (3) updating with the pocket part.
☐ Locate material in treatises in Westlaw, Lexis Advance, and Bloomberg Law by:
- Executing word searches in the databases for individual publications. View the table of contents for individual publications, if available.
- Executing a content-driven search, reviewing results for secondary sources, and filtering the content by source or other appropriate criteria.

3. LEGAL PERIODICALS

☐ Use legal periodicals for background information, citations to primary authority, in-depth analysis of a narrow topic, or information on a conflict in the law or an undeveloped area of the law.

- ☐ Locate citations to periodical articles with the *Index to Legal Periodicals* (ILP) or LegalTrac periodical indexes; execute a search to obtain a list of citations. Full text of some articles is available through these services.
- ☐ Locate legal periodicals in Westlaw, Lexis Advance, and Bloomberg Law by:
  - Executing word searches in the databases for multiple or individual publications.
  - Executing a content-driven search, reviewing results for secondary sources, and filtering the content by appropriate criteria.
- ☐ Locate legal periodicals in .pdf format using HeinOnline, SSRN, and the Digital Commons Network.
- ☐ Locate selected legal periodicals using a law-related website or general Internet search engine.

4. AMERICAN LAW REPORTS

- ☐ Use A.L.R. Annotations for an overview of an area of law and citations to primary authority (especially to locate nonbinding authority from other jurisdictions), but not for in-depth analysis of a topic.
- ☐ Locate material within A.L.R. in print by (1) using the A.L.R. Index; (2) locating relevant Annotations in the main volumes; and (3) updating with the pocket part.
- ☐ Locate A.L.R. Annotations in Westlaw and Lexis Advance by:
  - Executing word searches in the American Law Reports (ALR) database.
  - Executing a content-driven search, reviewing results for secondary sources, and filtering the content by source or other appropriate criteria.

5. RESTATEMENTS

- ☐ Use Restatements for research into common-law subjects and to locate binding and nonbinding authority from jurisdictions that have adopted a Restatement.
- ☐ Locate Restatements in print through the online catalog.
  - Locate information within a print Restatement by (1) using the subject index or table of contents to identify relevant sections within the Restatement volumes; (2) using the noncumulative Appendix volumes to find pertinent case summaries; and (3) using the pocket part in the latest Appendix volume to locate the most recent cases.
- ☐ Locate Restatements in Westlaw, Lexis Advance, and Bloomberg Law by (1) executing word searches in the appropriate database or viewing

the table of contents; or (2) executing a content-driven search, reviewing results for secondary sources, and filtering the content by source or other appropriate criteria.

- In Westlaw, Restatement rules (with comments and illustrations) and case annotations are combined; case annotations will follow individual Restatement rules.
- In Lexis Advance, Restatement rules (with comments and illustrations) and case annotations are separate; from a rule section, use the **Citators** link in **About This Document** to access case annotations.
- In Bloomberg Law, Restatement rules (with comments and illustrations) and case annotations are separate; search results will include separate documents with rule provisions and Appendix case summaries.

6. UNIFORM LAWS AND MODEL ACTS

☐ Use uniform laws and model acts to interpret a law adopted by a legislature and to locate nonbinding authority from other jurisdictions that have adopted the law.

☐ Locate uniform laws and model acts in print using *Uniform Laws Annotated, Master Edition* (ULA).

- Locate information in the ULA set by (1) using the *Directory of Uniform Acts and Codes: Tables and Index* to search by subject, by the name of the law, or by adopting jurisdiction; (2) locating relevant provisions in the main volumes; and (3) updating with the pocket part.

☐ Locate selected uniform laws and model acts in Westlaw, Lexis Advance, and Bloomberg Law by (1) executing word searches in the appropriate database or viewing the table of contents; or (2) executing a content-driven search and filtering the content by source or other appropriate criteria.

CHAPTER 5

Case Research

A. Introduction to cases
B. Researching cases in print
C. Researching cases online
D. Citing cases
E. Sample pages for case research
F. Checklist for case research

A. INTRODUCTION TO CASES

1. THE STRUCTURE OF THE COURT SYSTEM

The United States has more than 50 separate court systems, including the federal system, the 50 state systems, and the District of Columbia system. You may recall from Chapter 1 that there are three levels of courts in the federal system: the United States District Courts (the trial courts), the United States Courts of Appeals (the intermediate appellate courts), and the United States Supreme Court (the court of last resort). Most state court systems are structured the same way as the federal court system.

Judges from all of these courts issue written decisions, and their decisions are one source of legal rules. This chapter focuses on where these decisions are published, how they are organized, and how to locate them.

2. SOURCES OF CASES

When a court issues a written decision, the decision is a public document filed with the clerk of the court and is called a slip opinion. Written opinions are collected together and published in chronological order in print. The books containing court opinions, or cases, are called reporters. Although most cases are also available online, they are still largely organized and cited according to the print reporter system. Additionally, you can tell much about the authoritative value of a case from its citation if you understand the print reporter system. Therefore, you need to be familiar with both print and online sources of cases.

Many sets of reporters are limited to opinions from a single jurisdiction or level of court. Thus, for example, federal reporters contain opinions from federal courts, and state reporters contain opinions from state courts. In addition, each set of reporters may be subdivided into different series covering different time periods.

A reporter published under government authority is known as an official reporter.[1] Reporters published by commercial publishers are called unofficial reporters. Because these two types of reporters exist, the same opinion may be published in more than one reporter. The text of the opinion should be exactly the same in an official and an unofficial reporter; the only difference is that the former is published by the government, and the latter is not. When a case appears in more than one reporter, it is described as having parallel citations. This is because each set of reporters will have its own citation for the case.

The only federal cases published by the government are those of the U.S. Supreme Court; these are published in a reporter called *United States Reports*. State governments usually publish the decisions of their highest courts, and most also publish decisions from some of their lower courts.

Perhaps the largest commercial publisher of cases is Thomson Reuters/West, formerly West Publishing Company. West has created a network of unofficial reporters called the *National Reporter System*, which comprises reporters with decisions from almost every U.S. jurisdiction.

West publishes U.S. Supreme Court decisions in the *Supreme Court Reporter*. Decisions from the U.S. Courts of Appeals are published in the *Federal Reporter*, and those from U.S. District Courts are published in the *Federal Supplement*. West also publishes some specialized reporters that contain decisions from the federal courts. For example, *Federal Rules Decisions* (F.R.D.) contains federal district court decisions interpreting the Federal Rules of Civil and Criminal Procedure, and the *Federal Appendix* (F. App'x) contains non-precedential decisions from the federal courts of appeals. (Non-precedential decisions are discussed in more detail below.)

West publishes state court decisions in what are called regional reporters. West has divided the country into seven regions. The reporter for each region collects state court decisions from all of the states within that region.

Figure 5.1 shows where cases from the various state and federal courts can be found in West reporters. Decisions for most states can be

1. The government may publish the reporter itself, or it may arrange for the reporter to be published by a commercial publisher. As long as the government arranges for the publication, the reporter is official, even if it is physically produced by a commercial publisher.

FIGURE 5.1 **REPORTERS**

COURT or JURISDICTION	REPORTER (followed by reporter abbreviation; multiple abbreviations denote multiple series)
United States Supreme Court	*United States Reports* (U.S.)* *Supreme Court Reporter* (S. Ct.) *United States Supreme Court Reports, Lawyer's Edition* (L. Ed., L. Ed. 2d)
United States Courts of Appeals	*Federal Reporter* (F., F.2d, F.3d) *Federal Appendix* (F. App'x)
United States District Courts	*Federal Supplement* (F. Supp., F. Supp. 2d, F. Supp. 3d) *Federal Rules Decisions* (F.R.D.)
Atlantic Region states (Connecticut, Delaware, District of Columbia, Maine, Maryland, New Hampshire, New Jersey, Pennsylvania, Rhode Island, Vermont)	*Atlantic Reporter* (A., A.2d, A.3d)
North Eastern Region states (Illinois, Indiana, Massachusetts, New York, Ohio)	*North Eastern Reporter* (N.E., N.E.2d, N.E.3d) New York: *New York Supplement* (N.Y.S., N.Y.S.2d, N.Y.S.3d) Illinois: *Illinois Decisions* (Ill. Dec.)
South Eastern Region states (Georgia, North Carolina, South Carolina, Virginia, West Virginia)	*South Eastern Reporter* (S.E., S.E.2d)
Southern Region states (Alabama, Florida, Louisiana, Mississippi)	*Southern Reporter* (So., So. 2d, So. 3d)
South Western Region States (Arkansas, Kentucky, Missouri, Tennessee, Texas)	*South Western Reporter* (S.W., S.W.2d, S.W.3d)
North Western Region states (Iowa, Michigan, Minnesota, Nebraska, North Dakota, South Dakota, Wisconsin)	*North Western Reporter* (N.W., N.W.2d, N.W.3d)
Pacific Region states (Alaska, Arizona, California, Colorado, Hawaii, Idaho, Kansas, Montana, Nevada, New Mexico, Oklahoma, Oregon, Utah, Washington, Wyoming)	*Pacific Reporter* (P., P.2d, P.3d) California: *California Reporter* (Cal. Rptr., Cal. Rptr. 2d, Cal. Rptr. 3d)

*Official reporter published by the federal government.

found in the state's official reporter, as well as in the reporters listed in **Figure 5.1.**[2]

Almost all cases are identified by official reporter citations, West reporter citations, or both, and you can obtain a case from either of these types of print reporters. But you can obtain cases from other sources as well. Virtually any commercial research service, including Westlaw, Lexis Advance, Bloomberg Law, Casemaker, Fastcase, and others, will give you access to cases. Cases are also largely available for free on the Internet.

3. THE FORMAT OF A PUBLISHED CASE

Many appellate courts post their slip opinions online as soon as cases are decided. Because a slip opinion is issued before the case appears in a reporter, these opinions are ordinary typed documents. They are identified by case number or party names instead of by reporter citations.

After the court issues a slip opinion, the case may be published in print in an official reporter, an unofficial reporter, or both. A published case begins with a heading containing the case name, the court that rendered the decision, and the date of the decision. If the case has parallel citations, the heading may also include the citations to the other reporters where the case is published. After the heading, you will see the names of the attorneys who represented the parties and the judge or judges who decided the case. The opinion of the court follows these preliminary items. If the decision has any concurring or dissenting opinions, they will follow immediately after the majority or plurality opinion.

Published cases often include editorial enhancements to help you with your research. Commercial publishers frequently add this type of information, but free online sources typically do not. Editorial enhancements can include a synopsis of the case and one or more paragraphs summarizing the key points in the case. These summary paragraphs are called headnotes. Headnotes allow you to research cases by subject, as explained more fully in Sections B and C, below.

Editorial enhancements that accompany a case are written by case editors, not by the court. Although they are useful for research, anything that is not part of the court's opinion does not constitute primary authority. In a few jurisdictions, the court adds its own summary or syllabus that contains the holding of the case. Unless you see a notation indicating otherwise, however, you should treat only the text of the court's opinion as authoritative.

---

2. West also publishes separate unofficial state reporters for New York, California, and Illinois. Thus, New York, California, and Illinois cases may appear in three places: (1) an official state reporter; (2) a West regional reporter; and (3) a West unofficial state reporter. Some lower court opinions published in West's New York and California reporters are not published in the regional reporters covering those states. By contrast, all of the cases in *West's Illinois Decisions* are included in the regional reporter covering Illinois.

Figures 5.2 and 5.3 contain excerpts from the same case from two different sources. **Figure** 5.2 is from a free source, Google Scholar, which is explained in more detail in Section C, below. **Figure** 5.3 is from a West print reporter and contains editorial enhancements.

FIGURE 5.2 **GOOGLE SCHOLAR EXCERPT FROM *PADILLA-MANGUAL v. PAVIA HOSPITAL***

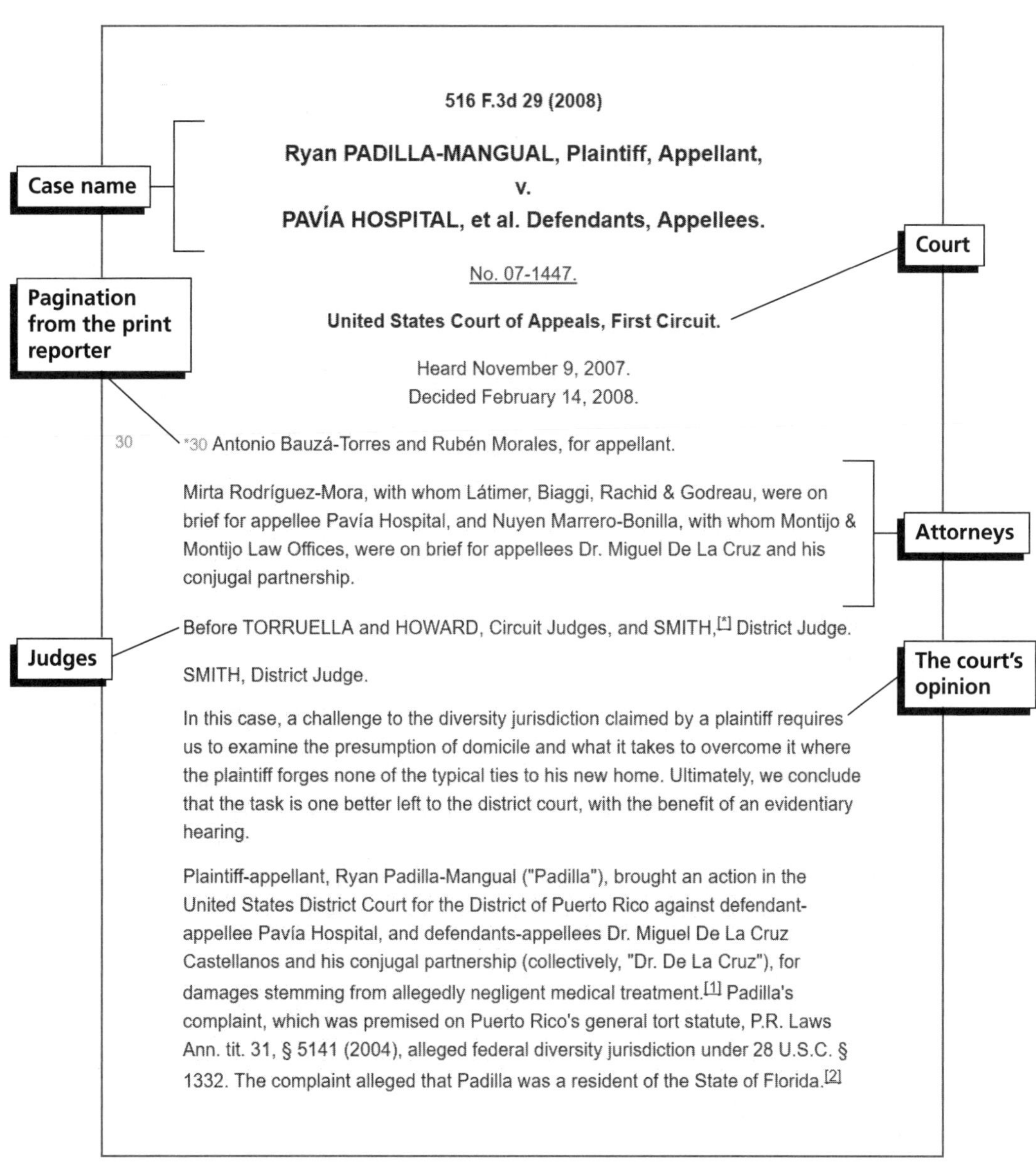

516 F.3d 29 (2008)

Ryan PADILLA-MANGUAL, Plaintiff, Appellant,
v.
PAVÍA HOSPITAL, et al. Defendants, Appellees.

No. 07-1447.

United States Court of Appeals, First Circuit.

Heard November 9, 2007.
Decided February 14, 2008.

30 *30 Antonio Bauzá-Torres and Rubén Morales, for appellant.

Mirta Rodríguez-Mora, with whom Látimer, Biaggi, Rachid & Godreau, were on brief for appellee Pavía Hospital, and Nuyen Marrero-Bonilla, with whom Montijo & Montijo Law Offices, were on brief for appellees Dr. Miguel De La Cruz and his conjugal partnership.

Before TORRUELLA and HOWARD, Circuit Judges, and SMITH,[*] District Judge.

SMITH, District Judge.

In this case, a challenge to the diversity jurisdiction claimed by a plaintiff requires us to examine the presumption of domicile and what it takes to overcome it where the plaintiff forges none of the typical ties to his new home. Ultimately, we conclude that the task is one better left to the district court, with the benefit of an evidentiary hearing.

Plaintiff-appellant, Ryan Padilla-Mangual ("Padilla"), brought an action in the United States District Court for the District of Puerto Rico against defendant-appellee Pavía Hospital, and defendants-appellees Dr. Miguel De La Cruz Castellanos and his conjugal partnership (collectively, "Dr. De La Cruz"), for damages stemming from allegedly negligent medical treatment.[1] Padilla's complaint, which was premised on Puerto Rico's general tort statute, P.R. Laws Ann. tit. 31, § 5141 (2004), alleged federal diversity jurisdiction under 28 U.S.C. § 1332. The complaint alleged that Padilla was a resident of the State of Florida.[2]

Reprinted with permission from Google Scholar, *Padilla-Mangual v. Pavia Hosp.*, 516 F.3d 29-30 (1st Cir. 2008).

FIGURE 5.3 **WEST PRINT REPORTER EXCERPT FROM *PADILLA-MANGUAL v. PAVIA HOSPITAL***

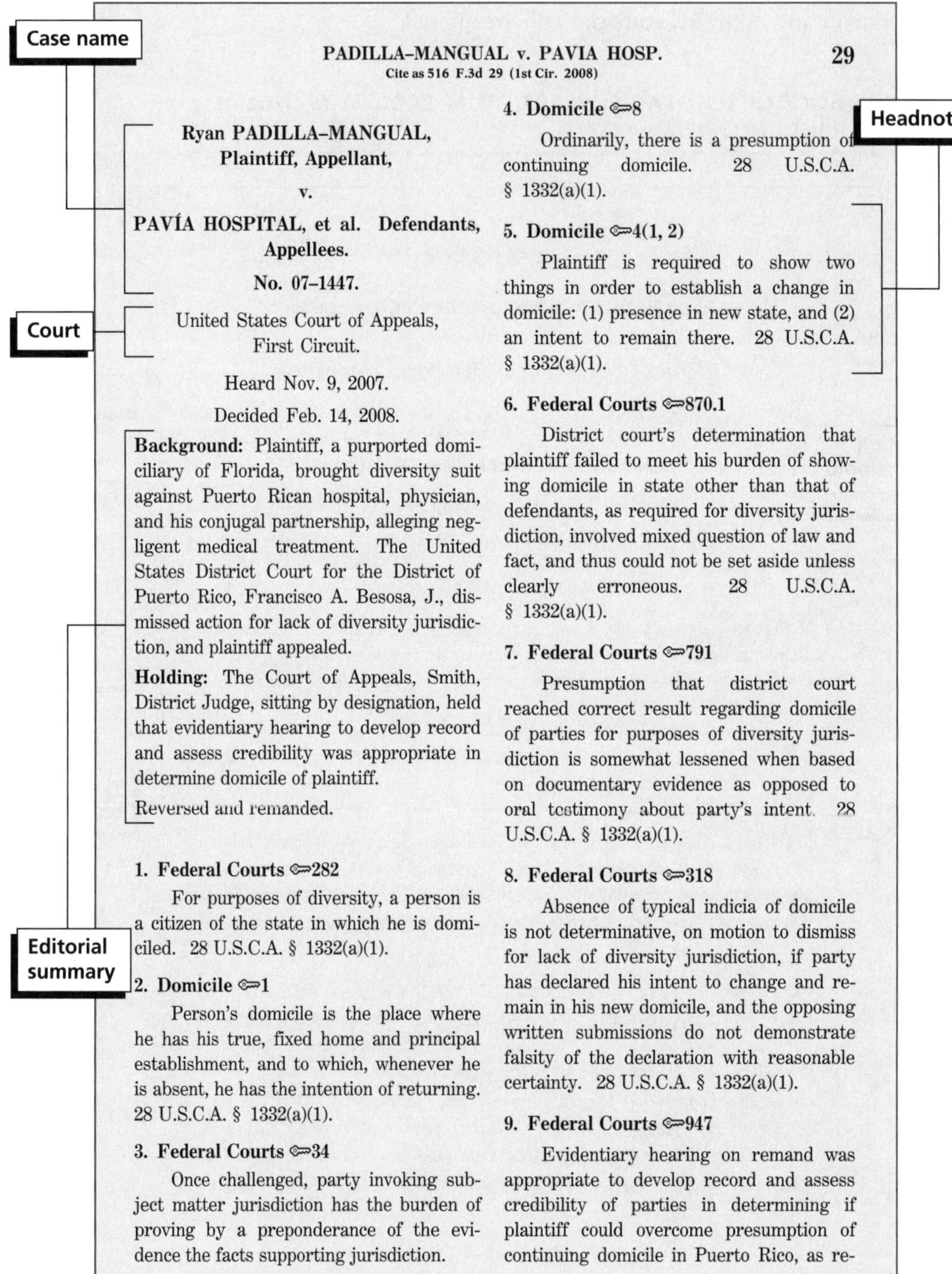

PADILLA-MANGUAL v. PAVIA HOSP. 29
Cite as 516 F.3d 29 (1st Cir. 2008)

Ryan PADILLA-MANGUAL, Plaintiff, Appellant,

v.

PAVÍA HOSPITAL, et al. Defendants, Appellees.

No. 07-1447.

United States Court of Appeals, First Circuit.

Heard Nov. 9, 2007.

Decided Feb. 14, 2008.

Background: Plaintiff, a purported domiciliary of Florida, brought diversity suit against Puerto Rican hospital, physician, and his conjugal partnership, alleging negligent medical treatment. The United States District Court for the District of Puerto Rico, Francisco A. Besosa, J., dismissed action for lack of diversity jurisdiction, and plaintiff appealed.

Holding: The Court of Appeals, Smith, District Judge, sitting by designation, held that evidentiary hearing to develop record and assess credibility was appropriate in determine domicile of plaintiff.

Reversed and remanded.

1. Federal Courts ⚷282

For purposes of diversity, a person is a citizen of the state in which he is domiciled. 28 U.S.C.A. § 1332(a)(1).

2. Domicile ⚷1

Person's domicile is the place where he has his true, fixed home and principal establishment, and to which, whenever he is absent, he has the intention of returning. 28 U.S.C.A. § 1332(a)(1).

3. Federal Courts ⚷34

Once challenged, party invoking subject matter jurisdiction has the burden of proving by a preponderance of the evidence the facts supporting jurisdiction.

4. Domicile ⚷8

Ordinarily, there is a presumption of continuing domicile. 28 U.S.C.A. § 1332(a)(1).

5. Domicile ⚷4(1, 2)

Plaintiff is required to show two things in order to establish a change in domicile: (1) presence in new state, and (2) an intent to remain there. 28 U.S.C.A. § 1332(a)(1).

6. Federal Courts ⚷870.1

District court's determination that plaintiff failed to meet his burden of showing domicile in state other than that of defendants, as required for diversity jurisdiction, involved mixed question of law and fact, and thus could not be set aside unless clearly erroneous. 28 U.S.C.A. § 1332(a)(1).

7. Federal Courts ⚷791

Presumption that district court reached correct result regarding domicile of parties for purposes of diversity jurisdiction is somewhat lessened when based on documentary evidence as opposed to oral testimony about party's intent. 28 U.S.C.A. § 1332(a)(1).

8. Federal Courts ⚷318

Absence of typical indicia of domicile is not determinative, on motion to dismiss for lack of diversity jurisdiction, if party has declared his intent to change and remain in his new domicile, and the opposing written submissions do not demonstrate falsity of the declaration with reasonable certainty. 28 U.S.C.A. § 1332(a)(1).

9. Federal Courts ⚷947

Evidentiary hearing on remand was appropriate to develop record and assess credibility of parties in determining if plaintiff could overcome presumption of continuing domicile in Puerto Rico, as re-

FIGURE 5.3 **WEST PRINT REPORTER EXCERPT FROM *PADILLA-MANGUAL v. PAVIA HOSPITAL (Continued)***

30 **516 FEDERAL REPORTER, 3d SERIES**

The court's opinion

quired to establish diversity of citizenship, notwithstanding absence of typical indicia of plaintiff's domicile in Florida other than issuance of driver's license, given plaintiff's expressed intent to remain in Florida, and failure of defendants to demonstrate falsity of that declaration with reasonable certainty in their written submissions. 28 U.S.C.A. § 1332(a)(1).

10. Federal Courts ⚿30, 33

In conducting a jurisdictional inquiry, the court enjoys broad authority to order discovery, consider extrinsic evidence, hold an evidentiary hearing, and hear testimony in order to determine its own jurisdiction.

Attorneys

Antonio Bauzá–Torres and Rubén Morales, for appellant.

Mirta Rodríguez–Mora, with whom Látimer, Biaggi, Rachid & Godreau, were on brief for appellee Pavía Hospital, and Nuyen Marrero–Bonilla, with whom Montijo & Montijo Law Offices, were on brief for appellees Dr. Miguel De La Cruz and his conjugal partnership.

Before TORRUELLA and HOWARD, Circuit Judges, and SMITH,* District Judge.

Judges

SMITH, District Judge.

In this case, a challenge to the diversity jurisdiction claimed by a plaintiff requires us to examine the presumption of domicile and what it takes to overcome it where the plaintiff forges none of the typical ties to his new home. Ultimately, we conclude that the task is one better left to the district court, with the benefit of an evidentiary hearing.

Plaintiff-appellant, Ryan Padilla–Mangual ("Padilla"), brought an action in the United States District Court for the District of Puerto Rico against defendant-appellee Pavía Hospital, and defendants-appellees Dr. Miguel De La Cruz Castellanos and his conjugal partnership (collectively, "Dr. De La Cruz"), for damages stemming from allegedly negligent medical treatment.[1] Padilla's complaint, which was premised on Puerto Rico's general tort statute, P.R. Laws Ann. tit. 31, § 5141 (2004), alleged federal diversity jurisdiction under 28 U.S.C. § 1332. The complaint alleged that Padilla was a resident of the State of Florida.[2]

On July 17, 2006, Dr. De La Cruz moved to dismiss for lack of subject matter jurisdiction on the grounds that diversity of citizenship was lacking.[3] Dr. De La Cruz claimed that as of January 30, 2006, the date that Padilla filed his complaint, Padil-

* Of the District of Rhode Island, sitting by designation.

1. The complaint originally named Nicole Freire (or, Freyre), Padilla's then-fiancée, as an additional plaintiff. However, she subsequently was voluntarily dismissed from the case.

2. Although Padilla's complaint actually alleged that he was a "resident" of Florida, rather than a "citizen" or "domiciliary" of Florida, the district court's analysis of domicile moots any concern as to whether Padilla's allegations, if defective, should preclude a finding of diversity jurisdiction. *See Cantellops v. Álvaro–Chapel*, 234 F.3d 741, 742–743 (1st Cir.2000) (district court's analysis of domicile reviewed for clear error even where complaint specifically alleged residency instead of domicile).

3. Dr. De La Cruz's motion also requested that the district court abstain from deciding the action based on the abstention doctrine set forth in *Colorado River Water Conservation Dist. v. United States*, 424 U.S. 800, 96 S.Ct. 1236, 47 L.Ed.2d 483 (1976). The district court did not discuss the issue of abstention in light of its decision to dismiss the complaint for lack of diversity jurisdiction.

4. UNPUBLISHED, OR NON-PRECEDENTIAL, OPINIONS

Not all cases are published; only those designated by the courts for publication appear in print reporters. The decisions not designated for publication are called unpublished decisions. In the past, the only ways to obtain copies of unpublished decisions were from the parties to the case or from the clerk's office at the courthouse. This is still true today for some unpublished decisions, especially those issued by state courts. Many unpublished decisions, however, are available online. The federal courts of appeals make many of their unpublished decisions available on their websites. In addition, unpublished decisions issued by the federal courts of appeals since 2001 are available in print in the *Federal Appendix*, a West reporter.

Because these decisions are increasingly available online and in print, the term "unpublished" opinion has become a misnomer. A more accurate term is "non-precedential" opinion. Non-precedential decisions are often subject to special court rules. For example, unlike decisions published in the *Federal Reporter*, those appearing in the *Federal Appendix* are not treated as binding precedent by the courts, which is why they are described as "non-precedential" decisions. In the past, the federal courts of appeals often limited the circumstances under which non-precedential decisions could be cited, although all non-precedential opinions issued on or after January 1, 2007 may now be cited without restriction. Because of restrictions on citations to earlier non-precedential opinions, many decisions in the *Federal Appendix* contain notations indicating that they are not binding precedent and cautioning readers to check court rules before citing the opinions. Non-precedential decisions by other courts may also be subject to special rules.

Although courts have issued non-precedential opinions for many years, the practice is not without controversy. The authoritative value of non-precedential decisions is a subject of ongoing debate in the legal community. Regardless of the controversy, non-precedential decisions can be valuable research tools. Therefore, you should not disregard them when you are conducting case research.

5. METHODS OF LOCATING CASES

You can locate cases in several ways. If you have the citation to a case that you have obtained from another source, such as a secondary source, you can easily locate the case in print or online.

When you do not have a citation, you can locate cases using either a source-driven or content-driven approach. If you use a source-driven approach, the first step will be deciding which jurisdiction's cases you want to research. Once you select a jurisdiction, you can search for cases by subject, by words in the document, or by party name.

Researching by subject is often a useful way to locate cases. Reviewing summaries of cases arranged by subject can help you identify those that address the topic of your research. You can search by subject in print using a research tool called a digest. You can also sort cases by subject categories in Lexis Advance, Westlaw, and other services. Word searching is another way to locate cases online. This option is available in free and fee-based commercial services as well as some court websites.

One additional search option is locating a case by party name. In print, you can use a directory of cases organized by party name. Online, you can use a party name as a term in a word search; many services also have search templates that allow you to enter party names.

If you choose content-driven searching in Lexis Advance, Westlaw, or Bloomberg Law, your search results will include cases. You will ordinarily pre-filter your search by jurisdiction unless you are researching the law of all U.S. jurisdictions. Once you execute the search, the results will include a section with cases. When you review the cases your search has retrieved, you can filter the results according to a number of criteria, such as cases from a particular level of court.

Sections B and C, below, explain how to research cases in print and online.

B. RESEARCHING CASES IN PRINT

1. LOCATING CASES BY SUBJECT USING A DIGEST

Reporters are published in chronological order; they are not organized by subject. Trying to research cases in chronological order would be impossible. The research tool that organizes cases by subject is called a digest, and that is the finding tool you will ordinarily use to locate cases by topic.

The term "digest" literally means to arrange and summarize, and that is exactly what a digest does. In a digest, the law is arranged into different subject categories, such as torts, contracts, or criminal law. Then, within each category, the digest provides summaries of cases that discuss the law on that subject. You can use the summaries to decide which cases you should read to find the answer to your research question.

The digest system created by West is the most commonly used print digest in legal research. West has divided the law into more than 400 subject categories, called topics. Under each topic, West provides summaries of cases relevant to the subject. Each topic is listed alphabetically in the digest. Because there are so many topics, a digest actually consists of a multivolume set of books. This is similar to a set of encyclopedias with multiple volumes covering topics in alphabetical order.

FIGURE 5.4 **BEGINNING OF THE WEST TOPIC FOR "DOMICILE"**

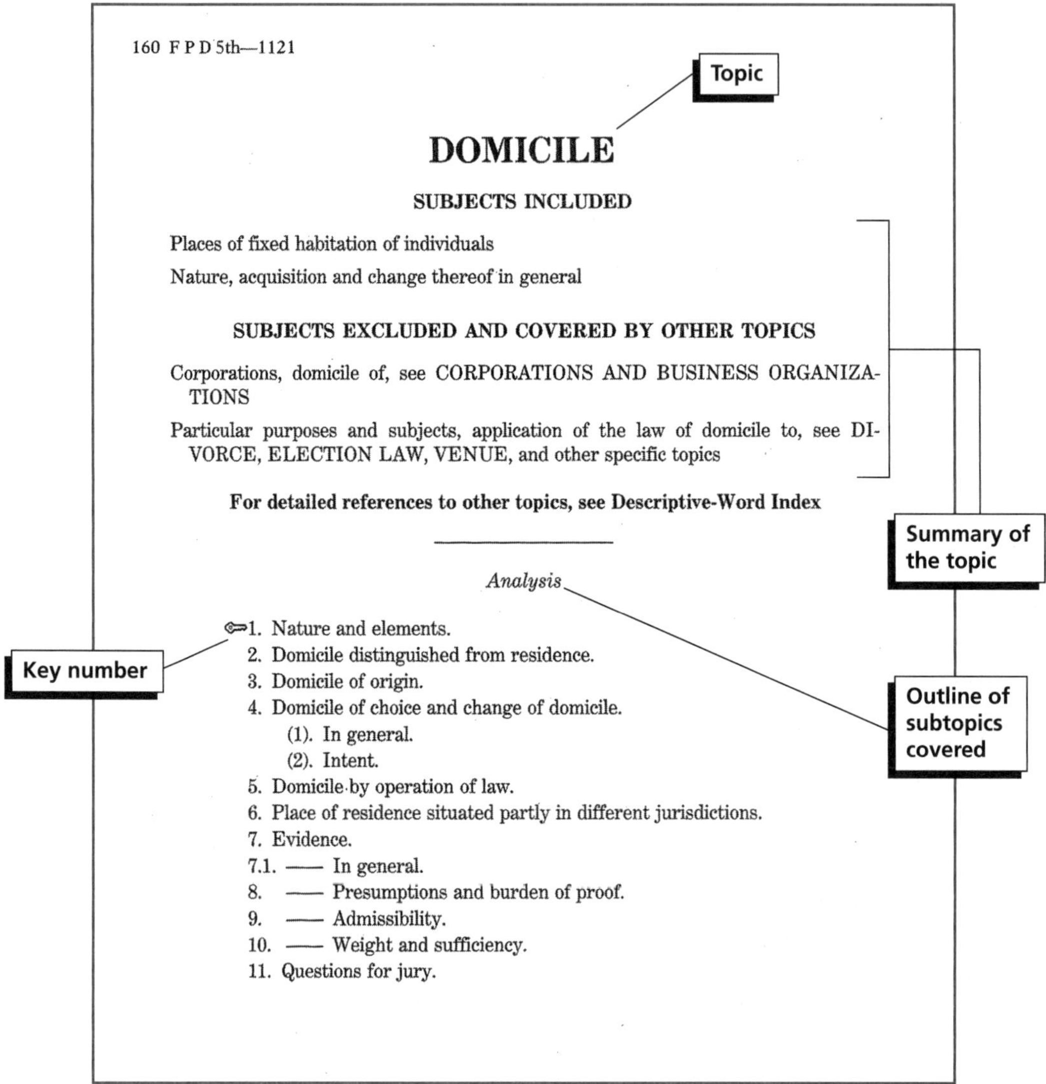

160 F P D 5th—1121

DOMICILE

SUBJECTS INCLUDED

Places of fixed habitation of individuals

Nature, acquisition and change thereof in general

SUBJECTS EXCLUDED AND COVERED BY OTHER TOPICS

Corporations, domicile of, see CORPORATIONS AND BUSINESS ORGANIZATIONS

Particular purposes and subjects, application of the law of domicile to, see DIVORCE, ELECTION LAW, VENUE, and other specific topics

For detailed references to other topics, see Descriptive-Word Index

Analysis

🔑1. Nature and elements.
2. Domicile distinguished from residence.
3. Domicile of origin.
4. Domicile of choice and change of domicile.
 (1). In general.
 (2). Intent.
5. Domicile by operation of law.
6. Place of residence situated partly in different jurisdictions.
7. Evidence.
7.1. —— In general.
8. —— Presumptions and burden of proof.
9. —— Admissibility.
10. —— Weight and sufficiency.
11. Questions for jury.

The West topics are quite broad. Subject areas such as torts or contracts generate thousands of cases. Therefore, the topics have been further subdivided into smaller categories. Each subdivision within a topic is assigned a number that West calls a key number. Thus, the case summaries within a West digest will appear under the relevant key number. Instead of requiring you to read summaries of all the cases on a very broad topic, the key number subdivisions allow you to focus more specifically on the precise issue you are researching.

FIGURE 5.5 **CASE SUMMARY UNDER THE "DOMICILE" TOPIC, KEY NUMBER 1**

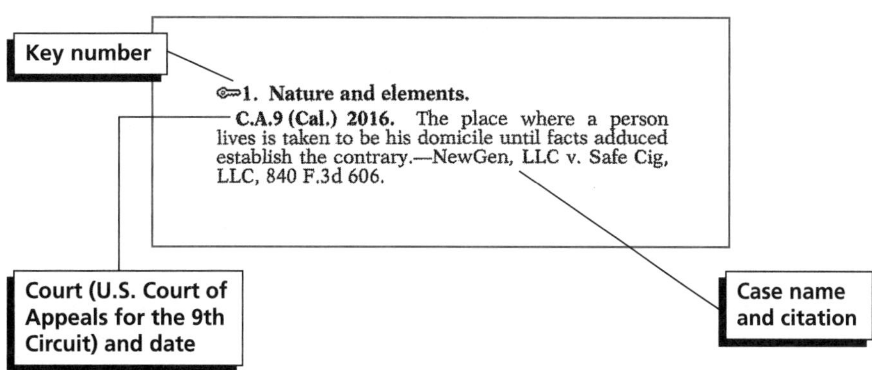

Reprinted with permission from Thomson Reuters/West, *West's Federal Practice Digest*, 4th & 5th Ser., February 2017 Pamphlet, p. 1238. © 2017 Thomson Reuters/West.

The topic, key number, and case summary that you find in a West digest will correspond exactly to one of the headnotes at the beginning of an opinion published in a West reporter.

Figures 5.4 and 5.5 illustrate some of the features of a West digest. **Figure** 5.4 shows the beginning of the West topic of "Domicile," including the outline of subtopics covered in each key number. **Figure** 5.5 shows a summary of a case under key number 1.

2. THE DIGEST RESEARCH PROCESS

The digest research process consists of four steps:

a. locating the correct digest set for the type of research you are doing;
b. locating relevant topics and key numbers within the digest;
c. reading the case summaries under the topics and key numbers;
d. updating your research to make sure you find summaries of the most recent cases.

a. Locating the Correct Digest Set

Reporters and digests are similar in several ways. Just as there are different reporters containing cases from different jurisdictions, there are also different sets of digests for finding cases from these various jurisdictions. And just as a case can be published in more than one reporter, a case can also be summarized in more than one digest. Thus, the first step in finding cases that will help you answer a research question is choosing the correct digest set.

Digest sets are organized by jurisdiction and by date. The four jurisdictional categories for digests are federal, state, regional, and combined. A federal digest, as you might imagine, summarizes federal cases. A state digest contains summaries of decisions from that state as well as opinions from the federal courts located in that state. A regional digest summarizes state court decisions from the states within the region, but it does not contain summaries of any federal cases. West publishes regional digests for some, but not all, of its regional reporters. A combined digest summarizes cases from all state and federal jurisdictions.

Within each category, the digest set may be divided into different series covering different time periods. For example, *West's Federal Practice Digest*, Fifth Series begins with 2003. Earlier cases, from the early 1980s to 2003, can be found in the Fourth Series of the digest. Ordinarily, you will want to begin your research in the most current series available. If you are unable to find information in the most current series, however, you could locate older cases by looking in the earlier series.

Figures 5.6 through 5.8 summarize some of the characteristics of West digests.

To decide which digest is the best choice for your research, you will need to consider the nature and scope of the project. Usually, you will want to choose the narrowest digest that still has enough information for you to find relevant legal authority. Sometimes you will need to use more than one digest to find all of the cases you need.

West's Federal Practice Digest is the best place to start looking for federal cases. If you are researching case law from an individual state, the digest from that state is usually the best starting place. If you do not have access to the state digest, the regional digest is another good place to look. It is also a good place to find nonbinding authority from surrounding jurisdictions. Remember, however, that regional digests summarize only state court decisions, not federal decisions. Therefore, if you also want to find cases from the federal courts located within an individual state, you will need to supplement your regional digest research by using *West's Federal Practice Digest.*

The combined digests have the most comprehensive coverage, but they are also the most difficult to use. *West's General Digest* summarizes the most recent cases. It is noncumulative. The Decennial Digests cover earlier time periods. Many libraries no longer carry the combined digests, so even if you conduct print research, you are not likely to use the combined digests.

FIGURE 5.6 **FEDERAL DIGESTS**

DESCRIPTION	*WEST'S FEDERAL PRACTICE DIGEST,* FIFTH SERIES	*WEST'S UNITED STATES SUPREME COURT DIGEST*
What is included	Summaries of cases from all federal courts	Summaries of United States Supreme Court cases
What is excluded	Summaries of state cases	Summaries of cases from lower federal courts and all state courts
Coverage	Summaries of cases from 2003–present. Older cases are summarized in prior series of set (e.g., *West's Federal Practice Digest*, Fourth Series).	Summaries of all United States Supreme Court cases

FIGURE 5.7 **STATE AND REGIONAL DIGESTS**

DESCRIPTION	STATE DIGESTS	REGIONAL DIGESTS
What is included	Summaries of cases from the state's courts and the federal courts within the state	Summaries of cases from the state courts within the region
What is excluded	Summaries of state and federal cases from courts outside the state	Summaries of state cases from states outside the region and all federal cases
Coverage	West publishes state digests for all states except Delaware, Nevada, and Utah. The *Virginia and West Virginia Digest* summarizes cases from both Virginia and West Virginia. The *Dakota Digest* summarizes cases from both North Dakota and South Dakota. Some state digests have multiple series.	West publishes Atlantic, North Western, Pacific, and South Eastern Digests. West *does not* publish North Eastern, Southern, or South Western Digests. All of the regional digests have multiple series.

FIGURE 5.8 **COMBINED DIGESTS**

DESCRIPTION	COMBINED DIGESTS	
What is included	Summaries of state and federal cases from all jurisdictions across the United States	
What is excluded	Nothing	
Coverage	The combined digests are divided into the *General*, *Decennial*, and *Century Digests*, covering the following dates:	
	General Digest, Fifteenth Series (each volume in the *General Digest* set is noncumulative)	2016-2019 (expected coverage)
	First through *Twelfth Decennial Digests* (each Decennial Digest covers a 10-year period)	1897-2016
	Century Digest	1658-1896

b. Locating Topics and Key Numbers

Once you have decided which set or sets of the digest to use, the next step is locating topics and key numbers relevant to your research issue. You can do this in three ways:

1. Using the headnotes in a case on point;
2. Using the Descriptive-Word Index;
3. Going directly to topics relevant to your research.

The easiest way to find relevant topics and key numbers is to use the headnotes in a case that you have already determined is relevant to your research. If you have read other chapters in this book, you already know that the digest is not the only way to locate cases. Many other research sources, including secondary sources (covered in Chapter 4) and statutes (covered in Chapter 7), can lead you to relevant cases. Therefore, when another source has led you to a relevant case that is published in a West reporter, you can use the headnotes to direct you to digest topics and key numbers.

If you do not already have a case on point, you will need to use the index to find topics and key numbers in the digest. The index in a West digest is called the Descriptive-Word Index (DWI). The DWI consists of several volumes that may be located either at the beginning or at the end of the digest set, and it lists subjects in alphabetical order. Once you have identified relevant topics and key numbers, you can look them up within the digest volumes. Digest topics appear alphabetically, and key numbers follow in numerical order.

Because digest topics are arranged alphabetically, you can bypass the DWI and go directly to the topic you are interested in researching. This can be a difficult way to start your research unless you are already familiar with that area of law and know which topics are likely to be relevant. For example, cases involving some types of real estate transactions are listed under the topic "Vendor and Purchaser," which might not be a topic you would have considered using.

Although you might not want to start your research by going directly to a digest topic, once you have identified useful topics through other means, you may want to review the overview section at the beginning of a topic. The list of subjects included and excluded and the outline of key numbers can provide additional helpful research leads.

c. Reading Case Summaries

Once you have reviewed the topic overview, you are ready to begin reading case summaries. In general, summaries are organized in descending order from highest to lowest court. If the digest contains summaries of both federal and state cases, federal cases will appear first. If the digest contains summaries of cases from multiple states, the states will be listed alphabetically. Summaries of multiple decisions from the same level of court and the same jurisdiction are listed in reverse chronological order.

One of the most difficult aspects of digest research is deciding which cases to read based on the summaries. The court and date abbreviations at the beginning of each entry will help you decide which cases to review. If you are using a digest with cases from more than one jurisdiction, paying attention to the abbreviations will help you stay focused on the summaries of cases from the appropriate jurisdiction. The abbreviations will also help you figure out which cases are from the highest court in the jurisdiction and which are the most recent decisions. In addition, many case summaries include not only a synopsis of the rule the court applied in the case, but also a concise description of the facts. You can use the factual summaries to narrow down the cases applicable to your issue.

Even a fact-specific summary, however, does not provide the full context of the case. Using the digest is only the first step in researching cases; all the digest can do is point you toward cases that may help answer your research question. Digest summaries, like headnotes, are editorial enhancements designed to assist you with your research. They are not authoritative, and you should never rely on one as a statement of the law. Always read the case in full before relying on it to answer a research question.

d. Updating Digest Research

The final step in digest research is updating. Each subject volume should have either a pocket part or a separate supplement on the shelf next to the hardcover book. This is the first place to look to update your research.

The pocket part is organized the same way as the main volume. The topics are arranged alphabetically, and the key numbers are arranged in numerical order within each topic. If newer cases have been decided since the main volume was published, you will find those summaries in the pocket part. If no reference to your topic and key number appears in the pocket part, no new decisions have been issued during the time period covered by the pocket part.

The pocket part is not the only supplement you should check. Pocket parts are generally published only once a year. For some digest sets, West also publishes softcover interim pamphlets to update for cases decided since the pocket part was published. They are usually shelved at the end of the digest set. The pamphlets contain summaries of new decisions under all of the topics and key numbers within the digest set. Just as with pocket parts, the topics in the interim pamphlets are arranged alphabetically.

Some interim pamphlets are cumulative, meaning you only need to look in the one book to update your research. Others, however, are noncumulative. If the pamphlets you are using are noncumulative, each one covers a specific time period, and you must check each one to update your research completely. To determine the dates covered by an interim pamphlet, check the dates on the spine or cover of the book. A table at the beginning of the interim pamphlet lists the latest volumes of each reporter covered by the supplement.

Each individual reporter volume contains a mini-digest summarizing cases within that volume. If necessary, you can further update by checking individual reporter volumes issued after the last volume covered by the interim pamphlet.

3. TABLE OF CASES

The Table of Cases lists cases alphabetically by the name of both the plaintiff and the defendant. Thus, if you know either party's name, you can find the case in the Table of Cases. In the Table of Cases, you will find the following items of information:

1. the full name of the case;
2. the court that decided the case;
3. the complete citation to the case, including the parallel citation (if any) to an official reporter;
4. a list of the topics and key numbers appearing in the headnotes to the case.

The Table of Cases usually appears at the end of the digest set. Often, it is contained in a separate volume or set of volumes, but in smaller digest sets it may be included in a volume containing other material.

C. RESEARCHING CASES ONLINE

1. WESTLAW

a. The Format of a Case in Westlaw

The format of a case in Westlaw is the same as the format of a case in a West print reporter. At the beginning of the document, you will see a caption with the name of the case and other identifying information. The caption will be followed by an editorial summary of the decision. In more recent cases, the summary is divided into two sections: background and holding. The summary will be followed by one or more numbered headnotes and then the full text of the opinion. Just as in the print version of a case, the editorial summary and headnotes, if any, are not part of the decision and are not authoritative.

In the body of the opinion, the pagination from the print version of the case will be indicated by starred numbers. For example, if a case begins on page 231 of the print reporter, the transition to the next page will be indicated by *232. Page references to parallel citations may be indicated with multiple stars: **345.

Figure 5.9 shows what a case looks like in Westlaw.

b. Search Options in Westlaw

You can retrieve a case in Westlaw from its citation or by party name if you do not have the citation. Westlaw allows source-driven searching by subject or words in the document, as well as content-driven word searching.

A good way to search by subject is with the online West digests. Recall that digests organize case summaries by topic so that you can locate cases on specific subjects. You can access the online versions of the West digests in Westlaw in three ways. One way is from a case on point. The headnotes at the beginning of each case summarize the content of the case and assign a topic name and key number subdivision to each headnote. By following the links in the headnotes, you can retrieve a list of summaries of cases that have been assigned the same topic and key number. You can filter the results or change the jurisdiction as appropriate.

The second way to access the West digest system is to search through the digest topic headings. The **Key Numbers** link under the **All Content** tab opens a list of topic headings. From the headings, you can drill down through the digest topics to individual key numbers. You can also execute a search within the Key Number System as a whole, without first selecting a specific topic, to generate a list of case summaries

FIGURE 5.9 EXAMPLE OF A CASE IN WESTLAW

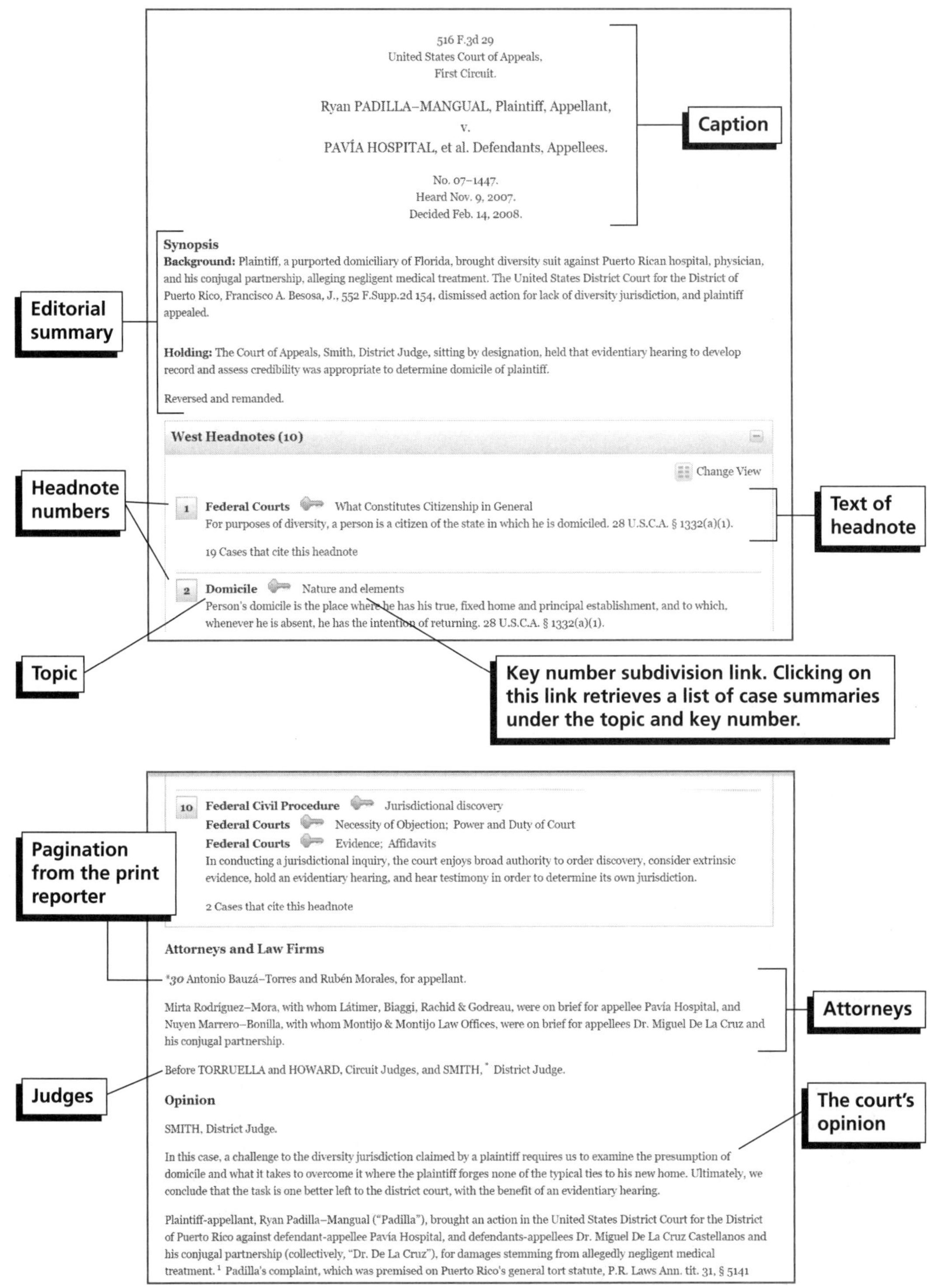

organized by subject. A third way is through a content-driven search, as explained below.

The **Practice Areas** tab offers another subject searching option, although this option offers only a limited number of broad subject categories without any subtopics.

You can also execute source-driven or content-driven word searches for cases. To execute a source-driven search for cases, pre-filter the search by following the appropriate links under the tabs on the **Browse** page. To execute a content-driven word search, you will usually want to pre-filter by jurisdiction(s). A content-driven search will retrieve many types of authority. The results will include cases (in the **Cases** section), as well links to digest topics and key numbers (in the **Key Numbers** section). The links under **Key Numbers** take you into the digest to view case summaries under the key number(s) you select. After you execute a word search, you will have a variety of options for filtering the search results.

The organization of the results may be by date or by relevance depending on the type of searching you do. You have some ability to modify the default sort options, again depending on the type of search. It is important to pay close attention to the date and level of court as you review the search results so you can assess whether each case is binding or nonbinding authority.

Chapter 10 contains more information on the process of word searching.

2. LEXIS ADVANCE

a. The Format of a Case in Lexis Advance

The format of a case in Lexis Advance is similar to the format of a case in Westlaw. At the beginning of the document, you will see a caption with the name of the case and other identifying information. The caption will be followed by information about the history of the case and the core terms used in the case. This information will be followed by an editorial summary of the decision. The summary is divided into three components: procedural posture, overview, and outcome. No key number headnotes appear in the Lexis Advance version of a case because the key number system is an editorial feature unique to West. Lexis Advance has a similar editorial feature, however, called LexisNexis Headnotes. These headnotes are summary paragraphs organized by subject that quote passages from the case. Even though the LexisNexis Headnotes usually quote the opinion verbatim, they are not part of the decision and are not authoritative.

In the body of the opinion, the pagination from the print version of the case will be indicated by numbers in brackets. For example, if a case begins on page 23 of the print reporter, the transition to the next page

FIGURE 5.10 EXAMPLE OF A CASE IN LEXIS ADVANCE

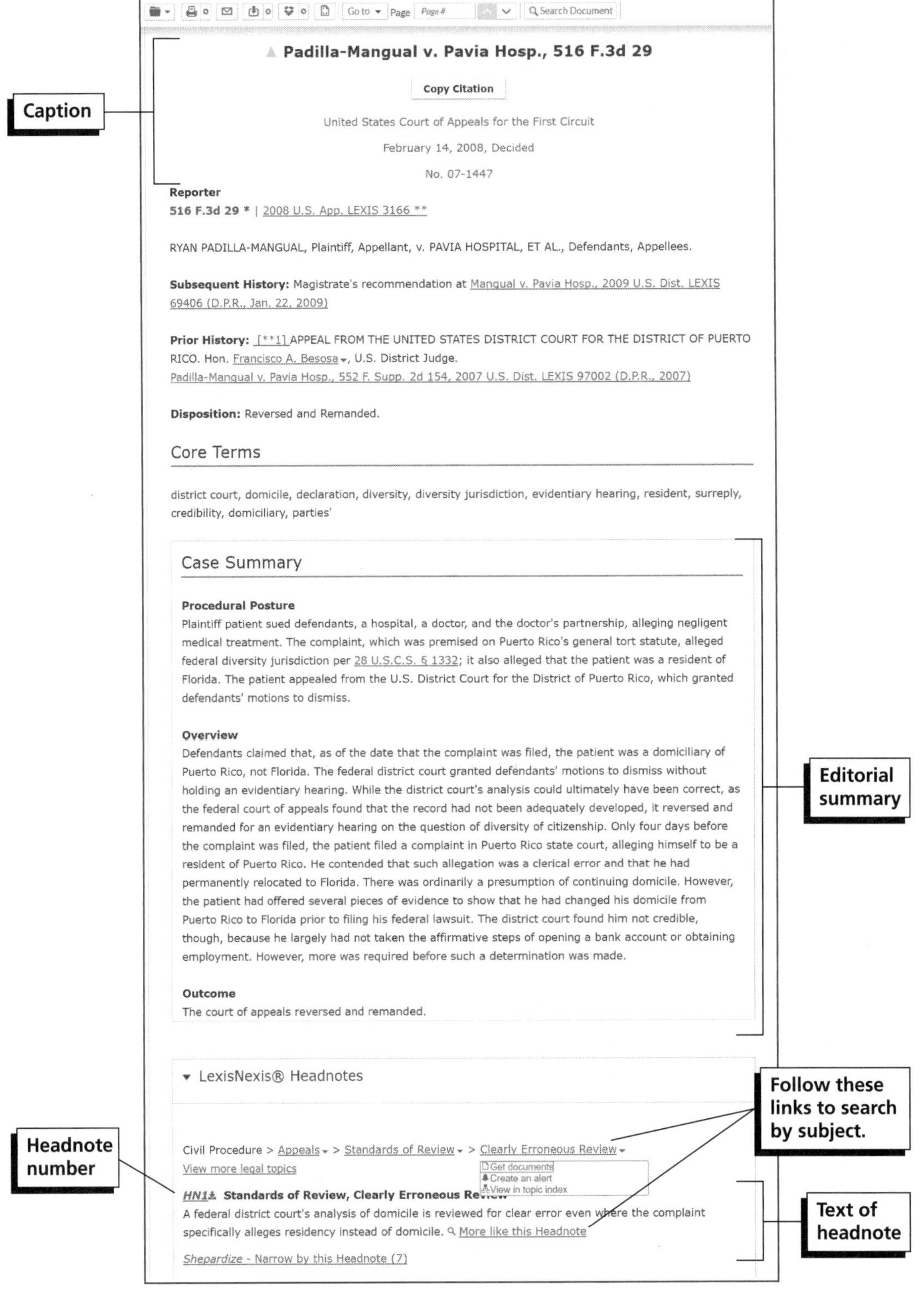

FIGURE 5.10 **EXAMPLE OF A CASE IN LEXIS ADVANCE *(Continued)***

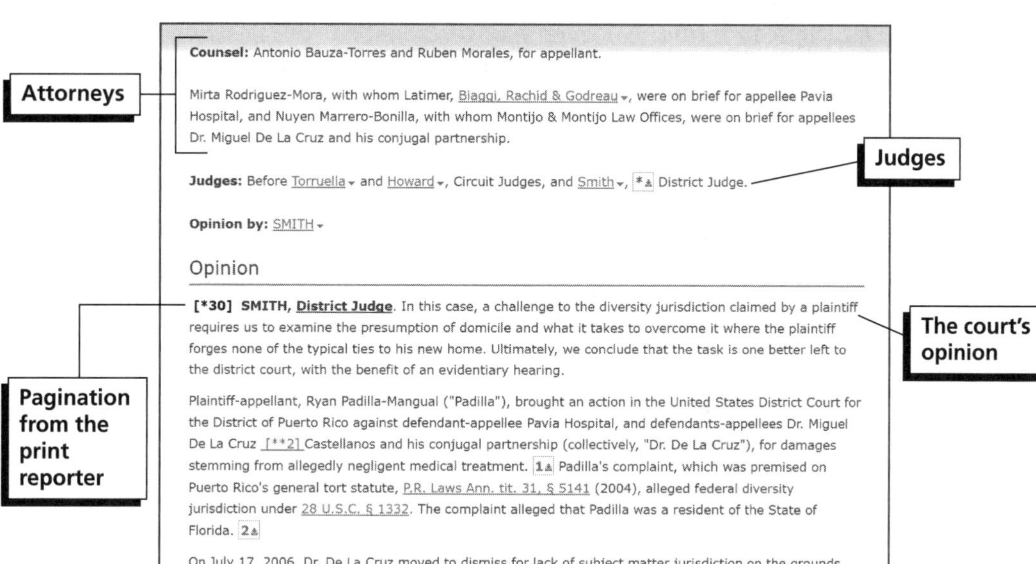

Counsel: Antonio Bauza-Torres and Ruben Morales, for appellant.

Mirta Rodriguez-Mora, with whom Latimer, Biaggi, Rachid & Godreau, were on brief for appellee Pavia Hospital, and Nuyen Marrero-Bonilla, with whom Montijo & Montijo Law Offices, were on brief for appellees Dr. Miguel De La Cruz and his conjugal partnership.

Judges: Before Torruella and Howard, Circuit Judges, and Smith, * District Judge.

Opinion by: SMITH

Opinion

[*30] SMITH, District Judge. In this case, a challenge to the diversity jurisdiction claimed by a plaintiff requires us to examine the presumption of domicile and what it takes to overcome it where the plaintiff forges none of the typical ties to his new home. Ultimately, we conclude that the task is one better left to the district court, with the benefit of an evidentiary hearing.

Plaintiff-appellant, Ryan Padilla-Mangual ("Padilla"), brought an action in the United States District Court for the District of Puerto Rico against defendant-appellee Pavia Hospital, and defendants-appellees Dr. Miguel De La Cruz [**2] Castellanos and his conjugal partnership (collectively, "Dr. De La Cruz"), for damages stemming from allegedly negligent medical treatment. 1 Padilla's complaint, which was premised on Puerto Rico's general tort statute, P.R. Laws Ann. tit. 31, § 5141 (2004), alleged federal diversity jurisdiction under 28 U.S.C. § 1332. The complaint alleged that Padilla was a resident of the State of Florida. 2

On July 17, 2006, Dr. De La Cruz moved to dismiss for lack of subject matter jurisdiction on the grounds that diversity [**3] of citizenship was lacking. 3 Dr. De La Cruz claimed that as of January 30, 2006, the date that Padilla filed his complaint, Padilla **[*31]** actually was a domiciliary of Puerto Rico, not Florida.

 Lexis Advance, 516 F.3d 29.

will be indicated by [24]. For cases with parallel citations (that is, those published in multiple reporters), the Reporter link near the top of the document allows you to select a reporter, and the bracketed numbers will reflect the pagination in the reporter you select.

Figure 5.10 shows what a case looks like in Lexis Advance.

b. Search Options in Lexis Advance

You can retrieve a case in Lexis Advance from its citation or by party name if you do not have the citation. Lexis Advance also allows source-driven searching by subject or words in the document, as well as content-driven searching.

If you have located a case on point, you can use that to search by subject. Clicking on the **More like this Headnote** link retrieves cases on the same topic. You can also use the drop-down menu next to a Lexis-Nexis Headnote topic. Choosing **Get documents** executes a search that retrieves cases organized under the same topic. **View in topic index** opens an outline of topics under the **Browse** menu, which you can also use to search by subject. If you do not start with a case on point, you can use the **Practice Area or Industry** menu to search by subject. If you do not start with a case on point, you can use the **Practice Area or Industry** menu to search by subject.

For a source-driven search, select the appropriate case filters from the **Explore Content** tabs or using the drop-down menu on the right side of the search box. Another way to execute a source-driven word search is through the **Browse** menu. Search or browse by **Source** to view a list of individual courts. When you find the source you want to search, add it as a search filter to execute a word search. Adding multiple sources as search filters allows you to search several sources simultaneously.

For content-driven searching, you can simply execute a search from the search box. You will usually want to filter by jurisdiction before executing the search. After you execute a word search, you will have a variety of options for filtering the search results.

Case law search results are typically sorted by relevance, but you can modify the default options to sort by court, date, or other criteria. It is important to pay close attention to the date and level of court as you review the search results so you can assess whether each case is binding or nonbinding authority. Additionally, Lexis has acquired another research provider—Ravel—that displays its search results with visual maps. Lexis Advance is integrating Ravel's tools to include visual maps highlighting the most important cases, the relationships among cases, and the evolution of precedent over time.

Chapter 10 contains more information on the process of word searching.

3. BLOOMBERG LAW

Bloomberg Law provides access to cases from all U.S. jurisdictions. You can execute a source-driven search for cases by following the options in the **Browse All Content** menu or the **Select Source** drop-down menu on the right side of the search box. You can also execute a content-driven search using the search box at the top of the screen. After you execute a search, you have a range of options for filtering the results. Results can be displayed by date, court, most cited, or relevance. Use the drop-down **Sort** menu to vary the display order.

Bloomberg Law does not add its own synopsis to a case. Some cases in Bloomberg Law include headnotes, but some do not. Bloomberg Law acquired the holdings of another publisher, the Bureau of National Affairs (BNA), which has its own specialized case reporters in specific subject areas of the law. Only cases on topics within BNA's coverage have headnotes, which are called BNA Headnotes. BNA Headnotes are unique to Bloomberg Law and are different from headnotes created by other publishers. For cases with BNA Headnotes, you can follow the links in the headnotes to identify additional cases on the same subject.

Even for a case without headnotes, however, Bloomberg Law has a **Points of Law** feature you can use to identify the opinion's main points.

You can browse highlighted passages using this feature. Clicking on a highlighted passage opens a window from which you can view additional cases stating the point of law, as well as a visual map of cases on the topic, and references to related topics. You can also use **Points of Law** to search by subject without retrieving a case first. From the **Browse** menu, select **Litigation and Dockets** to access **Points of Law Search**. Enter keywords and select a jurisdiction to locate relevant points of law.

Figure 5.11 shows a case in Bloomberg Law.

FIGURE 5.11 EXAMPLE OF A CASE IN BLOOMBERG LAW

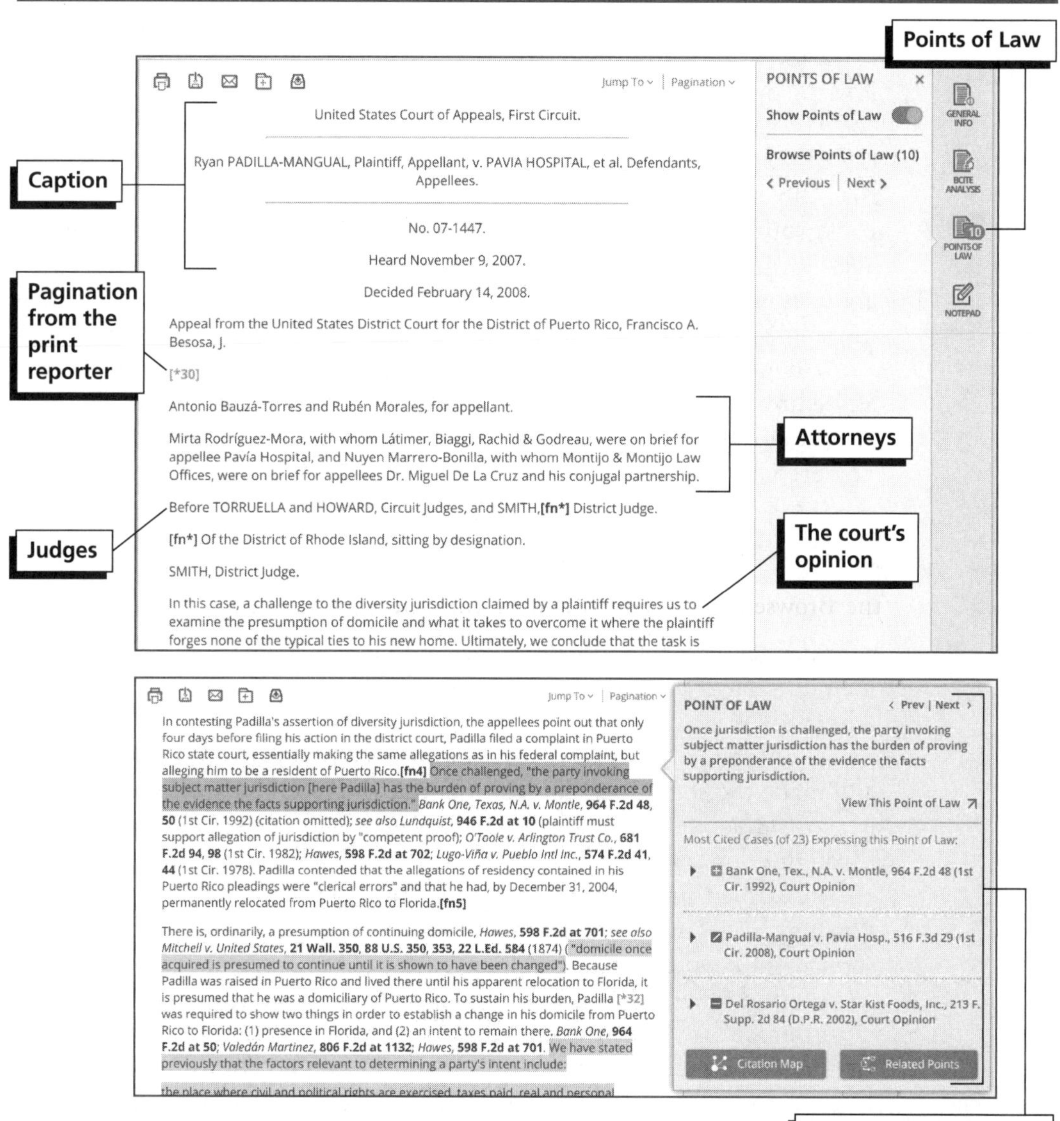

4. GOOGLE SCHOLAR

In addition to offering a general Internet search engine, Google also offers a specialized search vehicle called Google Scholar, which allows you to search for cases. The URL for Google Scholar appears in Appendix A.

Google Scholar's coverage includes published appellate opinions from all 50 states and the District of Columbia since 1950, opinions from the lower federal courts since 1923, and U.S. Supreme Court cases since 1791. Google Scholar does not include state trial court opinions or non-precedential or unpublished opinions.

On the Google Scholar search page you can choose to search articles or cases. To pre-filter the results by jurisdiction, select **Case law** and follow the options to select a jurisdiction before executing a search.

The search results are ranked by relevance, although you can change the list to date order. The Google Scholar search engine looks not only for your search terms within the text of documents, but also searches background information (meta-data). Therefore, the search is similar to a Westlaw plain language search described in Chapter 3. More information about how the type of search engine can affect search results, as well as more information on word searching generally, appears in Chapter 10.

When you view a case, you will see the text of the opinion, but not any editorial enhancements. By following the **How Cited** link, however, you can locate citations to other authorities that have referenced the case you are viewing.

5. OTHER COMMERCIAL SERVICES

Although Westlaw, Lexis Advance, and Bloomberg Law are well-known commercial services, other services are also available for case research, including Fastcase and Casetext. The URLs for these services appear in Appendix A.

A number of state and local bar associations subscribe to Fastcase and make the service available to members (including students), making it a cost-effective option for legal research. Fastcase may also be available through your law library's portal. (Casemaker is a similar service that is also available through some bar associations.) In an employment setting, you may be required to use one of these services before using more costly services to keep client research costs low. These services provide access to state and federal case law and offer a number of options for searching.

Fastcase has three search features to assist with case research: the Interactive Timeline, the tag cloud, and Forecite. The Interactive Time Line uses visual mapping to display search results. Cases are represented as circles on a timeline to give you a snapshot of the results. The tag cloud displays key terms in the results sized according to their prevalence. This can help you identify useful terms for narrowing your search. Forecite

FIGURE 5.12 SEARCH RESULTS IN FASTCASE

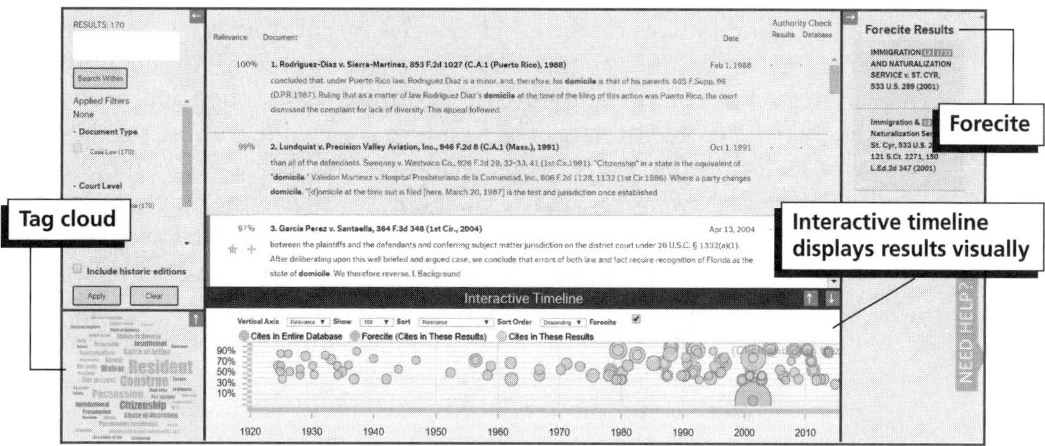

is a feature that retrieves documents that appear relevant to your search even if they do not contain your search terms. **Figure 5.12** is an example of search results in Fastcase.

Casetext is another commercial service for case research. Its content is free to all users, but premium search functionality requires a subscription. Students are eligible for free accounts while they are in school. Casetext's CARA function allows you to search without first developing a query. Instead, you upload a document, and CARA uses the citations in the document to generate search results. You can also add keywords to focus the search. **Figure 5.13** shows search results in Casetext.

FIGURE 5.13 SEARCH RESULTS IN CASETEXT

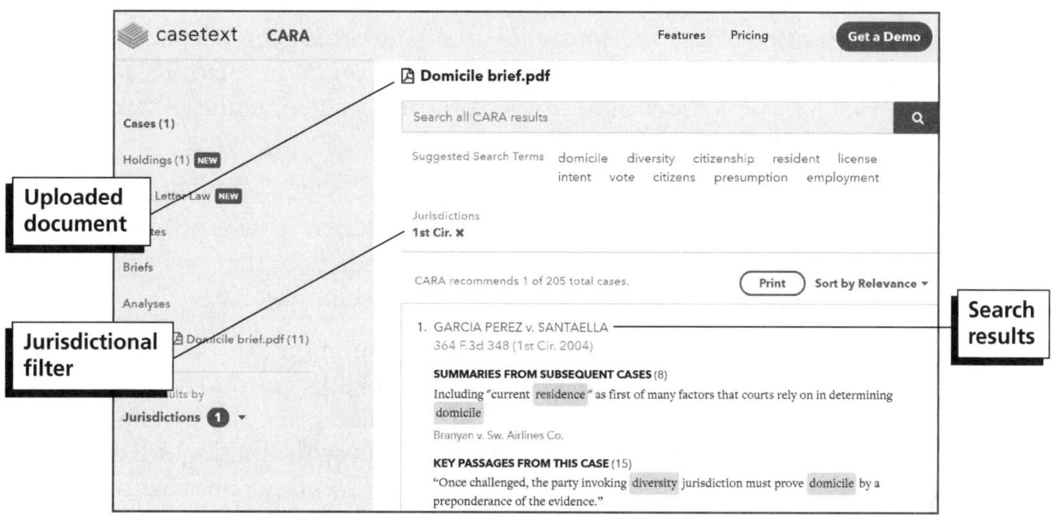

6. FREE ONLINE SOURCES

Free online sources can be good vehicles for locating cases, although using a general search engine like Google is not likely to be an efficient strategy for comprehensive case research. Two other approaches are likely to be more effective. The first is to review the website for the court whose decisions you are trying to locate. The second is to go to general legal research websites. Many of these websites either include links to websites with court opinions or index their own databases of cases. Appendix A lists a number of legal research websites that may be useful for case research.

Once you have located a source containing cases, several searching options may be available. You may be able to search by date, docket number, case name, or key word, depending on how the website is organized.

Searching free websites has some limitations. You may not have access to subject searching tools. Word searching functionality may not be as robust as in commercial services. The cases you find may not have editorial enhancements. Despite these limitations, free sites can be useful for targeted case research. Government websites may provide access to opinions unavailable elsewhere, including opinions of municipal courts or local agencies. In addition, the Internet is a more cost-effective way to access cases otherwise available in Lexis Advance, Westlaw, or other commercial services.

D. CITING CASES

As Chapter 1 explains, any time you report the results of your research in written form, you must cite your sources properly. This is especially important for cases because the information in the citation can help the reader assess the weight of the authority you are citing. A case citation has three basic components:

1. the case name;
2. information on the reporter in which the case is published;
3. a parenthetical containing the jurisdiction, the level of court that decided the case, and the year of decision.

You can find rules for each component in the *ALWD Guide* and the *Bluebook*. Using the *ALWD Guide* (6th ed.), you should read Rule 12 and use Appendices 1, 3, and 4 for any necessary abbreviations. Using the *Bluebook* (20th ed.), you should begin with Bluepages B10 and use Tables T1, T6, T7, and T10 to find any necessary abbreviations. **Figure 5.14** directs you to the citation rules for cases.

FIGURE 5.14 ***ALWD GUIDE* AND *BLUEBOOK* RULES GOVERNING CASE CITATIONS**

CITATION COMPONENT	*ALWD GUIDE* (6th ed.), RULE 12	*BLUEBOOK* (20th ed.), BLUEPAGES B10
Case name	Rule 12.2 & Appendix 3	Bluepages B10.1.1 & Tables T6 & T10
Reporter information	Rules 12.3-12.5 & Appendix 1	Bluepages B10.1.2, B10.1.3, & Table T1
Parenthetical	Rules 12.6-12.7 & Appendices 1 & 4	Bluepages B10.1.3 & Tables T1 & T7

The remainder of this section uses an example citation to illustrate each of these components. The example citation is to a fictional 2016 decision of the Delaware Court of Chancery in the case of Patricia Ellis and Sam Anson versus Acme Manufacturing Company, published in volume 145 of the *Atlantic Reporter*, Third Series, beginning on page 457.

1. THE CASE NAME

The name of the case appears first and must be underlined or *italicized*. The case name consists of the name of the first party on either side of the "v." In other words, if more than one plaintiff or defendant is listed in the full case name, give only the name of the first named plaintiff or first named defendant. In the example citation, Sam Anson would not be listed. Do not include "et al." when a case has multiple parties; simply refer to the first named party on both sides. If a person is named as a party, use only the person's last name, but if a company or other entity is listed, use the entity's full name.

Often, the case name will be abbreviated. You will need to read the rules and refer to the appropriate appendix or table to determine when words should be abbreviated and what the proper abbreviations are. The case name should be followed by a comma, which is not underlined or italicized.

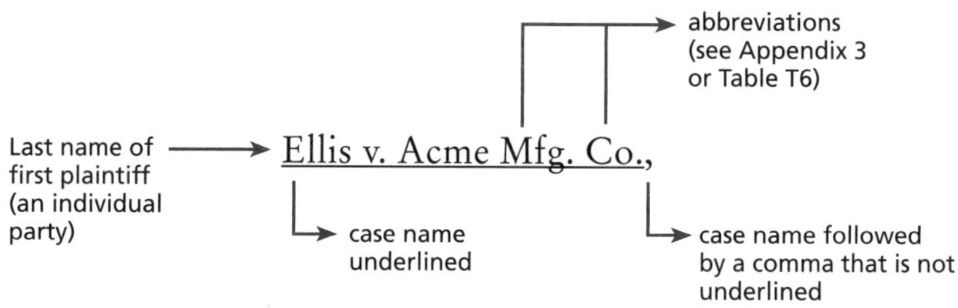

2. THE REPORTER

After the case name, the citation should list information on the reporter in which the case is published, as indicated in *ALWD Guide* Rule 12.4 and *Bluebook* Bluepages 10.1.2. In the citation, the name of the reporter will be abbreviated, so you must also determine the proper abbreviation. In the *ALWD Guide*, you can find this information in Appendix 1, which lists each jurisdiction in the United States along with reporter names and abbreviations. In the *Bluebook*, this same information appears in Table T1.

Ordinarily, you will list the volume of the reporter, the reporter abbreviation, and the starting page of the case. If you are citing a specific page within the case, you will also usually cite to that page as well, using what is called a pinpoint citation. A comma should appear between the starting page and the pinpoint citation, but the pinpoint citation should not be followed by a comma.

If the case is published in more than one reporter, you will need to refer to *ALWD Guide* Rule 12.4 and *Bluebook* Bluepages B10.1.3 to determine which reporter or reporters to cite.

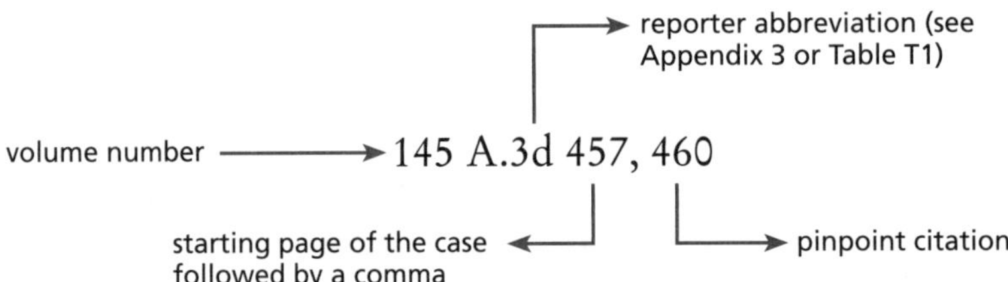

3. THE PARENTHETICAL

Following the information on the reporter, the case citation should include a parenthetical containing the abbreviated name of the jurisdiction, the abbreviated name of the level of court that decided the case, and the year the court issued its decision. This information is important because it can help the reader assess the weight of the authority you are citing.

The place to find the proper abbreviation for the jurisdiction and level of court is Appendix 1 in the *ALWD Guide* or Table T1 in the *Bluebook*. Appendix 1 and Table T1 list the levels of courts under each jurisdiction. Next to the name of each court, an abbreviation will appear in parentheses. This is the abbreviation for both the jurisdiction and the level of court, and this is what should appear in your parenthetical. You will notice that for the highest court in each state, the jurisdiction abbreviation is all that is necessary. This alerts the reader that the decision came from the highest court in the state; no additional court name abbreviation is necessary. Neither Appendix 1 nor Table T1 lists the abbreviations for all courts. If you do not find the abbreviations you need in Appendix 1 in the *ALWD Guide*, consult Appendix 4, which contains court abbreviations. In the *Bluebook*, Table T7 contains court names.

The last item to appear in the parenthetical is the year of the decision. The date when the court heard the case is not necessary in the citation; only the year of decision is required. No comma should appear before the year. After the year, the parenthetical should be closed.

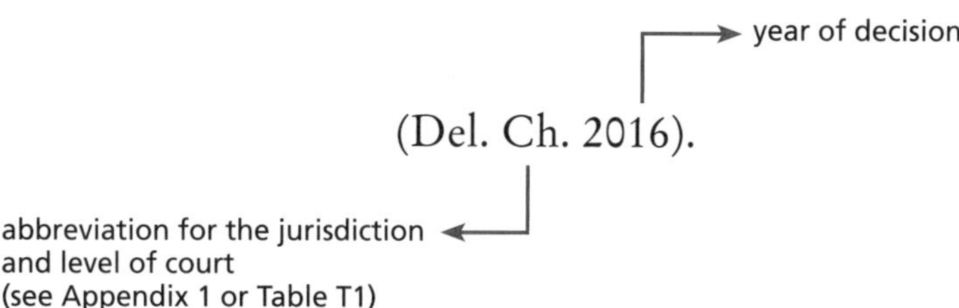

When all of the pieces are put together, the citation should look like this:

Ellis v. Acme Mfg. Co., 145 A.3d 457, 460 (Del. Ch. 2016).

E. SAMPLE PAGES FOR CASE RESEARCH

On the following pages, you will find sample pages illustrating the process of case research. For purposes of this illustration, assume that you need to determine whether the U.S. District Court for the District of Puerto Rico (which is in the First Circuit) has jurisdiction to hear your client's medical malpractice claim. This analysis requires you to determine your client's domicile as defined by federal case law. **Figures** 5.15 through 5.18 show what you would see in *West's Federal Practice Digest* if you were to research in print. **Figures** 5.19 through 5.21 show search results in Westlaw, Lexis Advance, and Bloomberg Law. **Figure** 5.22 is a case published in West's *Federal Reporter*, Third Series.

The first step in print digest research is using the Descriptive-Word Index to lead you to relevant topics and key numbers. One search term you might have used is *Domicile*. Under this heading, the index contains several entries with references to relevant topics and key numbers.

After checking the main index volume, you should check the pocket part for any updated index entries.

FIGURE 5.15 DESCRIPTIVE-WORD INDEX

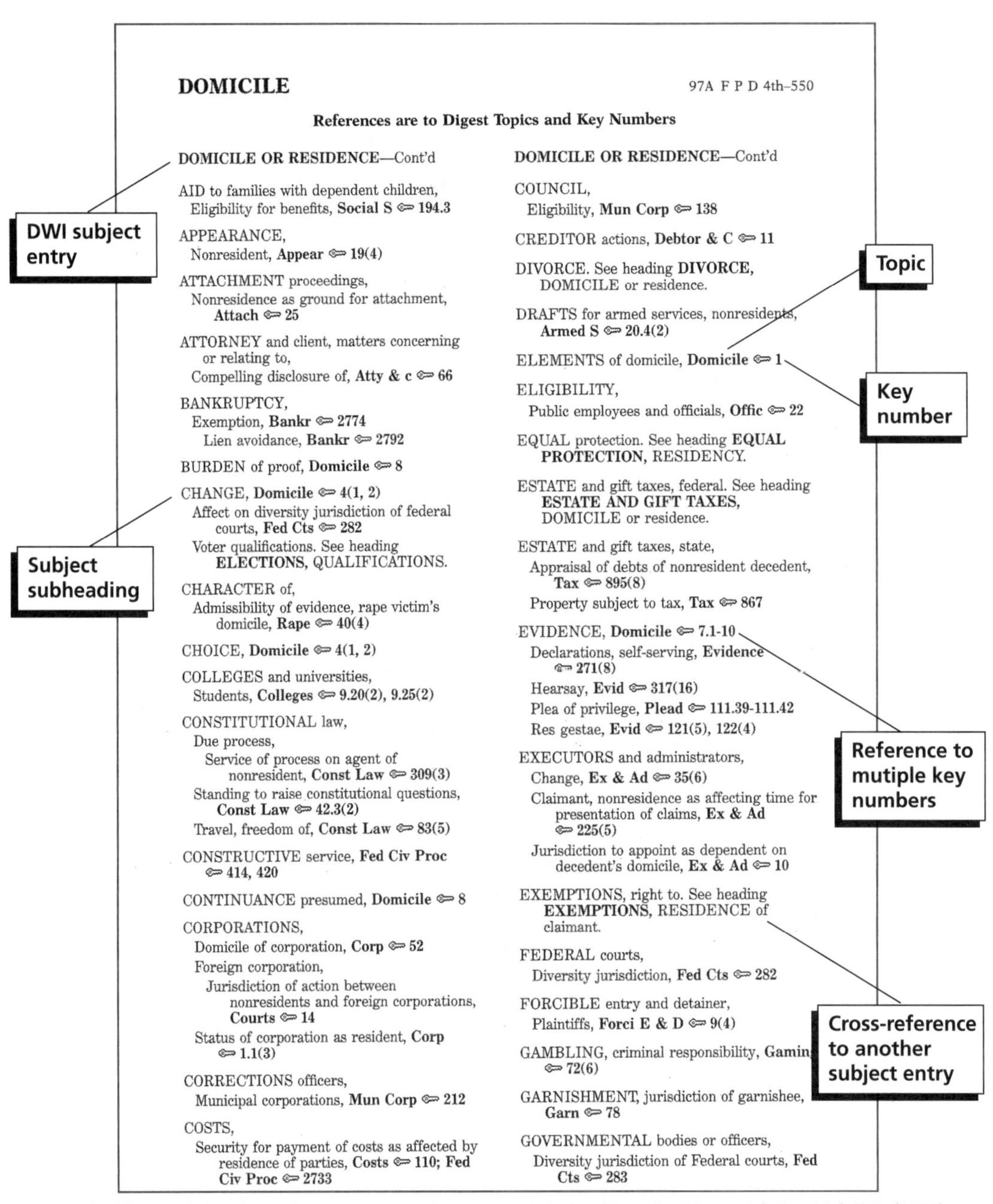

DOMICILE 97A F P D 4th–550

References are to Digest Topics and Key Numbers

DOMICILE OR RESIDENCE—Cont'd

AID to families with dependent children,
 Eligibility for benefits, **Social S 🔑 194.3**

APPEARANCE,
 Nonresident, **Appear 🔑 19(4)**

ATTACHMENT proceedings,
 Nonresidence as ground for attachment, **Attach 🔑 25**

ATTORNEY and client, matters concerning or relating to,
 Compelling disclosure of, **Atty & c 🔑 66**

BANKRUPTCY,
 Exemption, **Bankr 🔑 2774**
  Lien avoidance, **Bankr 🔑 2792**

BURDEN of proof, **Domicile 🔑 8**

CHANGE, **Domicile 🔑 4(1, 2)**
 Affect on diversity jurisdiction of federal courts, **Fed Cts 🔑 282**
 Voter qualifications. See heading **ELECTIONS**, QUALIFICATIONS.

CHARACTER of,
 Admissibility of evidence, rape victim's domicile, **Rape 🔑 40(4)**

CHOICE, **Domicile 🔑 4(1, 2)**

COLLEGES and universities,
 Students, **Colleges 🔑 9.20(2), 9.25(2)**

CONSTITUTIONAL law,
 Due process,
  Service of process on agent of nonresident, **Const Law 🔑 309(3)**
 Standing to raise constitutional questions, **Const Law 🔑 42.3(2)**
 Travel, freedom of, **Const Law 🔑 83(5)**

CONSTRUCTIVE service, **Fed Civ Proc 🔑 414, 420**

CONTINUANCE presumed, **Domicile 🔑 8**

CORPORATIONS,
 Domicile of corporation, **Corp 🔑 52**
 Foreign corporation,
  Jurisdiction of action between nonresidents and foreign corporations, **Courts 🔑 14**
 Status of corporation as resident, **Corp 🔑 1.1(3)**

CORRECTIONS officers,
 Municipal corporations, **Mun Corp 🔑 212**

COSTS,
 Security for payment of costs as affected by residence of parties, **Costs 🔑 110; Fed Civ Proc 🔑 2733**

DOMICILE OR RESIDENCE—Cont'd

COUNCIL,
 Eligibility, **Mun Corp 🔑 138**

CREDITOR actions, **Debtor & C 🔑 11**

DIVORCE. See heading **DIVORCE**, DOMICILE or residence.

DRAFTS for armed services, nonresidents, **Armed S 🔑 20.4(2)**

ELEMENTS of domicile, **Domicile 🔑 1**

ELIGIBILITY,
 Public employees and officials, **Offic 🔑 22**

EQUAL protection. See heading **EQUAL PROTECTION**, RESIDENCY.

ESTATE and gift taxes, federal. See heading **ESTATE AND GIFT TAXES**, DOMICILE or residence.

ESTATE and gift taxes, state,
 Appraisal of debts of nonresident decedent, **Tax 🔑 895(8)**
 Property subject to tax, **Tax 🔑 867**

EVIDENCE, **Domicile 🔑 7.1-10**
 Declarations, self-serving, **Evidence 🔑 271(8)**
 Hearsay, **Evid 🔑 317(16)**
 Plea of privilege, **Plead 🔑 111.39-111.42**
 Res gestae, **Evid 🔑 121(5), 122(4)**

EXECUTORS and administrators,
 Change, **Ex & Ad 🔑 35(6)**
 Claimant, nonresidence as affecting time for presentation of claims, **Ex & Ad 🔑 225(5)**
 Jurisdiction to appoint as dependent on decedent's domicile, **Ex & Ad 🔑 10**

EXEMPTIONS, right to. See heading **EXEMPTIONS**, RESIDENCE of claimant.

FEDERAL courts,
 Diversity jurisdiction, **Fed Cts 🔑 282**

FORCIBLE entry and detainer,
 Plaintiffs, **Forci E & D 🔑 9(4)**

GAMBLING, criminal responsibility, **Gaming 🔑 72(6)**

GARNISHMENT, jurisdiction of garnishee, **Garn 🔑 78**

GOVERNMENTAL bodies or officers,
 Diversity jurisdiction of Federal courts, **Fed Cts 🔑 283**

Reprinted with permission from Thomson Reuters/West, *West's Federal Practice Digest*, 4th Ser., Vol. 97A (2002), p. 550.

The next step is looking up the topic "Domicile" in the subject volumes. The outline at the beginning of the topic identifies several key numbers that may be relevant.

FIGURE 5.16 KEY NUMBER OUTLINE, "DOMICILE" TOPIC

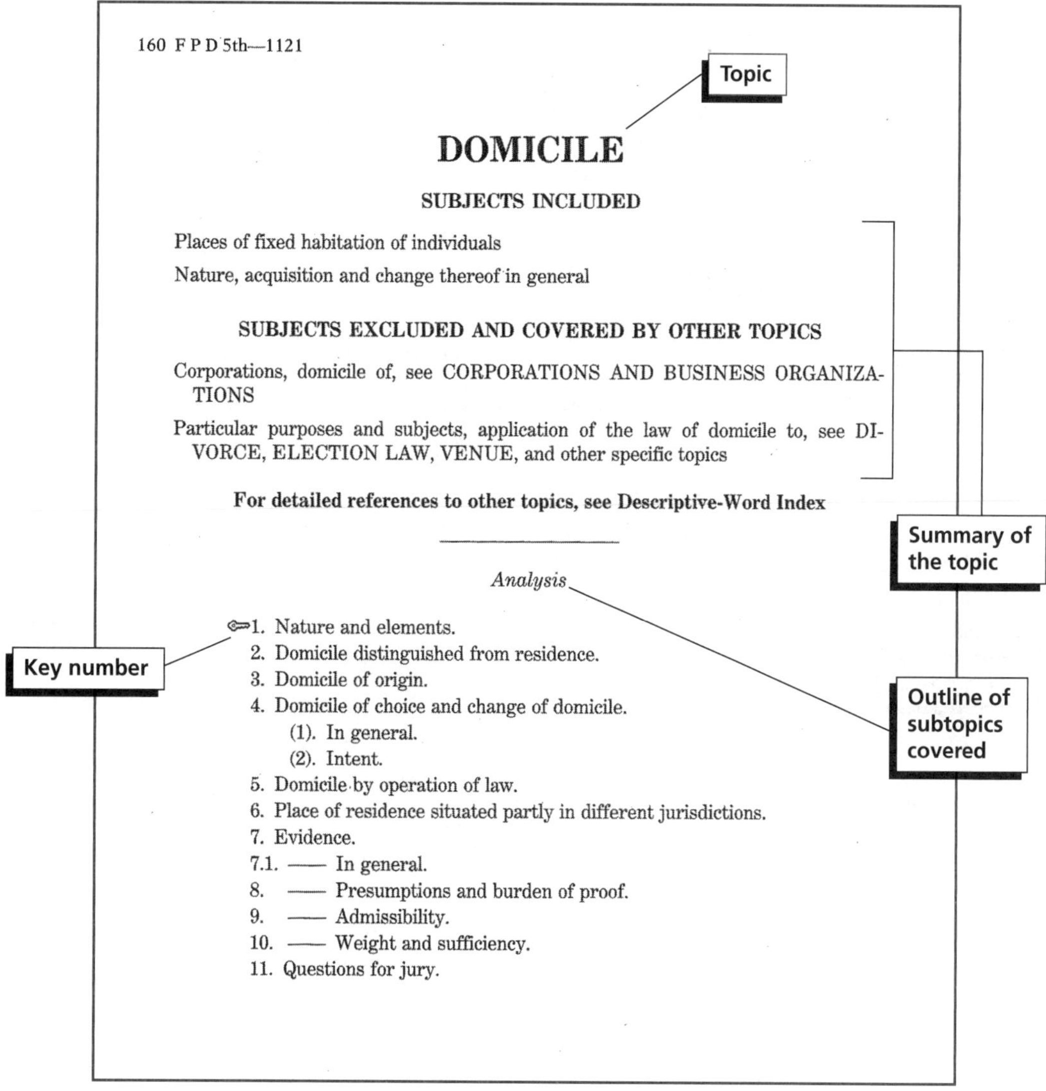
160 F P D 5th—1121

DOMICILE

SUBJECTS INCLUDED

Places of fixed habitation of individuals

Nature, acquisition and change thereof in general

SUBJECTS EXCLUDED AND COVERED BY OTHER TOPICS

Corporations, domicile of, see CORPORATIONS AND BUSINESS ORGANIZATIONS

Particular purposes and subjects, application of the law of domicile to, see DIVORCE, ELECTION LAW, VENUE, and other specific topics

For detailed references to other topics, see Descriptive-Word Index

Analysis

1. Nature and elements.
2. Domicile distinguished from residence.
3. Domicile of origin.
4. Domicile of choice and change of domicile.
   (1). In general.
   (2). Intent.
5. Domicile by operation of law.
6. Place of residence situated partly in different jurisdictions.
7. Evidence.

7.1. —— In general.
8. —— Presumptions and burden of proof.
9. —— Admissibility.
10. —— Weight and sufficiency.
11. Questions for jury.

Reprinted with permission from Thomson Reuters/West, *West's Federal Practice Digest*, 5th Ser., Vol. 160 (2015), p. 1121. © 2015 Thomson Reuters/West.

The case summaries under key number 1 include a potentially relevant case from the U.S. Court of Appeals for the First Circuit, as well as several from the federal district court in Puerto Rico.

FIGURE 5.17 CASE SUMMARIES UNDER "DOMICILE" TOPIC

⚷1 DOMICILE

160 F P D 5th—1122

For later cases, see same Topic and Key Number in Pocket Part

Research Notes

Federal jurisdiction, diversity of citizenship, see West's Federal Practice Manual.

See Wright & Miller, Federal Practice and Procedure: Civil.

⚷**1. Nature and elements.**

C.A.9 (Hawai'i) 2004. A person's domicile is her permanent home, where she resides with the intention to remain or to which she intends to return.
Gaudin v. Remis, 379 F.3d 631, transferred to 415 F.3d 1028, appeal after remand 334 Fed.Appx. 133, certiorari denied 131 S.Ct. 109, 178 L.Ed.2d 31.

A person generally assumes the domicile of his or her parents, and she may have only one domicile at a time.
Gaudin v. Remis, 379 F.3d 631, transferred to 415 F.3d 1028, appeal after remand 334 Fed.Appx. 133, certiorari denied 131 S.Ct. 109, 178 L.Ed.2d 31.

C.A.1 (Puerto Rico) 2008. Person's domicile is the place where he has his true, fixed home and principal establishment, and to which, whenever he is absent, he has the intention of returning. 28 U.S.C.A. § 1332(a)(1).
Padilla-Mangual v. Pavia Hosp., 516 F.3d 29, on remand 640 F.Supp.2d 128.

C.A.5 (Tex.) 2010. Domicile is established by physical presence in a location coupled with an intent to remain there indefinitely.
In re Ran, 607 F.3d 1017.

C.A.3 (Virgin Islands) 2011. Individual's "domicile" is his true, fixed and permanent home and place of habitation; it is place to which, whenever he is absent, he has intention of returning.
Washington v. Hovensa LLC, 652 F.3d 340, on remand 2011 WL 5563260.

Domicile is established by objective physical presence in state or territory coupled with subjective intention to remain there indefinitely.
Washington v. Hovensa LLC, 652 F.3d 340, on remand 2011 WL 5563260.

D.Conn. 2013. In general, for jurisdictional purposes, the domicile of an individual is his true, fixed and permanent home and place of habitation—i.e., the place to which, whenever he is absent, he has the intention of returning. 28 U.S.C.A. § 1332(a)(1).
Doe No. 1 v. Knights of Columbus, 930 F.Supp.2d 337.

D.D.C. 2014. Any analysis of a party's domicile, for purposes of diversity, must be fact-specific.
Lopes v. Jetsetdc, LLC, 4 F.Supp.3d 238.

S.D.Ind. 2011. "Domicile" is normally understood to mean (1) physical presence at a particular location, and (2) intent to remain somewhere indefinitely.
Hill-Jackson v. FAF, Inc., 808 F.Supp.2d 1083.

D.N.M. 2013. Person's "domicile" is place in which he or she has residence in fact and intent to remain indefinitely, as of time of filing of lawsuit.
Ullman v. Safeway Ins. Co., 995 F.Supp.2d 1196.

E.D.N.Y. 2013. Under New York law, a party can have only one domicile at a time, and the pertinent time for purposes of choice-of-law analysis is the time of the tort rather than any later time.
Youngman v. Robert Bosch LLC, 923 F.Supp.2d 411.

S.D.N.Y. 2014. A person's "domicile" is the place where a person has his true fixed home and principal establishment, and to which, whenever he is absent, he has the intention of returning.
Hai Yang Liu v. 88 Harborview Realty, LLC, 5 F.Supp.3d 443.

At any given time, a person can only have one domicile.
Hai Yang Liu v. 88 Harborview Realty, LLC, 5 F.Supp.3d 443.

S.D.N.Y. 2006. Under New York law, a party may have but one domicile at a time.
Hatfill v. Foster, 415 F.Supp.2d 353.

D.Puerto Rico 2008. A person's "domicile" is the place where he has his true, fixed home and principal establishment, and to which, whenever he is absent, he has the intention of returning.
Alexandrino v. Jardin de Oro, Inc., 573 F.Supp.2d 465.

Domicile requires both physical presence in a place and the intent to make that place one's home.
Alexandrino v. Jardin de Oro, Inc., 573 F.Supp.2d 465.

D.Puerto Rico 2007. Party can only have one domicile at a time.
Cruz-Martinez v. Hospital Hermanos Melendez, Inc., 475 F.Supp.2d 140.

D.Puerto Rico 2006. Party may only have one domicile at a time; however, a change of one's legal domicile could, very well, occur instantly.
Torres Vazquez v. Commercial Union Ins. Co., 417 F.Supp.2d 227.

† This Case was not selected for publication in the National Reporter System
For cited U.S.C.A. sections and legislative history, see United States Code Annotated

The next step is checking the pocket part for this volume. The entry under key number 1 in the pocket part lists several cases, although none from the District of Puerto Rico or the First Circuit. To complete your updating, you would also need to check the interim pamphlets for cases decided after the pocket part was published.

FIGURE 5.18 DIGEST VOLUME, POCKET PART

160 F P D 5th—109

DOMICILE ⚷8

were divorced at the time of ex-husband's death.—Stengel v. Medtronic Inc., 306 F.R.D. 230.

Bkrtcy.D.Vt. 2015. While divorce court may assign responsibility for payment of particular debts, this assignment does not affect which spouse is personally obligated to creditor, and creditor can use any remedies it had before the divorce to recover from either liable spouse.—In re Kadoch, 528 B.R. 626.

VII. FOREIGN DIVORCES.

Foreign custody decrees, Hague Convention, and other international issues as to custody, see CHILD CUSTODY. Foreign child support decrees and other international issues as to child support, see CHILD SUPPORT.

Pocket part entry for key number 1

DOMICILE

Research Notes

Federal jurisdiction, diversity of citizenship, see West's Federal Practice Manual.

See Wright & Miller, Federal Practice and Procedure: Civil.

⚷1. Nature and elements.

C.A.5 (Tex.) 2015. Under Texas law, person is domiciled in state if he or she: (1) resides within the state, and (2) intends to remain in that state for the indefinite future. V.T.C.A., Property Code § 41.001.—In re Brown, 807 F.3d 701.

N.D.Cal. 2015. Person's "domicile" is her permanent home, where she resides with intention of remaining or to which she intends to return.—In re Anthem, Inc., 129 F.Supp.3d 887.

D.D.C. 2015. In the District of Columbia Circuit, domicile is determined by two factors: physical presence in a state, and intent to remain there for an unspecified or indefinite period of time.—Core VCT PLC v. Hensley, 89 F.Supp.3d 104.

Bkrtcy.N.D.Ill. 2015. "Domicile" is place where one has his true, fixed, permanent home and principal establishment, and to which, whenever he is absent, he has the intention of returning, and where he exercises his political rights; there must exist, in combination, the fact of residence and animus manendi, i.e., an intention of remaining.—In re Husain, 533 B.R. 658.

Bkrtcy.D.S.C. 2015. Under South Carolina law, party's "residence" is the place where he actually lives or has his home, his dwelling place or place of habitation, his abode, house where his home is, or dwelling house.—In re Bycura, 540 B.R. 211.

⚷2. Domicile distinguished from residence.

Bkrtcy.N.D.Ill. 2015. "Residence" indicates permanency of occupation as distinguished from temporary occupation, but does not include so much as "domicile," which requires an intention continued with residence.—In re Husain, 533 B.R. 658.

⚷4(2). Intent.

C.A.5 (Tex.) 2015. Bankruptcy court did not clearly err in finding that Chapter 7 debtor was domiciled in Florida at time of his death, and that his widow's right to probate allowance was governed not by Texas but by Florida law, given that, while debtor still maintained some connections with Texas and had significant assets in that state, he had moved from Texas to Florida roughly two years prior to his death, he also possessed many valuable assets in Florida, and there was no evidence in record that, prior to his death, he had any intention of again relocating outside of Florida. V.T.C.A., Estates Code § 353.053.—In re Brown, 807 F.3d 701.

D.D.C. 2015. Evidence that judgment debtor applied for property tax discount with respect to property in Illinois, that he renewed his Illinois driver's license, that he filed federal and state income tax returns as Illinois resident, and that he was employed by United States entity, was insufficient to demonstrate that debtor intended to reestablish domicile in Illinois, as required for district court to have diversity subject matter jurisdiction in action by judgment creditor under Uniform Foreign-Country Money Judgments Recognition Act to enforce judgment obtained in England's High Court of Justice; when debtor renewed his Illinois driver's license, he still had long-term lease in Monaco and held valid residency card for that country, declaration of Illinois residency on tax returns was weak evidence of domiciliary intent, and debtor did not live anywhere in Illinois but had leased out his only property in Illinois when he moved to France. D.C. Code § 15-361.—Core VCT PLC v. Hensley, 89 F.Supp.3d 104.

Bkrtcy.N.D.Ill. 2015. "Domicile" is place where one has his true, fixed, permanent home and principal establishment, and to which, whenever he is absent, he has the intention of returning, and where he exercises his political rights; there must exist, in combination, the fact of residence and animus manendi, i.e., an intention of remaining.—In re Husain, 533 B.R. 658.

"Residence" is place where a person's habitation is fixed without any present intention of removing therefrom, and is lost by leaving the place where one has acquired a permanent home and removing to another place animo non revertendi, i.e., without intent to return.—Id.

⚷8. —— Presumptions and burden of proof.

D.D.C. 2015. Magistrate judge's determination that judgment debtor was "stateless" was not based on implicit adoption of "homeless wanderer" theory, for purposes of determining whether district court had subject matter jurisdiction, on basis of diversity, over judgment creditor's action under Uniform Foreign-Country Money Judgments Recognition Act to enforce judgment obtained in England's High Court of Justice; rather, Magistrate Judge found that debtor was stateless because, under presumption of continuing domicile, he moved to France, and then to Monaco, and therefore, was domiciliary of either France or Monaco at time creditors filed suit. D.C. Code § 15-361.—Core VCT PLC v. Hensley, 89 F.Supp.3d 104.

The presumption of "continuing domicile" dictates that a domicile once existing continues until another is acquired.—Id.

Under presumption of continuing domicile, once judgment debtor moved from France to Monaco, he remained domiciliary of Monaco until he moved back to United States, and thus, district court lacked subject matter jurisdiction, on basis of diversity, over action by judgment creditor under Uniform Foreign-Country Money Judgments Recognition Act to enforce judgment obtained in England's High Court of Justice, regardless of whether he became citizen of Monaco. D.C. Code § 15-361.—Id.

D.Vt. 2014. Presumption that a prisoner retains his preincarceration domicile is rebuttable only when a prisoner can show truly exceptional circumstances which would justify a finding that he has acquired a new domicile at the place of his incarceration.—Shovah v. Mercure, 44

† This Case was not selected for publication in the National Reporter System

In Westlaw, you can conduct a content-driven search that will retrieve cases and other authorities. You can also access the West Key Number System from the Key Numbers link under the All Content tab. Executing a word search within the West Key Number System and following the appropriate links retrieves a list of case summaries organized by topic. The search can also be pre-filtered by jurisdiction. Figure 5.19 shows the results of a search for *domicile* within the West Key Number System, as well as summaries of appellate cases from the First Circuit regarding *domicile*.

FIGURE 5.19 WEST KEY NUMBER SEARCH OPTIONS AND RESULTS

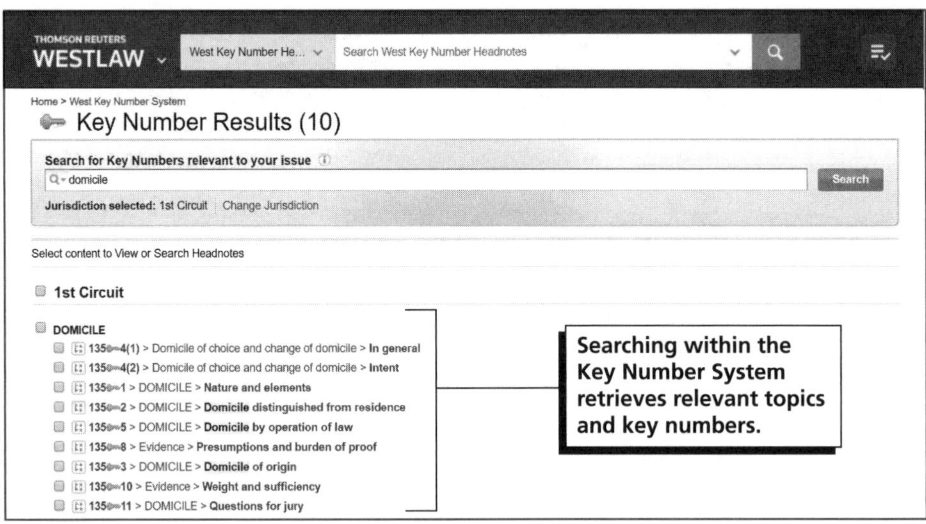

Jurisdiction is one filtering option

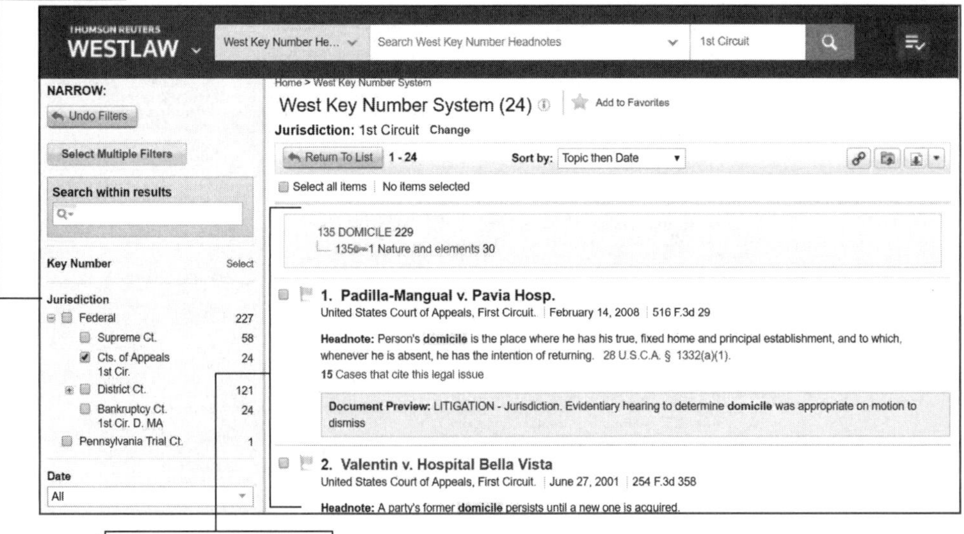

First Circuit cases concerning domicile

In Lexis Advance, you can execute a source-driven or content-driven search and use a variety of filters to narrow the search results. In Figure 5.20 a content-driven search for *domicile* in the First Circuit retrieves more than 10,000 total documents and roughly 1,400 cases. Filtering the case results by court to focus only on appellate cases from the First Circuit and searching within the search results for the term *malpractice* reduces the number to 11 cases.

FIGURE 5.20 RESULTS OF A WORD SEARCH IN LEXIS ADVANCE

Lexis Advance search results. Copyright 2017 LexisNexis, a division of Reed Elsevier Inc. All Rights Reserved. LexisNexis and the Knowledge Burst logo are registered trademarks of Reed Elsevier Properties Inc. and are used with the permission of LexisNexis.

In Bloomberg Law, you can execute source-driven or content-driven searches. Figure 5.21 shows the results of a source-driven search for appellate cases from the First Circuit containing the term *domicile*. Filtering options appear to the left of the search results. Once you open a case, you can access the Points of Law function to search for cases on specific issues.

FIGURE 5.21 RESULTS OF A WORD SEARCH IN BLOOMBERG LAW

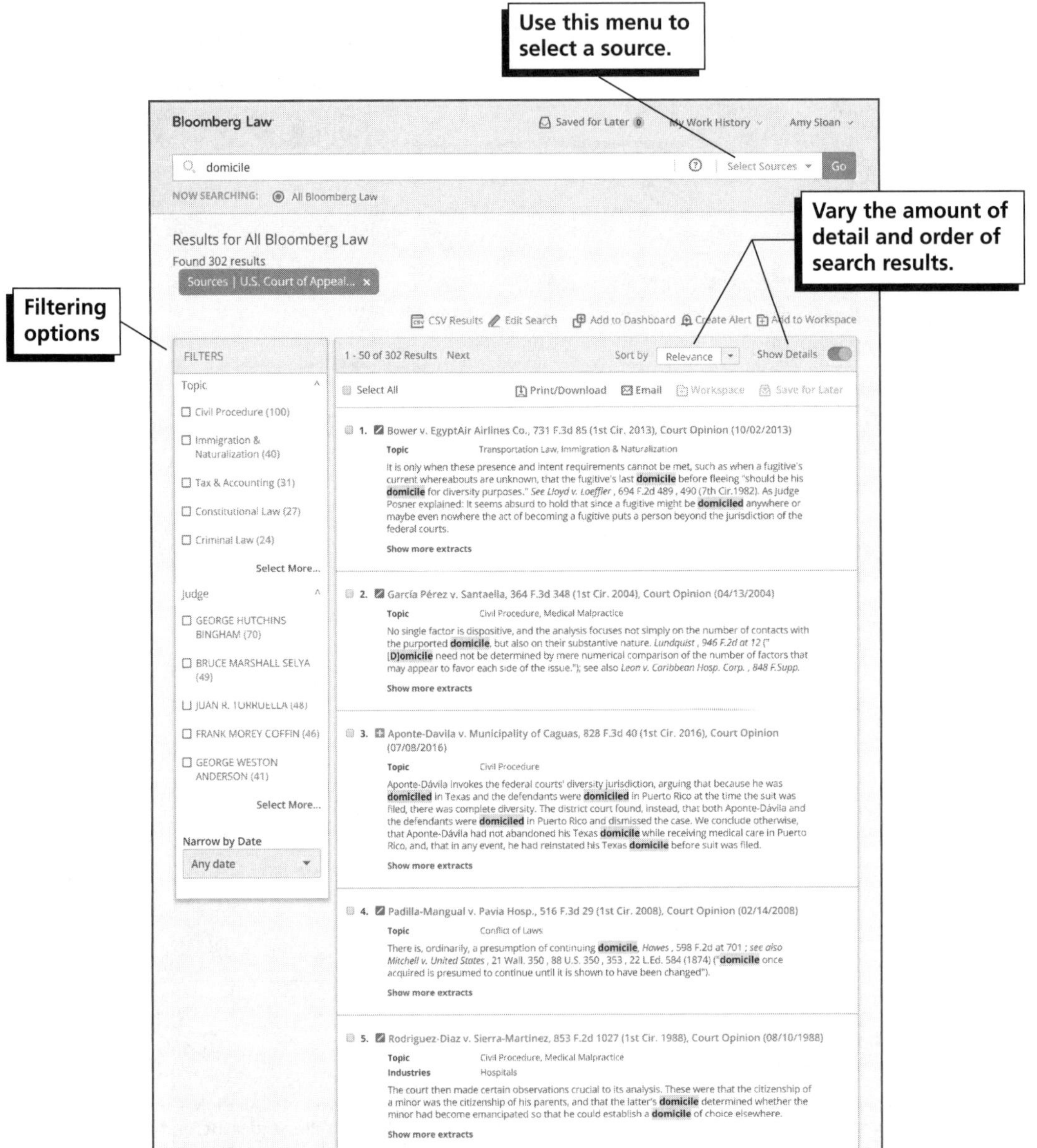

This is the opinion in *Padilla-Mangual v. Pavia Hospital*, a case that is summarized in the West print digest and within the search results in Westlaw, Lexis Advance, and Bloomberg Law. This is how the case would appear in print or as the original .pdf in Westlaw. You would want to review this case, as well as others, in conducting your research.

FIGURE 5.22 *PADILLA-MANGUAL v. PAVIA HOSP.*, 516 F.3D 29 (1ST CIR. 2008)

PADILLA-MANGUAL v. PAVIA HOSP. 29
Cite as 516 F.3d 29 (1st Cir. 2008)

Ryan PADILLA-MANGUAL, Plaintiff, Appellant,

v.

PAVÍA HOSPITAL, et al. Defendants, Appellees.

No. 07–1447.

United States Court of Appeals, First Circuit.

Heard Nov. 9, 2007.

Decided Feb. 14, 2008.

Background: Plaintiff, a purported domiciliary of Florida, brought diversity suit against Puerto Rican hospital, physician, and his conjugal partnership, alleging negligent medical treatment. The United States District Court for the District of Puerto Rico, Francisco A. Besosa, J., dismissed action for lack of diversity jurisdiction, and plaintiff appealed.

Holding: The Court of Appeals, Smith, District Judge, sitting by designation, held that evidentiary hearing to develop record and assess credibility was appropriate in determine domicile of plaintiff.

Reversed and remanded.

1. Federal Courts ⚷282

For purposes of diversity, a person is a citizen of the state in which he is domiciled. 28 U.S.C.A. § 1332(a)(1).

2. Domicile ⚷1

Person's domicile is the place where he has his true, fixed home and principal establishment, and to which, whenever he is absent, he has the intention of returning. 28 U.S.C.A. § 1332(a)(1).

3. Federal Courts ⚷34

Once challenged, party invoking subject matter jurisdiction has the burden of proving by a preponderance of the evidence the facts supporting jurisdiction.

4. Domicile ⚷8

Ordinarily, there is a presumption of continuing domicile. 28 U.S.C.A. § 1332(a)(1).

5. Domicile ⚷4(1, 2)

Plaintiff is required to show two things in order to establish a change in domicile: (1) presence in new state, and (2) an intent to remain there. 28 U.S.C.A. § 1332(a)(1).

6. Federal Courts ⚷870.1

District court's determination that plaintiff failed to meet his burden of showing domicile in state other than that of defendants, as required for diversity jurisdiction, involved mixed question of law and fact, and thus could not be set aside unless clearly erroneous. 28 U.S.C.A. § 1332(a)(1).

7. Federal Courts ⚷791

Presumption that district court reached correct result regarding domicile of parties for purposes of diversity jurisdiction is somewhat lessened when based on documentary evidence as opposed to oral testimony about party's intent. 28 U.S.C.A. § 1332(a)(1).

8. Federal Courts ⚷318

Absence of typical indicia of domicile is not determinative, on motion to dismiss for lack of diversity jurisdiction, if party has declared his intent to change and remain in his new domicile, and the opposing written submissions do not demonstrate falsity of the declaration with reasonable certainty. 28 U.S.C.A. § 1332(a)(1).

9. Federal Courts ⚷947

Evidentiary hearing on remand was appropriate to develop record and assess credibility of parties in determining if plaintiff could overcome presumption of continuing domicile in Puerto Rico, as re-

FIGURE 5.22 *PADILLA-MANGUAL v. PAVIA HOSP.*, 516 F.3D 29 (1ST CIR. 2008) *(Continued)*

quired to establish diversity of citizenship, notwithstanding absence of typical indicia of plaintiff's domicile in Florida other than issuance of driver's license, given plaintiff's expressed intent to remain in Florida, and failure of defendants to demonstrate falsity of that declaration with reasonable certainty in their written submissions. 28 U.S.C.A. § 1332(a)(1).

10. Federal Courts ⚷**30, 33**

In conducting a jurisdictional inquiry, the court enjoys broad authority to order discovery, consider extrinsic evidence, hold an evidentiary hearing, and hear testimony in order to determine its own jurisdiction.

Antonio Bauzá–Torres and Rubén Morales, for appellant.

Mirta Rodríguez–Mora, with whom Látimer, Biaggi, Rachid & Godreau, were on brief for appellee Pavía Hospital, and Nuyen Marrero–Bonilla, with whom Montijo & Montijo Law Offices, were on brief for appellees Dr. Miguel De La Cruz and his conjugal partnership.

Before TORRUELLA and HOWARD, Circuit Judges, and SMITH,* District Judge.

SMITH, District Judge.

In this case, a challenge to the diversity jurisdiction claimed by a plaintiff requires us to examine the presumption of domicile and what it takes to overcome it where the plaintiff forges none of the typical ties to his new home. Ultimately, we conclude that the task is one better left to the district court, with the benefit of an evidentiary hearing.

Plaintiff-appellant, Ryan Padilla–Mangual ("Padilla"), brought an action in the United States District Court for the District of Puerto Rico against defendant-appellee Pavía Hospital, and defendants-appellees Dr. Miguel De La Cruz Castellanos and his conjugal partnership (collectively, "Dr. De La Cruz"), for damages stemming from allegedly negligent medical treatment.[1] Padilla's complaint, which was premised on Puerto Rico's general tort statute, P.R. Laws Ann. tit. 31, § 5141 (2004), alleged federal diversity jurisdiction under 28 U.S.C. § 1332. The complaint alleged that Padilla was a resident of the State of Florida.[2]

On July 17, 2006, Dr. De La Cruz moved to dismiss for lack of subject matter jurisdiction on the grounds that diversity of citizenship was lacking.[3] Dr. De La Cruz claimed that as of January 30, 2006, the date that Padilla filed his complaint, Padil-

* Of the District of Rhode Island, sitting by designation.

1. The complaint originally named Nicole Freire (or, Freyre), Padilla's then-fiancée, as an additional plaintiff. However, she subsequently was voluntarily dismissed from the case.

2. Although Padilla's complaint actually alleged that he was a "resident" of Florida, rather than a "citizen" or "domiciliary" of Florida, the district court's analysis of domicile moots any concern as to whether Padilla's allegations, if defective, should preclude a finding of diversity jurisdiction. *See Cantellops v. Álvaro–Chapel,* 234 F.3d 741, 742–743 (1st Cir.2000) (district court's analysis of domicile reviewed for clear error even where complaint specifically alleged residency instead of domicile).

3. Dr. De La Cruz's motion also requested that the district court abstain from deciding the action based on the abstention doctrine set forth in *Colorado River Water Conservation Dist. v. United States,* 424 U.S. 800, 96 S.Ct. 1236, 47 L.Ed.2d 483 (1976). The district court did not discuss the issue of abstention in light of its decision to dismiss the complaint for lack of diversity jurisdiction.

FIGURE 5.22 *PADILLA-MANGUAL v. PAVIA HOSP.*, 516 F.3D 29 (1ST CIR. 2008) *(Continued)*

PADILLA-MANGUAL v. PAVIA HOSP. 31
Cite as 516 F.3d 29 (1st Cir. 2008)

la actually was a domiciliary of Puerto Rico, not Florida. On October 3, 2006, Pavía Hospital moved for summary judgment on Padilla's claims, also arguing that the district court lacked diversity jurisdiction. The district court granted both motions in a single order on February 1, 2007, without holding an evidentiary hearing. Padilla timely filed this appeal. While the district court's analysis ultimately may prove to be correct, because we find that the record has not been adequately developed, we reverse and remand for an evidentiary hearing on the question of diversity of citizenship.

[1, 2] Federal jurisdiction based on diversity of citizenship requires that the matter in controversy be between citizens of different states. 28 U.S.C. § 1332(a)(1) (2006). For purposes of diversity, a person is a citizen of the state in which he is domiciled. *Lundquist v. Precision Valley Aviation, Inc.*, 946 F.2d 8, 10 (1st Cir. 1991); *Rodríguez–Díaz v. Sierra–Martínez*, 853 F.2d 1027, 1029 (1st Cir.1988); *Valedón Martínez v. Hospital Presbiteriano de la Comunidad, Inc.*, 806 F.2d 1128, 1132 (1st Cir.1986). "A person's domicile 'is the place where he has his true, fixed home and principal establishment, and to which, whenever he is absent, he has the intention of returning.'" *Rodríguez–Díaz*, 853 F.2d at 1029 (quoting Charles Allen Wright, Arthur R. Miller, & Edward H. Cooper, *Federal Practice & Procedure* § 3612 (2d ed.1984)). Domicile is determined as of the time the suit is filed. *Lundquist*, 946 F.2d at 10; *Valedón Martínez*, 806 F.2d at 1132; *Hawes v. Club Ecuestre El Comandante*, 598 F.2d 698, 701 (1st Cir.1979).

[3] In contesting Padilla's assertion of diversity jurisdiction, the appellees point out that only four days before filing his action in the district court, Padilla filed a complaint in Puerto Rico state court, essentially making the same allegations as in his federal complaint, but alleging him to be a resident of Puerto Rico.[4] Once challenged, "the party invoking subject matter jurisdiction [here Padilla] has the burden of proving by a preponderance of the evidence the facts supporting jurisdiction." *Bank One, Texas, N.A. v. Montle*, 964 F.2d 48, 50 (1st Cir.1992) (citation omitted); *see also Lundquist*, 946 F.2d at 10 (plaintiff must support allegation of jurisdiction by "competent proof"); *O'Toole v. Arlington Trust Co.*, 681 F.2d 94, 98 (1st Cir.1982); *Hawes*, 598 F.2d at 702; *Lugo–Viña v. Pueblo Int'l, Inc.*, 574 F.2d 41, 44 (1st Cir.1978). Padilla contended that the allegations of residency contained in his Puerto Rico pleadings were "clerical errors" and that he had, by December 31, 2004, permanently relocated from Puerto Rico to Florida.[5]

[4, 5] There is, ordinarily, a presumption of continuing domicile, *Hawes*, 598 F.2d at 701; *see also Mitchell v. United States*, 21 Wall. 350, 88 U.S. 350, 353, 22 L.Ed. 584 (1874) ("domicile once acquired is presumed to continue until it is shown to have been changed"). Because Padilla was raised in Puerto Rico and lived there until his apparent relocation to Florida, it is presumed that he was a domiciliary of Puerto Rico. To sustain his burden, Padilla

4. The complaint filed in Puerto Rico state court on January 26, 2006, was actually an amended complaint. The original complaint, which also alleged that Padilla was a resident of Puerto Rico, was filed on August 22, 2005.

5. Padilla's representation that he relocated to Florida on December 31, 2004 appears to be contradicted by his own appellate brief, in which he asserts that he was flown (apparently from Puerto Rico) to the Mayo Clinic in Jacksonville, Florida, on or about January 18, 2005.

FIGURE 5.22 *PADILLA-MANGUAL v. PAVIA HOSP.*, 516 F.3D 29 (1ST CIR. 2008) *(Continued)*

was required to show two things in order to establish a change in his domicile from Puerto Rico to Florida: (1) presence in Florida, and (2) an intent to remain there. *Bank One,* 964 F.2d at 50; *Valedón Martínez,* 806 F.2d at 1132; *Hawes,* 598 F.2d at 701. We have stated previously that the factors relevant to determining a party's intent include:

> the place where civil and political rights are exercised, taxes paid, real and personal property (such as furniture and automobiles) located, driver's and other licenses obtained, bank accounts maintained, location of club and church membership and places of business or employment.

Bank One, 964 F.2d at 50 (citation omitted). While no single factor is controlling, some courts have presumed domicile in a state is established where a party is registered to vote. *Id.* This Court has not recognized such a presumption, but we have said that the place a person is registered to vote is a "weighty" factor in determining domicile. *Lundquist,* 946 F.2d at 12.

[6] The district court's conclusion that Padilla failed to meet his burden of proving that he changed his domicile to Florida at the time he filed his federal complaint is a "mixed question of law and fact and as such may not be set aside unless clearly erroneous." *Bank One,* 964 F.2d at 51; *Lundquist,* 946 F.2d at 11; *Valedón Martínez,* 806 F.2d at 1132; *O'Toole,* 681 F.2d at 98; *Hawes,* 598 F.2d at 702. "A finding is 'clearly erroneous' when, although there is evidence to support it, the reviewing court is left with the definite and firm conviction that a mistake has been committed." *Anderson v. Bessemer City,* 470 U.S. 564, 573, 105 S.Ct. 1504, 84 L.Ed.2d 518 (1985) (citation omitted). Though this presents a high hurdle for Padilla, we believe it has been cleared here—if only just—and we therefore cannot sustain, on the present record, the district court's finding of a lack of diversity jurisdiction. *See Fredyma v. AT & T Network Sys., Inc.,* 935 F.2d 368, 370 (1st Cir.1991) (reversing district court judgment for error in procedure, but expressing no opinion on "ultimate viability" of complaint).

The record before us reveals that Padilla offered several pieces of evidence to show that he had changed his domicile from Puerto Rico to Florida prior to filing his federal lawsuit: (1) two declarations, one his and the other his mother's, made under penalty of perjury, that he is a resident of Florida and has no intention of returning to Puerto Rico; (2) copies of four ledgers detailing payments and charges from four different addresses in Florida where Padilla claims to have resided since January 2005;[6] and (3) a copy of a driver's license issued to Padilla on January 20, 2005, by the state of Florida. In his declaration, Padilla stated that he moved to Florida on December 31, 2004 and has never returned to Puerto Rico. He also declared that he intends to continue living in Florida, has no intention of ever returning to Puerto Rico, and that all of his personal contacts are in Florida, with the exception of his mother in Puerto Rico who provides him with financial support. Padilla's mother's declaration echoed Padilla's claims and clarified that she pays all

6. As the district court noted, only one of the ledgers records Padilla as a co-tenant with Nicole Freire, Padilla's then-fiancée. Two others show only Freire as the tenant, and the fourth shows Padilla's mother as the tenant. The ledger recording Padilla as a cotenant overlaps with the date that Padilla filed his federal complaint, *i.e.* Padilla apparently was the cotenant of a Florida residence as of the day that he filed his federal complaint on January 30, 2006.

FIGURE 5.22 *PADILLA-MANGUAL v. PAVIA HOSP.*, 516 F.3D 29 (1ST CIR. 2008) *(Continued)*

of Padilla's expenses since he is unable to work or study.[7]

Based on these submissions, as well as the Puerto Rico state court pleadings alleging that Padilla was a domiciliary of Puerto Rico, the district court found that, "[g]iven the totality of the circumstances, the Court simply cannot find that Padilla has established his domicile in Florida for diversity purposes." The district court reasoned that, ultimately, "Padilla has not shown . . . that he has taken any affirmative steps to establish a domicile in Florida." Specifically, the district court focused on Padilla's apparent failure to cultivate the sort of ties traditionally viewed as manifesting an expression of domicile:

> Padilla does not work nor has he indicated that he is looking for work in Florida. He does not go to school. He does not own or rent any real property in Florida. He does not belong to any clubs or groups, nor does he attend a church. He does not have any bank accounts. He has not registered or exercised the right to vote. Other than his driver's license and a stated desire to stay there, Padilla doesn't seem to have established any real presence in Florida.

The district court also believed it to be contradictory that Padilla stated his physical condition prevented him from working or attending school, and yet Padilla also professed to live alone and far from family, to care for himself, and to drive a car.

In other words, the district court found that Padilla's declaration was not credible because he largely had not taken the affirmative steps described in *Bank One, e.g.* opening a bank account or obtaining employment. However, nothing we have said in our prior decisions implies that the typical indicia of domicile are required in order to change one's domicile; rather, we have described these as examples of indicia of intent.

[7–9] We recognize that the mode of proving diversity is normally left to the district court, but its discretion is not unfettered. *Bank One,* 964 F.2d at 51; *O'Toole,* 681 F.2d at 98. While the district court may rely on documentary evidence to establish whether jurisdiction attaches, and while the same clearly erroneous standard applies to findings based thereon, the presumption that the court reached a correct result is somewhat lessened relative

7. While Padilla argued in opposition to the motion to dismiss and motion for summary judgment that his Puerto Rico pleadings contained erroneous allegations of residency, he submitted no actual evidence to support this specific claim until he submitted the declaration of his former counsel with his surreply. This relates to an additional concern that we would prefer to see alleviated before terminating Padilla's right to seek relief in a federal forum. The district court apparently granted Padilla an extension of time to February 6, 2007 to file a surreply. Nonetheless, the district court entered its judgment dismissing Padilla's complaint one day sooner, on February 5. Padilla's surreply, filed on February 6, included the declaration from his former counsel, in which counsel stated that he inadvertently copied Padilla's mother's address into the Puerto Rico pleadings, as well as additional documentation purporting to evidence Padilla's Florida domiciliary. That same day, Padilla also filed a motion for reconsideration of the district court's decision, which the district court denied on February 7. In denying the motion for reconsideration, the district court stated that it reviewed Padilla's surreply and found "no reason to change its previous ruling." We are troubled by this apparent *sub silentio* reversal of the district court's decision to grant Padilla the opportunity to file a surreply. It is not inconceivable that the previous day's dismissal of Padilla's complaint colored the district court's review of his surreply. We think these events support our view that the best approach is for the district court to take a fresh look at all the evidence submitted and conduct an evidentiary hearing to assess the credibility of the declarants.

FIGURE 5.22 ***PADILLA-MANGUAL v. PAVIA HOSP., 516 F.3D 29 (1ST CIR. 2008) (Continued)***

to findings based on oral testimony. *Bose Corp. v. Consumers Union of United States, Inc.,* 466 U.S. 485, 500, 104 S.Ct. 1949, 80 L.Ed.2d 502 (1984). In *Prakash v. American University,* 727 F.2d 1174 (D.C.Cir.1984), the District of Columbia Circuit, remanding for further proceedings on the question of diversity, stated:

> [i]n many instances, and perhaps in most, a party's intent will appear, at least in part, from facts established by documents. When, however, as here, a party expressly declares his intent, and the opposing written submissions do not demonstrate the falsity of the declaration with reasonable certainty, the issue necessarily becomes one of the declarant's credibility. In that event, the court cannot rest its decision simply on the paper record, but must hold a hearing in order to adequately assess credibility. Only in that way is a sound decision on intent possible.

Id. at 1180 (citations omitted); *see also Rubin v. Buckman,* 727 F.2d 71, 73 (3d Cir.1984) (remanding for further proceedings on whether diversity might exist); *Williamson v. Tucker,* 645 F.2d 404, 414 (5th Cir.1981) (where subject matter jurisdiction is attacked "the district court must give the plaintiff an opportunity for discovery and for a hearing that is appropriate to the nature of the motion to dismiss"); *Shahmoon Indus., Inc. v. Imperato,* 338 F.2d 449, 451–52 (3d Cir.1964) (remanding case for further inquiry into the jurisdictional facts where the court had "serious doubts" as to the district court's jurisdiction based on the factual record and where the factual record only raised doubts as to the accuracy of one of the parties' affidavits). It is certainly possible that one might change his residence with no intent of returning, but not make those connections described in *Bank One.* Any number of explanations are possible—physical or mental incapacity, religious objections, to name a few. The point is that where a party has declared his intent to change and remain in his new domicile, and the opposing written submissions do not demonstrate the falsity of the declaration with reasonable certainty, the absence of typical indicia of domicile is not determinative. More is required of the district court before it concludes that a plaintiff has not met his burden and overcome the presumption. We agree with our sister circuits that in these circumstances an evidentiary hearing is appropriate.

Thus, while we note that the district court's decision is by no means wholly unsupported by the record, we are persuaded, for the reasons stated above, that Padilla's complaint should not be dismissed in the absence of an evidentiary hearing that will allow the district court to assess fully Padilla's credibility and resolve certain unanswered questions implicated by the parties' briefing.

[10] We stress that we are not predetermining the ultimate findings of the district court. In conducting a jurisdictional inquiry, the court enjoys broad authority to order discovery, consider extrinsic evidence, hold an evidentiary hearing, and hear testimony in order to determine its own jurisdiction. *Valentín v. Hospital Bella Vista,* 254 F.3d 358, 363 (1st Cir. 2001). We do not pretend to know what the district court may determine as a result of its inquiry; we request only that the inquiry be sufficiently thorough to assure that all parties receive a full and fair opportunity to be heard.[8]

Reversed and Remanded.

8. As a final note, we emphasize that, on remand, Padilla must establish by *preponder-*

F. CHECKLIST FOR CASE RESEARCH

1. RESEARCH CASES WITH A PRINT DIGEST

- ☐ Select an appropriate digest: *West's Federal Practice Digest* for federal cases; a state digest for state and federal cases from an individual state; a regional digest for state cases only within the region.
- ☐ Locate topics and key numbers from the headnotes in case on point, the Descriptive-Word Index, or a topic entry.
- ☐ Read the case summaries, using the court and date abbreviations to target appropriate cases.
- ☐ Update with the pocket part for the subject volume and any cumulative or noncumulative interim pamphlets.

2. ONLINE CASE RESEARCH—SEARCHING BY SUBJECT

- ☐ In Westlaw, search for cases by subject.
  - Use the West **Key Numbers** to find summaries of cases organized by topic and key number.
  - From a case on point, search for cases under a particular topic and key number by following the link to the key number in a relevant headnote.
  - Use the subject headings under the **Practice Areas** tab.
- ☐ In Lexis Advance, search for cases by subject.
  - Use the **Explore Content** tabs, drop-down menu in the search box, or **Browse** menu and select a topic area under **Practice Area or Industry** to search for cases by subject.
  - From a case on point, click on **More like this Headnote** or use the drop-down menu next to a LexisNexis Headnote topic to search for cases on the same headnote subject.
- ☐ In Bloomberg Law, search for cases by subject using **Points of Law** or from the headnote links in a case on point that has BNA Headnotes.

3. ONLINE CASE RESEARCH—WORD SEARCHING

- ☐ In Westlaw, Lexis Advance, and Bloomberg Law, execute word searches.
  - Source-driven searching: Pre-filter by jurisdiction and source or category to search for cases from a specific jurisdiction.
  - Content-driven searching: Pre-filter by jurisdiction (if possible) and execute a content-driven search; filter the results to target appropriate cases.
- ☐ In Google Scholar, execute word searches for published cases.

- ☐ In Fastcase, execute word searches; use the Fastcase Interactive Timeline, tag cloud, and Forecite to refine search results.
- ☐ Use Casetext's CARA to generate search results from an uploaded document instead of a search query.
- ☐ Use free research websites for targeted, cost-effective research; use websites for courts or other tribunals to locate very recent opinions, unpublished (non-precedential) opinions, or opinions unavailable from other sources.

CHAPTER 6

Research with Citators

A. INTRODUCTION TO CITATORS

1. THE PURPOSE OF A CITATOR

Virtually all cases contain citations to legal authorities, including other cases, secondary sources, statutes, and regulations. These decisions can affect the continued validity of the authorities they cite. For example, cases can be reversed or overruled, or statutes can be held unconstitutional. Even if an authority remains valid, the discussion of the authority in later cases can be helpful in your research. As a consequence, when you find an authority that helps you answer a research question, you will often want to know whether the authority has been cited elsewhere, and if so, what has been said about it.

The tool that helps you do this is called a citator. Citators catalog cases, secondary sources, and other authorities, analyzing what they say about the sources they cite. Some citators also track the status of statutes and regulations, indicating, for example, whether a statute has been amended or repealed. Citators will help you determine whether an authority is still "good law," meaning it has not been changed or invalidated since it was issued. They will also help you locate additional authorities that pertain to your research question.

Shepard's Citations is the best known citator. Shepard's was, for many years, the only citator most lawyers ever used, and checking citations came to be known as "Shepardizing." Generations of law students learned how to interpret print Shepard's entries, which are filled with symbols and abbreviations. Today, however, few legal researchers use Shepard's in print, and few libraries carry the print version. Instead, virtually all legal researchers use online citators. Shepard's is still a well-respected citator, and it is available in Lexis Advance. Westlaw also has its own citator—called KeyCite—and Bloomberg Law has a citator called BCite. Other online service providers offer their own citators.

Shepard's and KeyCite can be used in researching many types of authority, including cases, statutes, regulations, and some secondary sources. The process of using these citators, however, is the same for almost any type of authority. As this text goes to press, BCite is available only for cases. Accordingly, for purposes of introducing you to citators, this chapter focuses on their use in case research. Later chapters in this book discuss the use of Shepard's and KeyCite in researching other types of authority.

2. WHEN TO USE A CITATOR IN CASE RESEARCH

You must check every case on which you rely to answer a legal question to make sure it is still good law. In general, you will want to use a citator early in your research, after you have identified what appear to be a few key cases, to make sure you do not build your analysis on authority that is no longer valid. Using a citator at this stage will help direct you to other relevant authorities as well. You should also check every case you cite before handing in your work to make sure each one continues to be authoritative. Citing bad authority is every attorney's nightmare, and failing to check your citations can constitute professional malpractice. As a consequence, now is the time to get in the habit of updating your case research carefully.

3. CHOOSING AMONG CITATORS

Shepard's and KeyCite are the most widely used citators, and they enjoy the greatest acceptance as thorough and reliable services. BCite is newer, so its track record is not as established in the legal community. Other citators include **Authority Check** in Fastcase and **V.Cite** in VersusLaw. Google Scholar includes a **How Cited** tab with its search results. This is not a citator in the traditional sense, but it is a tool that can refer you to later cases that have cited the original case. (The URLs for all of these services appear in Appendix A.)

When you have a choice of citators, you must decide which one(s) to use in your research. The decision will depend on several factors. As noted above, Shepard's and KeyCite are the most accepted citators in legal research, but they are not identical. You should use both services enough to become comfortable with them while you are in law school. When you are out of school, you may continue to have access to one or both services. Shepard's and KeyCite are fairly economical to use, costing subscribers only a few dollars per citation, and many law libraries provide free public access to these services. If you do not have access to Shepard's or KeyCite but do have access to BCite or another citator, you should use it, understanding that the coverage of the citator may be limited to holdings within that service's database.

Using either Shepard's or KeyCite should be sufficient to verify the continued validity of a case as long as you carefully interpret the information they provide. Citators often characterize the treatment of a case by later sources as positive or negative, and this requires the exercise of editorial judgment. Different citators may characterize the status of a case differently. Therefore, if a case is especially important to your analysis, you would do well to check it in more than one citator.

If you are looking for research references, you may also want to use more than one citator. Any citator should provide references to later cases that you can use for research, but not all include references to secondary sources. Shepard's, KeyCite, and BCite include references to secondary sources, but they do not index all the same secondary sources. Thus, you may get slightly different research results in each service. Of course, there is more than one way to find almost any source, so a single citator—even one that does not include references to secondary sources—may be sufficient for your research when used in combination with other research tools. If you are having trouble finding relevant information, however, consider using a different citator to see if it identifies additional research references.

4. TERMS AND PROCEDURAL CONCEPTS USED IN CITATOR RESEARCH

Before you begin learning how to use citators, it is important to understand the terminology and procedural concepts used in the process. A case citator contains entries for decided cases that list the later authorities (cases, secondary sources, and other forms of authority) that have cited the case. This chapter uses the term "original case" to describe the case that is the subject of the citator entry. The terms "citing case" and "citing source" refer to the later authorities that cite the original case. Thus, for example, if you located the case of *Uddin v. Embassy Suites Hotel,* 165 Ohio App. 3d 699 (2005), and wanted to use a citator to verify its continued validity, *Uddin* would be referred to as the original case. The later authorities that cite *Uddin* would be referred to as citing cases or citing sources.

Two procedural concepts you need to understand are direct and indirect case history. Direct history refers to all of the opinions issued in conjunction with a single piece of litigation. One piece of litigation may generate multiple opinions. A case may be appealed to a higher court, resulting in opinions from both an intermediate appellate court and the court of last resort. A higher court may remand a case—that is, send a case back to a lower court—for reconsideration, again resulting in opinions issued by both courts. Or a court might issue separate opinions to resolve individual matters arising in a case. All of these opinions, whether issued before or after the original case, constitute direct history. Opinions issued before the original case may be called prior history; those issued after the original case may be called subsequent history or subsequent appellate history, as appropriate. Indirect history refers to an opinion generated from a different piece of litigation than the original case. Every unrelated case that cites the original case is part of the indirect history of the original case.

Both direct and indirect case history can be positive, negative, or neutral. Thus, if the original case is affirmed by a higher court, it has positive direct history, but if the original case is reversed, it has negative direct history. A related opinion in the same litigation on a different issue could be neutral; the opinion resolving the second issue could have no effect on the continued validity of the opinion resolving the first issue. Similarly, if the original case is relied upon by a court deciding a later, unrelated case, the original case has positive indirect history, but if the original case is overruled, it has negative indirect history. A citing case could discuss the original case in a way that does not include any positive or negative analysis. In that situation, the indirect history would be considered neutral.

B. USING SHEPARD'S IN LEXIS ADVANCE FOR CASE RESEARCH

To use Shepard's effectively, you need to know how to access the service, interpret the entries, and limit the display. You can also create a Shepard's Alert to continue updating your research over time.

1. ACCESSING SHEPARD'S

One way to access Shepard's is from a case. If you are viewing a case, a summary of Shepard's information appears to the right. You can view the complete Shepard's entry by selecting ***Shepardize*® this document**, or you can jump to a specific portion of the Shepard's entry using the links within the summary. **Figure 6.1** illustrates the Shepard's summary accom-

FIGURE 6.1 CASE WITH SHEPARD'S® SUMMARY

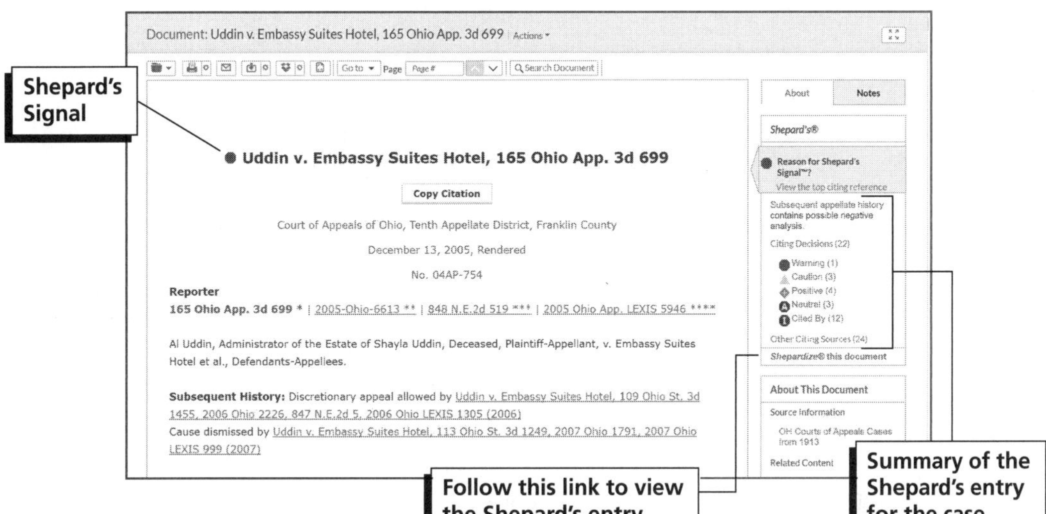

 Case with Shepard's® summary.

panying a case. The symbols in the entry are called "Shepard's Signals," and they are explained below. You can also access Shepard's without retrieving a case by typing *shep:* followed by the citation in the search box.

2. INTERPRETING AND LIMITING SHEPARD'S ENTRIES

Once you have retrieved the entry for the original case, you must evaluate the information you find. If appropriate to your research task, you may also want to limit the display to focus on specific information in the entry.

Shepard's uses symbols such as a red stop sign or a yellow triangle to indicate the type of treatment the original case has received from the citing cases. These symbols are called "Shepard's Signals." As noted above, Shepard's Signals also appear at the beginning of a case and in the Shepard's summary. A list of Shepard's Signals for cases and Lexis Advance's definition for each signal appear in **Figure 6.2.**

It is often difficult to reduce the status of a case to a single notation. Determining the continued validity of an original case often requires study of the citing cases. For example, an original case with a negative Shepard's Signal such as a red stop sign may no longer be good law for one of its points, but it may continue to be authoritative on other points. If you were to rely on the red stop sign without further inquiry, you might miss a case that is important for the issue you are researching. As a consequence, although Shepard's Signals can be helpful research tools,

FIGURE 6.2 **SHEPARD'S® SIGNALS FOR CASES**

SIGNAL	MEANS
Red stop sign	*Warning: Negative treatment is indicated.* This signal indicates that citing references in the Shepard's® Citations Service contain strong negative history or treatment of your case (e.g., overruled by or reversed).
Orange square surrounding the letter Q	*Questioned: Validity questioned by citing references.* This signal indicates that citing references in the Shepard's® Citations Service contain treatment that questions the continuing validity or precedential value of your case because of intervening circumstances, including judicial or legislative overruling.
Yellow triangle	*Caution: Possible negative treatment indicated.* This signal indicates that citing references in the Shepard's® Citations Service contain history or treatment that may have a significant negative impact on your case (e.g., limited or criticized by).
Green diamond surrounding a plus sign	*Positive treatment is indicated.* This signal indicates that citing references in the Shepard's® Citations Service contain history or treatment that has a positive impact on your case (e.g., affirmed or followed by).
Blue octagon surrounding the letter A	*Citing references with analysis available.* This signal indicates that citing references in the Shepard's® Citations Service contain treatment of your case that is neither positive nor negative (e.g., explained).
Blue octagon surrounding the letter I	*Citation information available.* This signal indicates that citing references are available in the Shepard's® Citations Service for your case, but the references do not have history or treatment analysis (e.g., the references are law review citations).

you should not rely on them in deciding whether the original case is valid. Always research the Shepard's entry and review the citing cases carefully to satisfy yourself about the status of the original case. You can view any document in the entry from the links provided. A Shepard's entry is divided into four sections:

- **Appellate History** contains the direct history of the original case.
- **Citing Decisions** lists citing cases in the indirect history of the original case.
- **Other Citing Sources** lists other sources that cite the original case.
- **Table of Authorities** lists the cases cited by the original case.

Figure 6.3 shows a portion of a Shepard's entry.

FIGURE 6.3 SHEPARD'S® ENTRY EXCERPT FOR 165 OHIO APP. 3D 699

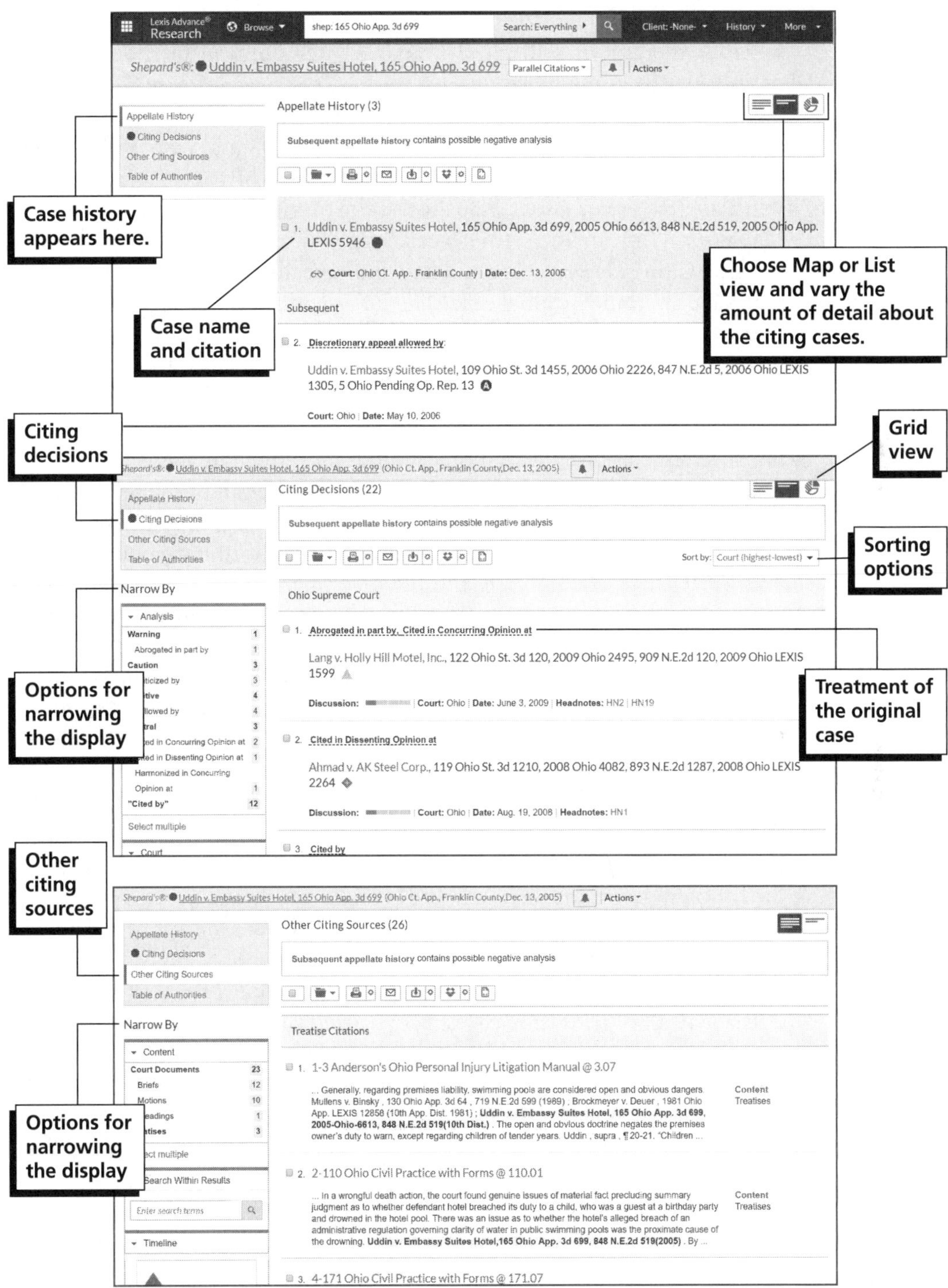

 SHEPARD'S® entry for 165 Ohio App. 3d 699.

The **Appellate History** section of a Shepard's entry lists the direct history of the case, meaning prior and subsequent opinions arising from the same litigation. The information in this section will help you determine whether the case is still good law. If a later opinion in the direct line of appeal affects the continued validity of the original case (e.g., reversing or affirming the original case), that information will be noted in the **Appellate History** section. The citation for the original case will be highlighted so you can identify it easily within the history. Lexis Advance will also give you a visual snapshot of the original case's history with the **Map** view. This can be useful if a case has an extensive or complex history.

The **Citing Decisions** section lists indirect history, meaning later cases that have cited the original case. The information in this section will help you determine whether the case is still good law. It will also help you identify additional cases that are relevant to your research issue.

When you Shepardize a federal case, the list of citing decisions will begin with U.S. Supreme Court citations. Federal cases divided according to circuit appear next. For each circuit, appellate cases will appear first, followed by federal district court cases. After all of the federal cases, state cases will be listed alphabetically by state, again with cases from higher courts first, followed by those from subordinate courts. When you Shepardize a state case, the list of citing decisions will begin with cases from the same state as the original case. Then you will see federal cases by circuit and cases from other states.

Along with the full name and citation to the citing case, the entry will note the treatment the citing case has given the original case. Often, the citing case will simply have "cited" the original case without significant analysis. If, however, the citing case has treated the original case in a way that could affect its continued validity (e.g., following, criticizing, or distinguishing it), Shepard's will note that.

The **Sort by** menu allows you to set the order of the citing cases with the following options: level of court (highest to lowest), type of analysis (red, meaning negative, to blue, meaning positive), depth of discussion (high to low), or date (newest to oldest).

The **Grid** view displays a color-coded grid that provides a snapshot of the way all of the citing cases have treated the original case. Click on a box in the grid to show the list view of the cases included in the category you selected. **Figure 6.4** shows the grid view.

Another feature in the **Citing Decisions** section is the headnote references. You may recall from Chapter 5, on case research, that headnotes are summary paragraphs added by case editors identifying the key points in the case. If a citing case cites the original case for a point that is summarized in a headnote at the beginning of the original case, the headnote will be referenced in the Shepard's entry. In the example citation, *Uddin* discusses a point of law that is summarized in headnote 9. A citing case, *Davis v. Accor North America, Inc.*, has cited *Uddin* for the

FIGURE 6.4 CITING DECISIONS GRID VIEW

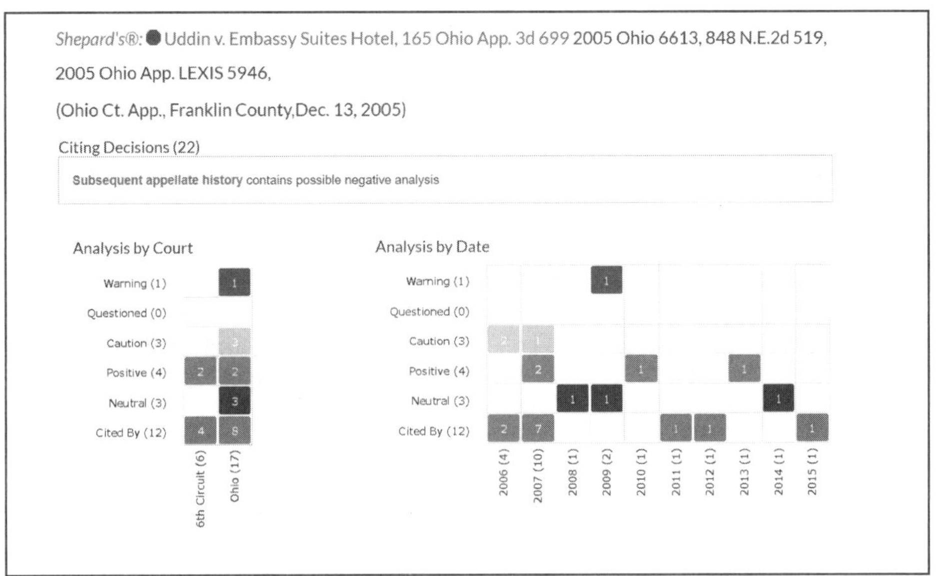

SHEPARD'S® entry for 165 Ohio App. 3d 699.

same proposition of law summarized in headnote 9. Thus, the Shepard's entry includes the reference to headnote 9. The illustrations in **Figures 6.5** through **6.7** trace a headnote from an original case to a Shepard's entry and then to a citing case. You may again recall from Chapter 5 that West publishes many state and federal reporters and adds headnotes to those cases. LexisNexis Headnotes are different from West headnotes, and the two sets of headnotes do not correspond to each other. The LexisNexis Headnotes are the ones that are displayed in the Shepard's entry.

The third section of the entry is **Other Citing Sources.** This section lists sources other than cases that have cited the original case. It will help you locate additional information on your research issue. Not all of the types of other authorities described here will appear in each entry. The authorities included will depend on where the original case has been cited.

If any statutory annotations include a summary of the original case, that information will appear first. Statutory annotations are research references in an annotated code. (Annotated codes are discussed in Chapter 7, on statutory research.) Secondary sources follow, divided by type of authority (law review articles, treatises, etc.). Shepard's entries do not include references to A.L.R. Annotations (a type of secondary source described in Chapter 4). Because A.L.R. is published by West, references to that publication appear only in KeyCite. The last item in this section

FIGURE 6.5 HEADNOTE 9 FROM THE ORIGINAL CASE, *UDDIN v. EMBASSY SUITES HOTEL*

Headnote 9 of *Uddin*

Torts > ... > Duty On Premises > Invitees > Business Invitees

View more legal topics

HN9 **Invitees, Business Invitees**

An owner or occupier of business premises owes business invitees a duty of ordinary care in maintaining the premises in a reasonably safe condition and has the duty to warn invitees of latent or hidden dangers. However, the owner or occupier of a business premise is not an insurer of a business invitee's safety. More like this Headnote

Shepardize - Narrow by this Headnote (6)

FIGURE 6.6 SHEPARD'S® ENTRY EXCERPT FOR *UDDIN v. EMBASSY SUITES HOTEL*

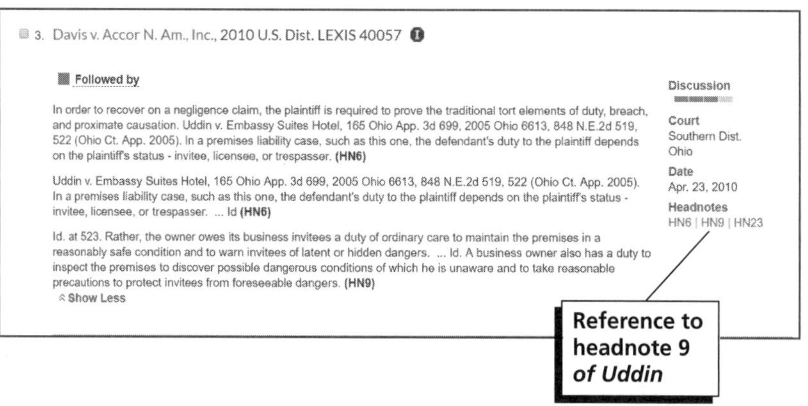

3. Davis v. Accor N. Am., Inc., 2010 U.S. Dist. LEXIS 40057

Followed by

In order to recover on a negligence claim, the plaintiff is required to prove the traditional tort elements of duty, breach, and proximate causation. Uddin v. Embassy Suites Hotel, 165 Ohio App. 3d 699, 2005 Ohio 6613, 848 N.E.2d 519, 522 (Ohio Ct. App. 2005). In a premises liability case, such as this one, the defendant's duty to the plaintiff depends on the plaintiff's status - invitee, licensee, or trespasser. **(HN6)**

Uddin v. Embassy Suites Hotel, 165 Ohio App. 3d 699, 2005 Ohio 6613, 848 N.E.2d 519, 522 (Ohio Ct. App. 2005). In a premises liability case, such as this one, the defendant's duty to the plaintiff depends on the plaintiff's status - invitee, licensee, or trespasser. ... Id **(HN6)**

Id. at 523. Rather, the owner owes its business invitees a duty of ordinary care to maintain the premises in a reasonably safe condition and to warn invitees of latent or hidden dangers. ... Id. A business owner also has a duty to inspect the premises to discover possible dangerous conditions of which he is unaware and to take reasonable precautions to protect invitees from foreseeable dangers. **(HN9)**

Show Less

Discussion

Court
Southern Dist. Ohio

Date
Apr. 23, 2010

Headnotes
HN6 | HN9 | HN23

Reference to headnote 9 *of Uddin*

FIGURE 6.7 *DAVIS v. ACCOR NORTH AMERICA, INC.*, CITING *UDDIN v. EMBASSY SUITES HOTEL*

A. A&K's Alleged Negligence

Plaintiff sues A&K for wrongful death, personal injuries, and negligent infliction of emotional distress to recover damages caused by A&K's alleged negligence in operating the swimming pool.

In order to recover on a negligence claim, the plaintiff is required to prove the traditional tort elements of duty, breach, and proximate causation. ***Uddin v. Embassy Suites Hotel*, 165 Ohio App. 3d 699, 2005 Ohio 6613, 848 N.E.2d 519, 522 (Ohio Ct. App. 2005)**. In a premises liability case, such as this one, the defendant's duty to the plaintiff depends on the plaintiff's status - invitee, licensee, or trespasser. ***Id.*** In this case, it is not disputed that the Davises and Shylettia were business invitees of A&K.

The owner of a business is not an insurer of the safety of its business invitees. ***Id.* at 523**. Rather, the owner owes its business invitees a duty of ordinary care to maintain the premises in a reasonably safe condition and to warn invitees of latent or hidden dangers. ***Id.*** A business owner also has a duty to inspect the **[*14]** premises to discover possible dangerous conditions of which he is unaware and to take reasonable precautions to protect invitees from foreseeable dangers. *Kirchner v. Shooters on the Water, Inc.*, 167 Ohio App. 3d 708, 2006 Ohio 3583, 856 N.E.2d 1026, 1032 (Ohio Ct. App. 2006).

Information summarized in headline 9 of *Uddin*

 LexisNexis, 165 Ohio App. 3d 699, Headnote 9; Shepard 's entry for 165 Ohio App. 3d 699; Davis v. Accor N. Am., Inc., 2010 U.S. Dist. LEXIS 40057.

is court documents. These are filings submitted by parties in other cases that have cited the original case, not documents issued by courts.

The last section in the Shepard's entry is **Table of Authorities**. This section lists the cases that the original case cites as authority. You can use this feature to determine the authoritative value of the cases the original case cites. If cases in the table of authorities have received negative treatment, that could affect the continued validity of the original case.

Although the full Shepard's entry provides the most complete information about the original case, you may want to view a more limited entry depending on your research task. Shepard's offers several options for filtering the display to focus on the information most relevant to you. The narrowing options appear in the left margin. See **Figure 6.3**. You can filter the results according to a number of criteria, including analysis, jurisdiction, and LexisNexis Headnote.

Additionally, Lexis has acquired another research provider—Ravel—that displays its search results with visual maps. Lexis Advance is integrating Ravel's tools with Shepard's to include visual maps to help you assess the strength of a case.

3. USING SHEPARD'S ALERT®

One additional feature you can use is Shepard's Alert®. If you find a case that is especially important in your research, you may want to monitor it over time to make sure it remains valid and to review any new citing cases or sources added to the Shepard's entry. This will be especially useful when you are working on a project over a long period of time. Shepard's Alert® automatically Shepardizes the authorities you select and delivers periodic reports to you. To set up a Shepard's Alert®, use the bell icon at the top of the screen and follow the instructions to specify the content, delivery format, and frequency of the report.

C. USING KEYCITE IN WESTLAW FOR CASE RESEARCH

Westlaw provides a citator called KeyCite. Like Shepard's, KeyCite is available for cases, statutes, and administrative materials. KeyCite is similar to Shepard's in the information it provides, and the process of using KeyCite is very similar to the process of Shepardizing. To use KeyCite effectively, you need to know how to access the service, interpret the entries, and filter the results to target the information you want. You can also create a KeyCite Alert to continue updating your research over time.

FIGURE 6.8 **KEYCITE TABS AND STATUS FLAG**

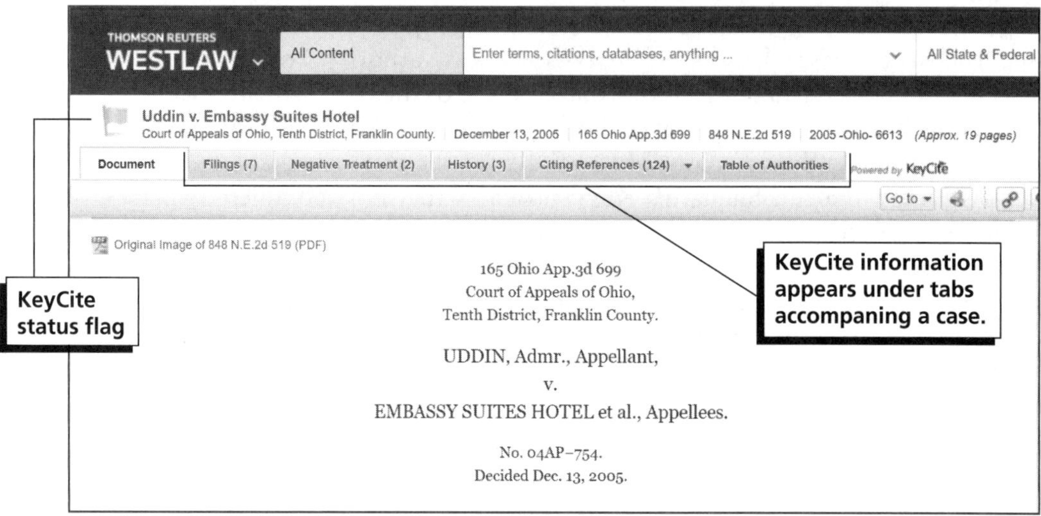

1. ACCESSING KEYCITE, INTERPRETING THE ENTRIES, AND FILTERING THE RESULTS

In Westlaw, you can access KeyCite simply by retrieving a case. Alternatively, you can type *kc:* followed by the citation in the search box.

As **Figure 6.8** illustrates, KeyCite information appears under tabs accompanying a document. KeyCite uses a symbol called a status flag to indicate the status of a case. Status flags are similar to Shepard's Signals in Lexis Advance. Westlaw's definitions of the status flags are explained in **Figure 6.9**. If a case has a status flag, the flag will appear both at the beginning of the case and within the KeyCite entry to give you some indication of the case's treatment in KeyCite. Like Shepard's Signals, KeyCite status flags are useful research tools, but they cannot substitute for your own assessment of the continued validity of a case. You should

FIGURE 6.9 **WESTLAW STATUS FLAGS**

STATUS FLAG	MEANS
Red flag	The case is no longer good law for at least one of the points it contains.
Yellow flag	The case has some negative history but has not been reversed or overruled.
Blue-striped flag	The case has been appealed to the U.S. Courts of Appeals or the U.S. Supreme Court.

FIGURE 6.10 KEYCITE "NEGATIVE TREATMENT" TAB

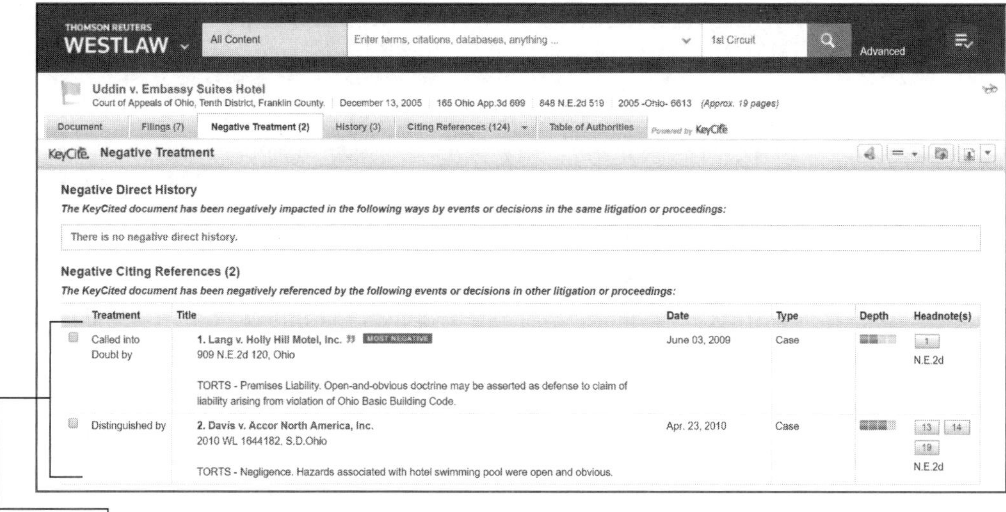

always research the KeyCite entry and review the citing sources carefully to satisfy yourself about the status of a case.

KeyCite information about the original case is contained under the following five tabs:

- **Filings**—This tab lists the court filings in the case you retrieved.
- **Negative Treatment**—This tab lists both direct and indirect negative history of the case, as illustrated in **Figure 6.10**.
- **History**—This tab shows the direct history of the case in both list and graphical form, as illustrated in **Figure 6.11**.
- **Citing References**—This tab shows the complete indirect history of the case, including citing cases and other citing sources, as illustrated in **Figure 6.12**.
- **Table of Authorities**—This tab lists the cases that the original case cites as authority and can help you determine the validity of the cases upon which the original case relies.

If the original case has received negative treatment, the citation to what West editors consider the most negative treatment will appear at the top of the document view to give you a sense of the status of the case. This may not include all the negative history of the case. You need to view the **Negative Treatment** and **History** tabs to get complete information about the original case.

The **Citing References** tab shows the complete indirect history of the original case along with other citing sources. The default organization of citing sources in Westlaw is by depth of treatment, without regard for type of document or jurisdiction. Westlaw uses green bars to indicate

FIGURE 6.11 KEYCITE "HISTORY" TAB

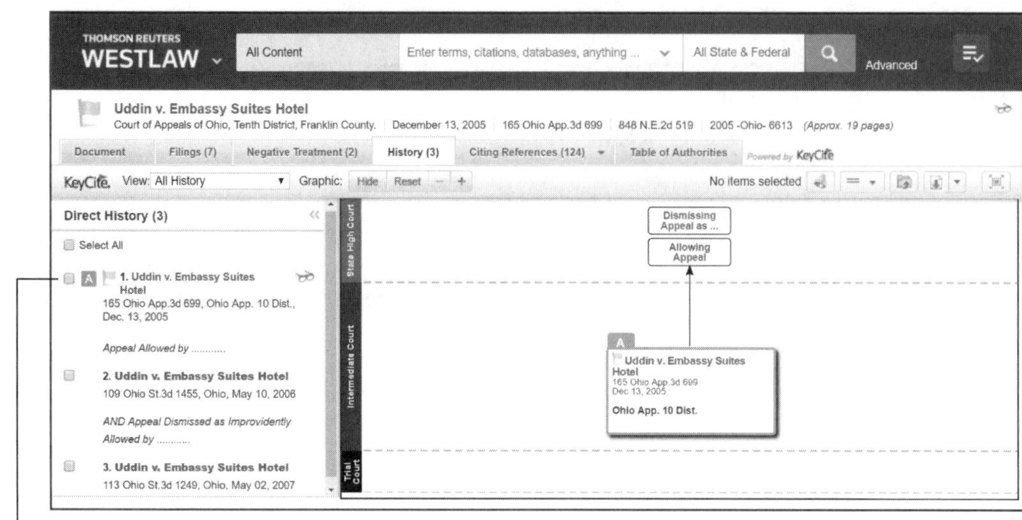

Reprinted with permission from Thomson Reuters/West, from Westlaw, KeyCite entry for 165 Ohio App. 3d 699. © 2017 Thomson Reuters/West.

FIGURE 6.12 KEYCITE "CITING REFERENCES" TAB

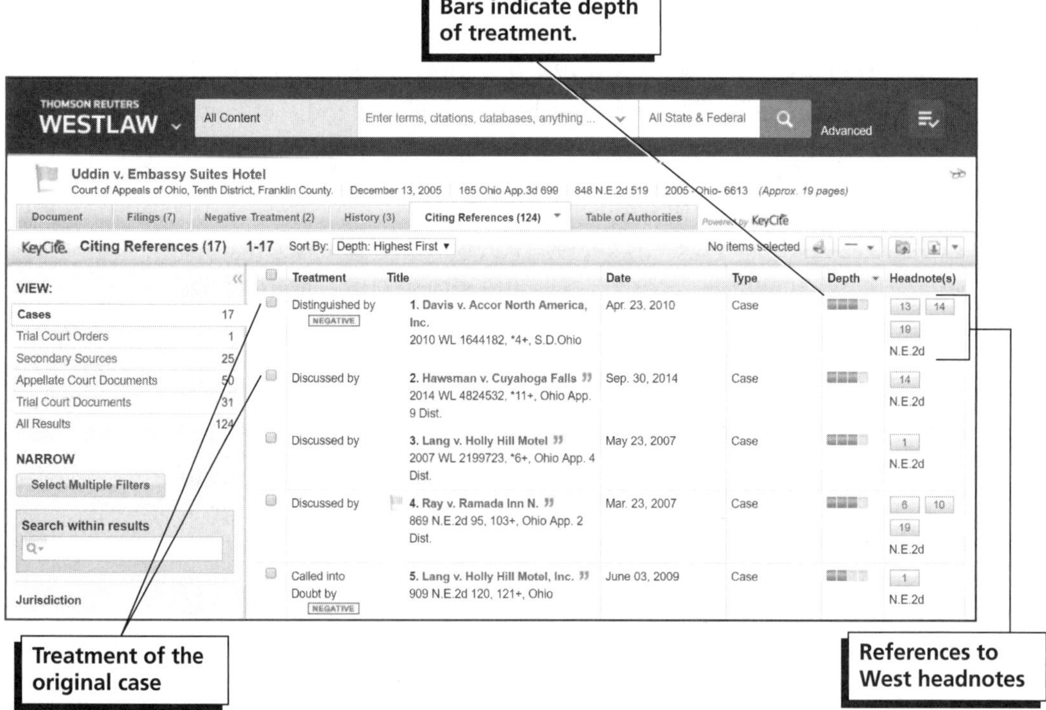

Reprinted with permission from Thomson Reuters/West, from Westlaw, KeyCite entry for 165 Ohio App. 3d 699. © 2017 Thomson Reuters/West.

FIGURE 6.13 **DEFINITIONS OF KEYCITE DEPTH OF TREATMENT CATEGORIES**

NUMBER OF BARS	MEANING	DEFINED
Four	Examined	Contains an extended discussion of the original case, usually more than a printed page of text.
Three	Discussed	Contains a substantial discussion of the original case, usually more than a paragraph but less than a printed page.
Two	Cited	Contains some discussion of the original case, usually less than a paragraph.
One	Mentioned	Contains a brief reference to the original case, usually in a string citation.

depth of treatment. See **Figure 6.13** for the depth of treatment categories. You can change the default search option to organize by date. The filtering options in the left margin will allow you to limit the results according to a number of criteria, including type of document, treatment, jurisdiction, and headnote. **Figure 6.14** shows some of the filtering options for cases.

Headnote references also accompany the citations to citing cases and sources. Headnote references in KeyCite work the same way as those

FIGURE 6.14 **KEYCITE FILTERING OPTIONS**

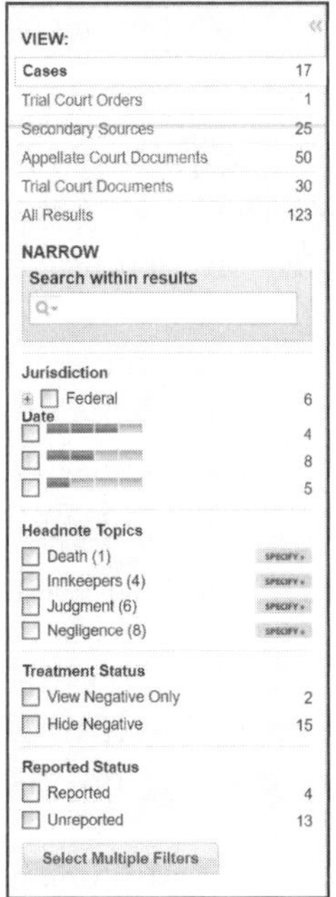

Reprinted with permission from Thomson Reuters/West, from Westlaw, KeyCite entry for 165 Ohio App. 3d 699. © 2017 Thomson Reuters/West.

in Shepard's. If a citing case cites the original case for a proposition of law summarized in a headnote at the beginning of the original case, the headnote reference will appear in the KeyCite entry. Headnote references in KeyCite correspond only to West headnotes, not to LexisNexis Headnotes or headnotes in an official reporter. You can see the text of a headnote by rolling your cursor over the headnote number. If a citing case quotes the original case, quotation marks will appear after the citation to the citing case in the KeyCite entry.

2. USING KEYCITE ALERT

Like Shepard's Alert®, KeyCite Alert automatically checks the authorities you select and delivers periodic reports to you. To set up a KeyCite Alert from a case you are viewing, click on the bell icon along the top of the display and follow the instructions to create a KeyCite Alert. You can also set up a KeyCite Alert by selecting the Alerts link at the top of the page and following the menu options.

D. USING BCITE IN BLOOMBERG LAW

To use BCite in Bloomberg Law effectively, you need to know how to access the service and interpret the entries. You must first retrieve the text of a case to access BCite information. Following the link for **BCite Analysis** opens a menu with the categories of BCite information. Choose any category to open the entry. Within the entry, the categories of BCite information appear across the top:

- **Direct History**—This tab lists the direct history of the original case.
- **Case Analysis**—This tab lists citing cases, that is, later cases that have cited the original case.
- **Table of Authorities**—This tab shows how the original case treated the cases it cites.
- **Citing Documents**—This tab lists citing sources, that is, all of the legal content within Bloomberg Law that cites the original case.

Bloomberg Law uses a system of indicators similar to Shepard's Signals and KeyCite status flags to give you some indication of the case's treatment in BCite. Bloomberg Law's definitions of the indicators appear in **Figure 6.15**. Like the other citators' symbols, BCite indicators are useful research tools that cannot substitute for your own assessment of the continued validity of a case.

Figure 6.16 shows a portion of a BCite entry.

FIGURE 6.15 BCITE INDICATORS

INDICATOR	MEANS
Red box with a white horizontal line	• The case has been reversed, vacated or depublished in full. • The court overrules the opinion in full or in part or states that the opinion has been overruled in full or in part by a prior decision.
Orange box with a white circle	• The court states that the opinion has been superseded, displaced, or rendered obsolete by an intervening statute, rule or regulation.
Yellow box with a white triangle	• The opinion has been modified, clarified, or amended by a subsequent decision. • One or more courts have criticized the legal reasoning of the opinion without overruling it.
Blue box with a white forward slash	• One or more courts have distinguished the opinion on the law or the facts.
Gray box with a white plus sign	• No courts have cited the opinion.
Green box with a white plus sign	• One or more courts cite to, discuss, or follow the opinion with approval.

FIGURE 6.16 BCITE DISPLAY

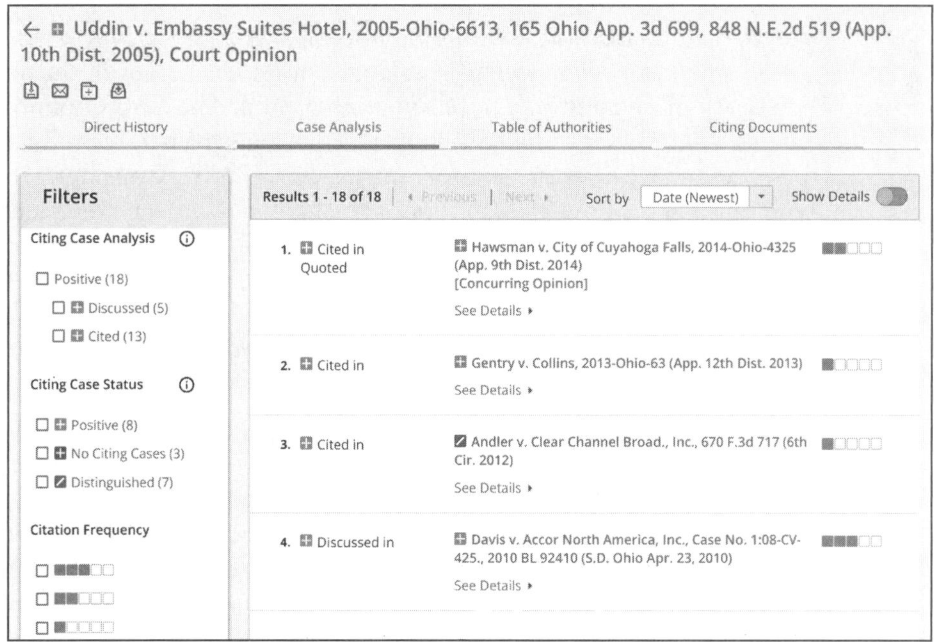

Unlike Shepard's and KeyCite, BCite organizes citing sources by date, rather than by jurisdiction or depth of treatment. Under **Case Analysis**, you can change the display order to list cases by citation frequency, the type of citing case analysis (distinguished, discussed, etc.), or court. You can also use menu options to filter the display by a number of criteria, which may include type of case analysis, citation frequency, court, judge, and date. Citation frequency is indicated with blue bars. The **See Details** link under each case will show the references to the original case within the citing case. Under **Citing Documents**, you cannot change the date-order display, but you can filter by content type or date. Additionally, you can execute a search within the listed documents.

E. SAMPLE PAGES FOR CASE RESEARCH WITH CITATORS

The sample pages that follow contain portions of the Shepard's, KeyCite, and BCite entries for *Uddin v. Embassy Suites Hotel,* 165 Ohio App. 3d 699. The entries in **Figures 6.17** through **6.19** show differences in how Shepard's, KeyCite, and Bloomberg Law analyze the citing sources and provide an example of differences in editorial judgment regarding the citing cases' analysis of the original case.

Uddin v. Embassy Suites Hotel involves a negligence claim for injuries to a child at a hotel swimming pool. *Davis v. Accor North America, Inc.* involves a negligence claim against a hotel arising out of the drowning death of an adult in a hotel swimming pool. The *Davis* opinion discusses *Uddin.* Reproduced below is a passage from *Davis.* Read this passage and review the citator entries for *Uddin.* Consider whether you agree with how the citators have characterized the treatment that *Davis* gave to *Uddin.* (The references to all cases except *Uddin v. Embassy Suites Hotel* have been omitted.)

***Excerpt from* Davis v. Accor North America, Inc., *discussing* Uddin v. Embassy Suites Hotel:**

> In order to recover on a negligence claim, the plaintiff is required to prove the traditional tort elements of duty, breach, and proximate causation. [Citing *Uddin.*] In a premises liability case, such as this one, the defendant's duty to the plaintiff depends on the plaintiff's status—invitee, licensee, or trespasser. [Citing *Uddin.*] In this case, it is not disputed that the [plaintiffs] were business invitees of [the defendant].
>
> The owner of a business is not an insurer of the safety of its business invitees. [Citing *Uddin.*] Rather, the owner owes its business

invitees a duty of ordinary care to maintain the premises in a reasonably safe condition and to warn invitees of latent or hidden dangers. [Citing *Uddin*.] A business owner also has a duty to inspect the premises to discover possible dangerous conditions of which he is unaware and to take reasonable precautions to protect invitees from foreseeable dangers.

Where, however, the hazard on the premises is open and obvious, a business owner owes no duty of care to invitees.... Where the open and obvious doctrine applies, it operates as a complete bar to negligence claims....

In Ohio, "a swimming pool presents an open and obvious condition that should be appreciated by both minors and adults."[4]

---

4. In *Uddin*, the court held that a swimming pool is not an open and obvious danger to children of tender years, i.e., ten years old or less. This aspect of the *Uddin* decision is inapposite, however, because the [plaintiff's] children were not at risk of drowning and [another family member in the pool] was age 17 at the time.

Figure 6.17 shows the Shepard's entry for *Uddin v. Embassy Suites Hotel*. The display is limited to citing cases that have given the original case positive treatment. *Davis v. Accor North America, Inc.* is listed as having followed the original case.

FIGURE 6.17 SHEPARD'S® DISPLAY

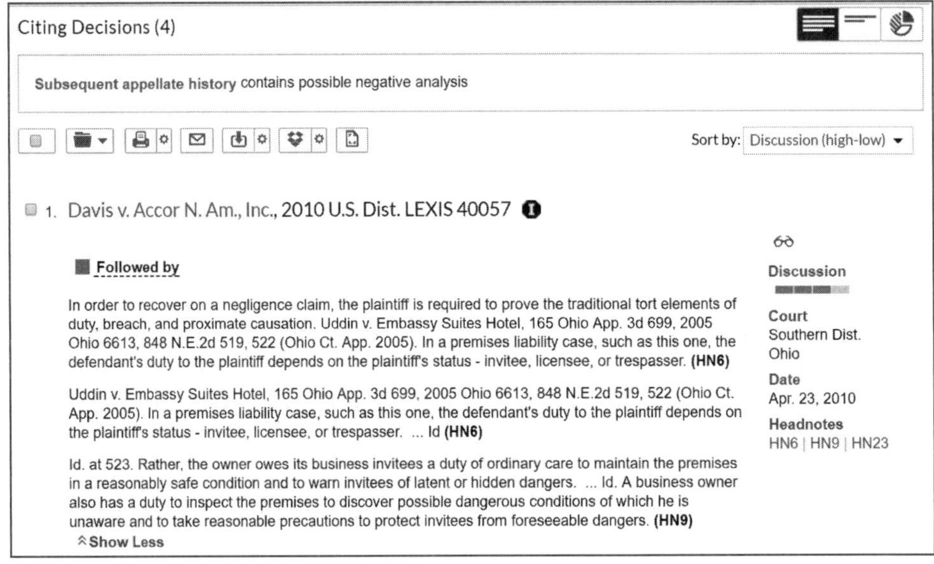

Citing Decisions (4)

Subsequent appellate history contains possible negative analysis

Sort by: Discussion (high-low)

1. Davis v. Accor N. Am., Inc., 2010 U.S. Dist. LEXIS 40057

Followed by

In order to recover on a negligence claim, the plaintiff is required to prove the traditional tort elements of duty, breach, and proximate causation. Uddin v. Embassy Suites Hotel, 165 Ohio App. 3d 699, 2005 Ohio 6613, 848 N.E.2d 519, 522 (Ohio Ct. App. 2005). In a premises liability case, such as this one, the defendant's duty to the plaintiff depends on the plaintiff's status - invitee, licensee, or trespasser. **(HN6)**

Uddin v. Embassy Suites Hotel, 165 Ohio App. 3d 699, 2005 Ohio 6613, 848 N.E.2d 519, 522 (Ohio Ct. App. 2005). In a premises liability case, such as this one, the defendant's duty to the plaintiff depends on the plaintiff's status - invitee, licensee, or trespasser. ... Id **(HN6)**

Id. at 523. Rather, the owner owes its business invitees a duty of ordinary care to maintain the premises in a reasonably safe condition and to warn invitees of latent or hidden dangers. ... Id. A business owner also has a duty to inspect the premises to discover possible dangerous conditions of which he is unaware and to take reasonable precautions to protect invitees from foreseeable dangers. **(HN9)**

Show Less

Discussion

Court Southern Dist. Ohio

Date Apr. 23, 2010

Headnotes HN6 | HN9 | HN23

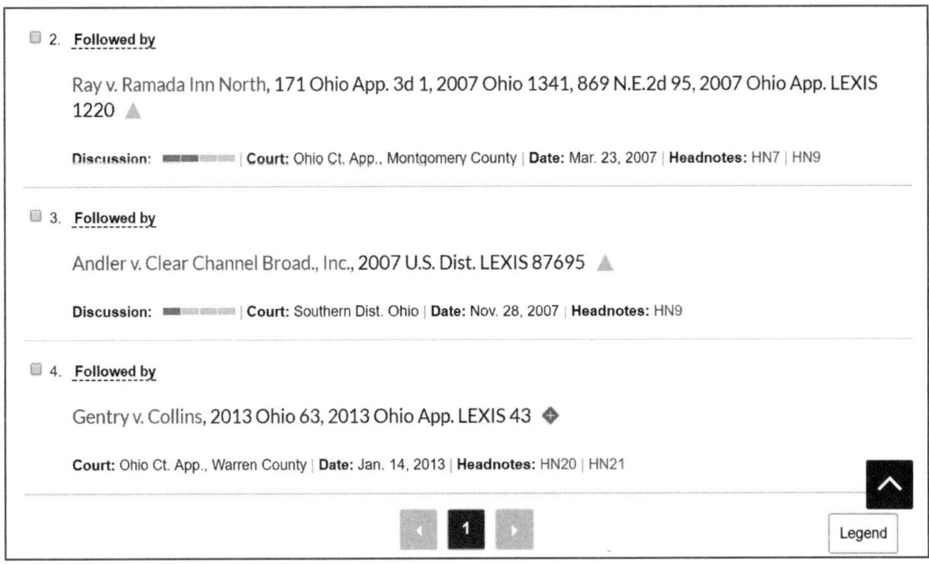

2. Followed by

Ray v. Ramada Inn North, 171 Ohio App. 3d 1, 2007 Ohio 1341, 869 N.E.2d 95, 2007 Ohio App. LEXIS 1220

Discussion: | **Court:** Ohio Ct. App., Montgomery County | **Date:** Mar. 23, 2007 | **Headnotes:** HN7 | HN9

3. Followed by

Andler v. Clear Channel Broad., Inc., 2007 U.S. Dist. LEXIS 87695

Discussion: | **Court:** Southern Dist. Ohio | **Date:** Nov. 28, 2007 | **Headnotes:** HN9

4. Followed by

Gentry v. Collins, 2013 Ohio 63, 2013 Ohio App. LEXIS 43

Court: Ohio Ct. App., Warren County | **Date:** Jan. 14, 2013 | **Headnotes:** HN20 | HN21

1

Legend

SHEPARD'S® entry for 165 Ohio App. 3d. 699.

Figure 6.18 shows the KeyCite entry for *Uddin v. Embassy Suites Hotel*. The display is limited to citing cases that have given the original case negative treatment. Notice the difference between the analyses of the citing cases in KeyCite and Shepard's. KeyCite does not characterize *Davis* as following the original case, but rather, as distinguishing it.

FIGURE 6.18 KEYCITE DISPLAY

Uddin v. Embassy Suites Hotel
Court of Appeals of Ohio, Tenth District, Franklin County. | December 13, 2005 | 165 Ohio App.3d 699 | 848 N.E.2d 519 | 2005 -Ohio- 6613 (Approx. 19 pages)

Document | Filings (7) | Negative Treatment (2) | History (3) | Citing References (124) | Table of Authorities | Powered by KeyCite

KeyCite. Citing References (2) 1-2 Sort By: Depth: Highest First

No items selected

Treatment	Title	Date	Type	Depth	Headnote(s)
Distinguished by NEGATIVE	1. Davis v. Accor North America, Inc. 2010 WL 1644182, *4+, S.D.Ohio TORTS - Negligence. Hazards associated with hotel swimming pool were open and obvious.	Apr. 23, 2010	Case		13 14 19 N.E.2d
Called into Doubt by NEGATIVE	2. Lang v. Holly Hill Motel, Inc. 909 N.E.2d 120, 121+, Ohio TORTS - Premises Liability. Open-and-obvious doctrine may be asserted as defense to claim of liability arising from violation of Ohio Basic Building Code.	June 03, 2009	Case		1 N.E.2d

Figure 6.19 shows the BCite entry for *Uddin v. Embassy Suites Hotel*. The display is limited to citing cases that have discussed (not just cited) the original case. Notice the difference in how Shepard's, KeyCite, and BCite analyze the case. BCite characterizes *Davis* as discussing *Uddin* positively. When the entry is expanded with See Details, however, it includes the footnote text that distinguishes *Uddin* from *Davis*.

FIGURE 6.19 BCITE DISPLAY

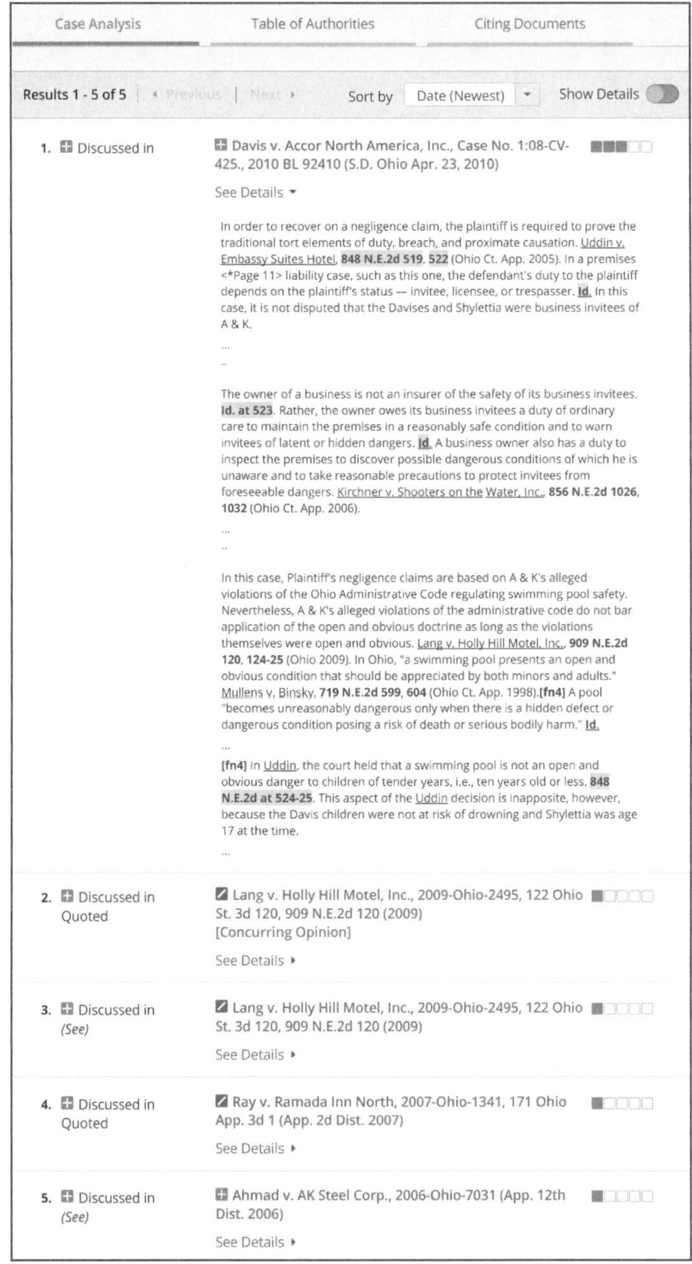

Reprinted with permission from Bloomberg Law, BCite entry for 165 Ohio App. 3d 699. © 2017 Bloomberg Law.

F. CHECKLIST FOR CASE RESEARCH WITH CITATORS

1. USE SHEPARD'S IN LEXIS ADVANCE

- ☐ Access Shepard's using the **Shepardize® this document** link from a relevant case.
- ☐ Interpret the entry.
  - Use the Shepard's Signal as a qualified indicator of case status, not a definitive determination.
  - View information in each component of the entry:
    - **Appellate History** contains the direct history of the original case.
    - **Citing Decisions** lists citing cases in the indirect history of the original case.
    - **Other Citing Sources** lists other sources that cite the original case.
    - **Table of Authorities** lists the cases cited by the original case.
  - Use the descriptions of the history (e.g., affirmed, reversed) and treatment (e.g., followed, distinguished, overruled) to identify citing cases that may affect the validity of the original case.
  - Use headnote references to identify citing cases that discuss propositions most relevant to your research.
  - Use the **Map** view for a snapshot of case history in chart form and the **Grid** view for a snapshot of treatment by later citing cases in chart form.
- ☐ Filter the display with the narrowing options in the left margin.
- ☐ Create a Shepard's Alert® for automatic updates to the Shepard's entry for the original case.

2. USE KEYCITE IN WESTLAW

- ☐ Access KeyCite from a relevant case.
- ☐ Interpret the entry.
  - Use the KeyCite status flag as a qualified indicator of case status, not a definitive determination.
  - View information under each tab:
    - **Filings** lists court filings in the original case.
    - **Negative Treatment** lists direct and indirect negative history of the original case.
    - **History** lists the direct history of the original case in list and chart form.
    - **Citing References** lists the indirect history of the original case (citing cases and other sources).
    - **Table of Authorities** lists the cases cited by the original case.

- Use the descriptions of the history (e.g., affirmed, reversed) and treatment (e.g., distinguished, disagreed with, overruled) to identify citing cases that may affect the validity of the original case.
- Use headnote references to identify citing cases that discuss propositions most relevant to your research.
- Use quotation marks to identify citing cases that quote the original case.

☐ Filter the display with the narrowing options in the left margin.
☐ Create a KeyCite Alert for automatic updates to the KeyCite entry for the original case.

3. USE BCITE IN BLOOMBERG LAW

☐ Access BCite from a relevant case using the **BCite Analysis** link.
☐ Interpret the entry.

- Use the BCite indicator as a qualified indicator of case status, not a definitive determination.
- View information in each component of the entry:
  - **Direct History** lists the direct history of the original case.
  - **Case Analysis** lists citing cases that have cited the original case.
  - **Table of Authorities** lists the cases cited by the original case.
  - **Citing Documents** lists citing sources available within Bloomberg Law that cite the original case.
- Use the descriptions of the history (e.g., affirmed, reversed) and treatment (e.g., followed, distinguished, overruled) to identify citing cases that may affect the validity of the original case.

☐ Filter the display with the narrowing options in the left margin.

CHAPTER 7

Statutory Research

A. INTRODUCTION TO STATUTORY LAW

Statutes enacted by a legislature are organized by subject matter into what is called a "code." Codes are published by jurisdiction; each jurisdiction that enacts statutes collects them in its own code. Thus, the federal government publishes the United States Code, which contains all federal statutes. Statutes for each state are published in individual state codes. Most state codes contain the text of the state constitution, and many include the text of the U.S. Constitution as well.

1. THE PUBLICATION PROCESS FOR FEDERAL STATUTES

When a federal law is enacted, it is published in three steps: (1) it is published as a separate document; (2) it is included in a chronological listing of all statutes passed within a session of Congress; and (3) it is reorganized by subject matter and placed within the code. In the first step of the process, every law passed by Congress is assigned a public law number. The public law number indicates the session of Congress in which the law was passed and the order in which it was passed. Thus, Public Law 103-416 was the 416th law passed during the 103rd session of Congress. Each public law is published in a separate booklet or pamphlet containing the full text of the law as it was passed by Congress. This booklet is known as a slip law and is identified by its public law number.

In the second step of the process, slip laws for a session of Congress are compiled together in chronological order. Laws organized within this chronological compilation are called session laws because they are organized according to the session of Congress during which they were enacted. Session laws are compiled in a publication called *United States Statutes at Large.* A citation to *Statutes at Large* will tell you the volume of *Statutes at Large* containing the law and the page number on which the text of the law begins. Thus, a citation to 108 Stat. 4305 tells you that this law can be located in volume 108 of *Statutes at Large,* beginning on page 4305. Both the slip law and session law versions of a statute should be identical. The only difference is the form of publication.

The third step in the process is the codification of the law. When Congress enacts a law, it enacts a block of legislation that may cover a wide range of topics. A single bill can contain provisions applicable to many different parts of the government. For example, a drug abuse prevention law could contain provisions applicable to subject areas such as food and drugs, crimes, and public health. If federal laws remained organized chronologically by the date of passage, it would be virtually impossible to research the law by subject. Laws relating to individual subjects could have been passed at so many different times that it would be extremely difficult to find all of the relevant provisions.

In the third step of the process, therefore, the pieces of the bill are reorganized according to the different subjects they cover, and they are placed by subject, or codified, within the federal code. Once legislation is codified, it is much easier to locate because it can be indexed by subject much the way cases are indexed by subject in a digest.

State statutes go through a similar codification process. State laws are organized by subject in each state's code.

Figure 7.1 illustrates the publication process.

2. THE ORGANIZATION OF STATUTORY CODES

As noted above, a code is a subject matter compilation. A statutory code, therefore, is arranged by subject area. Each subject area is then subdivided into smaller units. A section is the smallest individual unit of a code.

Although all codes are organized by subject, not all codes are numbered the same way. The federal code is organized into Titles. Each Title covers a different subject area. Title 18, for instance, contains the laws pertaining to federal crimes and criminal procedure, and Title 35 contains the laws pertaining to patents. For many years, the federal code had 50 Titles. In 2010, however, Congress enacted Title 51. As this text goes to press, the federal code has 54 Titles. Additional Titles may be enacted in the future. Each Title is subdivided into chapters and sections.

FIGURE 7.1 **PUBLICATION PROCESS FOR FEDERAL STATUTES**

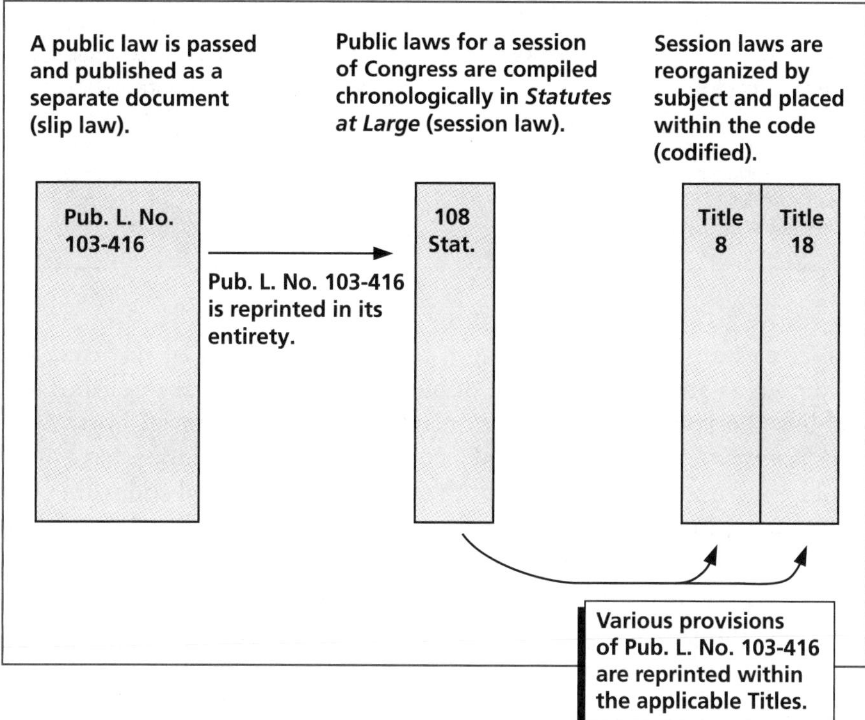

To locate a provision of the federal code, you need to know the Title and section number assigned to it. For example, 18 U.S.C. § 2113 is the provision of the federal code prohibiting bank robbery. The citation tells you that this provision appears in Title 18 of the United States Code in section 2113.

A state code can be organized in one of several ways. Some are organized by Title like the federal code. Some are organized by subject name. Some have their own unique numbering systems. Regardless of how the code as a whole is organized, state statutes are typically subdivided into chapters and sections.

To find a provision of a code organized by subject name, you need to know the subject area and the section number assigned to it. For example, New York Penal Law § 190.05 prohibits issuing a bad check. The citation tells you that this provision appears in the Penal Law (the subject area designation for criminal statutes) in section 190.05.

3. TYPES AND SOURCES OF CODES

Although there is only one "code" for each jurisdiction, in the sense that each jurisdiction has only one set of statutes in force, the text of the laws may be published in more than one set of books or online databases.

FIGURE 7.2 **CHARACTERISTICS OF OFFICIAL AND UNOFFICIAL CODES**

OFFICIAL CODES	UNOFFICIAL CODES
Published under government authority (e.g.,U.S.C.).	Published by a commercial publisher without government authorization (e.g., U.S.C.A. and U.S.C.S.).
May or may not contain research references (annotations). U.S.C. is not an annotated code.	Often contain research references (annotations). Both U.S.C.A. and U.S.C.S. are annotated codes.

Sometimes a government arranges for the publication of its laws; this is known as an "official" code. Sometimes a commercial publisher will publish the laws for a jurisdiction without government authorization; this is known as an "unofficial" code.[1] Some jurisdictions have both official and unofficial codes. If both official and unofficial codes are published for a jurisdiction, they will usually be organized and numbered identically (e.g., all sets will be organized by subject or by Title). For federal laws, the government publishes an official code, *United States Code* or U.S.C. Unofficial versions of the federal code are also available. For example, *United States Code Annotated* (U.S.C.A.) and *United States Code Service* (U.S.C.S.) are two unofficial versions of the federal code.

In addition, a published code can come in one of two formats: annotated or unannotated. An annotated code contains the text of the law, as well as different types of research references. The research references may include summaries of cases or citations to secondary sources discussing a statute. An unannotated code contains only the text of the law. It may have a few references to the statutes' original public law numbers, but other than that, it will not contain research references. An annotated code is a more useful research tool than an unannotated code.

Figure 7.2 summarizes the characteristics of official and unofficial codes, and **Figure** 7.3 shows some of the kinds of information that may be included in statutory annotations. Not all sections of an annotated code will contain all of these items, and some will not contain any references at all. The information provided depends on the research references appropriate for the specific section of the code and the content that the publisher chooses to include in the annotations.

Statutes are available from a number of sources, but not all sources provide access to the same information. U.S.C. (the official federal code) is an unannotated code, as are many official state codes. U.S.C. and the official codes for all 50 states and the District of Columbia are publicly

1. The government may publish the code itself, or it may arrange for a commercial publisher to publish the code. As long as the government arranges for the publication, the code is an official code, even if it is physically produced by a commercial publisher.

FIGURE 7.3 INFORMATION CONTAINED IN STATUTORY ANNOTATIONS

CATEGORIES OF INFORMATION IN ANNOTATIONS	CONTENTS
Statutory History Sometimes this section is called Historical and Statutory Notes.	Contains the history of the section, including summaries of amendments. This section can also refer to the legislative history of the statute (for more discussion of federal legislative history, see Chapter 8).
Cross-References	Contains cross-references to related provisions of the code.
Library or Research References Sometimes this section is subdivided into categories for different types of sources.	May contain references to related subjects in a digest, as well as references to legal encyclopedia sections, treatises, law review articles, or other secondary sources with information on the subject (see Chapter 5 for more discussion of the digest system and Chapter 4 for more discussion of secondary sources).
Code of Federal Regulations (Federal statutes only) Sometimes this appears as a separate section,and sometimes it is included with Library or Research References.	Contains references to administrative agency regulations implementing the statute (for more discussion of federal administrative regulations, see Chapter 9).
Case Annotations Sometimes this section is called Notes of Decisions or Case Notes.	Contains summaries of cases interpreting the statute. If the statute has been discussed in a large number of cases, the case annotations will be divided into subject categories, and each category will be assigned a number. Cases on each subject will be listed under the appropriate number.

available online. You can locate them through government websites as well as free and commercial legal research services.

Unofficial codes are also available from multiple sources. Unofficial codes are often (but not always) annotated. For example, U.S.C.A. and U.S.C.S. are annotated codes. Annotated codes are often available in print. Westlaw and Lexis Advance provide access to annotated state and federal codes. Bloomberg Law provides access to unofficial versions of state and federal codes. Although the codes in Bloomberg Law are not annotated the same way they are in Westlaw and Lexis, Bloomberg Law has search features that will allow you to find sources that have cited a code provision, as explained more fully in Section C, below.

Figures 7.4 and 7.5 show excerpts from the same section of the federal code from two different sources. **Figures** 7.4 is from U.S.C.A., an unofficial, annotated code published by Thomson Reuters/West.

FIGURE 7.4 18 U.S.C.A. § 915

Ch. 43 FALSE PERSONATION **18 § 915**

Notes of Decisions

Evidence 2
Offenses 1

1. Offenses

Defendant, in cashing United States Treasury check made out to another by representing herself as payee and by exhibiting, as proof of identity, card issued in name of payee violated this section proscribing receiving money by falsely impersonating holder of debt of United States, even if payee had theretofore negotiated check and received cash for it and even if payee was not holder of instrument at time defendant cashed check. U.S. v. McMillian, C.A.4 (Va.) 1971, 438 F.2d 980. False Pretenses ⚿ 19

One procuring payment of check of United States by falsely representing his authority was not guilty of "personating" lawful holder of debt of United States. Lane v. U.S., C.C.A.6 (Ohio) 1927, 17 F.2d 923. False Personation ⚿ 1

2. Evidence

Testimony of store proprietor that defendant had attempted to cash stolen social security check which had been endorsed in blank by named payee and had stated that check was his when questioned supported conclusion that defendant had represented himself to be payee of the check and sustained conviction of violation of this section prohibiting the false personation of a person entitled to any annuity, dividend, pension, wages, or other debt due from the United States. U.S. v. Johnson, C.A.5 (Fla.) 1973, 483 F.2d 444. False Personation ⚿ 6

§ 915. Foreign diplomats, consuls or officers

Whoever, with intent to defraud within the United States, falsely assumes or pretends to be a diplomatic, consular or other official of a foreign government duly accredited as such to the United States and acts as such, or in such pretended character, demands or obtains or attempts to obtain any money, paper, document, or other thing of value, shall be fined under this title or imprisoned not more than ten years, or both.

(June 25, 1948, c. 645, 62 Stat. 743; Pub.L. 103–322, Title XXXIII, § 330016(1)(K), Sept. 13, 1994, 108 Stat. 2147.)

HISTORICAL AND STATUTORY NOTES

Revision Notes and Legislative Reports

1948 Acts. Based on § 232 of Title 22, U.S.C., 1940 ed., Foreign Relations and Intercourse (June 15, 1917, c. 30, Title VIII, § 2, 40 Stat. 226; Mar. 28, 1940, c. 72, § 6, 54 Stat. 80).

Reference to "jurisdiction" of the United States was omitted as unnecessary in view of definition of "United States" in § 5 of this title.

Mandatory punishment provision was rephrased in the alternative.

Minor changes were made in phraseology.

1994 Acts. House Report Nos. 103–324 and 103–489, and House Conference Report No. 103–711, see 1994 U.S. Code Cong. and Adm. News, p. 1801.

Amendments

1994 Amendments. Pub.L. 103–322, § 330016(1)(K), substituted "under this title" for "not more than $5,000" wherever appearing.

CROSS REFERENCES

Jurisdiction of offenses, see 18 USCA § 3241
Letters, writings, etc., in violation of this section as nonmailable, see 18 USCA § 1717.

723

Code section number

Title of section

Statutory text

Histsorical notes

Cross-references

FIGURE 7.4 **18 U.S.C.A. § 915 *(Continued)***

18 § 915 CRIMES Part 1

Library and research references

LIBRARY REFERENCES

American Digest System
False Pretenses ⚷19.
Key Number System Topic No. 170.

Corpus Juris Secundum
CJS Postal Service & Offenses Against Postal Laws § 26, Nonmailable Matter.

Research References

Encyclopedias
Am. Jur. 2d False Personation § 5, Federal Statutes.
Am. Jur. 2d False Personation § 8, Federal Statutes.

Treatises and Practice Aids
Restatement (Third) of Foreign Relations § 464, Immunity of Diplomatic Agents of Other States.

Notes of Decisions

Summaries of cases applying the section

1. Offenses

For a person other than a diplomatic or consular official or attache to act in the United States as an agent of a foreign government without prior notification to the Secretary of State or falsely to assume or pretend to be an official of a foreign government accredited to the United States with intent to defraud anyone is a criminal offense under this section. U.S. v. Peace Information Center, D.C.D.C. 1951, 97 F.Supp. 255. International Law ⚷ 10.24

2. Indictment or information

Variance between corporate name of drawer of check as referred to in indictment charging offense of falsely assuming to be consular official of a foreign government and corporate name of drawer as shown by evidence was not prejudicial to defendant whose own testimony showed full familiarity with check. Cortez v. U.S., C.A.5 (Tex.) 1964, 328 F.2d 51, certiorari denied 85 S.Ct. 89, 379 U.S. 848, 13 L.Ed.2d 52. Criminal Law ⚷ 1167(1)

3. Evidence

Evidence supported defendant's conviction of wrongfully impersonating a diplomat in violation of this section which sought to correct evil of false pretense of foreign diplomatic authority to obtain something of value. U.S. v. Callaway, C.A.3 (N.J.) 1971, 446 F.2d 753, certiorari denied 92 S.Ct. 694, 404 U.S. 1021, 30 L.Ed.2d 670. False Pretenses ⚷ 49(1)

Evidence in prosecution for falsely assuming to be consular official of a foreign government was sufficient to justify finding that defendant had obtained check from individual in his pretended character as consul for the foreign government and not, as he claimed, as part of business transaction. Cortez v. U.S., C.A.5 (Tex.) 1964, 328 F.2d 51, certiorari denied 85 S.Ct. 89, 379 U.S. 848, 13 L.Ed.2d 52. False Pretenses ⚷ 49(6)

Evidence sustained jury finding that defendant, charged with falsely assuming to be consular official of foreign government, had intent to defraud when he obtained check from business firm in United States. Cortez v. U.S., C.A.5 (Tex.) 1964, 328 F.2d 51, certiorari denied 85 S.Ct. 89, 379 U.S. 848, 13 L.Ed.2d 52. False Pretenses ⚷ 49(2)

4. Instructions

Instructions in prosecution for falsely assuming to be consular official of foreign government, when taken as a whole, fairly set forth elements of offense and defendant's theory of case and contained no prejudicial error. Cortez v. U.S., C.A.5 (Tex.) 1964, 328 F.2d 51, certiorari denied 85 S.Ct. 89, 379 U.S. 848, 13 L.Ed.2d 52. Criminal Law ⚷ 822(6)

Court which had fully and adequately instructed jury on intent in prosecution for falsely assuming to be consular official of foreign government was not required to isolate and emphasize element of personal, good-faith belief of defen-

724

FIGURE 7.5 **18 U.S.C. § 915**

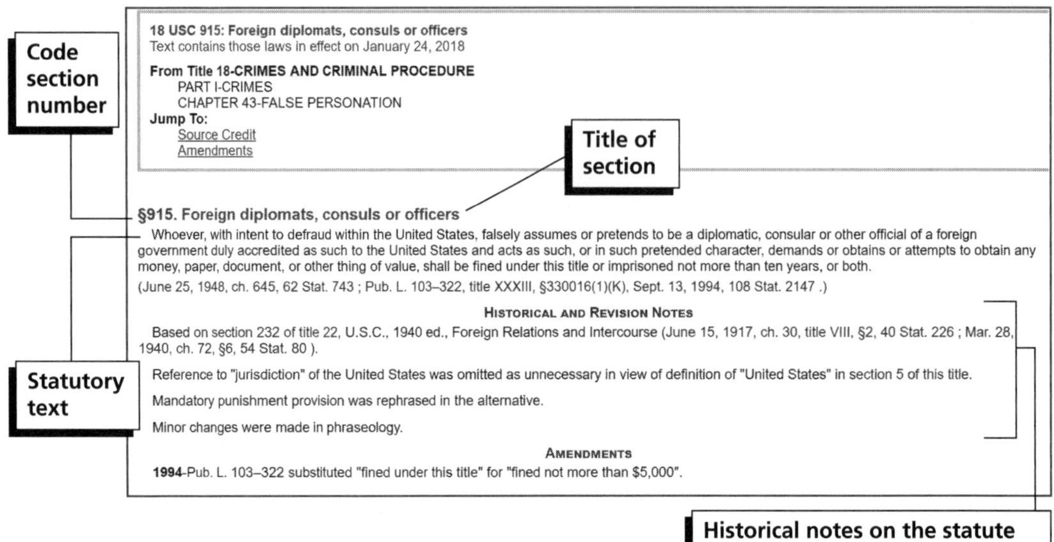
18 USC 915: Foreign diplomats, consuls or officers
Text contains those laws in effect on January 24, 2018

From Title 18-CRIMES AND CRIMINAL PROCEDURE
PART I-CRIMES
CHAPTER 43-FALSE PERSONATION
Jump To:
Source Credit
Amendments

§915. Foreign diplomats, consuls or officers

Whoever, with intent to defraud within the United States, falsely assumes or pretends to be a diplomatic, consular or other official of a foreign government duly accredited as such to the United States and acts as such, or in such pretended character, demands or obtains or attempts to obtain any money, paper, document, or other thing of value, shall be fined under this title or imprisoned not more than ten years, or both.

(June 25, 1948, ch. 645, 62 Stat. 743 ; Pub. L. 103–322, title XXXIII, §330016(1)(K), Sept. 13, 1994, 108 Stat. 2147 .)

HISTORICAL AND REVISION NOTES

Based on section 232 of title 22, U.S.C., 1940 ed., Foreign Relations and Intercourse (June 15, 1917, ch. 30, title VIII, §2, 40 Stat. 226 ; Mar. 28, 1940, ch. 72, §6, 54 Stat. 80).

Reference to "jurisdiction" of the United States was omitted as unnecessary in view of definition of "United States" in section 5 of this title.

Mandatory punishment provision was rephrased in the alternative.

Minor changes were made in phraseology.

AMENDMENTS

1994-Pub. L. 103–322 substituted "fined under this title" for "fined not more than $5,000".

Figure 7.5 is from a database maintained by the House of Representatives' Office of Law Revision Counsel. It is free to use, but it is unannotated. Although **Figure** 7.5 comes from a government source, it is not the official version of the code. Only the print code, available online from other sources in .pdf format, is the official federal code.

4. METHODS OF LOCATING STATUTES

a. Locating Codified Statutes

You can locate codified statutes in many ways. If you have the citation to a statute that you have obtained from another source, such as a secondary source, you can easily locate the statute in a print code or online.

When you do not have a citation, you can locate statutes using either a source-driven or content-driven approach. If you use a source-driven approach, the first step will be deciding which jurisdiction's statutes you want to research. Once you select a jurisdiction, you can search for statutes by subject, by words in the document, or by the name of an act.

Researching by subject is often a useful way to locate statutes. The index to a code will be organized by subject, and using an index is one of the most common subject searching techniques for statutory research. All print codes have subject indexes. If you are searching online, you may or may not have access to the index.

Every code also has a table of contents, which you can view in print or online. Reviewing the table of contents can be a difficult way to begin your research unless you know the subject area of the statute you are trying to find. Once you find a relevant provision of the code, however, viewing the table of contents can help you find related code sections, as described more fully below.

Word searching is another way to locate statutes. Because legislatures often use technical terms in statutes, however, word searching can be more difficult than subject searching if you are not already familiar with the statutory terminology.

An additional search option is locating a statute by name. Many statutes are known by their popular names, such as the Americans with Disabilities Act. In print, you can use a directory listing statutes according to their popular names. Online, you can use a statute's name as a word search; many services also have popular name search options.

If you choose content-driven searching in Westlaw, Lexis Advance, or Bloomberg Law, your search results will include statutes. You will ordinarily pre-filter your search by jurisdiction unless you are researching the law of all U.S. jurisdictions. Once you execute the search, the results will include a section with statutes.

Most search techniques will lead you to individual sections of a code. But a piece of legislation ordinarily will not appear in its entirety within a single code section. More often, a statutory scheme enacted by a legislature will be codified in a chapter or subchapter of the code comprising multiple code sections. Rarely will an individual code section viewed in isolation resolve your research question. You usually need to research the entire statutory scheme to ensure that you consider all potentially applicable code sections.

For example, assume you retrieved a code provision applicable to your research issue but failed to retrieve a nearby section containing definitions of terms used in the applicable provision. If you relied only on the one section your initial search revealed, your research would not be accurate. It is especially easy to lose sight of the need to research multiple sections when you work online because individual code sections ordinarily appear within search results as separate documents. Whether you use print or online sources for statutory research, however, be sure to research the entire statutory scheme to ensure that you consider all potentially applicable code sections.

Once you have located a relevant code section, the easiest way to research a statutory scheme is to use the statutory outline or table of contents to identify related code provisions. In print, you will often find a chapter or subchapter outline of sections. **Figure** 7.6 shows the outline for a chapter within Title 18 of the federal code in U.S.C.A. And of course, all you have to do is turn the pages to see preceding and subsequent code sections. Online sources often either display or provide links to statutory outlines or tables of contents, and most have functions that allow you to browse preceding and subsequent code sections.

Sections B and C, below, explain how to research codified statutes in print and online.

FIGURE 7.6 **CHAPTER OUTLINE IN TITLE 18**

CHAPTER 43—FALSE PERSONATION

Sec.
911. Citizen of the United States.
912. Officer or employee of the United States.
913. Impersonator making arrest or search.
914. Creditors of the United States.
915. Foreign diplomats, consuls or officers.
916. 4-H Club members or agents.
917. Red Cross members or agents.

Reprinted with permission from Thomson Reuters/West, *United States Code Annotated*, Title 18 (2015), p. 683.

b. Locating State and Federal Rules of Procedure

You are probably learning about rules of procedure governing cases filed in court in your Civil Procedure class. Whenever you are preparing to file a document or take some action that a court requires or permits, the court's rules of procedure will tell you how to accomplish your task. The rules of procedure for most courts are published as part of the code for the jurisdiction where the court is located. For example, the Federal Rules of Civil Procedure appear as an appendix to Title 28 in the federal code. In many states, court procedural rules are published in a separate Rules volume.

If you want to locate procedural rules, therefore, one way to find them is through the applicable code. Many procedural rules have been interpreted by cases, and you may need to research cases to understand the rules' requirements fully. If you locate rules in an annotated code, summaries of the cases will follow the rules, just as they do any other provision of the code.

A couple of caveats about rules of procedure are in order. First, understanding the rules can be challenging. As with any other type of research, you may want to locate secondary sources for commentary on the rules and citations to cases interpreting the rules to make sure you understand them. For the Federal Rules of Civil Procedure, two helpful treatises are *Moore's Federal Practice* and Wright & Miller's *Federal Practice and Procedure.* For state procedural rules, a state "deskbook," or handbook containing practical information for lawyers practicing in the jurisdiction, may contain both the text of the rules and helpful commentary on them. If you locate the rules through a secondary source, however, be sure to update your research because the rules can be amended at any time.

Second, virtually all jurisdictions have multiple types and levels of courts, and each of these courts may have its own procedural rules. Therefore, be sure you locate the rules for the appropriate court. Determining which court is the appropriate one may require separate research into the jurisdiction of the courts.

Third, many individual districts, circuits, or divisions of courts have local rules with which you must comply. Local rules cannot conflict with the rules of procedure published with the code, but they may add requirements that do not appear in the rules of procedure. Local rules usually are not published with the code, but you can obtain them from a number of sources, including the court itself, a secondary source such as a practice deskbook, a website, or an online database. To be sure that your work complies with the court's rules, do not neglect any local rules that may add to the requirements spelled out in the rules of procedure.

c. Locating Uniform Laws and Model Acts

Uniform laws and model acts, as explained in Chapter 4, are proposed statutes that can be adopted by legislatures. Technically, they are secondary sources; their provisions do not take on the force of law unless they are adopted by a legislature. If your research project involves a statute based on a uniform law or model act, however, you may want to research these sources.

Many uniform laws and model acts are published in a multivolume set of books entitled *Uniform Laws Annotated, Master Edition* (ULA). The ULA set is organized like an annotated code. It contains the text of the uniform law or model act and annotations summarizing cases from jurisdictions that have adopted the statute. It also provides commentary that can help you interpret the statute. Chapter 4, on secondary sources, explains how to use the ULA set. You can also search uniform laws and model acts online through Westlaw, Lexis Advance, and Bloomberg Law.

B. RESEARCHING STATUTES IN PRINT

The process of researching statutes is fairly uniform for state and federal codes. The examples in this section are drawn from U.S.C.A., but the process described here can be used to research state codes as well. Sample pages illustrating the process of state statutory research appear in Section E of this chapter. This section begins with a general discussion of the statutory research process. It then discusses options for federal statutory research. This section concludes with a discussion of statutory citators.

1. RESEARCHING STATUTES BY SUBJECT

The most common way to locate statutes by subject is through an index. The research process entails three steps:

a. Look up the topics you want to research in the index.
b. Locate the relevant code section(s) in the main volumes of the code, and evaluate the material in the accompanying annotations.
c. Update your research using the pocket part and any supplementary pamphlets that accompany the code.

If the code you are using contains the federal or state constitution, you can locate constitutional provisions by subject the same way you would locate a statute.

a. Using the Index

The index to a code is an ordinary subject index. It may consist of several hardcover or softcover books. The index will list topics alphabetically. Next to each topic, references to code provisions will appear. The abbreviation "et seq." means that the index is referring to a series of sections beginning with the section listed; often, this will be a reference to an entire chapter within the code. The index also contains cross-references to other subjects relevant to the topic.

b. Locating Statutes and Reading the Annotations

Once you have located code references in the index, the next step is finding the statute within the books. The books may be organized alphabetically or by Title, depending on how the code itself is organized. In U.S.C.A., the books are organized numerically by Title, although some Titles span more than one volume. Sections will be listed in numerical order within the volume.[2] As noted earlier, an outline of the statute usually appears at the beginning of each chapter or subchapter.

Following the text of the code section, you may find a series of annotations with additional information about the statute. See **Figure** 7.4 to review the annotations accompanying 18 U.S.C.A. § 915.

c. Updating Statutory Research Using Pocket Parts and Supplements

Like other hardcover books used in legal research, hardcover statutory volumes are updated with pocket parts. If the pocket part gets too big to

2. If the statute was enacted after the main volume was published, you will not find it in the hardcover book. More recent statutes will appear in the pocket part or supplement, which are explained in the next section.

fit in the back of the book, you should find a separate softcover supplement on the shelf next to the hardcover volume.

The pocket part or supplement is organized in the same way as the main volume. Therefore, to update your research, you need only look up the provision you located in the main volume. The pocket part or supplement will show any revisions to the statute, as well as additional annotations if, for example, new cases interpreting the section have been decided. If there is new statutory language, the text in the pocket part or supplement supersedes the text in the main volume. If you find no reference to the section, the statute has not been amended, and no new research references are available. **Figure** 7.7 shows the pocket part update for 18 U.S.C.A. § 915.

The pocket part for each volume is published only once a year. Statutes can be amended and cases interpreting a statute can be decided at any time. Therefore, some print codes have supplements to update beyond the pocket part.

Supplementary pamphlets may be cumulative or noncumulative. Cumulative pamphlets include all available updates since the pocket part was printed. Noncumulative pamphlets cover a specific time period. The dates of coverage of each pamphlet should appear on the cover. To update your research thoroughly in a code with noncumulative supplements, you must look for your code section in each pamphlet published since the pocket part.

The supplementary pamphlets are organized the same way as the rest of the code. The pamphlet, like the pocket part, will list any changes to the statute, as well as additional annotations. If no reference to the section appears in the supplementary pamphlet, then there is no additional information for you to research.

2. RESEARCHING STATUTES BY POPULAR NAME

Research using a subject-matter index is appropriate when you know the subject you want to research but do not know the exact statute you need to find. Sometimes, however, you will know the name of the statute you need to find. In that situation, the easiest way to find the citation may be by popular name.

The index to the code may include entries for acts known by their popular names (e.g., the Americans with Disabilities Act). The code may also contain a separate alphabetical list or table of acts by popular name. The popular name table will tell you where the act is codified. Remember that when a law is passed by a legislature, it may affect many different areas of the law and, therefore, may be codified in many different places within the code. Thus, the popular name table may refer you to a number of different areas within the code. For many well-known statutes, however, the popular name table is an efficient way to locate the law within the code.

FIGURE 7.7 POCKET PART UPDATE FOR 18 U.S.C.A. § 915

18 § 911 CRIMES AND CRIMINAL PROCEDURE
Note 11

lent letter on behalf of aide, signing letter on behalf of aide, copying Representative's official letterhead into letter, and falsely stating in letter that Representative's office had taken certain steps on behalf of defendant's tax services client. U.S. v. Tomsha-Miguel, C.A.9 (Cal.) 2014, 766 F.3d 1041. False Personation ⚷ 2

14. Harmless or prejudicial error

Even assuming that it was hearsay or other nonconstitutional error, in prosecution of defendant for illegal reentry offense and for falsely claiming to be United States citizen, to allow government to introduce evidence of place of defendant's birth through affidavit of border patrol agents not yet called as witnesses at trial, error was harmless beyond reasonable doubt, in light of overwhelming evidence, including Mexican birth certificate, that defendant was born in Mexico. U.S. v. Macias, C.A.9 (Cal.) 2015, 789 F.3d 1011, certiorari denied 136 S.Ct. 1168, 194 L.Ed.2d 190. Criminal Law ⚷ 1169.1(9)

Several of prosecutor's comments during trial for false personation of United States officer or employee were well within normal bounds of advocacy, did not prejudice defendant, and did not render her trial fundamentally unfair, and thus permitting such comments did not constitute plain error; during his opening statement, prosecutor asked jurors to imagine what would happen if people had reason to doubt whether letter or phone call from government office was legitimate, during his closing argument, prosecutor cautioned that such doubt could lead people to stop paying attention to government communications, and, during his rebuttal, prosecutor reminded jurors that he had warned them that defense counsel would try to distract or confuse jurors. U.S. v. Tomsha-Miguel, C.A.9 (Cal.) 2014, 766 F.3d 1041. Criminal Law ⚷ 1037.1(2)

§ 912. Officer or employee of the United States

Notes of Decisions

29. —— Double jeopardy, defenses

Sequence of events, in that Commonwealth of Puerto Rico brought charges against defendant for impersonating a federal officer or employee six months after offense conduct occurred and that federal charges arising from same conduct were filed over three years after charges were dismissed in state court, did not bar defendant's subsequent trial for same offense in United States on double jeopardy grounds under exception to dual sovereignty doctrine; six-month period between alleged offense conduct and filing of indictment in state court could hardly be described as a delay and had no relevance on whether Commonwealth acted as pawn for federal government, three year gap between state and federal charges did not somehow transform state prosecution into a sham for federal government, and, given nature of alleged crime, it was only natural that a level of intergovernmental cooperation would be necessary. U.S. v. Barros-Villahermosa, D.Puerto Rico 2015, 91 F.Supp.3d 261. Double Jeopardy ⚷ 186

No new statutory language

§ 914. Creditors of the United States

FEDERAL SENTENCING GUIDELINES

See Federal Sentencing Guidelines § 2B1.1, 18 USCA.

§ 915. Foreign diplomats, consuls or officers

FEDERAL SENTENCING GUIDELINES

See Federal Sentencing Guidelines § 2B1.1, 18 USCA.

Notes of Decisions

3. Evidence

Evidence sustained conviction for impersonating a foreign diplomatic officer; police officer testified that after he stopped defendant's vehicle, defendant handed him a diplomatic identification card identifying defendant as an ambassador of the Conch Republic, card stated that, based on his status as a diplomat, defendant was an official immune from traffic infractions, detention, arrest, or civil and criminal prosecution, and officer testified that that notice led him to give defendant a warning rather than a speeding ticket. United States v. The-Nimrod Sterling, C.A.8 (Ark.) 2016, 828 F.3d 649. False Personation ⚷ 2; False Pretenses ⚷ 19

New research references

§ 917. Red Cross members or agents

FEDERAL SENTENCING GUIDELINES

See Federal Sentencing Guidelines § 2B1.1, 18 USCA.

34

3. OPTIONS FOR RESEARCHING FEDERAL STATUTES

As noted earlier in this chapter, you can research federal statutes with the official federal code (U.S.C.) or either of the unofficial codes (U.S.C.A. and U.S.C.S.).

The index and popular name methods of locating statutes are available with U.S.C. The main difference in researching U.S.C. concerns updating. The index and main volumes of the code are published every six years. In the intervening years, U.S.C. is not updated with pocket parts. Instead, it is updated with hardcover cumulative supplements. A new supplement is issued each year until the next publication of the main set.

In theory, using the supplements should be sufficient to update your research. In practice, however, the system presents some difficulties. Laws can be changed more frequently than the supplements are published, and the government is often several years behind in publishing the supplements. To update completely, you would need to research session and slip laws published since the latest supplement. Therefore, U.S.C. usually is not the best source for locating the most current version of a statute, and because it lacks the research references contained in the annotated federal codes, it is not the most useful statutory research tool.

The examples in the prior section illustrate research options in U.S.C.A. The U.S.C.A. General Index is a softcover set of books updated annually. Acts are listed by popular name in the General Index and in the Popular Name Table. Hardcover volumes are updated with pocket parts and noncumulative supplementary pamphlets.

U.S.C.S. is organized much the same way as U.S.C.A. The index and popular name methods of locating statutes are available with U.S.C.S. Annotations in U.S.C.S. often have fewer references to cases than the Notes of Decisions in U.S.C.A., but the references to administrative materials are often more comprehensive than those in U.S.C.A.[3] The nature of your research project and the materials available in your library will determine whether it is more appropriate for you to use U.S.C.S. or U.S.C.A. for federal statutory research.

The process of updating U.S.C.S. research is basically the same as that for U.S.C.A. Hardcover main volumes are updated with pocket parts. In addition, at the end of U.S.C.S., you will find softcover supplements to the code as a whole called the Cumulative Later Case and Statutory Service. Unlike the supplements to U.S.C.A., the U.S.C.S. supplements are cumulative, so you only need to check the most recent one. The supplements are organized by Title and section number and will reflect both changes to the statutory language and additional annotations.

3. Chapter 9 explains administrative materials and administrative law research.

4. USING A CITATOR FOR STATUTORY RESEARCH

Chapter 6 discusses citators and how to use them in conducting case research. Citators are also available as research and updating tools for state and federal statutes. Statutory citator entries typically include information about the history of a statute (i.e., whether it has been amended or repealed), as well as lists of citing cases and sources. As noted in Chapter 6, most law libraries no longer carry Shepard's in print. Therefore, specific information about statutory citators appears in the next section on online research. As explained in more detail below, Shepard's for statutes is available in Lexis Advance, and KeyCite for statutes is available in Westlaw.

C. RESEARCHING STATUTES ONLINE

Much statutory material is available online. This section discusses search options for researching statutes using Westlaw, Lexis Advance, Bloomberg Law, and additional online sources. The features of the online statutory citators (Shepard's in Lexis Advance and KeyCite in Westlaw) are also explained in this section.

1. WESTLAW

Westlaw contains annotated versions of the federal code, all 50 state codes, and the District of Columbia code. The annotated version of the federal code in Westlaw is derived from U.S.C.A. For most jurisdictions, you will find court rules of procedure included with the code, and for some you will find local court rules as well.

a. Viewing an Individual Code Section in Westlaw

You can retrieve an individual code section using a citation or by executing a search and selecting a code section from the search results. The display for an individual code section begins with a heading containing, among other things, the citation for the section and a **Currentness** link to tell you the date through which the statute has been updated.

The display of statutory information depends on how you access the statute. If you retrieve the document from its citation, you will see the text of the statute on the opening page, with additional information under accompanying tabs. Information from the annotations appears under the **Notes of Decisions** and **Context & Analysis** tabs. The **Notes of Decisions** tab contains brief summaries of the most important cases that have analyzed the statute. The **Context & Analysis** tab lists secondary sources and other research references that refer to the statute.

The **History** and **Citing References** tabs contain the KeyCite information for the statute. The **History** tab lists amendments and other legislative action affecting the statute, along with legislative history documents if they are available. (Federal legislative history is discussed in Chapter 8.) The **Citing References** tab will list every case or other source that has cited the statute. Because KeyCite's **Citing References** list is comprehensive, everything under **Notes of Decisions** and **Context & Analysis** will also appear under **Citing References,** but the reverse is not true. You may find the presentation of the material in **Notes of Decisions** and **Context & Analysis** easier to use.

If you execute a word search and select the statute from the search results, the opening page will show the text of the statute and portions of the annotations that contain your search terms. The complete information from the annotations and KeyCite appear under the accompanying tabs.

When you view an individual code section, you can see the table of contents for the statutory chapter and the entire code using the **Table of Contents** link. You can also browse the previous or next section using the arrows near the top of the screen. **Figure 7.8** shows how a federal statute appears in Westlaw.

FIGURE 7.8 EXCERPT FROM 18 U.S.C.A. § 915 IN WESTLAW

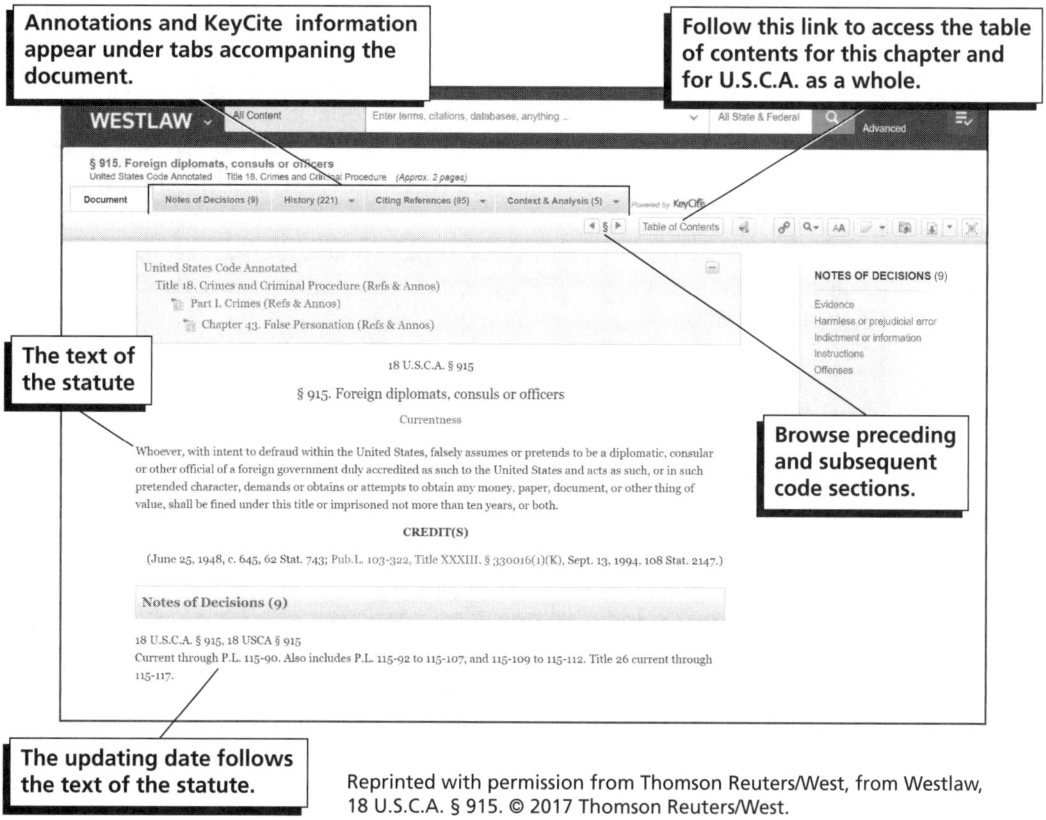

Annotations and KeyCite information appear under tabs accompaning the document.

Follow this link to access the table of contents for this chapter and for U.S.C.A. as a whole.

WESTLAW All Content Enter terms, citations, databases, anything ... All State & Federal Advanced

§ 915. Foreign diplomats, consuls or officers
United States Code Annotated Title 18. Crimes and Criminal Procedure (Approx. 2 pages)

Document | Notes of Decisions (9) | History (221) | Citing References (95) | Context & Analysis (5) | Powered by KeyCite

Table of Contents

United States Code Annotated
Title 18. Crimes and Criminal Procedure (Refs & Annos)
Part I. Crimes (Refs & Annos)
Chapter 43. False Personation (Refs & Annos)

NOTES OF DECISIONS (9)
Evidence
Harmless or prejudicial error
Indictment or information
Instructions
Offenses

The text of the statute

18 U.S.C.A. § 915

§ 915. Foreign diplomats, consuls or officers

Currentness

Whoever, with intent to defraud within the United States, falsely assumes or pretends to be a diplomatic, consular or other official of a foreign government duly accredited as such to the United States and acts as such, or in such pretended character, demands or obtains or attempts to obtain any money, paper, document, or other thing of value, shall be fined under this title or imprisoned not more than ten years, or both.

Browse preceding and subsequent code sections.

CREDIT(S)

(June 25, 1948, c. 645, 62 Stat. 743; Pub.L. 103-322, Title XXXIII, § 330016(1)(K), Sept. 13, 1994, 108 Stat. 2147.)

Notes of Decisions (9)

18 U.S.C.A. § 915, 18 USCA § 915
Current through P.L. 115-90. Also includes P.L. 115-92 to 115-107, and 115-109 to 115-112. Title 26 current through 115-117.

The updating date follows the text of the statute.

b. Searching for Statutes in Westlaw

Westlaw offers several search options for statutory research. If you know you want to research statutes, you should use a source-driven strategy to search within a statutory database. You can select a database by following the links on the **Browse** page for type of content (statutes and court rules), jurisdiction, or topic.

Once you select a database for statutes from a particular jurisdiction, the table of contents for the code will be displayed. You can execute a word search within the code using the search box at the top of the screen. Word searching is useful when you are searching for unique terms that are not likely to be included in the statutory index or table of contents. If you execute a word search in a database that includes an annotated version of a code, the search will retrieve documents that contain your search terms not only in the text of the statute but also in any of the annotations. Sometimes this is an advantage in your research. If the statute uses technical terms that are not in your search but the research references contain your search terms, executing a search that includes the annotations can improve your search results. But sometimes searching both statutes and annotations can retrieve irrelevant results if you are trying to search only statutory language.

If you want to search only the statutory language, you can execute your search in an unannotated version of the code or use special search commands to limit your search to words in the statute itself. (Word searching in general and techniques for limiting a search are discussed in Chapter 10, on online legal research.)

You can browse the code's table of contents by expanding the main headings to view chapters and individual code sections. You can also execute a word search within individual parts of the code by selecting the specific portions you want to search from the table of contents. Table of contents searching is a good option when you are familiar enough with the code to know which subject areas are likely to contain relevant statutes but do not have specific statutory citations. It is also an excellent feature for viewing an entire statutory scheme.

In the **Tools and Resources** section on the right, you will see additional search options, including the following:

- The **Find Template** displays a list of templates you can use to retrieve statutory citations. You do not have to choose a statutory database to retrieve a statute from its citation, but the template may be useful if you are unsure about the citation form for statutes from a particular jurisdiction.
- The code's **Index** allows you to search the code's subject index just as you would if you were researching in print. The index entries will refer you to statutory provisions. This is a good research option when you want to search by subject because the index is organized around concepts instead of individual terms in a document and contains cross-references to related terms and concepts.

FIGURE 7.9 **WESTLAW U.S.C.A. TABLE OF CONTENTS AND SEARCH OPTIONS**

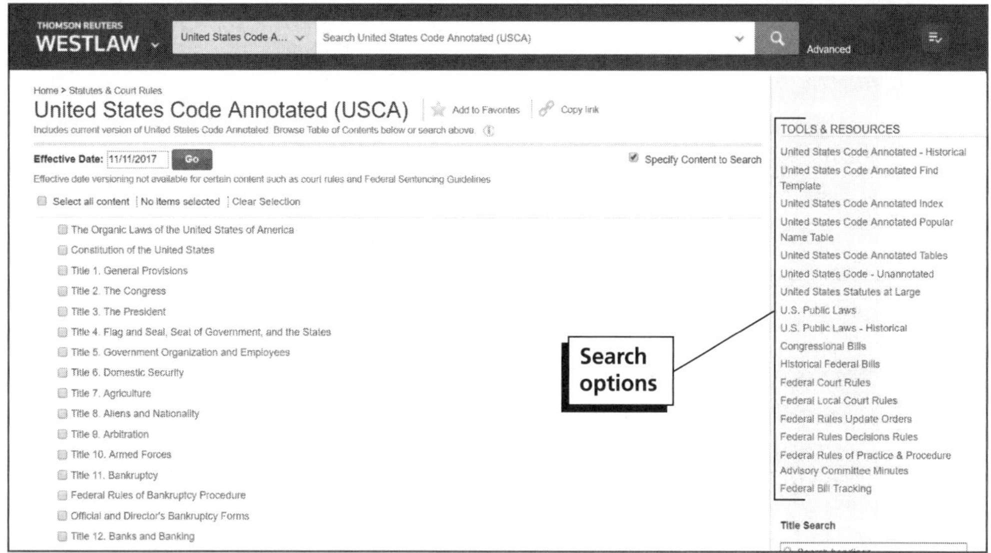

- The **Popular Name Table** lists laws by their popular names. Choosing the **Popular Name Table** option displays an alphabetical list of acts by their popular names. The link to an act's popular name will retrieve an entry listing the Title(s) and section(s) where the act is codified. When you know the popular name of a statute but do not have its citation, this is a good research option.

Figure 7.9 shows the table of contents and search options for U.S.C.A.

Westlaw will also allow you to execute a word search without first selecting a database. If you use this content-driven approach, you will ordinarily want to pre-filter by jurisdiction. Your search results will include many types of authority, including statutes, which you can view in the **Statutes** section, and the results screen will show a variety of options for filtering the search results.

The organization of the results of a statutory search is usually by relevance. You can modify the default sort options to view results in a different order.

c. Using KeyCite for Statutory Research

Even though the statutes in Westlaw's databases are usually up to date, you may still want to use KeyCite in your research. Statutory annotations are not comprehensive and may not contain information that is useful for your research issue. The KeyCite entry will often contain more information because it lists every case that has cited the statute and may be more up to date than the statutory annotations.

KeyCite information is automatically included under the **History** and **Citing References** tabs when you view a statutory provision. You can also type *kc:* and a citation to go directly to a statute's KeyCite entry.

KeyCite history lists amendments and other legislative action affecting the statute, along with legislative history documents if they are available. KeyCite citing references will list every case or other source that has cited the statute. You can monitor a statutory KeyCite entry by creating a KeyCite Alert.

2. LEXIS ADVANCE

Lexis Advance contains annotated versions of the federal code, all 50 state codes, and the District of Columbia code. The annotated version of the federal code in Lexis Advance is derived from U.S.C.S. For most jurisdictions, you will find court rules of procedure included with the code, and for some you will find local court rules as well.

a. Viewing an Individual Code Section in Lexis Advance

The display for an individual code section begins with a heading containing, among other things, the citation for the section and a notation with the date through which it is updated. The text of the statute then appears, followed by any annotations.

When you retrieve an individual code section, you have several options for viewing the complete statutory outline. You can view the table of contents for the statutory chapter and the entire code from the **Table of Contents** tab along the left margin of the statutory language. You can also browse preceding or subsequent code sections using the links in the table of contents or the **Previous** and **Next** links at the top of the document. **Figure** 7.10 shows a federal statute in Lexis Advance.

b. Searching For Statutes in Lexis Advance

Lexis Advance offers several search options for statutory research. If you know you want to research statutes, you should use a source-driven strategy to search within a statutory database. You can select a database by following the links on the **Explore Content** page for type of content (statutes and court rules), jurisdiction, or topic.

Once you select a database for the code from a particular jurisdiction, the code's table of contents will be displayed. You can execute a word search within the code using the search box at the top of the screen. Word searching is useful when you are searching for unique terms that are not likely to be included in the statutory index or table of contents. If you execute a word search in a database that includes an annotated version of a code, the search will retrieve documents that contain your search terms not only in the text of the statute but also in any of the

FIGURE 7.10 **EXCERPT FROM 18 U.S.C.S. § 915 IN LEXIS ADVANCE**

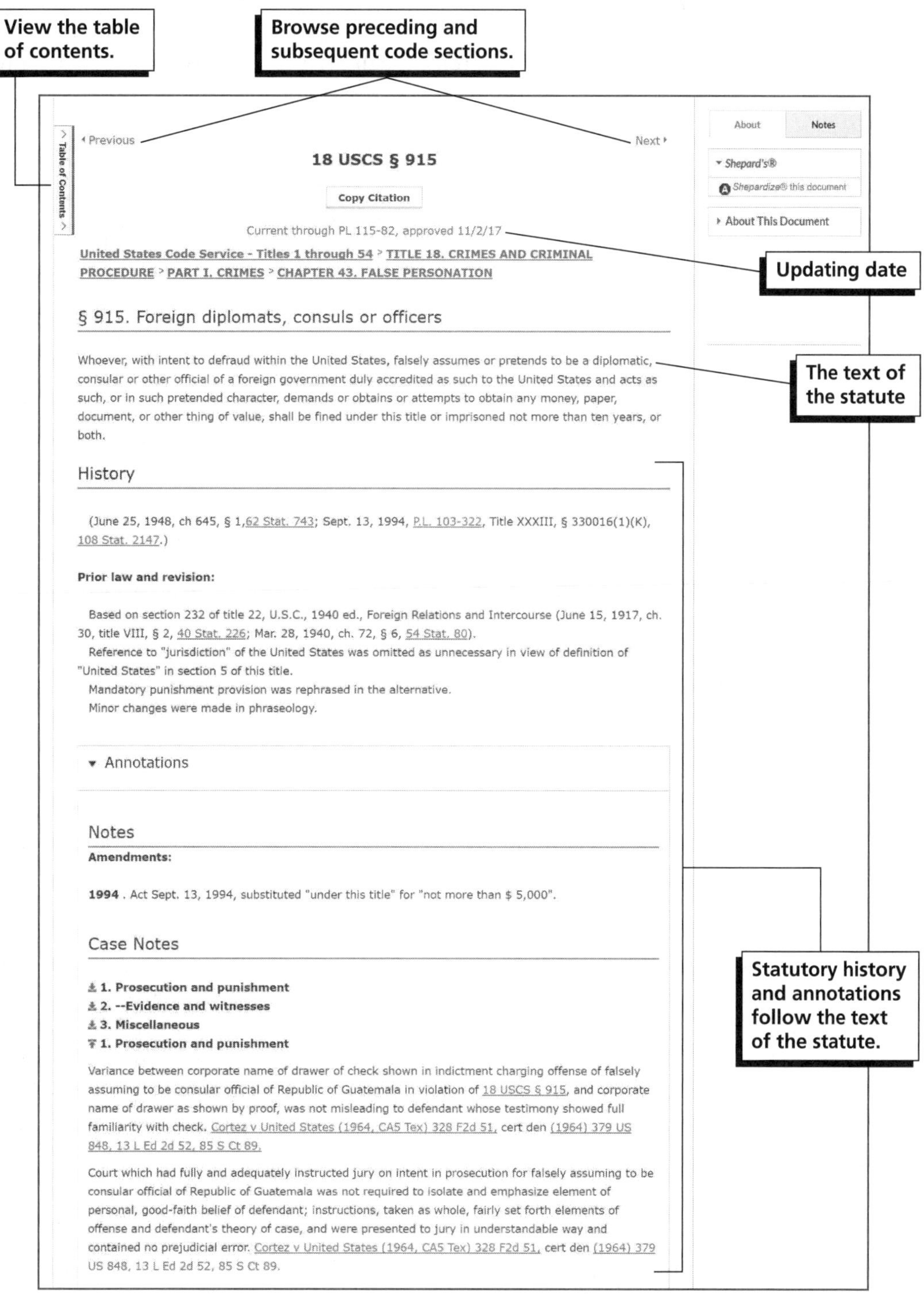

annotations. Sometimes this is an advantage in your research. If the statute uses technical terms that are not in your search but the research references contain your search terms, executing a search that includes the annotations can improve your search results. But sometimes searching both statutes and annotations can retrieve irrelevant results if you are trying to search only statutory language.

If you want to search only the statutory language, you can execute your search in an unannotated version of the code or use special search commands to limit your search to words in the statute itself. (Word searching in general and techniques for limiting a search are discussed in Chapter 10, on online legal research.)

You can browse the code's table of contents by expanding the main headings to view chapters and individual code sections. You can also execute a word search within individual parts of the code by selecting the specific portions you want to search from the table of contents. Table of contents searching is a good option when you are familiar enough with the code to know which subject areas are likely to contain relevant statutes but do not have specific statutory citations. It is also an excellent feature for viewing an entire statutory scheme.

Lexis Advance will also allow you to execute a word search without first selecting a database. If you use this content-driven approach, you will ordinarily want to pre-filter by jurisdiction using the drop-down menu on the right side of the search bar or the menu options under **Explore Content**. Your search results will include many types of authority, including statutes, which you can view in the **Statutes and Legislation** section, and the results screen will show a variety of options for filtering the search results.

The organization of the results of a statutory search is usually by relevance. You can modify the default sort options to view results in a different order.

Another way to search for statutes is through the **Browse** menu. Browse by **Source** and then by **Category** or **Jurisdiction** to view a list of individual sources. When you find the code you want to search, you have several search options. You can add the source as a search filter to execute a word search within the source. You can also open the table of contents to view the statutory outline and search within specific portions of the code. (Lexis Advance also allows you to access the index to U.S.C.S. and selected state codes through the **Browse** menu.) **Figure 7.11** shows the U.S.C.S. table of contents.

c. Using Shepard's For Statutory Research

Even though statutes in Lexis Advance are usually up to date, you may still want to use Shepard's in your research. As noted above, using a statutory citator ensures that your research is fully updated. In addition, a citator will provide the most complete research references because it lists

FIGURE 7.11 **LEXIS ADVANCE U.S.C.S. TABLE OF CONTENTS**

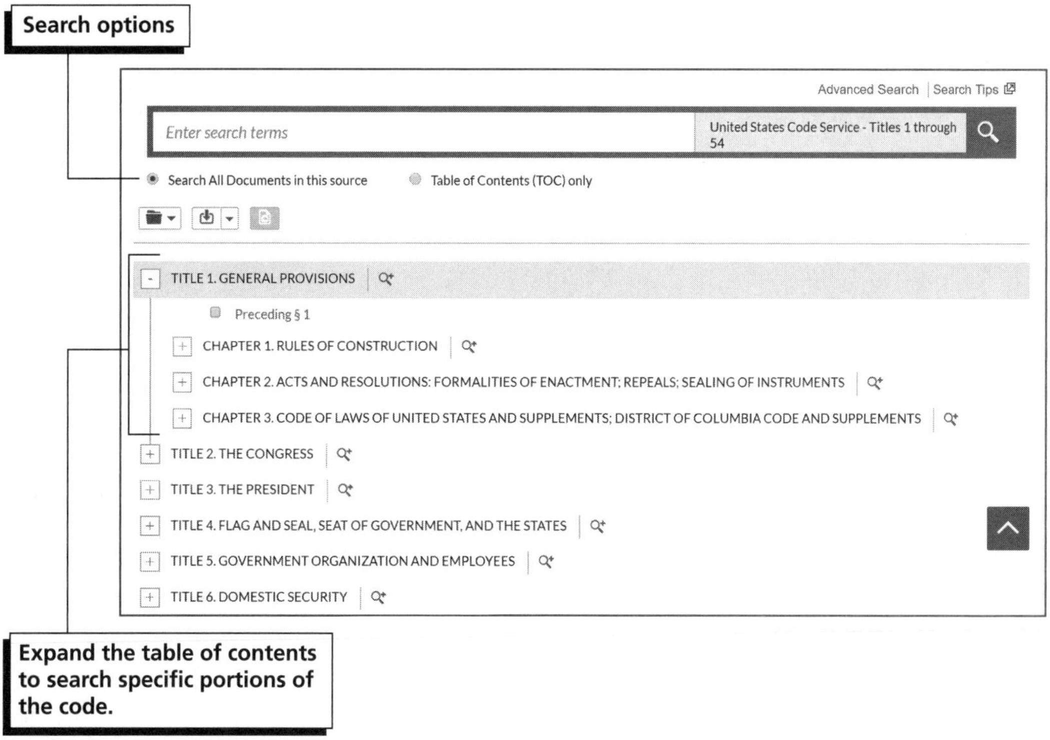

every case that has cited the statute and may be more up to date than the statutory annotations.

The process of using Shepard's for statutes is virtually identical to the process of using it for cases. You can enter a citation or access the service from a statute you are viewing. A Shepard's entry is divided into three sections: **History, Citing Decisions**, and **Other Citing Sources.** The **History** section shows the history of the statute, indicating, for example, whether the statute has been amended. The **Citing Decisions** section shows cases that have cited the statute, and the section with **Other Citing Sources** shows statutory annotations, law review articles, treatises, and other forms of authority that have cited the statute. You can limit the display to focus on the information most relevant to your research, and you can monitor a statutory Shepard's entry with Shepard's Alert®.

3. BLOOMBERG LAW

Bloomberg Law provides access to unofficial versions of the federal code, all 50 state codes, and the District of Columbia code. **Figure** 7.12

FIGURE 7.12 **18 U.S.C. § 915 IN BLOOMBERG LAW**

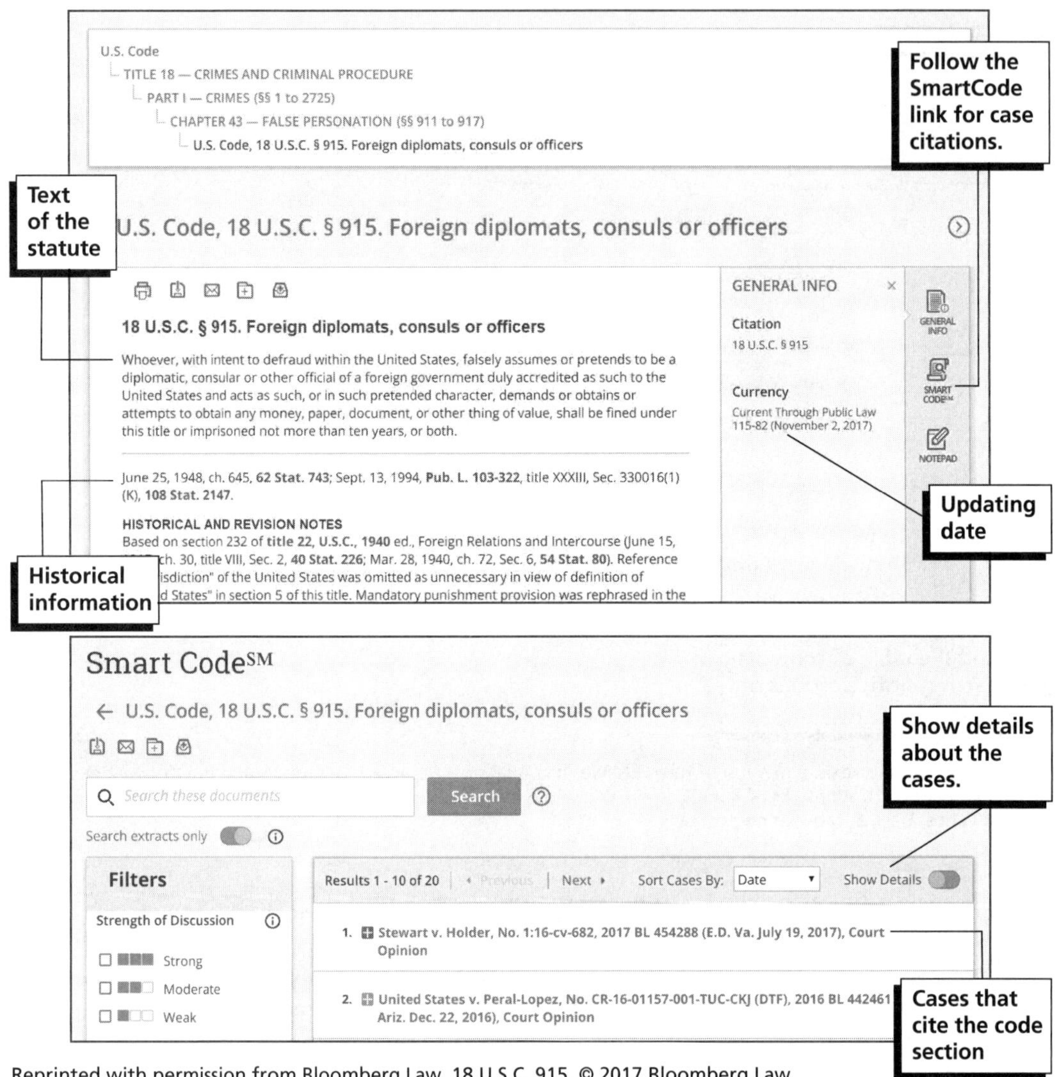

Reprinted with permission from Bloomberg Law, 18 U.S.C. 915. © 2017 Bloomberg Law.

shows a federal statute in Bloomberg Law. The **General Info** section indicates how current the statute is.

You can retrieve a code section by citation using the search box at the top of the screen. You can execute a source-driven search for statutes by selecting a code from the **Browse All Content** menu on the left or the **Select Sources** drop-down menu on the right side of the search box. Once you identify the code you want to search, you can view the table of contents and expand the headings to view chapters and individual sections. You can execute a search within the code using the search box or check off individual sections to limit the search to those portions of the code. You can also search the **Popular Name Table** for federal statutes.

To execute a content-driven search, use the search box at the top of the screen or select **All Legal Content** as your source. After you execute the search, you will have a range of options for filtering the results. Statutory search results are listed in numerical order by citation. If you do not pre-filter by jurisdiction, federal statutes will appear first and state statutes will be listed in alphabetical order.

Statutes in Bloomberg Law are not annotated, but Bloomberg Law has a search function to help you locate cases that cite a statute. When you view a code section, you can select **SmartCode** to run a search for cases that include the citation to the code section. **Figure** 7.12 shows **SmartCode** search results. This feature is available for federal statutes and is being added to state statutes as well. The search retrieves every case that cites the section, not an edited selection of case summaries like those in an annotated code. Consequently, you will likely need to filter the results or change the default display order to locate the most relevant case summaries. You can also use the **Strength of Discussion** filter to target cases with the most discussion of the statute. A small number of federal statutes have similar search functions for other types of authority, but for most statutes, this search function is limited to cases that cite the statute.

4. ADDITIONAL ONLINE SOURCES

The federal code, all 50 state codes, and the District of Columbia code are available online from many sources, including commercial services such as Fastcase and Casemaker; government websites, such as the website for the House of Representatives' Office of Law Revision Counsel; or general legal research websites. Often these sites have search functions that will allow you to retrieve statutes using word, subject, or table of contents searches. As this text goes to press, index searching is available for only a few states. Cornell Law School's Legal Information Institute site offers a popular name table for the *United States Code.* Appendix A lists websites that may be useful for statutory research. In addition, court rules of procedure, including local court rules, are often available on court websites. If the code or rules of procedure you need to research are available and up to date online, this can be an economical alternative to research with a commercial service.

Two caveats, however, are important to mention. First, with the exception of Fastcase, the versions of the codes available from these other online sources are usually unannotated, so you will only find the statutory text, not any additional research references. Second, it is important to check the date of any statutory material you use. Statutory compilations available online may be updated only as frequently as official print sources. If the material is not up to date, you will need to update your research.

D. CITING STATUTES

The general rules for citing statutes can be found in Rule 14 in the *ALWD Guide* (6th ed.) and Bluepages B12 in the *Bluebook* (20th ed.). Citations to statutes can be broken into two components: (a) information identifying the code and code section; and (b) parenthetical information containing the date of the code and any relevant supplements; this section may also include a reference to the publisher of the code. To find out the exact requirements for a citation to a particular code, you must look at Appendix 1 in the *ALWD Guide* or Table T1 in the *Bluebook,* both of which tell you how to cite codes from every jurisdiction in the U.S. Appendix 1 and Table T1 include information on which code to cite if more than one is published, how to abbreviate the name of the code, and whether the name of the publisher must be included with the date in the parenthetical.

In a citation to a Title code, you will ordinarily give the Title number, the abbreviated name of the code, the section symbol, the section number, and a parenthetical containing the date the book was published and, if necessary, the publisher.

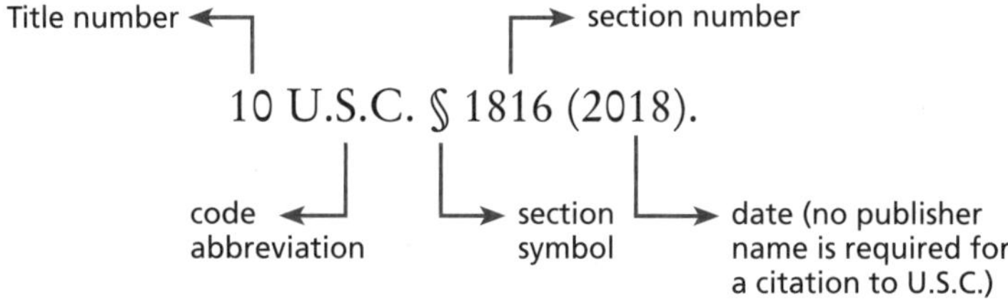

In a citation to a subject-matter code, you will ordinarily list the abbreviated name of the code, the section symbol, the section number, and a parenthetical containing the date the book was published and, if necessary, the publisher.

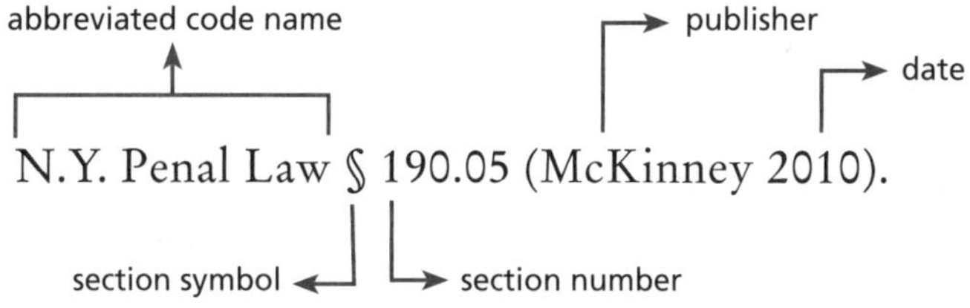

In this example, Appendix 1 and Table T1 provide that citations to McKinney's Consolidated Laws of New York Annotated must include the name of the publisher in the parenthetical, which is why you see the reference to McKinney in this citation. In both examples above, note that there is a space between the section symbol (§) and the section number.

Sometimes determining which date or dates to include in the parenthetical can be confusing. The answer is always a function of where a reader would have to look to find the full and up-to-date language of the statute in the print code. If the full statute is contained in the main volume of the code, the date in the parenthetical should refer only to the main volume. If the full statute is contained only in the pocket part, the date should refer only to the pocket part. If the reader must refer both to the main volume and to the pocket part, the parenthetical should list both dates. In making this determination, you should consider *only* the language of the statute itself, not the annotations. If the full text of the statute itself is in the main volume, you do not need to cite the pocket part even if it contains additional annotations. Once you have determined which date to place in the parenthetical, you should then refer to Appendix 1 or Table T1 to determine whether the publisher must also be included. The following are examples of citations with different date information included in the parenthetical.

N.Y. Penal Law § 190.05 (McKinney 2010).

In this example, Appendix 1 and Table T1 require the name of the publisher, and the full text of the statute can be found in the main volume.

N.Y. Penal Law § 190.05 (McKinney Supp. 2018).

In this example, Appendix 1 and Table T1 require the name of the publisher, and the full text of the statute can be found in the pocket part.

N.Y. Penal Law § 190.05 (McKinney 2010 & Supp. 2018).

In this example, Appendix 1 and Table T1 require the name of the publisher, and the reader must refer both to the main volume and to the pocket part to find the full text of the statute.

In citations to a code for which no publisher is required, the only difference would be the omission of the publisher's name, as in the example below.

Haw. Rev. Stat. § 328-1 (2010).

When you look at the entries in Table T1 of the *Bluebook,* you will notice that the names of the codes are in large and small capital letters, e.g., N.Y. PENAL LAW § 190.05 (McKinney 2010). Remember that this is the type style for law review footnotes. According to Bluepages B2, you may use regular type when citing statutes in briefs and memoranda.

E. SAMPLE PAGES FOR STATUTORY RESEARCH

Beginning on the next page, **Figures** 7.13 through 7.16 contain sample pages from West's *Annotated Code of Maryland* showing the print research process. For purposes of this example, assume that your client owns a car that was involved in an accident while she was a passenger in the car, not the driver. Although she was not injured, others involved in the accident were hurt. You need to determine whether your client had a duty to remain at the scene of the accident. **Figures 7.17** through **7.23** illustrate the same process using Westlaw, Lexis Advance, and Bloomberg Law.

The first step in researching the Maryland Code in print is using the most recent General Index to locate relevant code sections. This example shows what you would find if you looked under "Traffic Rules and Regulations."

FIGURE 7.13 EXCERPT FROM MARYLAND CODE ANNOTATED GENERAL INDEX

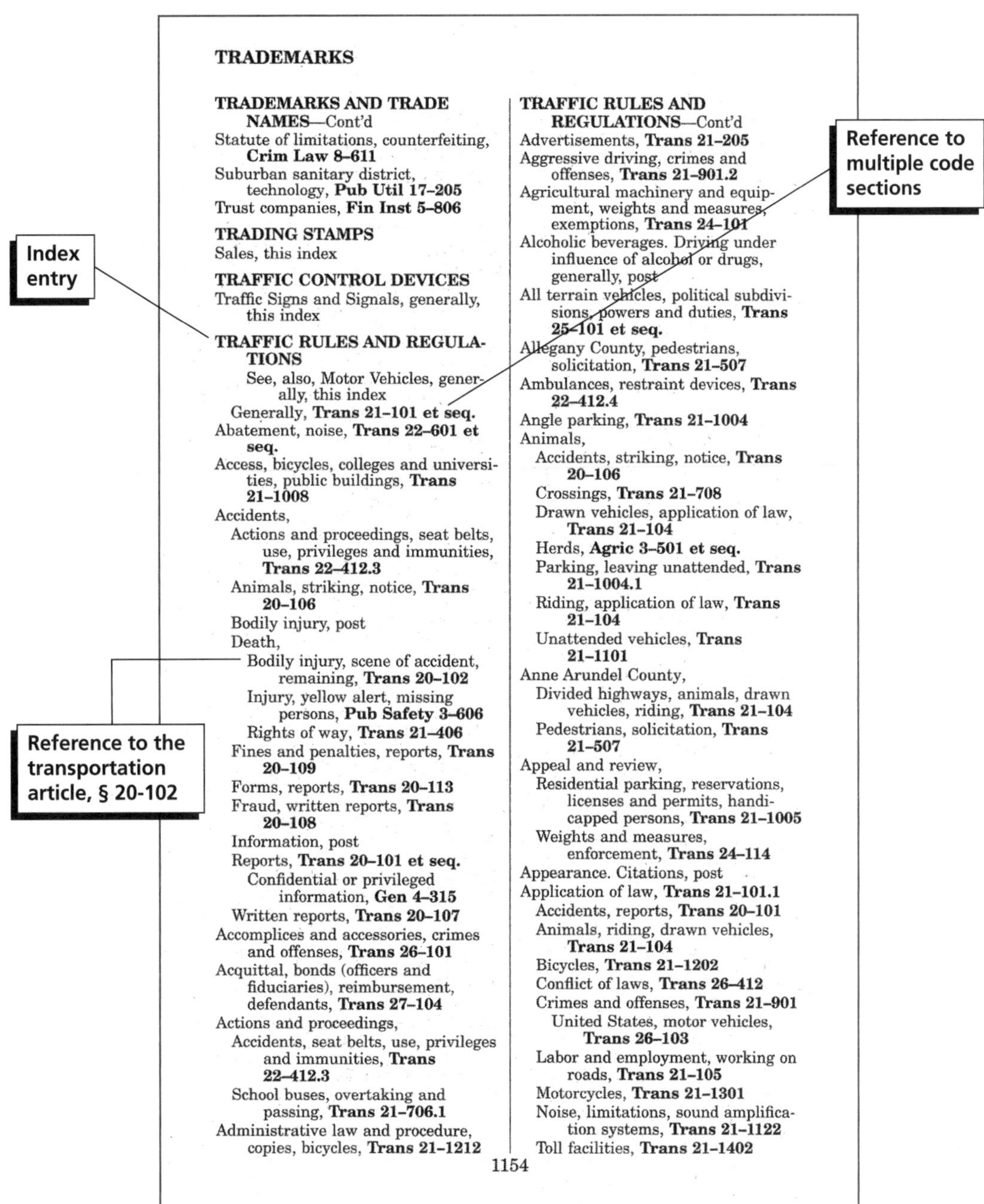

TRADEMARKS

TRADEMARKS AND TRADE NAMES—Cont'd
Statute of limitations, counterfeiting, **Crim Law 8–611**
Suburban sanitary district, technology, **Pub Util 17–205**
Trust companies, **Fin Inst 5–806**

TRADING STAMPS
Sales, this index

TRAFFIC CONTROL DEVICES
Traffic Signs and Signals, generally, this index

TRAFFIC RULES AND REGULATIONS
See, also, Motor Vehicles, generally, this index
Generally, **Trans 21–101 et seq.**
Abatement, noise, **Trans 22–601 et seq.**
Access, bicycles, colleges and universities, public buildings, **Trans 21–1008**
Accidents,
Actions and proceedings, seat belts, use, privileges and immunities, **Trans 22–412.3**
Animals, striking, notice, **Trans 20–106**
Bodily injury, post
Death,
Bodily injury, scene of accident, remaining, **Trans 20–102**
Injury, yellow alert, missing persons, **Pub Safety 3–606**
Rights of way, **Trans 21–406**
Fines and penalties, reports, **Trans 20–109**
Forms, reports, **Trans 20–113**
Fraud, written reports, **Trans 20–108**
Information, post
Reports, **Trans 20–101 et seq.**
Confidential or privileged information, **Gen 4–315**
Written reports, **Trans 20–107**
Accomplices and accessories, crimes and offenses, **Trans 26–101**
Acquittal, bonds (officers and fiduciaries), reimbursement, defendants, **Trans 27–104**
Actions and proceedings,
Accidents, seat belts, use, privileges and immunities, **Trans 22–412.3**
School buses, overtaking and passing, **Trans 21–706.1**
Administrative law and procedure, copies, bicycles, **Trans 21–1212**

TRAFFIC RULES AND REGULATIONS—Cont'd
Advertisements, **Trans 21–205**
Aggressive driving, crimes and offenses, **Trans 21–901.2**
Agricultural machinery and equipment, weights and measures, exemptions, **Trans 24–101**
Alcoholic beverages. Driving under influence of alcohol or drugs, generally, post
All terrain vehicles, political subdivisions, powers and duties, **Trans 25–101 et seq.**
Allegany County, pedestrians, solicitation, **Trans 21–507**
Ambulances, restraint devices, **Trans 22–412.4**
Angle parking, **Trans 21–1004**
Animals,
Accidents, striking, notice, **Trans 20–106**
Crossings, **Trans 21–708**
Drawn vehicles, application of law, **Trans 21–104**
Herds, **Agric 3–501 et seq.**
Parking, leaving unattended, **Trans 21–1004.1**
Riding, application of law, **Trans 21–104**
Unattended vehicles, **Trans 21–1101**
Anne Arundel County,
Divided highways, animals, drawn vehicles, riding, **Trans 21–104**
Pedestrians, solicitation, **Trans 21–507**
Appeal and review,
Residential parking, reservations, licenses and permits, handicapped persons, **Trans 21–1005**
Weights and measures, enforcement, **Trans 24–114**
Appearance. Citations, post
Application of law, **Trans 21–101.1**
Accidents, reports, **Trans 20–101**
Animals, riding, drawn vehicles, **Trans 21–104**
Bicycles, **Trans 21–1202**
Conflict of laws, **Trans 26–412**
Crimes and offenses, **Trans 21–901**
United States, motor vehicles, **Trans 26–103**
Labor and employment, working on roads, **Trans 21–105**
Motorcycles, **Trans 21–1301**
Noise, limitations, sound amplification systems, **Trans 21–1122**
Toll facilities, **Trans 21–1402**

1154

The next step is looking up the statute in the main volume. Section 20-102 sets out a driver's duty to remain at the scene of an accident that results in bodily injury.

FIGURE 7.14 CODE SECTION

§ 20–102 **TRANSPORTATION**

§ 20–102. Duty of driver to remain at scene of accident resulting in bodily injury or death

Duty of driver to stop vehicle close to scene of accident resulting in bodily injury

(a)(1) The driver of each vehicle involved in an accident that results in bodily injury to another person immediately shall stop the vehicle as close as possible to the scene of the accident, without obstructing traffic more than necessary.

(2) The driver of each vehicle involved in an accident that results in bodily injury to another person immediately shall return to and remain at the scene of the accident until the driver has complied with § 20–104 of this title.

Duty of driver to stop vehicle close to scene of accident resulting in death

(b)(1) The driver of each vehicle involved in an accident that results in the death of another person immediately shall stop the vehicle as close as possible to the scene of the accident, without obstructing traffic more than necessary.

(2) The driver of each vehicle involved in an accident that results in the death of another person immediately shall return to and remain at the scene of the accident until the driver has complied with § 20–104 of this title.

Added by Acts 1977, c. 14, § 2, eff. July 1, 1977. Amended by Acts 1986, c. 472, § 1; Acts 1988, c. 6, § 1; Acts 1991, c. 346, § 1; Acts 1998, c. 781, § 1, eff. Oct. 1, 1998; Acts 2001, c. 483, § 1, eff. Oct. 1, 2001; Acts 2002, c. 461, § 1, eff. Oct. 1, 2002; Acts 2002, c. 462, § 1, eff. Oct. 1, 2002; Acts 2005, c. 482, § 1, eff. Oct. 1, 2005.

Formerly Art. 66½, § 10–102.

Historical and Statutory Notes

2001 Legislation

Acts 2001, c. 483, § 1, repealed and reenacted this section without amendment.

2002 Legislation

Acts 2002, c. 461, § 1, and Acts 2002, c. 462, § 1, repealed and reenacted this section without amendment.

2005 Legislation

Acts 2005, c. 482, § 1, rewrote this section, which previously read:

"(a) The driver of each vehicle involved in an accident that results in bodily injury to or death of another person immediately shall stop the vehicle as close as possible to the scene of the accident, without obstructing traffic more than necessary.

"(b) The driver of each vehicle involved in an accident that results in bodily injury to or death of another person immediately shall return to and remain at the scene of the accident until the driver has complied with § 20–104 of this title."

Cross References

Authority to arrest without warrant, failure to remain at accident scene, see Transportation, § 26–202.

Vehicle offenses, effect given to certain convictions under Driver License Compact, see Transportation, § 16–707.

Vehicle offenses, expungement of driving record prohibited, see Transportation, § 16–117.1.

Vehicle offenses, limitation period for prosecution for failure to remain at accident scene, see Courts and Judicial Proceedings, § 5–106.

Vehicle offenses, punishment for failure to remain at accident scene, see Transportation, § 27–101.

Library References

Automobiles ⚿336.
Westlaw Topic No. 48A.
C.J.S. Motor Vehicles §§ 1488 to 1504.

270

FIGURE 7.14 **CODE SECTION *(continued)***

Research References

ALR Library
26 ALR 5th 1, Necessity and Sufficiency of Showing, in Criminal Prosecution Under "Hit-And-Run" Statute, Accused's Knowledge of Accident, Injury, or Damage.

Encyclopedias
Maryland Law Encyclopedia Autos & Motor Vehicles § 17, Accidents and Accident Reports.

Maryland Law Encyclopedia Autos & Motor Vehicles § 309.5, Other Offenses.

Summaries of cases applying the statute

Notes of Decisions

Damages 6
Defenses 4
Involved in an accident 2
Jury instructions 5
Knowledge 3
Purpose 1

1. Purpose

Purpose of "hit and run" statute is to discourage driver of vehicle which has been involved in injury-causing accident from abandoning persons in need of medical care and to prevent driver from attempting to avoid possible liability. Code, Transportation, § 20–102. Comstock v. State, 1990, 573 A.2d 117, 82 Md.App. 744. Automobiles ⚿ 336

2. Involved in an accident

Word "accident," as used in statutes requiring a driver to remain at the scene of an accident and establishing duty of driver to give information and render aid when vehicle is involved in accident, relates solely to occurrences actually resulting in death, personal injury, or property damage. General v. State, 2002, 789 A.2d 102, 367 Md. 475. Automobiles ⚿ 336

Driver whose vehicle went from the right southbound lane to the left southbound lane, crossing the middle lane without stopping, cutting off victim's vehicle, and allegedly causing victim to swerve into northbound lane and collide head-on with tractor trailer truck, resulting in victim's death, was "involved in an accident" within meaning of "hit and run" statute, even though driver's vehicle did not collide with another vehicle. Code, Transportation, § 20–102. Comstock v. State, 1990, 573 A.2d 117, 82 Md. App. 744. Automobiles ⚿ 336

Physical contact is not required for one to be "involved in an accident" within meaning of "hit and run" statute. Code, Transportation, § 20–102. Comstock v. State, 1990, 573 A.2d 117, 82 Md.App. 744. Automobiles ⚿ 336

3. Knowledge

Convictions under statutes requiring a driver to remain at the scene of an accident resulting in bodily injury or death and establishing the duty to give information and render aid when vehicle is involved in accident resulting in injury, death, or property damage require knowledge that the accident resulted in such injury, death, or property damage. General v. State, 2002, 789 A.2d 102, 367 Md. 475. Automobiles ⚿ 336

Where conditions were such that driver should have known that accident occurred or should have reasonably anticipated that accident resulted in injury to person, requisite proof of knowledge for conviction of leaving the scene of personal injury accident is present. Code, Transportation, § 20–102. Comstock v. State, 1990, 573 A.2d 117, 82 Md.App. 744. Automobiles ⚿ 336

Evidence, including testimony by passenger in driver's vehicle that he informed driver that vehicle cut off by driver had lost control of vehicle and defendant's testimony that he was told by passenger of accident, in which other vehicle crossed center median and collided head-on with tractor trailer truck, was sufficient to support finding that driver should have known he was "involved in an accident" after he learned that he had forced other car off road and that driver should have been aware of probable injury resulting from accident, and thus was sufficient to support conviction of leaving scene of personal injury accident. Code, Transportation, § 20–102. Comstock v. State, 1990, 573 A.2d 117, 82 Md.App. 744. Automobiles ⚿ 355(8)

Conviction of leaving the scene of a personal injury accident requires knowledge of both underlying accident and injury. Code, Transportation, § 20–102. Comstock v. State, 1990, 573 A.2d 117, 82 Md.App. 744. Automobiles ⚿ 336

4. Defenses

If defendant did not know that he struck a person with automobile and reasonably believed that he merely struck a white bag, then his mistake of fact was a defense to charged crimes of failure to remain at the scene of an accident and failure to render reasonable assistance. General v. State, 2002, 789 A.2d 102, 367 Md. 475. Criminal Law ⚿ 33

Because the statute may contain interrelated code sections, it is important to review the chapter outline in addition to the section referenced in the General Index. Section 20-101 specifies that the chapter's requirements apply to a vehicle owner present at an accident even if the owner was not the driver.

FIGURE 7.15 CHAPTER OUTLINE AND CODE SECTION

Chapter outline

TITLE 20

VEHICLE LAWS—ACCIDENTS AND ACCIDENT REPORTS

Section

20–101. Application of title.
20–102. Duty of driver to remain at scene of accident resulting in bodily injury or death.
20–103. Duty of driver to stop or return to scene of accident resulting in damage to vehicle.
20–104. Duty of driver to render reasonable assistance to persons injured in accident.
20–105. Duty of driver involved in accident with unattended vehicle or property.
20–105.1. Additional information required of driver of vehicle involved in accident.
20–106. Duty of driver upon striking domestic animal with vehicle.
20–107. Written accident report required by each driver involved in accident.
20–108. False oral or written reports prohibited.
20–109. Penalties for failure to file written accident report.
20–110. Repealed.
20–111, 20–112. Reserved.
20–113. Form and contents of written accident reports.

Historical and Statutory Notes

1977 Legislation

Acts 1977, c. 14, § 2, added Title 20, Vehicle Laws—Accidents and Accident Reports.

§ 20–101. Application of title

Application of title throughout State

(a) This title applies throughout this State, whether on or off a highway.

Sections 20–101 to 20–105 applicable to owner of vehicle

(b) All of the provisions of §§ 20–101 through 20–105 of this title apply to the owner of any vehicle who is present when the accident occurs, whether or not the owner is the driver.

Added by Acts 1977, c. 14, § 2, eff. July 1, 1977.

Formerly Art. 66½, §§ 10–101, 10–105.1.

Related provision indicates the chapter applies to an owner present at an accident.

Library References

Automobiles ⚷336.
Westlaw Topic No. 48A.
C.J.S. Motor Vehicles §§ 1488 to 1504.

Research References

Encyclopedias

Maryland Law Encyclopedia Autos & Motor Vehicles § 17, Accidents and Accident Reports.

Maryland Law Encyclopedia Autos & Motor Vehicles § 143, Persons or Property Not on Highway.

269

The next step is checking the pocket part. The pocket part entry for Maryland's Transportation Code § 20-102 shows both changes to the statutory language and additional research references.

FIGURE 7.16 **POCKET PART ENTRY FOR MARYLAND TRANSPORTATION CODE § 20-102**

TRANSPORTATION § 20–102

TITLE 20

VEHICLE LAWS—ACCIDENTS AND ACCIDENT REPORTS

§ 20–101. Application of title

Research References

Encyclopedias
Maryland Law Encyclopedia Autos & Motor Vehicles § 17, Accidents and Accident Reports.
Maryland Law Encyclopedia Autos & Motor Vehicles § 143, Persons or Property Not on Highway.

§ 20–102. Duty of driver to remain at scene of accident resulting in bodily injury or death

Duty of driver to stop vehicle close to scene of accident resulting in bodily injury

(a)(1) The driver of each vehicle involved in an accident that results in bodily injury to another person immediately shall stop the vehicle as close as possible to the scene of the accident, without obstructing traffic more than necessary.

(2) The driver of each vehicle involved in an accident that results in bodily injury to another person immediately shall return to and remain at the scene of the accident until the driver has complied with § 20–104 of this title.

New statutory language supersedes the language in the main volume.

Duty of driver to stop vehicle close to scene of accident resulting in death

(b)(1) The driver of each vehicle involved in an accident that results in the death of another person immediately shall stop the vehicle as close as possible to the scene of the accident, without obstructing traffic more than necessary.

(2) The driver of each vehicle involved in an accident that results in the death of another person immediately shall return to and remain at the scene of the accident until the driver has complied with § 20–104 of this title.

Fines and penalties

(c)(1) In this subsection, "serious bodily injury" means an injury that:

(i) Creates a substantial risk of death;

(ii) Causes serious permanent or serious protracted disfigurement;

(iii) Causes serious permanent or serious protracted loss of the function of any body part, organ, or mental faculty; or

(iv) Causes serious permanent or serious protracted impairment of the function of any body part or organ.

(2)(i) Except as provided in paragraph (3) of this subsection, a person convicted of a violation of subsection (a) of this section is subject to imprisonment not exceeding 1 year or a fine not exceeding $3,000 or both.

(ii) Except as provided in paragraph (3) of this subsection, a person convicted of a violation of subsection (b) of this section is subject to imprisonment not exceeding 5 years or a fine not exceeding $5,000 or both.

(3)(i) A person who violates this section and who knew or reasonably should have known that the accident might result in serious bodily injury to another person and serious bodily injury actually occurred to another person, is guilty of a felony and on conviction is subject to imprisonment not exceeding 5 years or a fine not exceeding $5,000 or both.

137

FIGURE 7.16 POCKET PART ENTRY FOR MARYLAND TRANSPORTATION CODE § 20-102 *(continued)*

§ 20–102 **TRANSPORTATION**

(ii) A person who violates this section and who knew or reasonably should have known that the accident might result in the death of another person and death actually occurred to another person, is guilty of a felony and on conviction is subject to imprisonment not exceeding 10 years or a fine not exceeding $10,000 or both.

Added by Acts 1977, c. 14, § 2, eff. July 1, 1977. Amended by Acts 1986, c. 472, § 1; Acts 1988, c. 6, § 1; Acts 1991, c. 346, § 1; Acts 1998, c. 781, § 1, eff. Oct. 1, 1998; Acts 2001, c. 483, § 1, eff. Oct. 1, 2001; Acts 2002, c. 461, § 1, eff. Oct. 1, 2002; Acts 2002, c. 462, § 1, eff. Oct. 1, 2002; Acts 2005, c. 482, § 1, eff. Oct. 1, 2005; Acts 2017, c. 55, § 1, eff. Oct. 1, 2017.

Formerly Art. 66½, § 10–102.

Legislative Notes

Revisor's Note (Acts 2017 c. 55):

Subsection (c) of this section is new language derived without substantive change from former §§ 27–113 and 27–101(*o*) of this article.

In subsection (c)(1)(iv) of this section, the reference to any "body part" is substituted for the former reference to any "bodily member" for consistency with subsection (c)(1)(iii) of this section.

The Department of Legislative Services notes, for consideration by the General Assembly, that the definition of "serious bodily injury" in subsection (c)(1)(iii) of this section includes an injury that causes serious permanent or serious protracted loss of the function of any body part, organ, or mental faculty. The definition also includes, in subsection (c)(1)(iv) of this section, an injury that causes serious permanent or serious protracted impairment of the function of any body part or organ, but does not include an injury that causes serious permanent or serious protracted impairment of the function of any mental faculty. The General Assembly may wish to address this inconsistency.

Historical and Statutory Notes

2017 Legislation

Acts 2017, c. 55, § 1, added (c).

New research references and case summaries

Research References

ALR Library

26 ALR 5th 1, Necessity and Sufficiency of Showing, in Criminal Prosecution Under "Hit-And-Run" Statute, Accused's Knowledge of Accident, Injury, or Damage.

101 ALR 911, Constitutionality, Construction, and Effect of Statutes in Relation to Conduct of Driver of Automobile After Happening of Accident.

Encyclopedias

Maryland Law Encyclopedia Autos & Motor Vehicles § 17, Accidents and Accident Reports.

Maryland Law Encyclopedia Autos & Motor Vehicles § 309.50, Other Offenses.

Maryland Law Encyclopedia Criminal Law § 537, Generally; "Crime" Defined.

Notes of Decisions

1. Purpose

The purpose of "hit and run" statute is to discourage the driver of a vehicle which has been involved in an injury-causing accident from abandoning persons who are in need of medical care, and to prevent that same driver from attempting to avoid possible liability. DeHogue v. State, 2010, 989 A.2d 759, 190 Md.App. 532. Automobiles ⚡ 336

2. Involved in an accident

Word "accident," as used in statutes requiring a driver to remain at the scene of an accident and establishing duty of driver to give information and render aid when vehicle is involved in accident, relates solely to occurrences actually resulting in death, personal injury, or property damage. General v. State, 2002, 789 A.2d 102, 367 Md. 475. Automobiles ⚡ 336

3. Knowledge

There was sufficient evidence that defendant, who struck with her pickup truck a pedestrian pushing a toddler in a stroller, knew or should have known that death or serious bodily injury had occurred to support conviction for failing to remain at the scene of an accident; passenger in defendant's vehicle testified that defendant had actual knowledge that she had hit pedestrian, and serious bodily injury actually occurred to pedestrian, and death occurred to toddler. DeHogue v. State, 2010, 989 A.2d 759, 190 Md.App. 532. Automobiles ⚡ 355(8)

Knowledge of both the underlying accident and injury is logically and legally necessary for one to be guilty of leaving the scene of a personal injury accident. DeHogue v. State, 2010, 989 A.2d 759, 190 Md.App. 532. Automobiles ⚡ 336

138

To research statutes online, you can browse the code's table of contents or execute a word search. In Westlaw, you can also use a statutory index.

To use an index in Westlaw, select the code you want to research. Choose the index option, and search alphabetically through the topics. Figure 7.18 shows the index to *West's Annotated Code of Maryland*, which you can use to locate the statute that sets out the duty to remain at the scene of a car accident that involves bodily injuries.

FIGURE 7.17 WEST'S *ANNOTATED CODE OF MARYLAND* INDEX

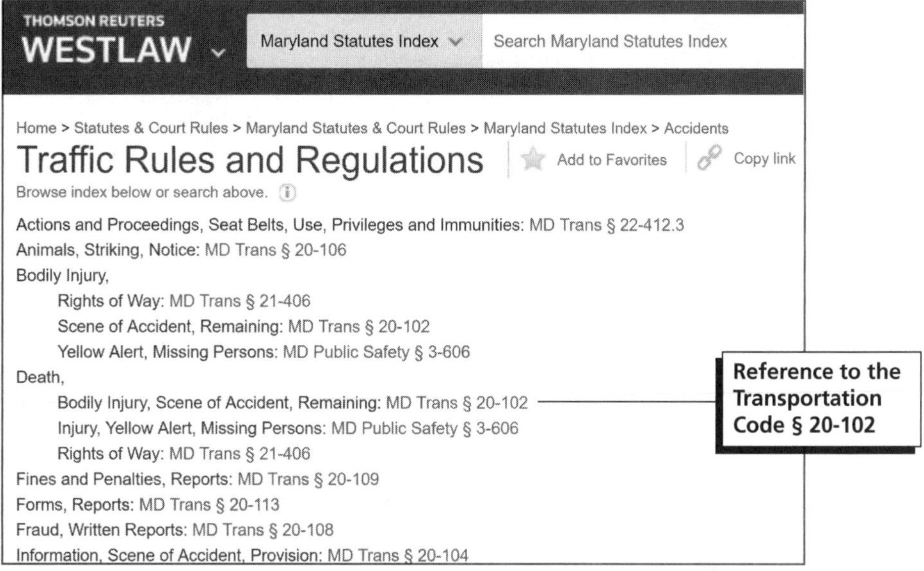

Following the link in the index retrieves the code section. You can browse preceding or subsequent sections or view the title's table of contents using the appropriate links. Annotations and KeyCite information appear under the tabs accompanying the document.

FIGURE 7.18 MARYLAND TRANSPORTATION CODE § 20-102

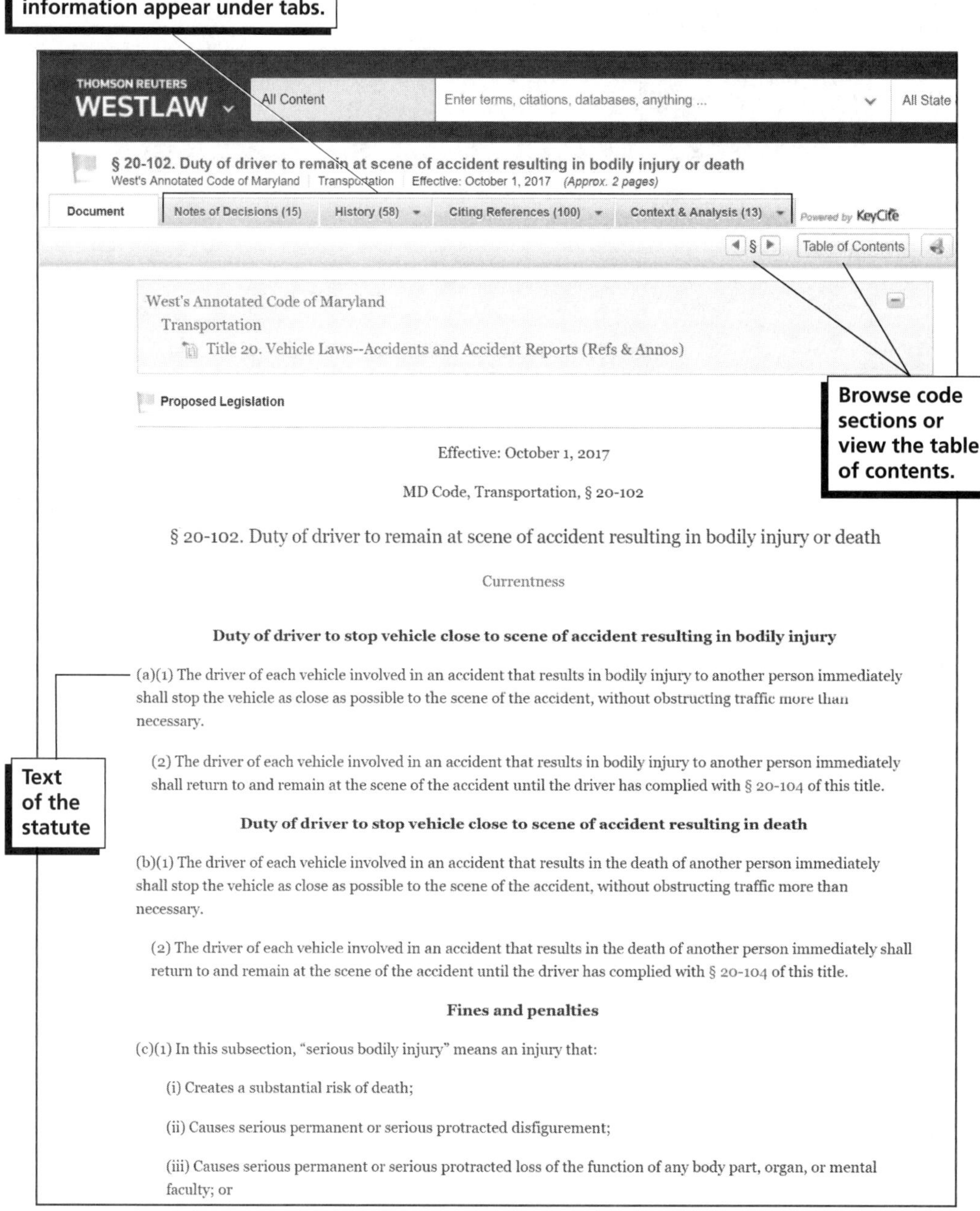

Reprinted with permission from Thomson Reuters/West, from Westlaw, West's *Annotated Code of Maryland* Transportation Code § 20-102. © 2017 Thomson Reuters/West.

Viewing the table of contents allows you to see all of the sections in the title. To open any section, click on the link. Following the link to § 20-101, Application of title, reveals that the duty described in § 20-102 applies to owners as well as drivers.

FIGURE 7.19 OUTLINE OF TITLE 20, MARYLAND TRANSPORTATION CODE

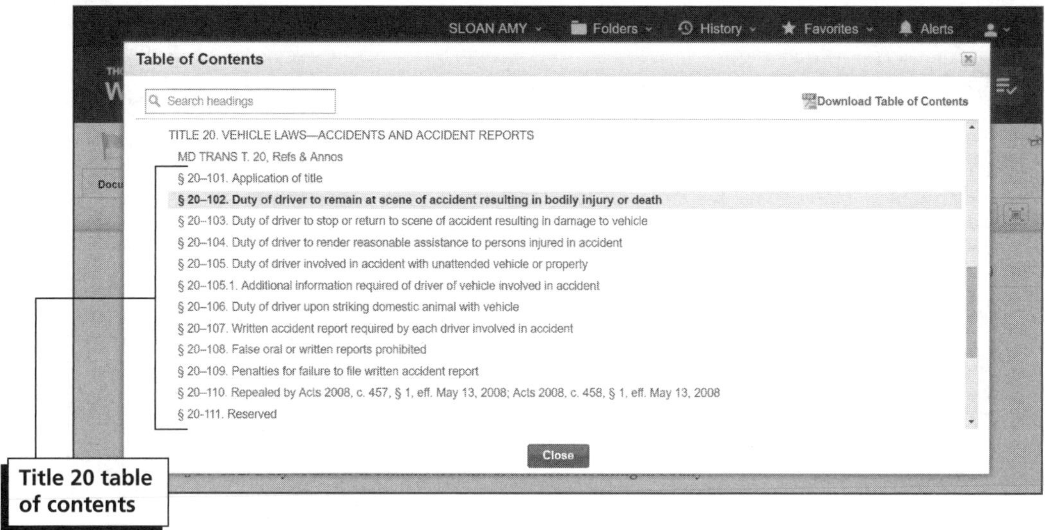

FIGURE 7.20 RELATED CODE SECTION

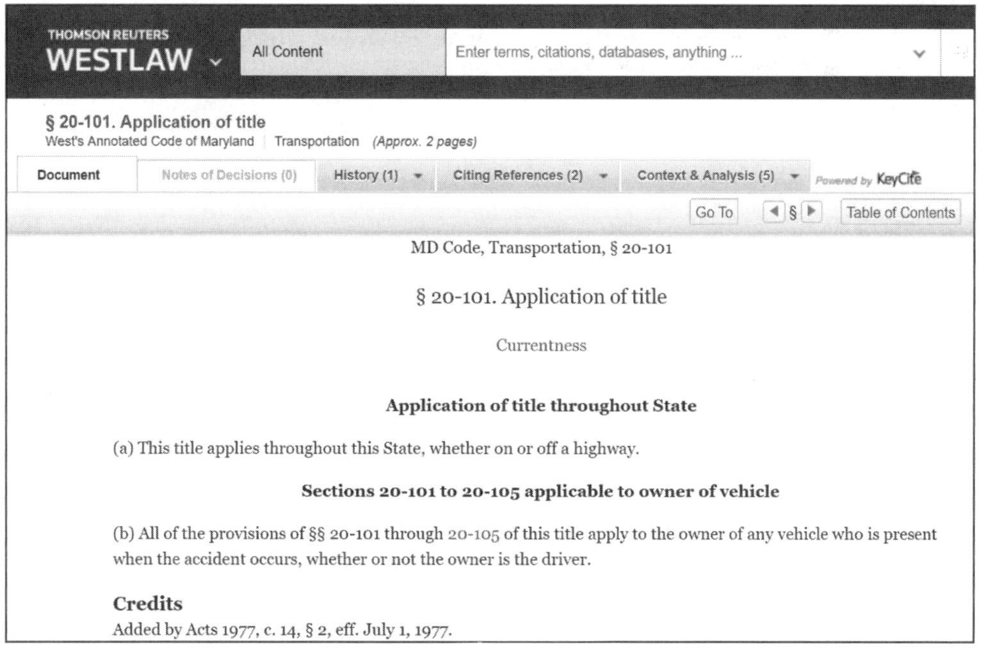

Another way to search for statutes is by word searching. In Lexis Advance, you can pre-filter by category (Statutes and Legislation) and jurisdiction (Maryland) before executing a search for *remain scene accident.*

FIGURE 7.21 LEXIS ADVANCE SEARCH RESULTS

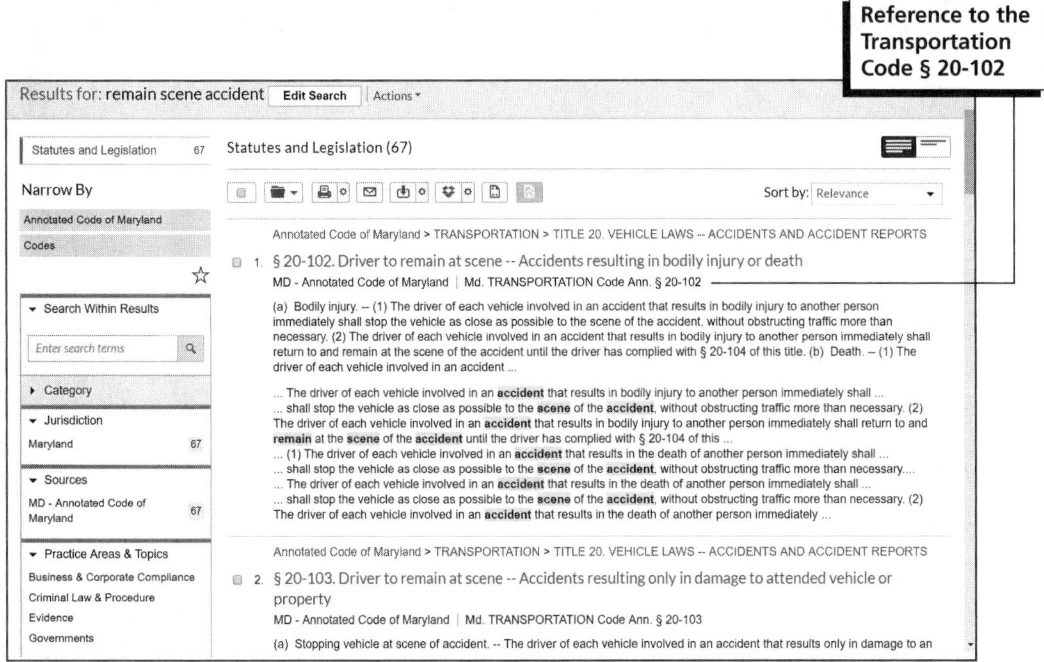

 From Lexis Advance, statutory search results.

Following the link to Maryland Transportation Code § 20-102 retrieves the code section. Annotations follow the statutory language. You can browse preceding or subsequent sections, view the chapter table of contents, or Shepardize the section using the appropriate links.

FIGURE 7.22 MARYLAND TRANSPORTATION CODE § 20-102

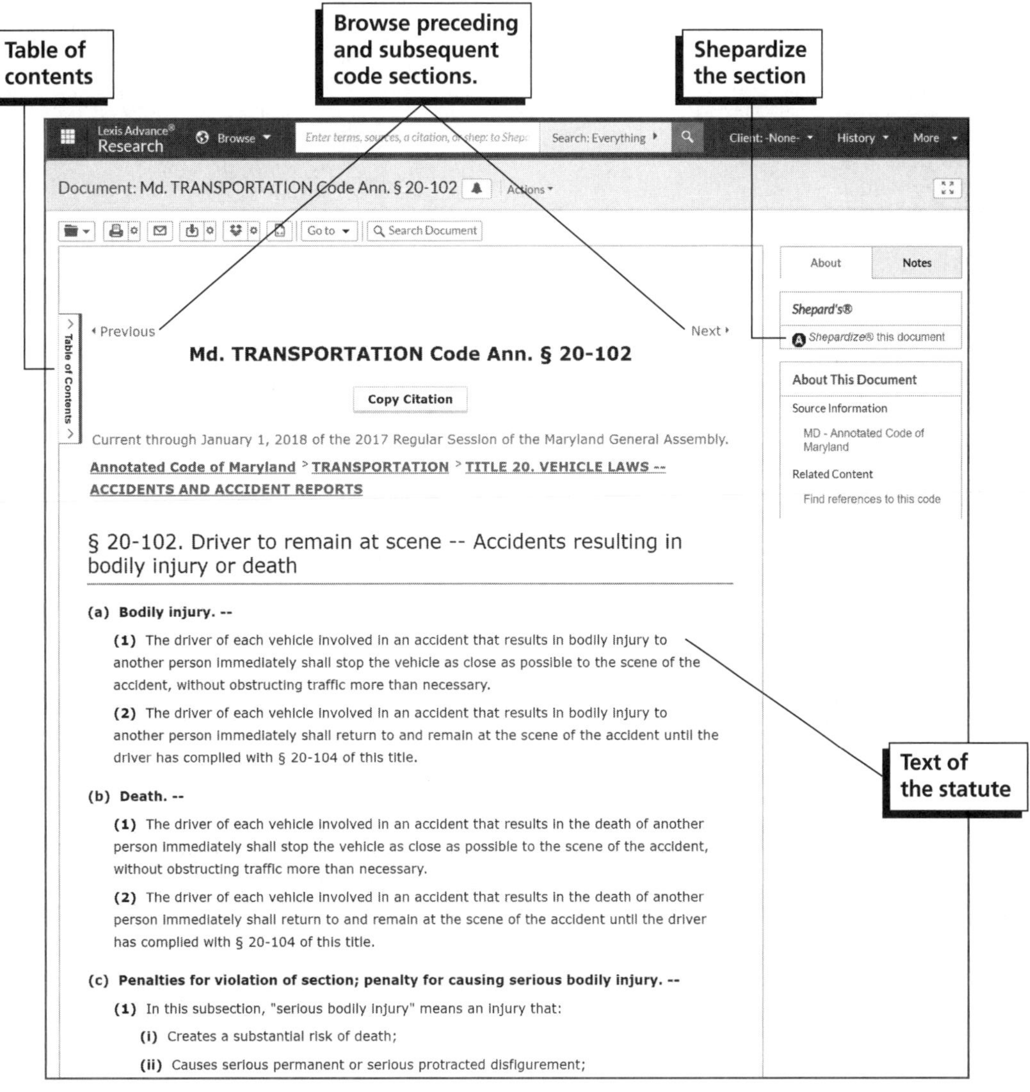

FIGURE 7.22 MARYLAND TRANSPORTATION CODE § 20-102 *(continued)*

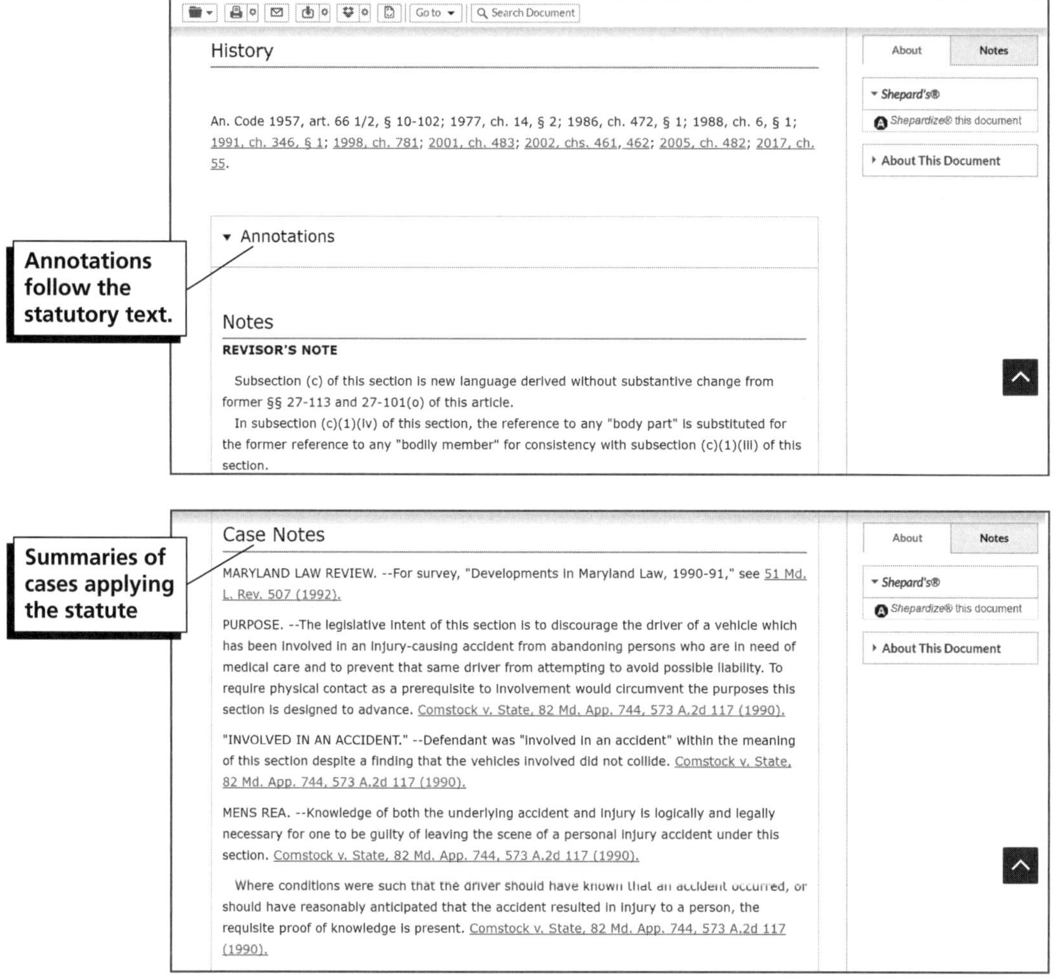

History

An. Code 1957, art. 66 1/2, § 10-102; 1977, ch. 14, § 2; 1986, ch. 472, § 1; 1988, ch. 6, § 1; 1991, ch. 346, § 1; 1998, ch. 781; 2001, ch. 483; 2002, chs. 461, 462; 2005, ch. 482; 2017, ch. 55.

▾ Annotations

Notes

REVISOR'S NOTE

Subsection (c) of this section is new language derived without substantive change from former §§ 27-113 and 27-101(o) of this article.

In subsection (c)(1)(iv) of this section, the reference to any "body part" is substituted for the former reference to any "bodily member" for consistency with subsection (c)(1)(iii) of this section.

Case Notes

MARYLAND LAW REVIEW. --For survey, "Developments in Maryland Law, 1990-91," see 51 Md. L. Rev. 507 (1992).

PURPOSE. --The legislative intent of this section is to discourage the driver of a vehicle which has been involved in an injury-causing accident from abandoning persons who are in need of medical care and to prevent that same driver from attempting to avoid possible liability. To require physical contact as a prerequisite to involvement would circumvent the purposes this section is designed to advance. Comstock v. State, 82 Md. App. 744, 573 A.2d 117 (1990).

"INVOLVED IN AN ACCIDENT." --Defendant was "involved in an accident" within the meaning of this section despite a finding that the vehicles involved did not collide. Comstock v. State, 82 Md. App. 744, 573 A.2d 117 (1990).

MENS REA. --Knowledge of both the underlying accident and injury is logically and legally necessary for one to be guilty of leaving the scene of a personal injury accident under this section. Comstock v. State, 82 Md. App. 744, 573 A.2d 117 (1990).

Where conditions were such that the driver should have known that an accident occurred, or should have reasonably anticipated that the accident resulted in injury to a person, the requisite proof of knowledge is present. Comstock v. State, 82 Md. App. 744, 573 A.2d 117 (1990).

In Bloomberg Law, as in Westlaw and Lexis Advance, you can execute a content-driven search. Limiting the search to authority from Maryland and executing a search for *remain scene accident* retrieves statutes as well as other types of authority. The display in Figure 7.23 shows the search results as a list of citations, but you can vary the display to show document summaries as well.

FIGURE 7.23 BLOOMBERG LAW SEARCH RESULTS

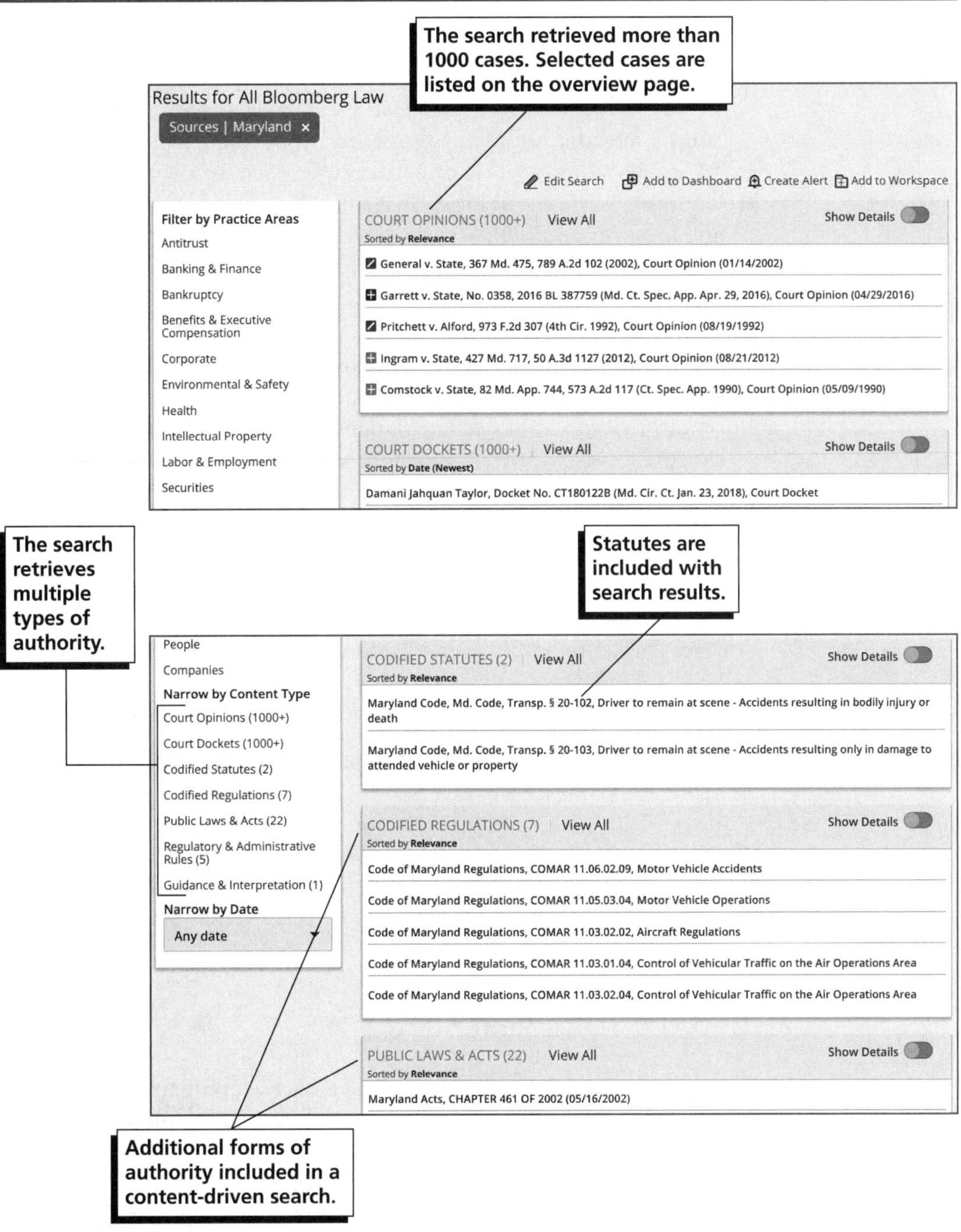

F. CHECKLIST FOR STATUTORY RESEARCH

1. LOCATE A STATUTE

☐ In print:
- Use an index to search by subject.
- Use the popular name table to locate a statute by its popular name.

☐ In Westlaw:
- Source-driven searching: Select a database to search for statutes from a specific jurisdiction; search by popular name, browse the statutory index or table of contents, or execute a word search.
- Content-driven searching: Pre-filter by jurisdiction (if possible) and execute a content-driven search; filter the results to target appropriate statutes.

☐ In Lexis Advance:
- Source-driven searching: Select a source to search for statutes using options under **Explore Content**, the drop-down menu on the right side of the search bar, or the **Browse** menu; search by type of authority (**Statutes & Legislation**), jurisdiction, and/or topic and execute a search; filter the results to target appropriate statutes.
- Content-driven searching: Pre-filter by jurisdiction (if possible) and execute a content-driven search; filter the results to target appropriate statutes.

☐ In Bloomberg Law, search for statutes with source-driven or content-driven searches.

☐ For free online research, locate statutes on government or general legal research websites.

2. READ THE STATUTE AND ANY ACCOMPANYING RESEARCH REFERENCES

☐ In an annotated code, use the annotations to find cases, secondary sources, and other research materials interpreting the statute.

☐ In Bloomberg Law, use **SmartCode** to retrieve cases that have cited the statute.

3. UPDATE YOUR RESEARCH

☐ With print research, check the pocket part accompanying the main volume and any cumulative or noncumulative supplements accompanying the code.

☐ With state or federal statutory research, update your research or find additional research references using a statutory citator such as Shepard's in Lexis Advance or KeyCite in Westlaw.

☐ With free online sources, check the date of the statute and update your research accordingly; consider using a statutory citator to update your research and find additional research references.

CHAPTER 8

Federal Legislative History Research

A. INTRODUCTION TO FEDERAL LEGISLATIVE HISTORY

When a legislature passes a statute, it does so with a goal in mind, such as prohibiting or regulating certain types of conduct. Despite their best efforts, however, legislators do not always draft statutes that express their intentions clearly, and it is almost impossible to draft a statute that contemplates every possible situation that may arise under it. Accordingly, lawyers and judges are often called upon to determine the meaning of an ambiguous statute. Lawyers must provide guidance about what the statute permits or requires their clients to do. In deciding cases, judges must determine what the legislature intended when it passed the statute.

If you are asked to analyze an ambiguous statute, you have a number of tools available to help with the task. If the courts have already resolved the ambiguity, secondary sources, statutory annotations, citators, or other research resources can lead you to cases that explain the meaning of the statute.

If the ambiguity has not yet been resolved, however, you face a bigger challenge. You could research similar statutes to see if they shed light on the provision you are interpreting. You could also look to the language of the statute itself for guidance. You may have studied what are called "canons of construction" in some of your other classes. These canons are principles used to determine the meaning of a statute. For example, one canon provides that statutory terms are to be construed according to their ordinary and plain meaning. Another states that remedial statutes are to be broadly construed, while criminal statutes are to be narrowly construed.[1] Although these tools can be helpful in interpreting statutes, they rarely provide the complete answer to determining the legislature's intent.

One of the best ways to determine legislative intent is to research the paper trail of documents that legislators create during the legislative process. These documents are known as the legislative history of the statute. This chapter discusses various types of documents that make up a statute's legislative history and explains how to locate and use them. At the state level, the types of legislative history documents produced and their ease of accessibility vary widely; therefore, this chapter discusses only federal legislative history.

1. THE PROCESS OF ENACTING A LAW

"Legislative history" is a generic term used to refer to a variety of documents produced during the legislative process; it does not refer to a single document or research tool. Courts consider some legislative history documents more important than others, depending on the type of information in the document and the point in the legislative process when the document was created. Understanding what legislative history consists of, as well as the value of different legislative history documents, requires an understanding of the legislative process. **Figure 8.1** illustrates this process.

The legislative process begins when a bill is introduced into the House of Representatives or the Senate by a member of Congress. After the bill is introduced, it is usually referred to a committee. The committee can hold hearings on the bill to obtain the views of experts and interested parties, or it can refer the bill to a subcommittee to hold hearings. If the committee is not in favor of the bill, it usually takes no action. This ordinarily causes the bill to expire in the committee, although the sponsor is free to reintroduce the bill in a later session of Congress. If the committee is in favor of the bill, it will recommend passage to the full chamber of the House or Senate. The recommendation is presented in a committee report that contains the full text of the bill and an analysis of each provision. Because the committee presents its views in a report, this process is called "reporting out" the bill.

---

1. *See generally* Abner J. Mikva & Eric Lane, AN INTRODUCTION TO STATUTORY INTERPRETATION AND THE LEGISLATIVE PROCESS (Aspen Publishers 1997).

FIGURE 8.1 HOW A BILL BECOMES A LAW

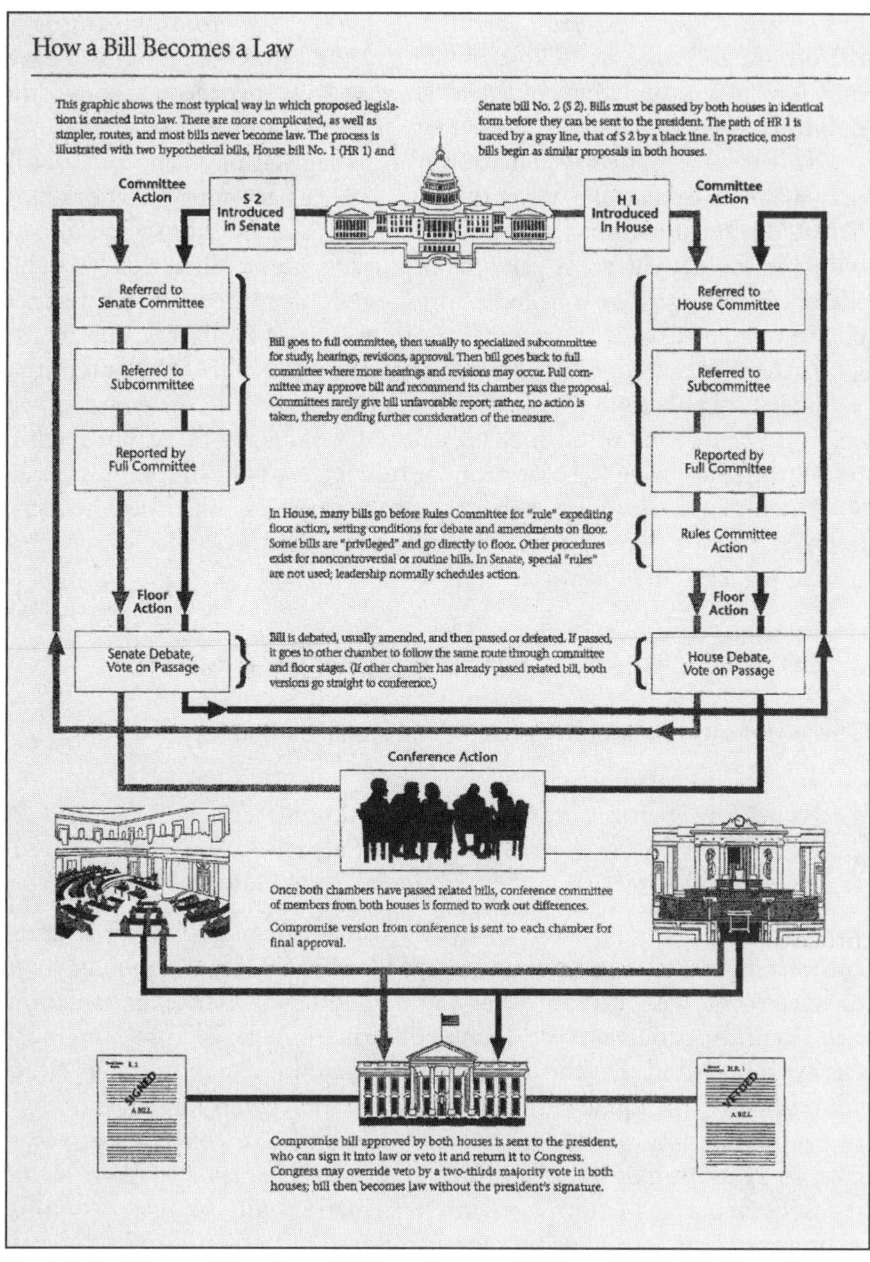

Reprinted with permission from *Guide to Congress*, CQ Press, 7th Ed. (2013), p. 1364.

The bill then goes before the full House or Senate, where it is debated and may be amended. The members of the House or Senate vote on the bill. If it is passed, the bill goes before the other chamber of Congress, where the same process is repeated. If both chambers pass the bill, it goes to the President. The President can sign the bill into law, allow it to become law without a signature, or veto it. If the bill is vetoed, it goes back to Congress. Congress can override the President's veto if two-thirds of the House and the Senate vote in favor of the bill. Once a bill is passed into law, it is assigned a public law number and proceeds through the publication process described in Chapter 7, on statutory research.

This is a simplified explanation of how legislation is enacted. A bill may make many detours along this path before becoming a law or being defeated. One situation that often occurs is that the House and Senate will pass slightly different versions of the same bill. When this happens, the bill is sent to what is called a conference committee. The conference committee consists of members of both houses of Congress, and its job is to attempt to reconcile the two versions of the bill. If the committee members are able to agree on the provisions of the bill, the compromise version is sent back to both chambers of Congress to be reapproved. If both houses approve the compromise bill, it then goes to the President.

Documents created at each stage of this process constitute the legislative history of a law. The next section describes the major sources that make up a legislative history.

2. SOURCES OF FEDERAL LEGISLATIVE HISTORY

There are four major sources of federal legislative history:

a. the bills introduced in Congress;
b. hearings before committees or subcommittees;
c. floor debates in the House and the Senate;
d. committee reports.

These sources are listed in order from least authoritative to most authoritative. Although some of these sources are generally considered to have more weight than others, none should be viewed in isolation. Each item contributes to the documentation of the legislature's intent. In fact, you may find that the documents contain information that is either contradictory or equally as ambiguous as the underlying statute. It is rare when an inquiry into legislative history will give you a definitive answer to a question of statutory interpretation. What is more likely is that the documents will equip you with information you can use to support your arguments for the proper interpretation of the statute.

a. Bills

The bill as introduced into Congress, and any later versions of the bill, can be helpful in determining congressional intent. Changes in language and addition or deletion of specific provisions may shed light on the goal the legislature was attempting to accomplish with the bill. Analysis of changes to a bill, however, requires speculation about the reasons behind the changes. Consequently, this is often considered an insufficient indication of legislative intent unless it is combined with other materials indicating intent to achieve a particular objective.

b. Hearings

Hearings before committees and subcommittees consist of the testimony of experts and interested parties called to give their views on the bill. Documents from these hearings may contain transcripts of testimony, reports, studies, or any other information requested by or submitted to the hearing committee. Unlike interpretation of different versions of a bill, interpretation of hearings does not require speculation. The individuals or groups providing information usually give detailed explanations and justifications for their positions.

Congress uses hearings to gather information. As a consequence, individuals or groups with opposing views are often represented, and their goal is to persuade Congress to act in a particular way. This results in the inclusion of information both for and against the legislation in the hearing documents. Sometimes it is possible to ascertain whether material from a particular source motivated Congress to act in a particular way, but this is not always the case. Therefore, hearing documents must be used carefully in determining congressional intent.

c. Floor Debates

Floor debates are another source of legislative history. They are published in a daily record of congressional proceedings called the *Congressional Record.* Unlike hearings, which include commentary that may or may not have been persuasive to the committee, floor debates consist of statements by the legislators themselves. Thus, the debates can be a source of information about Congress's intent in passing a bill. Debates may consist of transcripts of comments or exchanges taking place on the floor of Congress. In addition, members of Congress are permitted to submit prepared statements setting forth their views. Statements by a bill's sponsors may be especially useful in determining legislative intent. Different members of Congress may give different reasons for supporting legislation, however, and they are permitted to amend or supplement their statements after the fact. As a consequence, floor debates are not a definitive source for determining legislative intent.

d. Committee Reports

Committee reports are generally considered to be the most authoritative legislative history documents. They usually contain the committee's reasons for recommending the bill, a section-by-section analysis of the bill, and the views of any committee members who dissent from the committee's conclusions. If a bill is sent to a conference committee to work out compromise language, the conference committee usually prepares a report. This report discusses only the provisions that differed before the House and the Senate. It usually contains the agreed-upon language of the bill and an explanation of the compromise.

3. METHODS OF LOCATING FEDERAL LEGISLATIVE HISTORY DOCUMENTS

You can locate federal legislative history documents the same ways you locate most other forms of legal authority: by citation; by subject; and, for documents available online, by words in the document. Although federal legislative history documents have their own citations, those created in conjunction with legislation that is enacted into law are often organized by the bill number, public law number, or *Statutes at Large* citation associated with the legislation. Not all federal legislative history documents, however, are associated with legislation enacted into law. As a consequence, the methods you choose to research federal legislative history will depend on the type of material you need. If you are researching the history of an individual statute, your approach will be different than if you are looking for legislative activity on a particular subject without regard for whether a statute was passed on the topic.

If you are researching the history of an individual statute, it is important to remember that not all legislation is accompanied by all of the documents described above. A committee might elect not to hold hearings. Or the bill could be amended during floor debate, in which case the amendment would not have any history to be documented elsewhere. In addition, you may not always need to look at all of these documents to resolve your research question. If you are trying to determine Congress's intent in enacting a specific provision within a statute, and a committee report sets out the goals Congress was attempting to accomplish with that provision, you might not need to go any further in your research. Often, however, the committee reports will not discuss the provision you need to interpret. In that case, you may need to delve further into the legislative history, reviewing floor debates or hearings to see if the provision was discussed in either of those sources. In other instances, you may need to compile a complete legislative history.

Your research path will depend largely on the scope of your assignment. You will almost always begin with the statute itself. From there, you should be able to use the bill number, public law number, or *Statutes at Large* citation to locate documents relating to the statute. In most cases, you will want to begin by reviewing committee reports. If the committee reports do not address your question, you will then need to assess which other sources of legislative history are likely to assist you and which research tools provide the most efficient means of accessing those documents. If your research takes you beyond readily accessible committee reports, you may want to consult with a reference librarian for assistance in compiling the relevant documents. Remember also that a statute may be amended after its original enactment. Legislative history documents relevant to any amendments will be associated with the bill numbers, public law numbers, or *Statutes at Large* citations of the amending legislation.

If you are trying to find out about legislative activity on a specific topic, rather than the history of an individual statute, you will need to conduct subject or word searches. Because most bills are not passed into law, you may find documents relating to bills that have expired. In addition, you may locate documents unrelated to a bill. For example, committees can hold hearings on any subject within their jurisdiction, even if no legislation on the subject has been introduced.

Some research tools lend themselves more easily than others to subject and word searching, and some are more comprehensive in their coverage than others. Therefore, you will need to determine how much information you need, such as whether you need information on bills that have expired as well as existing legislation, and how far back in time you want to search. Again, you would be well advised to consult with a reference librarian for assistance in developing your research plan for this type of research.

The remainder of this chapter discusses methods for locating legislative history documents. The next section discusses print research tools that are accessible at many law libraries. Legislative history, however, is often easiest to research online. In particular, using government websites and commercial subscription services may be the most economical and user-friendly ways to locate federal legislative history.

B. RESEARCHING FEDERAL LEGISLATIVE HISTORY IN PRINT

Two print sources of legislative history are available in many law libraries:

1. compiled legislative histories containing all of the legislative history documents on a statute;
2. *United States Code Congressional and Administrative News,* or U.S.C.C.A.N., which contains selected committee reports on bills passed into law.

1. COMPILED LEGISLATIVE HISTORIES

Legislative histories for major pieces of legislation are sometimes compiled and published as separate volumes. In this situation, an author or publisher collects all of the legislative history documents on the legislation and publishes them in a single place. If a legislative history on the statute you are researching has already been compiled, your work has been done for you. Therefore, if you are researching a major piece of legislation, you should begin by looking for a compiled legislative history.

There are two ways to locate a compiled legislative history. The first is to look in the online catalog in your library. Compiled legislative histories can be published as individual books that are assigned call numbers and placed on the shelves. The second is to look for the statute in a reference source listing compiled legislative histories. One example of this type of reference book is *Sources of Compiled Legislative Histories: A Bibliography of Government Documents, Periodical Articles, and Books,* by Nancy P. Johnson. This book will refer you to books, government documents, and periodical articles that either reprint the legislative history for the statute or, at a minimum, contain citations to and discussion of the legislative history. This book is organized by public law number, so you would need to know the public law number of the statute to get started. You should be able to find the public law number following code sections in U.S.C. or an annotated code. HeinOnline, a subscription service discussed more fully below, has an online directory of compiled legislative histories derived from Professor Johnson's book. Another good reference for compiled legislative histories is *Federal Legislative Histories: An Annotated Bibliography and Index to Officially Published Sources,* by Bernard D. Reams, Jr.

2. UNITED STATES CODE CONGRESSIONAL AND ADMINISTRATIVE NEWS

United States Code Congressional and Administrative News, or U.S.C.C.A.N., is a readily available source of committee reports on bills passed into law. For each session of Congress, U.S.C.C.A.N. publishes a series of volumes containing, among other things, the text of laws passed by Congress (organized by *Statutes at Large* citation) and selected committee reports. References to reports in U.S.C.C.A.N. usually include the year the book was published and the starting page of the document. Thus, to find a report cited as 1996 U.S.C.C.A.N. 2166, you would need to locate the 1996 edition of U.S.C.C.A.N., find the volumes labeled "Legislative History," and turn to page 2166. U.S.C.C.A.N. does not reprint all committee reports for all legislation. Nevertheless, U.S.C.C.A.N. is often a good starting place for research into committee reports because it is available at many law libraries and is fairly easy to use.

FIGURE 8.2 EXCERPT FROM ANNOTATIONS ACCOMPANYING 18 U.S.C.A. § 2441

U.S.C.C.A.N. references

HISTORICAL AND STATUTORY NOTES

Revision Notes and Legislative Reports

1996 Acts. House Report No. 104–698, see 1996 U.S. Code Cong. and Adm. News, p. 2166.

House Report No. 104–788, see 1996 U.S. Code Cong. and Adm. News, p. 4021.

1997 Acts. House Conference Report No. 105–401, see 1997 U.S. Code Cong. and Adm. News, p. 2896.

2002 Acts. House Conference Report No. 107–685 and Statement by President, see 2002 U.S. Code Cong. and Adm. News, p. 1120.

2006 Acts. Statement by President, see 2006 U.S. Code Cong. and Adm. News, p. S61.

References in Text

Section 101 of the Immigration and Nationality Act, referred to in subsec. (b), is section 101 of Act June 27, 1952, c. 477, Title I, 66 Stat. 166, which is classified to section 1101 of Title 8, Aliens and Nationality.

Common Article 3, referred to in subsec. (c)(3) and (d), probably means Common Article 3 of the Geneva Convention Relative to the Treatment of Prisoners of War, Aug. 12, 1949, 6 U.S.T. 3316, 75 U.N.T.S. 135; the text of Common Arti-

U.S.C.C.A.N. is a West publication; therefore, you can find cross-references to it in the annotations in U.S.C.A. The cross-references are usually listed in the Historical and Statutory Notes section of the annotations. If the statute has been amended, the Historical and Statutory Notes section will explain the major changes resulting from later enactments, and the legislative history section of the Historical and Statutory Notes will refer you to the year and page number of any committee reports reprinted in U.S.C.C.A.N. **Figure 8.2** shows U.S.C.C.A.N. references in U.S.C.A., and **Figure 8.3** shows the starting page of a committee report in U.S.C.C.A.N.

C. RESEARCHING FEDERAL LEGISLATIVE HISTORY ONLINE

Most legislative history research is conducted online. In particular, government websites can be extremely useful in legislative history research. No matter which online source you use, your research strategy will still largely be governed by whether you are looking for information on an individual statute or searching by subject.

As with print research, online research into the legislative history of an individual statute is easiest if you have a citation identifying the legislation. Most online services will allow you to search using a bill number, public law number, or *Statutes at Large* citation. Conducting a word search using the popular name of an act is also an effective strategy. Simply searching by topic or with general keywords is the least effi-

FIGURE 8.3 **STARTING PAGE, HOUSE JUDICIARY COMMITTEE REPORT ON THE WAR CRIMES ACT OF 1996**

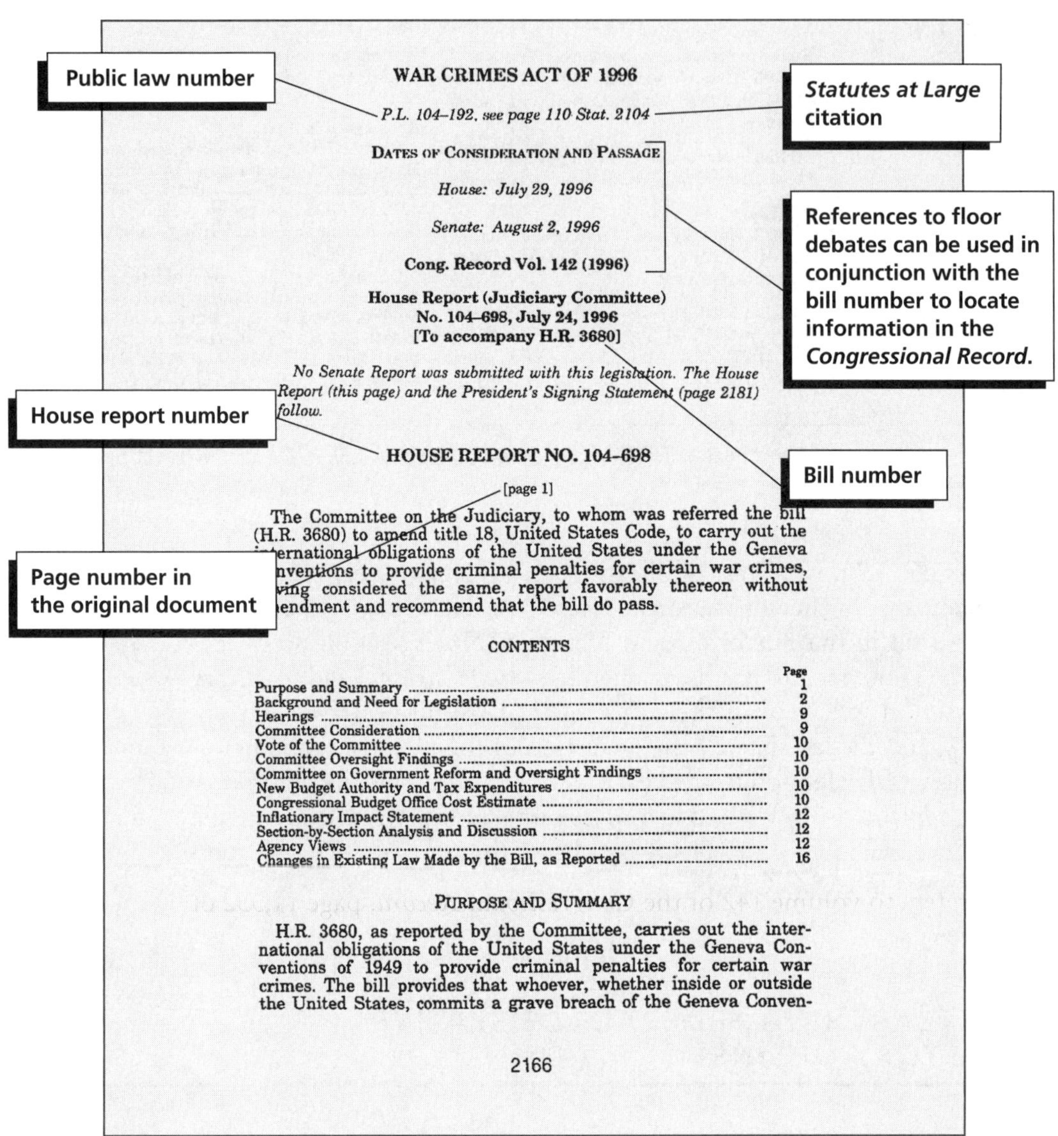

WAR CRIMES ACT OF 1996

P.L. 104–192, see page 110 Stat. 2104

DATES OF CONSIDERATION AND PASSAGE

House: July 29, 1996

Senate: August 2, 1996

Cong. Record Vol. 142 (1996)

House Report (Judiciary Committee)
No. 104–698, July 24, 1996
[To accompany H.R. 3680]

No Senate Report was submitted with this legislation. The House Report (this page) and the President's Signing Statement (page 2181) follow.

HOUSE REPORT NO. 104–698

[page 1]

The Committee on the Judiciary, to whom was referred the bill (H.R. 3680) to amend title 18, United States Code, to carry out the international obligations of the United States under the Geneva Conventions to provide criminal penalties for certain war crimes, having considered the same, report favorably thereon without amendment and recommend that the bill do pass.

CONTENTS

PURPOSE AND SUMMARY

H.R. 3680, as reported by the Committee, carries out the international obligations of the United States under the Geneva Conventions of 1949 to provide criminal penalties for certain war crimes. The bill provides that whoever, whether inside or outside the United States, commits a grave breach of the Geneva Conven-

2166

cient means of researching material on an individual statute. It is possible that you could miss important documents if you do not have the correct terms in the search; in addition, you are likely to retrieve material on other pieces of legislation unrelated to your research. By contrast, topic or keyword searching is most effective when you want to find out about legislative activity on a particular subject.

The scope of your project will also affect which online source you choose. Some provide access to the full range of legislative history documents (bill versions, hearings, floor debates, and committee reports). Others are more limited in their coverage. It is important to choose a service that includes the documents you need.

One form of legislative history you can research online is floor debates in the *Congressional Record.* The *Congressional Record* is the record of all activity on the floor of the House and Senate. To research the *Congressional Record* effectively, you need to understand how it is published.

A new volume of the *Congressional Record* is published for each session of Congress. While Congress is in session, the current volume of the *Congressional Record* is published daily in print as a softcover pamphlet; this is called the daily edition. **Figure 8.4** is an excerpt from the daily edition. At the end of each session of Congress, the daily editions are compiled into a hardbound print set; this is called the permanent edition.

The material in these two editions should be identical, but the pages in each are numbered differently. The daily edition is separated into different sections, including sections for House (H) and Senate (S) materials, and the pages within each section are numbered separately. In the permanent edition, all of the pages are numbered consecutively. References to the *Congressional Record* will vary, therefore, depending on whether they are to the permanent or daily edition. References to either edition will give the volume and page number, but the page numbering will differ for each edition. Thus, 142 Cong. Rec. H8620 refers to volume 142 of the *Congressional Record,* page 8,620 of the House section of the daily edition. The "H" before the page number alerts you that the reference is to the daily edition. By contrast, a citation to 142 Cong. Rec. 11,352 refers to volume 142 of the *Congressional Record,* page 11,352 of the permanent edition. Because the page number contains no letter designation, the reference is to the permanent edition.

Some online services provide access only to the daily edition. This can affect your research in two ways. First, if you have a citation to a floor debate in the permanent edition of the *Congressional Record,* you may not be able to retrieve it in a service that only provides access to the daily edition. Second, if you locate a floor debate using a word search, the document you retrieve may be from the daily edition even if it is several years old. This may affect your ability to cite the material properly.

Another thing to be aware of when you conduct online legislative history research concerns hearings. Some online services provide access to testimony provided at hearings, which consists of transcripts of testimony and prepared statements of witnesses, but not to reports, studies, or other documents submitted to the committee. Therefore, if you need the complete content of a congressional hearing, you must choose your research source carefully and may need to obtain the document in print or microfiche.

FIGURE 8.4 *CONGRESSIONAL RECORD*, DAILY EDITION

Comments on the War Crimes Act in the House of Representatives

H8620 CONGRESSIONAL RECORD—HOUSE *July 29, 1996*

Mr. Speaker, H.R. 740, introduced by the gentleman from New Mexico [Mr. SCHIFF] and the gentleman from New Mexico [Mr. SKEEN] would permit the Pueblo of Isleta Indian Tribe to file a claim in the U.S. Court of Federal Claims for certain aboriginal lands acquired from the tribe by the United States. The tribe was erroneously advised by the Bureau of Indian Affairs in regard to this claim, and as a result never filed a claim for aboriginal lands before the expiration of the statute of limitations.

The court's jurisdiction would apply only to claims accruing on or before August 13, 1946, as provided in the Indian Claims Commission Act.

The Pueblo of Isleta Tribe seeks the opportunity to present the merits of its aboriginal land claims, which otherwise would be barred as untimely. The tribe cites numerous precedents for conferring jurisdiction under similar circumstances, such as the case of the Zuni Indian Tribe in 1978.

An identical bill passed the Senate in the 103d Congress, but was not considered by the House. In the 102d Congress, H.R. 1206, amended to the current language, passed the House, but was not considered by the Senate before adjournment. On June 11, 1996, the Judiciary Committee favorably reported this bill by unanimous voice vote.

Mr. Speaker, I reserve the balance of my time.

Mr. SCOTT. Mr. Speaker, I yield myself such time as I may consume.

Mr. Speaker, I think the bill has been explained that was introduced by the gentleman from New Mexico [Mr. SKEEN] and the gentleman from New Mexico [Mr. SCHIFF]. It is a fair bill, and I would just urge colleagues to support it at this time.

Mr. Speaker, I yield back the balance of my time.

Mr. RICHARDSON. Mr. Speaker, I wish to extend my strong support for H.R. 740 which deals with the Pueblo of Isleta Indian land claims. H.R. 740 comes before Congress for a vote which will correct a 45-year-old injustice. In 1951, the Pueblo of Isleta was given erroneous advice by employees of the Bureau of Indian Affairs regarding the nature of the claim the Pueblo could mount under the Indian Claims Commission Act of 1946. This is documented and supported by testimony. The Pueblo was not made aware of the fact that a land claim could be made based upon aboriginal use and occupancy. As a result, it lost the opportunity to make such a claim.

The Pueblo of Isleta was a victim of circumstances beyond its control, and this bill is an opportunity for us to correct this wrong. No expenditure or appropriations of funds are provided for in this bill: only the opportunity for the Pueblo to make a claim for aboriginal lands which the Isletas believe to be rightfully theirs. This bill may be the last chance for the United States to correct an injustice which occurred many years ago because of misinformation from the BIA.

Therefore, I urge my colleagues to support H.R. 740.

Mr. SMITH of Texas. Mr. Speaker, I have no further requests for time, and I yield back the balance of my time.

The SPEAKER pro tempore. The question is on the motion offered by the gentleman from Texas [Mr. SMITH] that the House suspend the rules and pass the bill, H.R. 740.

The question was taken; and (two-thirds having voted in favor thereof) the rules were suspended and the bill was passed.

A motion to reconsider was laid on the table.

WAR CRIMES ACT OF 1996

Mr. SMITH of Texas. Mr. Speaker, I move to suspend the rules and pass the bill (H.R. 3680) to amend title 18, United States Code, to carry out the international obligations of the United States under the Geneva Conventions to provide criminal penalties for certain war crimes.

The Clerk read as follows:

H.R. 3680

Be it enacted by the Senate and House of Representatives of the United States of America in Congress assembled,

SECTION 1. SHORT TITLE.

This Act may be cited as the "War Crimes Act of 1996".

SEC. 2. CRIMINAL PENALTIES FOR CERTAIN WAR CRIMES.

(a) IN GENERAL.—Title 18, United States Code, is amended by inserting after chapter 117 the following:

"CHAPTER 118—WAR CRIMES

"Sec.

"2401. War crimes.

"§ 2401. War crimes

"(a) OFFENSE.—Whoever, whether inside or outside the United States, commits a grave breach of the Geneva Conventions, in any of the circumstances described in subsection (b), shall be fined under this title or imprisoned for life or any term of years, or both, and if death results to the victim, shall also be subject to the penalty of death.

"(b) CIRCUMSTANCES.—The circumstances referred to in subsection (a) are that the person committing such breach or the victim of such breach is a member of the armed forces of the United States or a national of the United States (as defined in section 101 of the Immigration and Nationality Act).

"(c) DEFINITIONS.—As used in this section, the term 'grave breach of the Geneva Conventions' means conduct defined as a grave breach in any of the international conventions relating to the laws of warfare signed at Geneva 12 August 1949 or any protocol to any such convention, to which the United States is a party."

(b) CLERICAL AMENDMENT.—The table of chapters for part I of title 18, United States Code, is amended by inserting after the item relating to chapter 117 the following new item:

"118. War crimes .... 2401".

The SPEAKER pro tempore. Pursuant to the rule, the gentleman from Texas [Mr. SMITH] and the gentleman from Virginia [Mr. SCOTT] each will control 20 minutes.

The Chair recognizes the gentleman from Texas [Mr. SMITH].

GENERAL LEAVE

Mr. SMITH of Texas. Mr. Speaker, I ask unanimous consent that all Members may have 5 legislative days to revise and extend their remarks on the bill under consideration.

The SPEAKER pro tempore. Is there objection to the request of the gentleman from Texas?

There was no objection.

Mr. SMITH of Texas. Mr. Speaker, I yield myself such time as I may consume.

Mr. Speaker, H.R. 3680 is designed to implement the Geneva conventions for the protection of victims of war. Our colleague, the gentleman from North Carolina, WALTER JONES, should be commended for introducing this bill and for his dedication to such a worthy goal.

☐ 1445

Mr. Speaker, the Geneva Conventions of 1949 codified rules of conduct for military forces to which we have long adhered. In 1955 Deputy Under Secretary of State Robert Murphy testified to the Senate that—

> The Geneva Conventions are another long step forward towards mitigating the severity of war on its helpless victims. They reflect enlightened practices as carried out by the United States and other civilized countries, and they represent largely what the United States would do, whether or not a party to the Conventions. Our own conduct has served to establish higher standards and we can only benefit by having them incorporated in a stronger body of wartime law.

Mr. Speaker, the United States ratified the Conventions in 1955. However, Congress has never passed implementing legislation.

The Conventions state that signatory countries are to enact penal legislation punishing what are called grave breaches, actions such as the deliberate killing of prisoners of war, the subjecting of prisoners to biological experiments, the willful infliction of great suffering or serious injury on civilians in occupied territory.

While offenses covering grave breaches can in certain instances be prosecutable under present Federal law, even if they occur overseas, there are a great number of instances in which no prosecution is possible. Such nonprosecutable crimes might include situations where American prisoners of war are killed, or forced to serve in the Army of their captors, or American doctors on missions of mercy in foreign war zones are kidnapped or murdered. War crimes are not a thing of the past, and Americans can all too easily fall victim to them.

H.R. 3680 was introduced in order to implement the Geneva Conventions. It prescribes severe criminal penalties for anyone convicted of committing, whether inside or outside the United States, a grave breach of the Geneva Conventions, where the victim or the perpetrator is a member of our Armed Forces. In future conflicts H.R. 3680 may very well deter acts against Americans that violate the laws of war.

Mr. Speaker, I urge my colleagues to support this legislation, and I reserve the balance of my time.

Mr. SCOTT. Mr. Speaker, I yield myself such time as I may consume.

Mr. Speaker, as the gentleman from Texas has fully explained, H.R. 3680 implements this country's international

1. COMMERCIAL SERVICES

Westlaw, Lexis Advance, and Bloomberg Law provide access to many legislative history documents.

Westlaw provides access to the full text of bills introduced in Congress, selected committee reports, floor debates in the *Congressional Record*, and congressional testimony, although not complete hearing documents. If you are searching for the history of an individual statute, the **History** tab accompanying the statute will list references to legislative history documents and will link to those available through Westlaw. Additionally, if you retrieve a statute by public law number, Westlaw provides the legislative history documents associated with the bill.

Westlaw also provides access to compiled legislative histories for certain major pieces of legislation. To locate this collection, select **Legislative History** and follow the link to **Arnold & Porter Legislative Histories.** You can access the **Legislative History** link from the **All Content** tab or by selecting **Statutes & Court Rules** and looking in the **Tools & Resources** section on the right.

Lexis Advance provides access to similar legislative history material, including full text of bills introduced in Congress, selected committee reports, and floor debates in the *Congressional Record.* The dates of coverage and access to congressional hearings may vary depending on the type of subscription a user has. The easiest way to search for information on a specific statute is by public law number. The search results will include a link to the public law document. A link to **View references to** the public law appears in the top left corner of the search result screen. Following this link will open a list of documents that refer to the public law, including any legislative history documents available in Lexis Advance. If you open the document containing the public law, you can view a **Bill Tracking** report, which also contain links to some legislative documents. Additionally, filtering options under **Statutes & Legislation** in word searches or within the **Browse** menu will allow you to identify legislative history documents.

Bloomberg Law also provides access to the full text of bills introduced in Congress, selected committee reports, floor debates in the *Congressional Record,* and testimony from congressional hearings, but not always complete hearing documents. If you are searching for the history of an individual statute, you can execute a source-driven search by searching **U.S. Legislative** and using the public law number or the popular name of the act as a search term. If you execute a content-driven search, legislative history documents will be included in the search results.

2. GOVERNMENT WEBSITES

The federal government provides free access to many legislative history documents through Congress.gov and govinfo, a website maintained by the Government Printing Office (GPO). The URLs for both of these sites are listed in Appendix A.

Congress.gov will provide you with the text of bills introduced, House and Senate roll call votes, public laws, the text of the *Congressional Record,* committee reports, and other information on the legislative process, although not congressional hearings or testimony. You have several search options in Congress.gov. You can browse or search by public law number, report number, or committee name. Word searching is also available. You can search for documents issued during a particular

FIGURE 8.5 INTRODUCTORY SCREEN FOR CONGRESS.GOV

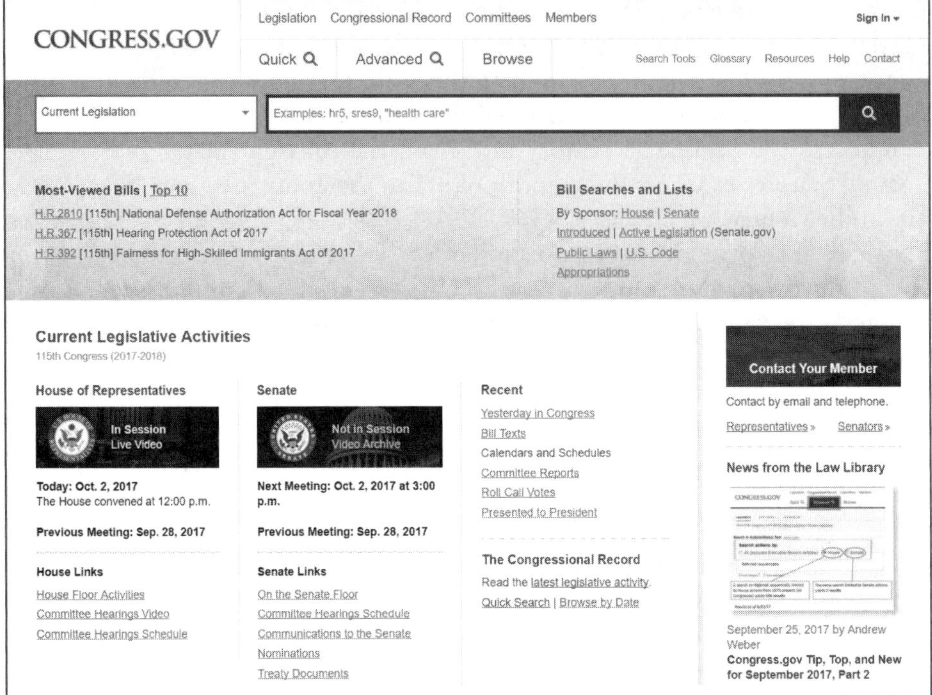

session of Congress, or you can search multiple sessions simultaneously. To access the *Congressional Record*, you can retrieve an individual issue, browse the contents of individual issues, or execute a word search. The introductory screen for Congress.gov appears in **Figure 8.5**.

An effective way to locate the history of an individual piece of legislation in Congress.gov is with the public law or bill number. You can use either number to retrieve an entry with information about the legislation. The tabs in the entry contain the text of the statute and links to all of the legislative history documents in Congress.gov's database, including committee reports and floor debates in the *Congressional Record.*

GPO's govinfo also provides access to legislative information. It is a relatively new site that is the successor to the Federal Digital System (FDSys), GPO's prior repository for government information. **Figure 8.6** shows some of the search options on govinfo. It provides access to the text of bills introduced into Congress, selected reports and hearings, and the *Congressional Record.* If you search for a bill or public law, you can download a text or .pdf version of the document. The **Related Documents** tab will list and link to legislative history documents on the legislation. You can also use govinfo to access congressional hearings. The hearing documents are .pdf versions of the print documents, so they contain the complete hearing content, including attachments and other documents, not just testimony.

FIGURE 8.6 INTRODUCTORY SCREEN FOR GOVINFO

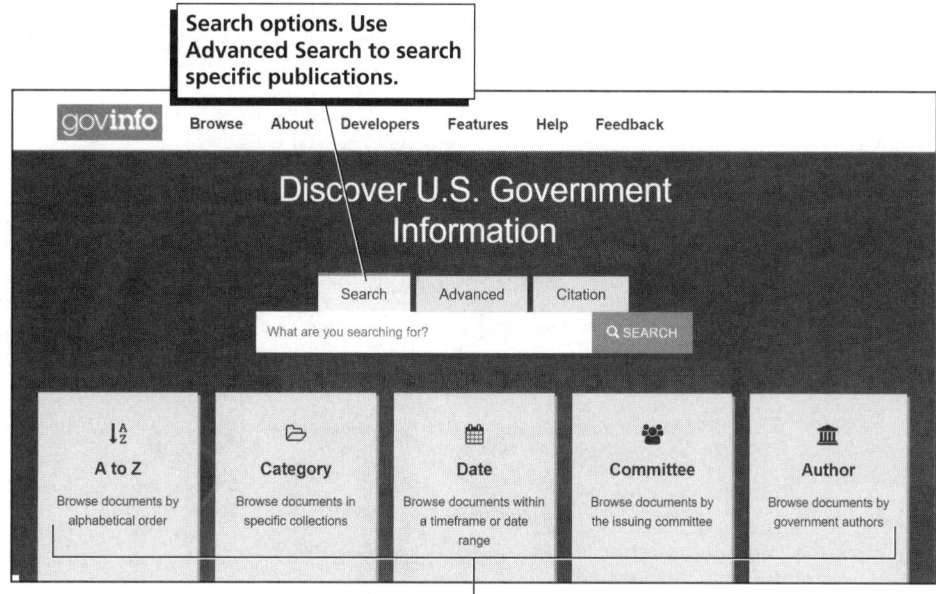

You will find it easiest to locate legislative history documents on a statute by searching with the public law number, bill number, or popular name of the act. Otherwise, if you know the type of document you want, you can retrieve it directly by citation or by browsing by session of Congress. General word searching is the least efficient way to search for information on a specific statute.

Congress.gov and govinfo add documents to their databases regularly, but neither provides complete historical access to legislative documents. For many types of information, coverage extends to the early 1970s. Unless you are researching older legislative documents, however, these government websites are excellent tools to use.

3. SUBSCRIPTION SERVICES

HeinOnline and ProQuest Congressional are two subscription services available at many law libraries that you can use for federal legislative history research. HeinOnline is best known for its comprehensive database of legal periodicals, but it also contains many other types of information, including legislative documents. HeinOnline has a database of compiled legislative histories derived from Nancy P. Johnson's reference book, *Sources of Compiled Legislative Histories: A Bibliography of Government Documents, Periodical Articles, and Books.* This database provides citations to many compiled legislative histories and full-text access to

FIGURE 8.7 HEINONLINE *SOURCES OF COMPILED LEGISLATIVE HISTORIES* ENTRY

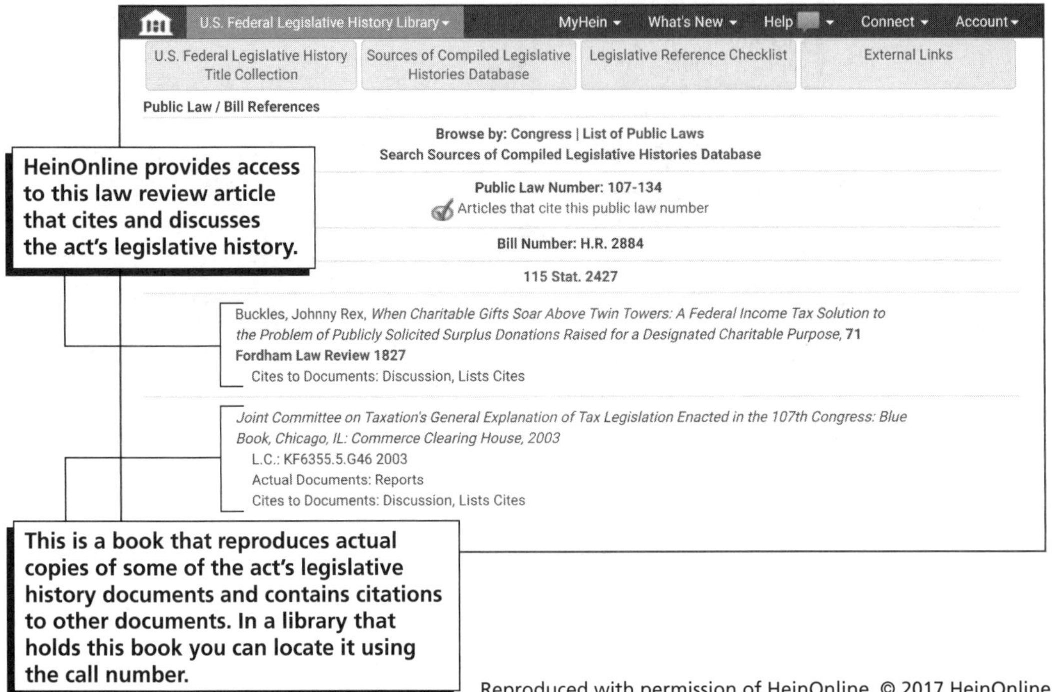

some. **Figure 8.7** shows an entry from this directory. HeinOnline also has its own collection of compiled legislative histories, the U.S. Federal Legislative History Title Collection. This is a database containing full-text legislative histories on major pieces of legislation. Many of these compiled legislative histories contain complete .pdf versions of the legislative documents, including hearings.

In addition to the compiled legislative histories, HeinOnline also has databases with individual congressional documents such as committee reports and complete hearing documents. Another feature, the *Congressional Record* Daily to Bound Locator, allows you to use a citation to the daily edition of the *Congressional Record* within the permanent edition.

ProQuest Congressional is a commercial research service that provides online access to a comprehensive set of legislative documents. Its Legislative Insight database is useful for legislative history research and includes committee reports, bills, and the *Congressional Record.* Access to hearings depends on the type of subscription your library has. You may have access to hearing testimony or complete hearing documents.

Within Legislative Insight, you can search the full text of the documents in its database, or you can search by number. The easiest way to locate all of the available documents on a piece of legislation is to search by number using the bill number, public law number, or *Statutes at Large* citation. Searching this way retrieves an entry that lists the legislative history documents associated with the statute. You can retrieve the full text

FIGURE 8.8 SEARCH OPTIONS FOR CONGRESSIONAL PUBLICATIONS IN PROQUEST LEGISLATIVE INSIGHT

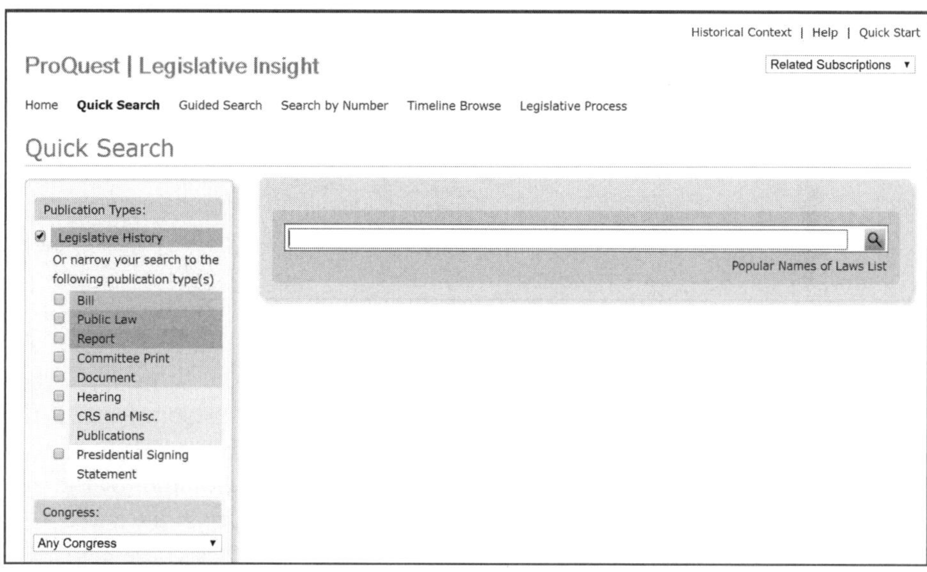

Reprinted with permission of ProQuest, ProQuest Legislative Insight search options. © 2017 ProQuest Congressional.

of a document by following the appropriate link. Full-text searching is also an option and is a good way to search for legislative information by topic. You can search for multiple types of documents, such as reports or hearings, simultaneously. **Figure 8.8** shows some of the search options for congressional documents.

D. CITING FEDERAL LEGISLATIVE HISTORY

Citations to legislative history documents are covered in the *ALWD Guide* (6th ed.) in Rule 15 and the *Bluebook* (20th ed.) in Bluepages B13 and Rule 13. This chapter discusses citations to committee reports and floor debates because those are the sources you are most likely to cite in a brief or memorandum.

In the *Bluebook*, the examples contained in Rule 13 show some of the congressional document abbreviations in large and small capital letters. According to Bluepages B2, however, citations to legislative documents in briefs and memoranda may appear in ordinary type.

1. COMMITTEE REPORTS

A citation to a committee report consists of four elements: (1) the abbreviation for the type of document; (2) the report number; (3) the pinpoint reference to the cited material; and (4) a parenthetical containing the date of the report. Here is an example:

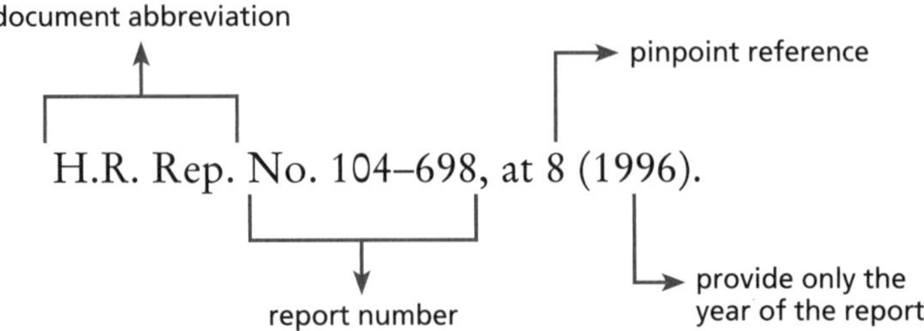

You should provide a parallel citation to U.S.C.C.A.N. if the report is reprinted there. A citation to a report reprinted in U.S.C.C.A.N. consists of six elements: (1) the report citation, as discussed above; (2) a notation that the citation is to a reprint of the document; (3) the year of the U.S.C.C.A.N. volume; (4) the publication name (U.S.C.C.A.N.); (5) the starting page of the report in U.S.C.C.A.N.; and (6) the pinpoint reference to the page in U.S.C.C.A.N. containing the cited material. Here is an example:

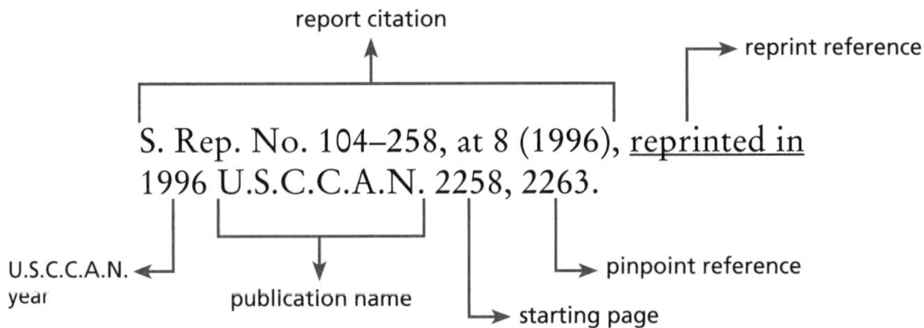

If you locate a report in U.S.C.C.A.N., you can still find the page numbers for the original document. Throughout the report, U.S.C.C.A.N. provides the page numbers of the original document in brackets.

2. FLOOR DEBATES

Floor debates are published in the *Congressional Record.* As explained earlier in this chapter, two versions of the *Congressional Record* are published. The daily edition is published during the current session of Congress, and the permanent edition is published at the close of the session. You should cite the permanent edition if possible. A citation to the permanent edition consists of four elements: (1) the volume number of the *Congressional Record;* (2) the abbreviation Cong. Rec.; (3) the page number with the information cited; and (4) a parenthetical containing the year.

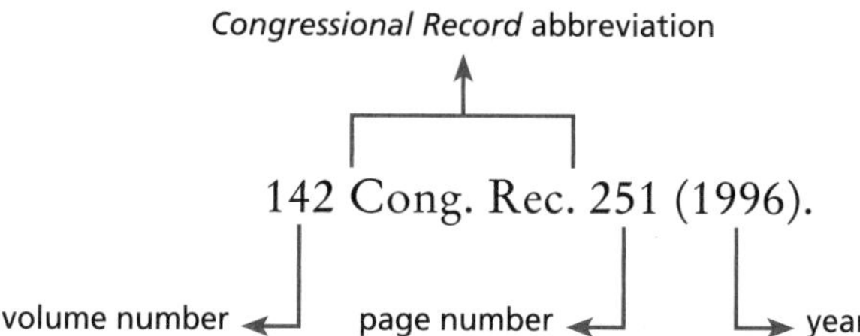

A citation to the daily edition contains the same elements, except that the parenthetical must indicate that the citation is to the daily edition and provide the exact date of the daily edition.

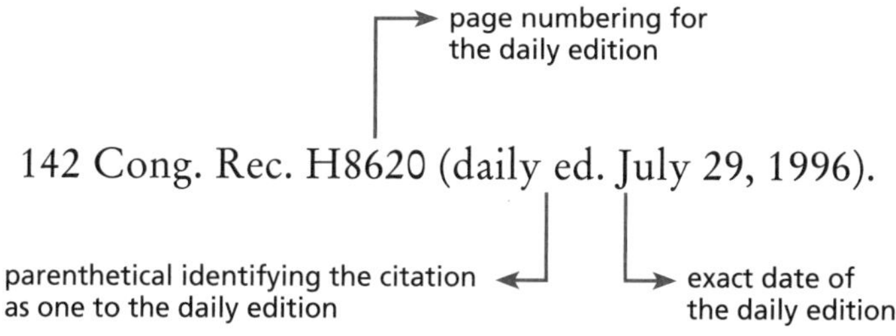

E. SAMPLE PAGES FOR FEDERAL LEGISLATIVE HISTORY RESEARCH

Beginning on the next page **Figures 8.9** through **8.12** contain sample pages illustrating what you would find if you researched legislative history documents associated with the War Crimes Act of 1996 using Congress.gov and govinfo.

Legislative history documents associated with the War Crimes Act of 1996 are available in Congress.gov. Searching by bill number, public law number, or the name of the act retrieves documents related to the legislation. Viewing the document with the bill text retrieves an entry that summarizes the legislation and includes tabs linking to reports, debates, and other information about the act.

FIGURE 8.9 **BILL SUMMARY IN CONGRESS.GOV**

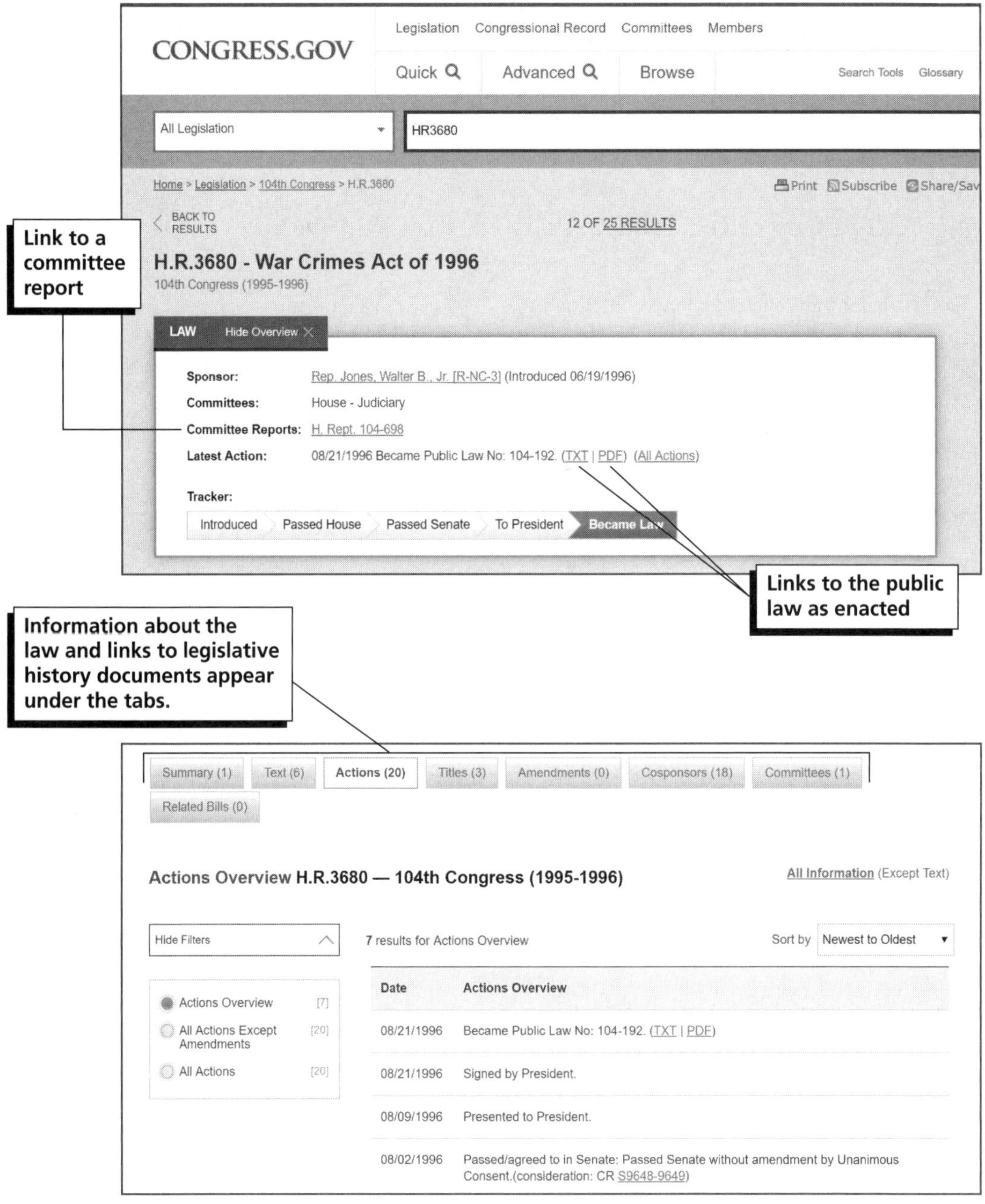

Following the link to House Report 104-698 retrieves the House Judiciary Committee report. Figure 8.10 shows the .pdf version of the report.

FIGURE 8.10 HOUSE JUDICIARY COMMITTEE REPORT IN CONGRESS.GOV

104TH CONGRESS 2d Session } HOUSE OF REPRESENTATIVES { REPORT 104–698

WAR CRIMES ACT OF 1996

JULY 24, 1996.—Committed to the Committee of the Whole House on the State of the Union and ordered to be printed

Mr. SMITH of Texas, from the Committee on the Judiciary, submitted the following

REPORT

[To accompany H.R. 3680]

[Including cost estimate of the Congressional Budget Office]

The Committee on the Judiciary, to whom was referred the bill (H.R. 3680) to amend title 18, United States Code, to carry out the international obligations of the United States under the Geneva Conventions to provide criminal penalties for certain war crimes, having considered the same, report favorably thereon without amendment and recommend that the bill do pass.

CONTENTS

PURPOSE AND SUMMARY

H.R. 3680, as reported by the Committee, carries out the international obligations of the United States under the Geneva Conventions of 1949 to provide criminal penalties for certain war crimes. The bill provides that whoever, whether inside or outside the United States, commits a grave breach of the Geneva Conven-

29–006

To locate legislative documents in govinfo, retrieve the public law by number to access an entry on the law.

FIGURE 8.11 SEARCH RESULTS IN GOVINFO, SUMMARY TAB

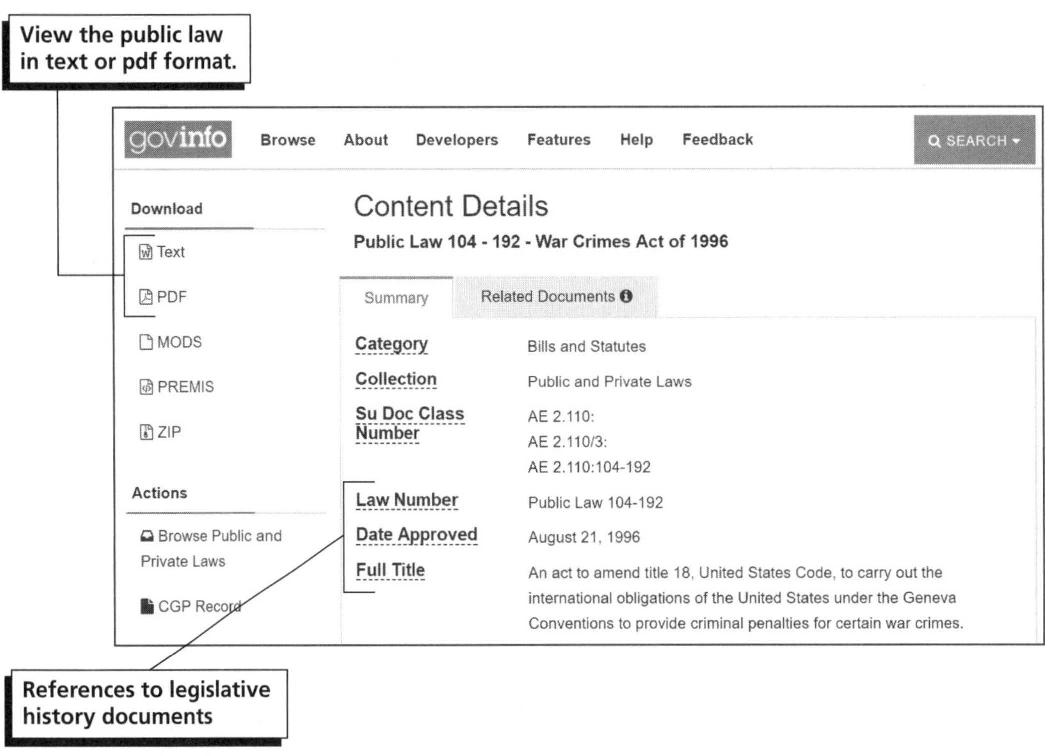

govinfo Browse About Developers Features Help Feedback SEARCH

Share

Bill Number: H.R. 3680

Report Number: H Rept. 104-698

Statutes at Large Citations: 110 Stat. 2104

Legislative History: LEGISLATIVE HISTORY--H.R. 3680:

HOUSE REPORTS: No. 104-698 (Comm. on the Judiciary).
CONGRESSIONAL RECORD, Vol. 142 (1996):
July 29, considered and passed House.
Aug. 2, considered and passed Senate.
WEEKLY COMPILATION OF PRESIDENTIAL DOCUMENTS, Vol. 32 (1996):
Aug. 21, Presidential statement.

References to legislative history documents

Under the Related Documents tab, you will find links to legislative history documents pertaining to the statute.

FIGURE 8.12 **SEARCH RESULTS IN GOVINFO, RELATED DOCUMENTS TAB**

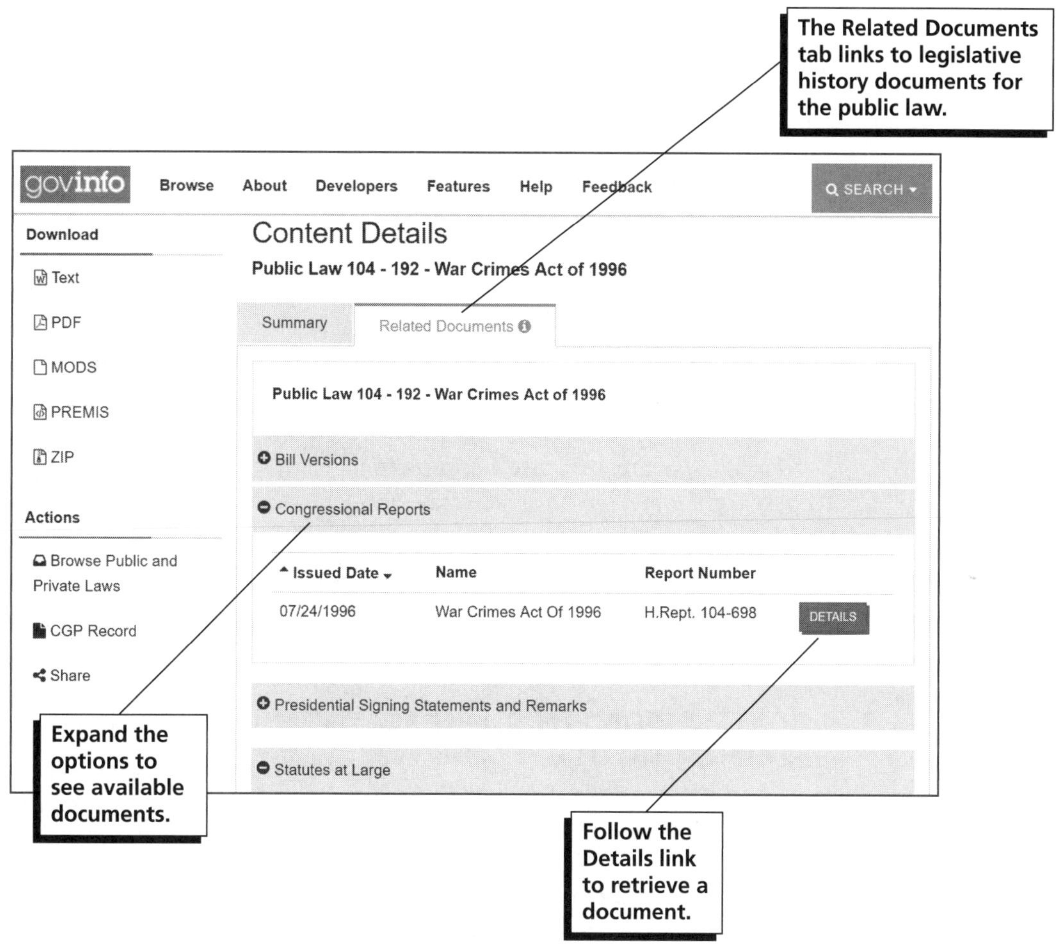

F. CHECKLIST FOR FEDERAL LEGISLATIVE HISTORY RESEARCH

1. IDENTIFY THE SCOPE OF YOUR RESEARCH

- ☐ Determine whether you need the history of an individual statute or material on a general subject.
- ☐ To research the history of an individual statute, begin by locating the statute.
  - The public law number should follow the statute in U.S.C. or an annotated code.
  - To determine congressional intent, start with committee reports; use U.S.C.C.A.N., a compiled legislative history, or an online source to locate committee reports.
  - For more comprehensive legislative history research, locate floor debates, hearings, and prior versions of the bill in addition to committee reports; use a compiled legislative history or an online source to locate a statute's complete legislative history.
- ☐ To research material on a general subject, use an online source to search by subject or keyword.
- ☐ If necessary, consult a reference librarian for assistance in determining the appropriate scope of your research and locating necessary documents.

2. LOCATE A COMPILED LEGISLATIVE HISTORY FOR A SPECIFIC STATUTE

- ☐ Search the library's online catalog for separately published legislative histories.
- ☐ Locate compiled legislative histories for major pieces of legislation in Westlaw under **Legislative History**.
- ☐ Use Johnson, *Sources of Compiled Legislative Histories,* U.S. Federal Legislative History Title Collection in HeinOnline, or Reams, *Federal Legislative Histories.*
- ☐ Search for legislative history by bill number, public law number, or *Statutes at Large* citation to collect all legislative history documents on an individual statute.

3. LOCATE COMMITTEE REPORTS, FLOOR DEBATES, AND OTHER LEGISLATIVE HISTORY DOCUMENTS FOR A SPECIFIC STATUTE

- ☐ In print, use annotations in U.S.C.A. to locate cross-references to committee reports reprinted in U.S.C.C.A.N.

- ☐ In Westlaw, retrieve a code section and locate references to legislative history documents under the **History** tab; retrieve a complete statute by public law number to locate selected legislative history documents for the statute.
- ☐ In Lexis Advance, search by public law number and use the link to **View references to** the bill or open the public law to review **Bill Tracking**; use choices under **Statutes & Legislation** in search results or the **Browse** menu to identify legislative history documents.
- ☐ In Bloomberg Law, use the public law or popular name of the act as a search term in **U.S. Legislative** to locate selected legislative history documents.
- ☐ In Congress.gov, search by bill number or public law number to retrieve the act; follow the links provided to view legislative history documents related to the statute.
- ☐ In govinfo, search by bill or public law number to retrieve the act; view the act in .pdf or text form; use the **Related Documents** tab for links to legislative history documents.
- ☐ In ProQuest Congressional, use Legislative Insight to search by bill number, public law number, or *Statutes at Large* citation to locate an entry listing documents related to the statute; use the links to retrieve the documents.

CHAPTER 9

Federal Administrative Law Research

A. INTRODUCTION TO FEDERAL ADMINISTRATIVE LAW

1. ADMINISTRATIVE AGENCIES AND REGULATIONS

Administrative agencies exist at all levels of government. Examples of federal administrative agencies include the Food and Drug Administration (FDA), the Environmental Protection Agency (EPA), and the Federal Communications Commission (FCC). Agencies are created by statute, but they are part of the executive branch because they "enforce" or implement a legislatively created scheme. In creating an agency, a legislature will pass what is known as "enabling" legislation. Enabling legislation defines the scope of the agency's mission and "enables" it to perform its functions, which may include promulgating regulations and adjudicating controversies, among other functions. If an agency is empowered to create regulations, those regulations cannot exceed the authority granted by the legislature. Thus, for example, while the FCC may be able to establish regulations concerning television licenses, it would not be able to promulgate regulations concerning the labeling of drugs because that would exceed the authority granted to it by Congress in its enabling legislation.

Federal agencies often create regulations to implement statutes passed by Congress. Sometimes Congress cannot legislate with the level of detail necessary to implement a complex legislative scheme. In those circumstances, Congress charges an agency with enforcing the statute, and the agency will develop procedures for implementing more general legislative mandates. In the Family and Medical Leave Act, for instance, Congress mandated that an employer allow an employee with a "serious health condition" to take unpaid medical leave. Pursuant to the statute, the Department of Labor has promulgated more specific regulations defining what "serious health condition" means.

In format, a regulation looks like a statute. It is, in essence, a rule created by a government entity, and many times administrative regulations are called "rules." In operation, they are indistinguishable from statutes, although the methods used to create, modify, and repeal them are different from those applicable to statutes. Federal administrative agencies are required to conform to the procedures set out in the Administrative Procedure Act (APA) in promulgating regulations. State agencies may be required to comply with similar statutes at the state level. Without going into too much detail, the APA frequently requires agencies to undertake the following steps: (1) notify the public when they plan to promulgate new regulations or change existing ones; (2) publish proposed regulations and solicit comments on them before the regulations become final; and (3) publish final regulations before they go into effect to notify the public of the new requirements.

At the federal level, regulations and proposed regulations are published in the *Federal Register.* The *Federal Register* is a daily publication reporting the activities of the executive branch of government. A new volume is published each year. It begins on the first business day of the new year with page one and is consecutively paginated from that point on until the last business day of the year.

After final regulations are published in the *Federal Register,* they are codified in the *Code of Federal Regulations* (C.F.R.). The C.F.R. is divided into 50 "Titles." The C.F.R. Titles are subdivided into chapters, which are usually named for the agencies issuing the regulations. Chapters are subdivided into Parts covering specific regulatory areas, and Parts are further subdivided into sections. To find a regulation, you would need to know its Title, Part, and section number. Thus, a citation to 16 C.F.R. § 1000.3 tells you that the regulation is published in Title 16 of the C.F.R. in Part 1000, section number 1000.3. **Figure 9.1** illustrates what federal regulations look like.

The C.F.R. is updated once a year in four separate installments. Titles 1 through 16 are updated on January 1 of each year, Titles 17 through 27 on April 1, Titles 28 through 41 on July 1, and Titles 42 through 50 on October 1. Because a new set of C.F.R. volumes is published annually, the C.F.R. is not updated with pocket parts. Instead, new or amended

FIGURE 9.1 **REGULATIONS IN 16 C.F.R. PART 1000**

SUBCHAPTER A—GENERAL

PART 1000—COMMISSION ORGANIZATION AND FUNCTIONS

AUTHORITY: 5 U.S.C. 552(a).

SOURCE: 71 FR 5165, Feb. 1, 2006, unless otherwise noted.

§ 1000.1 The Commission.

(a) The Consumer Product Safety Commission is an independent regulatory agency formed on May 14, 1973, under the provisions of the Consumer Product Safety Act (Pub. L. 92–573, 86 Stat. 1207, as amended (15 U.S.C. 2051, *et seq.*)). The purposes of the Commission under the CPSA are:

(1) To protect the public against unreasonable risks of injury associated with consumer products;

(2) To assist consumers in evaluating the comparative safety of consumer products;

(3) To develop uniform safety standards for consumer products and to minimize conflicting State and local regulations; and

(4) To promote research and investigation into the causes and prevention of product-related deaths, illnesses, and injuries.

(b) The Commission is authorized to consist of five members appointed by the President, by and with the advice and consent of the Senate, for terms of seven years. However, the Departments of Veterans Affairs and Housing and Urban Development, and Independent Agencies Appropriations Act, 1993, Public Law 102–389, limited funding to that for three Commissioners for fiscal year 1993 and thereafter.

§ 1000.2 Laws administered.

The Commission administers five acts:

(a) The Consumer Product Safety Act (Pub. L. 92–573, 86 Stat. 1207, as amended (15 U.S.C. 2051, *et seq.*)).

(b) The Flammable Fabrics Act (Pub. L. 90–189, 67 Stat. 111, as amended (15 U.S.C. 1191, *et seq.*)).

(c) The Federal Hazardous Substances Act (Pub. L. 86–613, 74 Stat. 380, as amended (15 U.S.C. 1261, *et seq.*)).

(d) The Poison Prevention Packaging Act of 1970 (Pub. L. 91–601, 84 Stat. 1670, as amended (15 U.S.C. 1471, *et seq.*)).

(e) The Refrigerator Safety Act of 1956 (Pub. L. 84–930, 70 Stat. 953, (15 U.S.C. 1211, *et seq.*)).

§ 1000.3 Hotline.

(a) The Commission operates a toll-free telephone Hotline by which the public can communicate with the Commission. The number for use in all 50 states is 1–800–638–CPSC (1–800–638–2772).

(b) The Commission also operates a toll-free Hotline by which hearing or speech-impaired persons can communicate with the Commission by teletypewriter. The teletypewriter number for use in all states is 1–800–638–8270.

9

regulations are published in the *Federal Register.* They are not codified within the C.F.R. until a new set is published.

2. METHODS OF LOCATING REGULATIONS

You can locate federal regulations in several ways. Three common techniques are searching by citation, by subject, or by words in the document. Once you know the Title and Part or section number of a regulation, you can locate it in within the C.F.R. An easy way to find citations to relevant regulations is through an annotated code. Because regulations implement statutory schemes, you will often begin regulatory research by consulting the enabling statute, and the statute's annotations may include citations to regulations. The annotations will not ordinarily direct you to a specific regulation; instead, they will direct you to the Title and Part of the C.F.R. with regulations applicable to the area of law you are researching.

Researching by subject is another useful way to locate regulations if you have access to the C.F.R. index. Each Title and Part of the C.F.R. also has a table of contents, which you can review to browse by subject. Reviewing the table of contents can be a difficult way to begin your research unless you know which agency promulgated the regulations you are trying to find. Once you find a relevant regulation, however, viewing the table of contents can help you find related regulations, as described more fully below.

Word searching is another way to locate regulations online. You can do a source-driven word search in a database limited to federal regulations or to a specific subject area. You can also do a content-driven search in Westlaw, Lexis Advance, or Bloomberg Law. As long as the search includes federal materials, federal regulations will appear in the search results. Because regulators often use technical terms in regulations, however, word searching can be more difficult than subject searching if you are not already familiar with the regulatory terminology.

Two additional avenues for regulatory research are the telephone and e-mail. Agency staff can be an invaluable resource for understanding the agency's operations, as well as for staying up to date on the agency's activities. If you practice in an area of law subject to agency regulation, do not hesitate to contact agency staff for information. Regulatory notices published in the *Federal Register* typically provide the name and contact information of an agency staff member who can provide additional information about the regulations.

Regulatory research is similar to statutory research in that you will often need to research interrelated regulations, not individual sections of the C.F.R., to answer your research question. Therefore, regardless of the search method you use initially to locate a relevant regulation, you should plan to expand your search to consider the entire regulatory scheme. Because online sources often retrieve individual regulations as separate documents, it is especially easy to lose sight of the need to research multiple sections. You can view the detailed outline of sections at the beginning of the Part, as illustrated in **Figure 9.1,** and browse preceding and subsequent sections of the C.F.R. to ensure that you consider all potentially applicable regulations.

Sections B and C, below, explain how to research regulations in print and online. Most researchers conduct C.F.R. research online because the federal government has made much regulatory material available through the Government Printing Office and agency websites. The online versions of official government sources, however, are updated on the same schedule as the print versions, and the process of updating regulations with official government sources, whether print or online, is the same. Therefore, information on updating regulatory research with official government sources appears in Section C, on online research. If you are updating federal regulations in print, you can follow the same steps using the print versions of the updating tools.

B. RESEARCHING FEDERAL REGULATIONS IN PRINT

1. LOCATING AND UPDATING REGULATIONS IN PRINT

Researching federal regulations entails two steps:

a. locating regulations;
b. updating your research.

This section describes how to complete these steps using print research resources.

a. Locating Regulations

The C.F.R. is published as a set of softcover books. Once you locate the C.F.R. set, the next question is how to find regulations relevant to your research issue. There are two ways to accomplish this. One way is to use the cross-references to the C.F.R. in U.S.C.S. or U.S.C.A. The other is to go directly to the C.F.R. itself, using a subject index to refer you to relevant C.F.R. provisions.

Because regulations are often used to implement statutory schemes, U.S.C.S. and U.S.C.A. frequently contain cross-references to applicable regulations. Thus, if your research leads you to statutes, the annotations are a useful tool to guide you toward regulations that bear on the area of law you are researching. You may recall from Chapter 7 that U.S.C.S. contains more extensive regulatory annotations than U.S.C.A. does. **Figure 9.2** shows C.F.R. cross-references in U.S.C.S. annotations.

FIGURE 9.2 **ANNOTATIONS TO 42 U.S.C.S. § 300V-1**

Cross-references to applicable regulations in U.S.C.S. statutory annotations

CODE OF FEDERAL REGULATIONS

Office of the Secretary of Agriculture—Protection of human subjects, 7 CFR 1c.101 et seq.

Department of Energy—Protection of human subjects, 10 CFR 745.101 et seq.

National Aeronautics and Space Administration—Protection of human subjects, 14 CFR 1230.101 et seq.

Office of the Secretary of Commerce—Protection of human subjects, 15 CFR 27.101 et seq.

Consumer Product Safety Commission—Protection of human subjects, 16 CFR 1028.101 et seq.

Agency for International Development—Protection of human subjects, 22 CFR 225.101 et seq.

Office of the Secretary, Department of Housing and Urban Development—Protection of human subjects, 24 CFR 60.101 et seq.

Department of Justice—Protection of human subjects, 28 CFR 46.101 et seq.

Office of the Secretary of Defense—Protection of human subjects, 32 CFR 219.101 et seq.

Office of the Secretary, Department of Education—Protection of human subjects, 34 CFR 97.101 et seq.

Department of Veterans Affairs—Protection of human subjects, 38 CFR 16.101 et seq.

Environmental Protection Agency—Protection of human subjects, 40 CFR 26.101 et seq.

Department of Health and Human Services—Protection of human subjects, 45 CFR 46.101 et seq.

Another way to locate regulations is to use the CFR Index and Finding Aids. This is a subject index within the C.F.R. set itself. Like all other C.F.R. volumes, it is a softcover book, and it is published annually.

b. Updating Regulations

As noted above, the C.F.R. is published once a year in four separate installments and is updated through the *Federal Register*, not with pocket parts. Updating C.F.R. research with the *Federal Register* is a two-step process:

- Use a monthly publication called the List of CFR Sections Affected (LSA) to find any *Federal Register* notices indicating that the regulation has been affected by agency action. Each monthly issue of the LSA is cumulative. Therefore, the current month's LSA will contain updates from the date of the latest C.F.R. volume through the end of the previous month.

- Use a cumulative table of CFR Parts Affected by agency action in the *Federal Register.* This table is published daily. It lists updates for the current month and will update your research from the last day covered by the LSA until the present.

These are the same steps you would follow to update your research using official government sources online. Therefore, they are explained in more detail in Section C, below.

2. USING A CITATOR FOR REGULATORY RESEARCH

Chapter 6 discusses citators and how to use them in conducting case research. Citators are also available for researching federal regulations. Regulatory citator entries typically contain lists of cases and other sources that have cited a regulation. As noted in Chapter 6, most law libraries no longer carry Shepard's in print. The online citators (Shepard's in Lexis Advance and KeyCite in Westlaw) are available for federal regulations, and they are explained in more detail in Section C, below.

Using a citator in regulatory research is useful for locating research references. Some administrative regulations are reproduced as part of the U.S.C.S. and U.S.C.A. print sets and may have limited annotations; however, the coverage is very limited. If you are researching in print you are likely to be working with unannotated regulations and will find a citator useful for locating cases interpreting a regulation. Even if you are using an annotated version of the C.F.R., the regulatory annotations often do not list every source that has cited the regulation. If the annotations are too sparse to give you the information you need about a regulation, you may find more complete information in a citator.

C. RESEARCHING FEDERAL REGULATIONS ONLINE

Lexis Advance, Westlaw, Bloomberg Law, and government websites are all useful sources for regulatory research. This section discusses search options in all of these sources. It also discusses use of online citators for regulatory research.

1. COMMERCIAL SOURCES

The C.F.R. is available in Lexis Advance, Westlaw, and Bloomberg Law. These services incorporate changes to regulations as they appear in the

Federal Register so that the version of the C.F.R. in these services is ordinarily up to date. You can verify whether the regulation is current by checking the updating date for the regulation. The *Federal Register* is also available in these services, although the continuous updating of the C.F.R. makes it unnecessary to use the *Federal Register* for updating regulations. The continuous updates also mean, however, that the versions of the C.F.R. in these services are not official sources for regulations. If you need the official source, you must use a print or online government source for the C.F.R. and *Federal Register.*

The C.F.R. in Lexis Advance is annotated. Annotations follow the regulation's text. You can retrieve federal regulations and *Federal Register* entries by entering a citation in the search box. The U.S.C.S. annotations in Lexis Advance also provide links to regulations.

To execute a source-driven search from the **Explore Content** menu, select the C.F.R. under the **Federal** tab. You can also use the **Browse** menu to search for the C.F.R. as a **Source**. Going through the **Browse** menu allows you to browse the table of contents or execute a word search in the C.F.R. If you execute a content-driven search that includes federal materials, use the narrowing options to filter the results for references to the C.F.R.

You can Shepardize a regulation you are viewing by following the ***Shepardize*® this document** link. You can also type *shep:* and the citation in the search box to access Shepard's. The Shepard's entry will list cases and other sources that have cited the regulation.

Westlaw also provides access to an annotated version of the C.F.R. The document will be accompanied by tabs with annotations and KeyCite information. You can retrieve federal regulations and *Federal Register* entries from their citations. In addition, the U.S.C.A. annotations in Westlaw provide some links to regulations.

You can execute a source-driven search by selecting the C.F.R. database from the **Browse** on the home page. Once you select the database, the table of contents will appear, and you can execute a search within the C.F.R. using the search box at the top of the screen. In the **Tools and Resources** section on the right, you will see additional search options, including the CFR Index. The search results screen will show a variety of options for filtering the search results. If you execute a content-driven search that includes federal materials, the results will include a section with **Regulations.**

Similarly, Bloomberg Law allows you to retrieve regulations and *Federal Register* entries from their citations. You can execute a source-driven search by selecting the Code of Federal Regulations database, and a content-driven search that includes federal materials will retrieve federal regulations. You can sort the search results according to a number of criteria. Bloomberg Law does not offer an annotated version of the C.F.R. But if you view a regulation, selecting the **SmartCode** function will execute a search for the citation and retrieve citations to cases that have cited the regulation.

2. GOVERNMENT SOURCES

Because the C.F.R. and *Federal Register* are government publications, they are widely available on online free of charge. The Government Printing Office's govinfo site is one of the best places to research federal regulations because it provides the official version of the C.F.R. in .pdf format. You can enter a citation, execute a word search or browse the C.F.R. table of contents. **Figure 9.3** shows the main search page for govinfo. Sites for individual agencies can also be good sources for federal regulations. The URLs for several useful sites for federal regulatory research are listed in Appendix A.

If you use a government source to locate C.F.R. provisions, pay careful attention to the date of the material you are using. Government

FIGURE 9.3 **GOVINFO SEARCH OPTIONS**

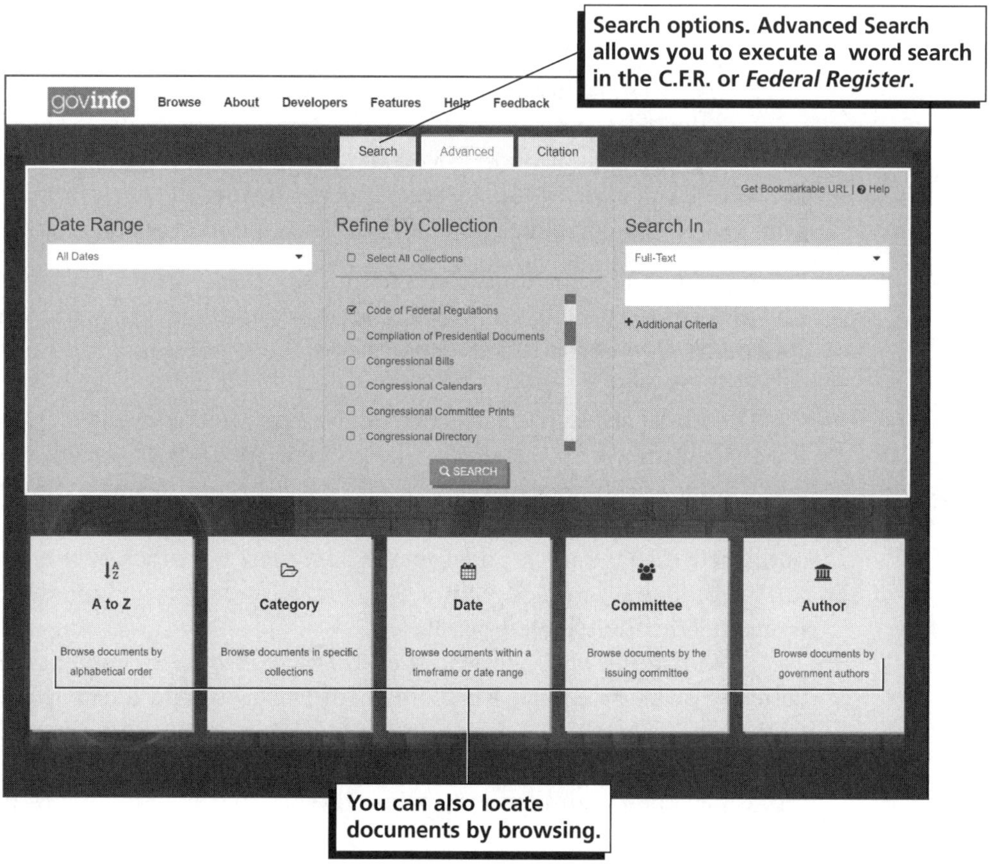

sources of regulations usually are no more up to date than the print version of the C.F.R. In govinfo, for example, the official C.F.R. database is only updated four times per year as the new print editions of the C.F.R. become available, although the *Federal Register* database is updated daily.

The Government Printing Office offers an unofficial version of the C.F.R. called the *Electronic Code of Federal Regulations* (e-CFR). The e-CFR is updated daily to incorporate changes to regulations as they are published in the *Federal Register,* in the same way that commercial services continually update their C.F.R. databases. Although the e-CFR is not an official source for regulations, it is a useful research tool. By comparing the official C.F.R. text with the e-CFR version, you can determine quickly and easily whether a regulation has been changed since the latest official edition of the C.F.R. was published. If you need an official source and citation for the change, you can then retrieve the *Federal Register* page containing the change in the govinfo *Federal Register* database. You can access the e-CFR from the e-CFR website (listed in Appendix A) or using the **Browse** A-Z option in govinfo.

Although no reason exists to doubt the accuracy of the e-CFR, there may be times when, out of an abundance of caution, you want to double check your research by updating it with official government sources. An alternate method of updating in govinfo requires you to research two sources:

- Use a monthly publication called the List of CFR Sections Affected (LSA) to find any *Federal Register* notices indicating that the regulation has been affected by agency action.
- Use the table of CFR Parts Affected during the current month in the most current *Federal Register* to update from the date of the LSA until the present.

The official updating sources available online are the same as those available in print. Therefore, these are also the steps you must follow to update print research.

The LSA lists each C.F.R. part and section affected by agency action. It is a cumulative publication. The current month's LSA will contain updates from the date of the latest C.F.R. volume through the end of the previous month. For example, if the latest C.F.R. volume had been published on January 1 and today's date were October 5, the current LSA would be dated September, and it would contain updates from January 1 through September 30.

To locate the LSA, choose the option to **Browse** documents alphabetically or by category (Regulatory Information) and locate the **List of CFR Sections Affected.** Expand the list under **Monthly LSA** to the latest LSA and then to the Title of the C.F.R. for the regulation you are updating. Open the document and review the list to see if the C.F.R. provision you are updating appears. If you do not find the section listed in the LSA, there have been no changes to the regulation. If you do find the provision listed, the LSA will refer you to the page or pages of the *Federal Register* containing information on the agency's action. **Figure 9.4** is an example of a page from the .pdf version of the September 2017 LSA. It indicates a change to 16 C.F.R. Part 1028, which includes § 1028.101.

The easiest way to find the *Federal Register* page with the change to the regulation is to retrieve it by citation from the govinfo home page. You can also browse the *Federal Register* by date to find the page or pages you need. Once you find the page, you can read about the change the regulation. **Figure 9.5** shows a page from the *Federal Register* with part of the change to 16 C.F.R. § 1028.101.

The second updating step requires you to use a table of CFR Parts Affected during the month to date. This table lists all of the C.F.R. Parts affected by notices published in the *Federal Register* during the current month and will update your research from the last day covered by the LSA until the present. Thus, if today's date were October 5, the list of CFR Parts Affected During October would contain updates since the September LSA, covering the period from October 1 through October 5. See **Figure 9.6.**

To locate this table, access today's issue of the ***Federal Register***, which may be easiest to do by browsing publications A-Z or by date. View the entire issue or use the TOC link to locate the **Reader Aids** section at the end of the issue. On this page you will see a table of CFR Parts Affected for the current month. (Note that a different table of CFR Parts Affected appears in a section with the title page at the beginning of the *Federal Register.* This table is a daily listing that is not cumulative for the month. Be sure to use the monthly table in the **Reader Aids** section.)

The table lists only the Parts affected by agency action, not individual sections. Therefore, if the table contains a reference to the C.F.R. Part you are researching, you need to retrieve the relevant page from the *Federal Register* to determine the section or sections within the C.F.R. Part affected by agency action. If the table does not list the Part you are researching, your updating is complete. **Figure 9.6** shows the cumulative table of CFR Parts Affected During October. No entry for Title 16 appears, so no additional changes occurred during the period covered.

FIGURE 9.4 LSA PAGE INDICATING CHANGES TO REGULATIONS

Changes to regulations in Title 16 of the C.F.R. are listed here.

SEPTEMBER 2017 35

CHANGES JANUARY 3, 2017 THROUGH SEPTEMBER 29, 2017

30 45528
200—299 (Ch. II) 40248
300—399 (Ch. III) 40248
700—799 (Ch. VII) 40248
800—899 (Ch. VIII) 40248
801 34894
900—999 (Ch. IX) 40248
922 .... 2254, 2269, 19195
1100—1199 (Ch. XI) 40248
2301 32776

TITLE 16—COMMERCIAL PRACTICES

Chapter I—Federal Trade Commission (Parts 0—999)

1.98 Revised 8137
1.125—1.129 (Subpart Q) Added 30966
1.130 (Subpart R) Added 30966
4.8 (b)(2)(iii), (6)(i), (7), (e)(2)(i)(C) and (i) revised 21686
259 Revised 43687
300.4 (c) and (e) revised 43691
301.26 (a), (b)(2) and (d) revised 43691
303.20 Revised 43692
305.11 (d) introductory text, (f)(9)(i), (iv) and (vii) through (x) revised; (d)(3) added 29235
305.13 (a)(1)(xii) revised; eff. 9-17-18 29236
305.16 (a)(3), (4), (b)(3) and (4) revised 29236
305.20 (b)(1)(i)(F) revised 29236
305 Appendix D5 revised 29236
803 Appendix revised 32124

Chapter II—Consumer Product Safety Commission (Parts 1000—1799)

1015 Authority citation revised 37007
1015.1 Revised 37007
1015.2 Revised 37008
1015.3 Heading revised; (a), (b), (d) and (e) amended 37008
1015.4 Amended 37008
1015.5 (a) revised; (e), (f) and (g) redesignated as (f), (g) and (h); new (e) added; (b) introductory text, (1), (d), (2), new (f), (g) introductory text, (5) and (h) amended; new (g)(2) and (3) revised 37008
1015.6 (a), (b) introductory text and (4) revised; (b)(5) added; (c) amended 37008
1015.7 Heading, (a), (b), (e), authority citation following (g) revised; (c) and (g) amended 37009
1015.9 (f)(6) redesignated as (f)(7); new (f)(6) added; (a), (e)(9), (f)(4), (5), (e)(1) and new (f)(7) amended; (b), (c)(2), (3) and (8) revised 37009
1015.10 Removed 37010
1015.11 Revised 37010
1015.15 Revised 37010
1015.16 Removed 37010
1015.17 Removed 37010
1015.20 (a) amended 37010
1028 Revised; eff. 1-19-18 43460
1112 Authority citation revised 8993
1112.15 (b)(39) added; eff. 1-30-18 8687
(b)(32 introductory text, (ii) introductory text and (c)(1)(ii) revised (b)(32)(i) and (c)(1)(iii) removed; (b)(32)(ii)(JJ) and (KK) added 8993
(b)(41) added 15627
(b)(42) added; eff. 3-19-18 ....
1217.2 Revised ....
1228 Added; eff. 1-30-18 ....
1229 Added; eff. 3-19-18 ....
1234 Added ....
1240 Removed 12717
1250 Added 8993
1308 Added 41171
1500.42 (a)(1) amended; CFR correction 2193

Federal Register page indicating a change

Proposed Rules:

0—999 (Ch. I) 29259
303 29251
312 19009
316 29254
410 29256
1000—1799 (Ch. II) 27636, 36705, 40392
1015 59
1112 .... 16963, 22925
1130 16963
1236 16963
1237 22925
1240 8907
1245 .... 22190, 31035
1420 42960

FIGURE 9.5 *FEDERAL REGISTER* PAGE SHOWING REGULATORY CHANGE

Revised section

43460 **Federal Register** / Vol. 82, No. 179 / Monday, September 18, 2017 / Rules and Regulations

HHS regulations in 45 CFR part 46, subpart A, CPSC proposed to adopt the amended regulatory text provided in the Common Rule final rule by providing a cross-reference to the HHS regulations in 45 CFR part 46, subpart A, rather than restating the text of HHS's regulation in CPSC's rule. However, at the direction of the Office of the Federal Register, for the final rule, CPSC is codifying the text of the revised Common Rule in CPSC's regulations at 16 CFR part 1028. CPSC's final rule is substantively identical to the HHS regulations in 45 CFR part 46, subpart A. Accordingly, CPSC now adopts the final Common Rule. The effective date of the Common Rule is January 19, 2018, with a compliance date of January 19, 2018, except for the section on cooperative research (§ 1028.114), which has a compliance date of January 20, 2020.

List of Subjects in 16 CFR Part 1028

Human research subjects, Reporting and recordkeeping requirements, Research.

For the reasons stated in the preamble, the Consumer Product Safety Commission amends Title 16 of the Code of Federal Regulations by revising part 1028 to read as follows:

PART 1028—PROTECTION OF HUMAN SUBJECTS

Sec.
1028.101 To what does this policy apply?
1028.102 Definitions for purposes of this policy.
1028.103 Assuring compliance with this policy—research conducted or supported by any Federal department or agency.
1028.104 Exempt research.
1028.105 [Reserved]
1028.106 [Reserved]
1028.107 IRB membership.
1028.108 IRB functions and operations.
1028.109 IRB review of research.
1028.110 Expedited review procedures for certain kinds of research involving no more than minimal risk, and for minor changes in approved research.
1028.111 Criteria for IRB approval of research.
1028.112 Review by institution.
1028.113 Suspension or termination of IRB approval of research.
1028.114 Cooperative research.
1028.115 IRB records.
1028.116 General requirements for informed consent.
1028.117 Documentation of informed consent.
1028.118 Applications and proposals lacking definite plans for involvement of human subjects.
1028.119 Research undertaken without the intention of involving human subjects.
1028.120 Evaluation and disposition of applications and proposals for research to be conducted or supported by a Federal department or agency.
1028.121 [Reserved]
1028.122 Use of Federal funds.
1028.123 Early termination of research support: Evaluation of applications and proposals.
1028.124 Conditions.

Authority: 5 U.S.C. 301; 42 U.S.C. 300v–1(b).

§ 1028.101 To what does this policy apply?

(a) Except as detailed in § 1028.104, this policy applies to all research involving human subjects conducted, supported, or otherwise subject to regulation by any Federal department or agency that takes appropriate administrative action to make the policy applicable to such research. This includes research conducted by Federal civilian employees or military personnel, except that each department or agency head may adopt such procedural modifications as may be appropriate from an administrative standpoint. It also includes research conducted, supported, or otherwise subject to regulation by the Federal Government outside the United States. Institutions that are engaged in research described in this paragraph and institutional review boards (IRBs) reviewing research that is subject to this policy must comply with this policy.

(b) [Reserved]

(c) Department or agency heads retain final judgment as to whether a particular activity is covered by this policy and this judgment shall be exercised consistent with the ethical principles of the Belmont Report.[1]

(d) Department or agency heads may require that specific research activities or classes of research activities conducted, supported, or otherwise subject to regulation by the Federal department or agency but not otherwise covered by this policy comply with some or all of the requirements of this policy.

(e) Compliance with this policy requires compliance with pertinent federal laws or regulations that provide additional protections for human subjects.

(f) This policy does not affect any state or local laws or regulations (including tribal law passed by the official governing body of an American Indian or Alaska Native tribe) that may otherwise be applicable and that provide additional protections for human subjects.

(g) This policy does not affect any foreign laws or regulations that may otherwise be applicable and that provide additional protections to human subjects of research.

(h) When research covered by this policy takes place in foreign countries, procedures normally followed in the foreign countries to protect human subjects may differ from those set forth in this policy. In these circumstances, if a department or agency head determines that the procedures prescribed by the institution afford protections that are at least equivalent to those provided in this policy, the department or agency head may approve the substitution of the foreign procedures in lieu of the procedural requirements provided in this policy. Except when otherwise required by statute, Executive Order, or the department or agency head, notices of these actions as they occur will be published in the **Federal Register** or will be otherwise published as provided in department or agency procedures.

(i) Unless otherwise required by law, department or agency heads may waive the applicability of some or all of the provisions of this policy to specific research activities or classes of research activities otherwise covered by this policy, provided the alternative procedures to be followed are consistent with the principles of the Belmont Report.[2] Except when otherwise required by statute or Executive Order, the department or agency head shall forward advance notices of these actions to the Office for Human Research Protections, Department of Health and Human Services (HHS), or any successor office, or to the equivalent office within the appropriate Federal department or agency, and shall also publish them in the **Federal Register** or in such other manner as provided in department or agency procedures. The waiver notice must include a statement that identifies the conditions under which the waiver will be applied and a justification as to why the waiver is appropriate for the research, including how the decision is consistent with the principles of the Belmont Report.

(j) Federal guidance on the requirements of this policy shall be issued only after consultation, for the purpose of harmonization (to the extent appropriate), with other Federal departments and agencies that have adopted this policy, unless such consultation is not feasible.

(k) [Reserved]

(l) Compliance dates and transition provisions:

(1) For purposes of this section, the *pre-2018 Requirements* means this

[1] The National Commission for the Protection of Human Subjects of Biomedical and Behavioral Research—Belmont Report. Washington, DC: U.S. Department of Health and Human Services. 1979.

[2] *Id.*

The *Federal Register* contains the amendments to the regulations.

FIGURE 9.6 *FEDERAL REGISTER*, CUMULATIVE MONTHLY LIST OF CFR PARTS AFFECTED

Cumulative table of parts affected for the month to date. No changes to Title 16 are listed.

i

Reader Aids

Federal Register

Vol. 82, No. 192

Thursday, October 5, 2017

CUSTOMER SERVICE AND INFORMATION

Federal Register/Code of Federal Regulations

General Information, indexes and other finding aids	**202–741–6000**
Laws	**741–6000**
Presidential Documents	
Executive orders and proclamations	**741–6000**
The United States Government Manual	**741–6000**
Other Services	
Electronic and on-line services (voice)	**741–6020**
Privacy Act Compilation	**741–6050**
Public Laws Update Service (numbers, dates, etc.)	**741–6043**

ELECTRONIC RESEARCH

World Wide Web

Full text of the daily Federal Register, CFR and other publications is located at: **www.fdsys.gov.**

Federal Register information and research tools, including Public Inspection List, indexes, and Code of Federal Regulations are located at: **www.ofr.gov.**

E-mail

FEDREGTOC (Daily Federal Register Table of Contents Electronic Mailing List) is an open e-mail service that provides subscribers with a digital form of the Federal Register Table of Contents. The digital form of the Federal Register Table of Contents includes HTML and PDF links to the full text of each document.

To join or leave, go to **https://public.govdelivery.com/accounts/USGPOOFR/subscriber/new**, enter your email address, then follow the instructions to join, leave, or manage your subscription.

PENS (Public Law Electronic Notification Service) is an e-mail service that notifies subscribers of recently enacted laws.

To subscribe, go to **http://listserv.gsa.gov/archives/publaws-l.html** and select *Join or leave the list (or change settings);* then follow the instructions.

FEDREGTOC and **PENS** are mailing lists only. We cannot respond to specific inquiries.

Reference questions. Send questions and comments about the Federal Register system to: **fedreg.info@nara.gov**

The Federal Register staff cannot interpret specific documents or regulations.

CFR Checklist. Effective January 1, 2009, the CFR Checklist no longer appears in the Federal Register. This information can be found online at **http://bookstore.gpo.gov/.**

FEDERAL REGISTER PAGES AND DATE, OCTOBER

45679–45954	2
45955–46122	3
46123–46368	4
46369–46654	5

CFR PARTS AFFECTED DURING OCTOBER

At the end of each month the Office of the Federal Register publishes separately a List of CFR Sections Affected (LSA), which lists parts and sections affected by documents published since the revision date of each title.

3 CFR

Proclamations:

9646 46353
9647 46355
9648 46357
9649 46359
9650 46361
9651 46653

Executive Orders:

13522 (Revoked by EO 13812) 46367
13708 (Superseded by EO 13811) 46363
13805 (Revoked by EO 13811) 46363
13811 46363
13812 46367

Administrative Orders:

Memorandums:
Memorandum of September 25, 2017 46649

7 CFR

319 45955

Proposed Rules:

33 46425
35 46425

12 CFR

271 45679
1002 45680
1101 45697

Proposed Rules:

740 46173

13 CFR

102 46369

14 CFR

36 46123
39 ..... 45697, 45701, 45703, 45705, 45710, 46379, 46382
71 ..... 45713 45714, 45715, 45716, 45717, 45719, 45720, 45957, 45958
73 45721
91 46123
97 ..... 46385, 46386

Proposed Rules:

Ch. I 45750
Ch. II 45750
Ch. III 45750
39 45743
71 ..... 45747, 45749, 46426

15 CFR

730 45959
732 45959
734 45959
736 45959
738 45959
740 45959
742 45959
743 45959
744 45959
746 45959
748 45959
750 45959
754 45959
756 45959
758 45959
760 45959
762 45959
764 45959
766 45959
768 45959
770 45959
772 45959
774 45959

17 CFR

227 45722
230 45722

21 CFR

876 45725

Proposed Rules:

101 45753

23 CFR

Proposed Rules:

Ch. I 45750
Ch. II 45750
Ch. III 45750
490 46427

26 CFR

1 46388

30 CFR

56 46411
57 46411
583 45962

33 CFR

100 ..... 45977, 45979, 46413
117 ..... 45728, 45729, 45980, 45981
165 ..... 45729, 45981, 45984, 45986, 45988, 46132

Proposed Rules:

110 46004
165 46007

38 CFR

Proposed Rules:

17 45756

39 CFR

Proposed Rules:

111 46010

40 CFR

9 45990

FIGURE 9.7 **UPDATING C.F.R. RESEARCH USING OFFICIAL SOURCES**

DATE	JANUARY 1, 2017	JANUARY 1, 2017 – SEPTEMBER 30, 2017	OCTOBER 1, 2017 – OCTOBER 5, 2017
Source	Title 16 C.F.R.	September 2017 List of CFR Sections Affected (LSA)	List of CFR Parts Affected During August
Use	Locate regulations in the C.F.R. Note the date of the C.F.R.	Use the latest monthly issue. Look up the Title and section number of the regulation. If it is listed, look up the page in the *Federal Register* to locate the change.	Use the cumulative table in the Reader Aids section in back of the latest daily issue of the *Federal Register*. If the C.F.R. Part is not listed, no changes have taken place during the month to date. If the C.F.R. Part is listed, each page reference must be checked to see which individual sections have been affected.

The chart in **Figure 9.7** summarizes the process of updating C.F.R. research with official sources, using the example of a regulation within Title 16 of the C.F.R. published on January 1, 2017, an LSA dated September 30, 2017, and the list of CFR Parts Affected dated October 5, 2017.

D. CITING FEDERAL REGULATIONS

Citations to administrative materials are governed by Rule 18 in the *ALWD Guide* (6th ed.) and Bluepages B14 and Rule 14.2 in the *Bluebook* (20th ed.).

A citation to the C.F.R. is very similar to a citation to a federal statute. It consists of the Title number, the abbreviation C.F.R., the pinpoint reference to the section number, and a parenthetical containing the year.

Here is an example:

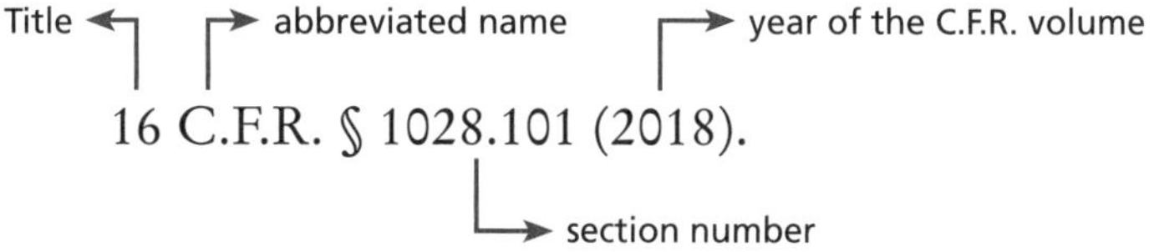

Citations to the *Federal Register* are also fairly simple. They require the volume number, the abbreviation Fed. Reg., the page number, and a parenthetical containing the exact date.

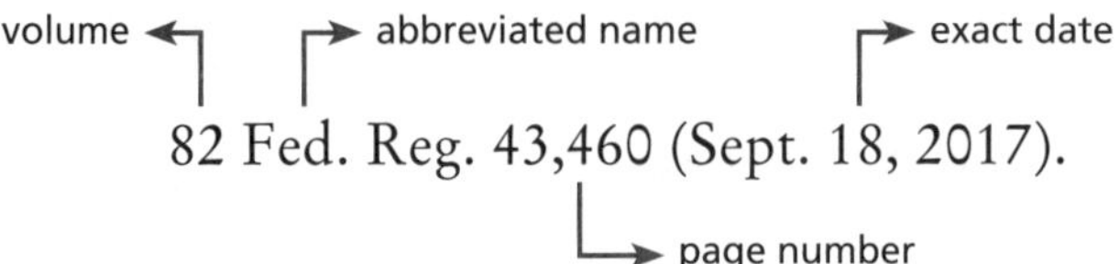

If appropriate, you should also provide a pinpoint reference to the specific page or pages containing the cited material. Additional requirements apply to citations to regulations appearing in the *Federal Register* that are not codified in the C.F.R.

E. SAMPLE PAGES FOR FEDERAL ADMINISTRATIVE LAW RESEARCH

Beginning on the next page, **Figures 9.8** through **9.12** contain sample pages from the C.F.R. showing the process of researching regulations pertaining to the protection of human research subjects using govinfo and the e-CFR.

The first step is locating relevant regulations. You could use a subject index such as the CFR Index and Finding Aids, cross-references in statutory annotations, or a word search to locate relevant regulations. Retrieving the regulations in govinfo allows you to view the official version in .pdf format. Once you know the relevant Part, you can use the outline of the Part to review the regulatory scheme.

FIGURE 9.8 16 C.F.R. PART 1028 TABLE OF CONTENTS

§ 1027.8 16 CFR Ch. II (1–1–17 Edition)

debt claim from another agency, deductions will be scheduled to begin at the next established pay interval. The employee must receive written notice that CPSC has received a certified debt claim from the creditor agency, the amount of the debt, the date salary offset will begin, and the amount of the deduction(s). CPSC shall not review the merits of the creditor agency's determination of the validity or the amount of the certified claim.

(2) If the employee transfers to another agency after the creditor agency has submitted its debt claim to CPSC and before the debt is collected completely, CPSC must certify the amount collected. One copy of the certification must be furnished to the employee. A copy must be furnished to the creditor agency with notice of the employee's transfer.

§ 1027.8 Procedures for salary offset.

(a) Deductions to liquidate an employee's debt will be by the method and in the amount stated in the Executive Director's notice of intention to offset as provided in § 1027.4. Debts will be collected in one lump sum where possible. If the employee is financially unable to pay in one lump sum, collection must be made in installments.

(b) Debts will be collected by deduction at officially established pay intervals from an employee's current pay account unless alternative arrangements for repayment are made.

(c) Installment deductions will be made over a period not greater than the anticipated period of employment. The size of installment deductions must bear a reasonable relationship to the size of the debt and the employee's ability to pay. The deduction for the pay intervals for any period must not exceed 15% of disposable pay unless the employee has agreed in writing to a deduction of a greater amount.

(d) Unliquidated debts may be offset against any financial payment due to a separated employee including but not limited to final salary or leave payment in accordance with 31 U.S.C. 3716.

§ 1027.9 Refunds.

(a) CPSC will promptly refund to an employee any amounts deducted to satisfy debts owed to CPSC when the debt is waived, found not owed to CPSC, or when directed by an administrative or judicial order.

(b) Another creditor agency will promptly return to CPSC any amounts deducted by CPSC to satisfy debts owed to the creditor agency when the debt is waived, found not owed, or when directed by an administrative or judicial order.

(c) Unless required by law, refunds under this paragraph shall not bear interest.

§ 1027.10 Statute of limitations.

(a) If a debt has been outstanding for more than 10 years after CPSC's right to collect the debt first accrued, the agency may not collect by salary offset unless facts material to the Government's right to collect were not known and could not reasonably have been known by the official or officials who were charged with the responsibility for discovery and collection of such debts.

(b) [Reserved]

§ 1027.11 Non-waiver of rights.

An employee's involuntary payment of all or any part of a debt collected under these regulations will not be construed as a waiver of any rights that the employee may have under 5 U.S.C. 5514 or any other provision of law.

§ 1027.12 Interest, penalties, and administrative costs.

Charges may be assessed on a debt for interest, penalties, and administrative costs in accordance with 31 U.S.C. 3717 and the Federal Claims Collection Standards, 4 CFR 101.1 *et seq.*

PART 1028—PROTECTION OF HUMAN SUBJECTS

Sec.

108

The table of contents refers to a specific regulation on the applicability of the policy.

The outline of the part will direct you to specific regulations.

FIGURE 9.9 16 C.F.R. § 1028.101

Regulation referenced in the table of contents

Consumer Product Safety Commission **§ 1028.101**

AUTHORITY: 5 U.S.C. 301; 42 U.S.C. 300v–1(b).

SOURCE: 56 FR 28012, 28019, June 18, 1991, unless otherwise noted.

§ 1028.101 To what does this policy apply?

(a) Except as provided in paragraph (b) of this section, this policy applies to all research involving human subjects conducted, supported or otherwise subject to regulation by any federal department or agency which takes appropriate administrative action to make the policy applicable to such research. This includes research conducted by federal civilian employees or military personnel, except that each department or agency head may adopt such procedural modifications as may be appropriate from an administrative standpoint. It also includes research conducted, supported, or otherwise subject to regulation by the federal government outside the United States.

(1) Research that is conducted or supported by a federal department or agency, whether or not it is regulated as defined in § 1028.102(e), must comply with all sections of this policy.

(2) Research that is neither conducted nor supported by a federal department or agency but is subject to regulation as defined in § 1028.102(e) must be reviewed and approved, in compliance with §§ 1028.101, 1028.102, and 1028.107 through 1028.117 of this policy, by an institutional review board (IRB) that operates in accordance with the pertinent requirements of this policy.

(b) Unless otherwise required by department or agency heads, research activities in which the only involvement of human subjects will be in one or more of the following categories are exempt from this policy:

(1) Research conducted in established or commonly accepted educational settings, involving normal educational practices, such as (i) research on regular and special education instructional strategies, or (ii) research on the effectiveness of or the comparison among instructional techniques, curricula, or classroom management methods.

(2) Research involving the use of educational tests (cognitive, diagnostic, aptitude, achievement), survey procedures, interview procedures or observation of public behavior, unless:

(i) Information obtained is recorded in such a manner that human subjects can be identified, directly or through identifiers linked to the subjects; and

(ii) Any disclosure of the human subjects' responses outside the research could reasonably place the subjects at risk of criminal or civil liability or be damaging to the subjects' financial standing, employability, or reputation.

(3) Research involving the use of educational tests (cognitive, diagnostic, aptitude, achievement), survey procedures, interview procedures, or observation of public behavior that is not exempt under paragraph (b)(2) of this section, if:

(i) The human subjects are elected or appointed public officials or candidates for public office; or

(ii) Federal statute(s) require(s) without exception that the confidentiality of the personally identifiable information will be maintained throughout the research and thereafter.

(4) Research, involving the collection or study of existing data, documents, records, pathological specimens, or diagnostic specimens, if these sources are publicly available or if the information is recorded by the investigator in such

109

FIGURE 9.9 16 C.F.R. § 1028.101 *(Continued)*

a manner that subjects cannot be identified, directly or through identifiers linked to the subjects.

(5) Research and demonstration projects which are conducted by or subject to the approval of department or agency heads, and which are designed to study, evaluate, or otherwise examine:

(i) Public benefit or service programs;

(ii) Procedures for obtaining benefits or services under those programs;

(iii) Possible changes in or alternatives to those programs or procedures; or

(iv) Possible changes in methods or levels of payment for benefits or services under those programs.

(6) Taste and food quality evaluation and consumer acceptance studies, (i) if wholesome foods without additives are consumed or (ii) if a food is consumed that contains a food ingredient at or below the level and for a use found to be safe, or agricultural chemical or environmental contaminant at or below the level found to be safe, by the Food and Drug Administration or approved by the Environmental Protection Agency or the Food Safety and Inspection Service of the U.S. Department of Agriculture.

(c) Department or agency heads retain final judgment as to whether a particular activity is covered by this policy.

(d) Department or agency heads may require that specific research activities or classes of research activities conducted, supported, or otherwise subject to regulation by the department or agency but not otherwise covered by this policy, comply with some or all of the requirements of this policy.

(e) Compliance with this policy requires compliance with pertinent federal laws or regulations which provide additional protections for human subjects.

(f) This policy does not affect any state or local laws or regulations which may otherwise be applicable and which provide additional protections for human subjects.

(g) This policy does not affect any foreign laws or regulations which may otherwise be applicable and which provide additional protections to human subjects of research.

(h) When research covered by this policy takes place in foreign countries, procedures normally followed in the foreign countries to protect human subjects may differ from those set forth in this policy. (An example is a foreign institution which complies with guidelines consistent with the World Medical Assembly Declaration (Declaration of Helsinki amended 1989) issued either by sovereign states or by an organization whose function for the protection of human research subjects is internationally recognized.) In these circumstances, if a department or agency head determines that the procedures prescribed by the institution afford protections that are at least equivalent to those provided in this policy, the department or agency head may approve the substitution of the foreign procedures in lieu of the procedural requirements provided in this policy. Except when otherwise required by statute, Executive Order, or the department or agency head, notices of these actions as they occur will be published in the FEDERAL REGISTER or will be otherwise published as provided in department or agency procedures.

(i) Unless otherwise required by law, department or agency heads may waive the applicability of some or all of the provisions of this policy to specific research activities or classes of research activities otherwise covered by this policy. Except when otherwise required by statute or Executive Order, the department or agency head shall forward advance notices of these actions to the Office for Human Research Protections, Department of Health and Human Services (HHS), or any successor office, and shall also publish them in the FEDERAL REGISTER or in such other manner as provided in department or agency procedures.[1]

[56 FR 28012, 28019, June 18, 1991; 56 FR 29756, June 28, 1991, as amended at 70 FR 36328, June 23, 2005]

Federal Register notices with the original regulation and later amendments

[1] Institutions with HHS-approved assurances on file will abide by provisions of title 45 CFR part 46, subparts A-D. Some of the other Departments and Agencies have incorporated all provisions of title 45 CFR part 46 into their policies and procedures as well. However, the exemptions at 45 CFR 46.101(b)

You can update C.F.R. research in govinfo using the LSA and the *Federal Register*. You can also use the unofficial e-CFR to find regulatory changes.

FIGURE 9.10 e-CFR SEARCH SCREEN

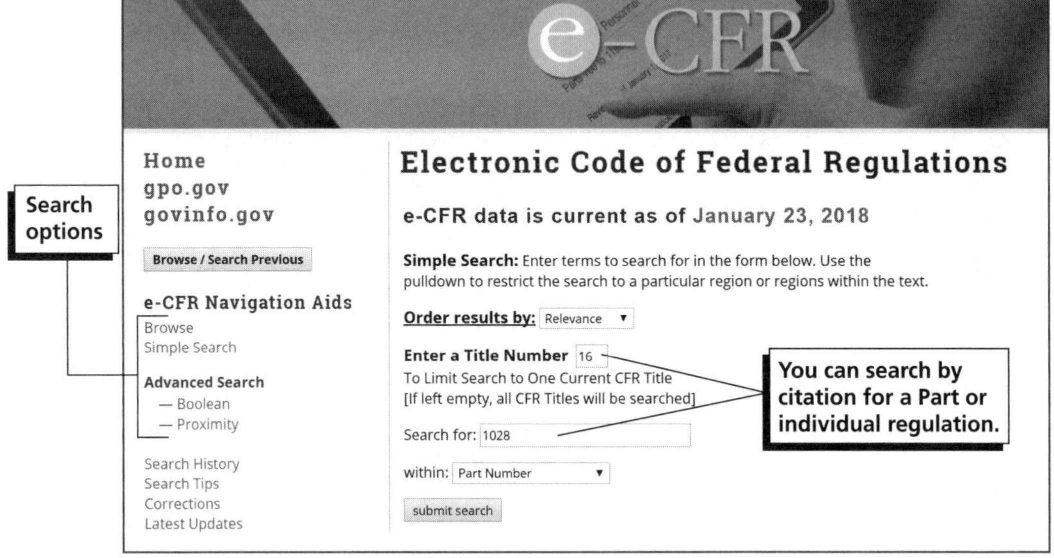

The regulation is displayed in textual form. Because the pending change to the regulation has been adopted but has not yet gone into effect, the e-CFR displays the existing regulation and links to the revised version. References indicating where the regulation and any amendments were originally published in the *Federal Register* follow the regulatory text. After the revised version takes effect, the e-CFR will be updated with the new language and the latest *Federal Register* notice.

FIGURE 9.11 e-CFR VERSION OF 16 C.F.R. § 1028.101

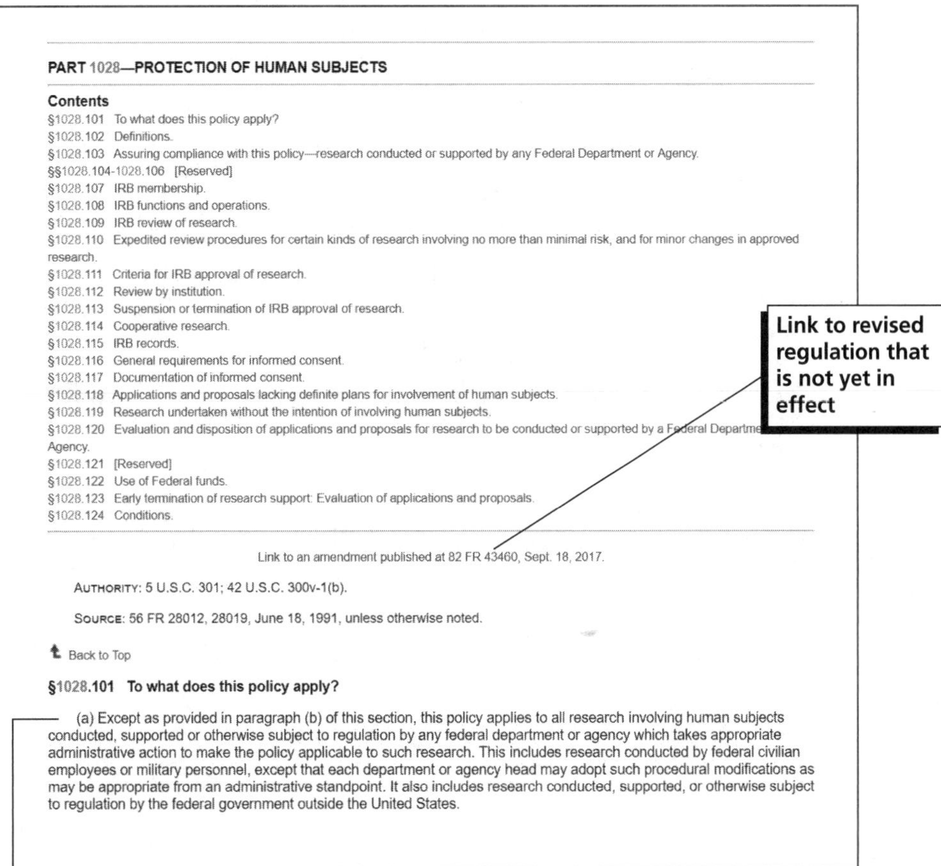

PART 1028—PROTECTION OF HUMAN SUBJECTS

Contents

Link to an amendment published at 82 FR 43460, Sept. 18, 2017.

AUTHORITY: 5 U.S.C. 301; 42 U.S.C. 300v-1(b).

SOURCE: 56 FR 28012, 28019, June 18, 1991, unless otherwise noted.

Back to Top

§1028.101 To what does this policy apply?

(a) Except as provided in paragraph (b) of this section, this policy applies to all research involving human subjects conducted, supported or otherwise subject to regulation by any federal department or agency which takes appropriate administrative action to make the policy applicable to such research. This includes research conducted by federal civilian employees or military personnel, except that each department or agency head may adopt such procedural modifications as may be appropriate from an administrative standpoint. It also includes research conducted, supported, or otherwise subject to regulation by the federal government outside the United States.

FIGURE 9.11 e-CFR VERSION OF 16 C.F.R. § 1028.101 *(Continued)*

(6) Taste and food quality evaluation and consumer acceptance studies, (i) if wholesome foods without additives are consumed or (ii) if a food is consumed that contains a food ingredient at or below the level and for a use found to be safe, or agricultural chemical or environmental contaminant at or below the level found to be safe, by the Food and Drug Administration or approved by the Environmental Protection Agency or the Food Safety and Inspection Service of the U.S. Department of Agriculture.

(c) Department or agency heads retain final judgment as to whether a particular activity is covered by this policy.

(d) Department or agency heads may require that specific research activities or classes of research activities conducted, supported, or otherwise subject to regulation by the department or agency but not otherwise covered by this policy, comply with some or all of the requirements of this policy.

(e) Compliance with this policy requires compliance with pertinent federal laws or regulations which provide additional protections for human subjects.

(f) This policy does not affect any state or local laws or regulations which may otherwise be applicable and which provide additional protections for human subjects.

(g) This policy does not affect any foreign laws or regulations which may otherwise be applicable and which provide additional protections to human subjects of research.

(h) When research covered by this policy takes place in foreign countries, procedures normally followed in the foreign countries to protect human subjects may differ from those set forth in this policy. (An example is a foreign institution which complies with guidelines consistent with the World Medical Assembly Declaration (Declaration of Helsinki amended 1989) issued either by sovereign states or by an organization whose function for the protection of human research subjects is internationally recognized.) In these circumstances, if a department or agency head determines that the procedures prescribed by the institution afford protections that are at least equivalent to those provided in this policy, the department or agency head may approve the substitution of the foreign procedures in lieu of the procedural requirements provided in this policy. Except when otherwise required by statute, Executive Order, or the department or agency head, notices of these actions as they occur will be published in the FEDERAL REGISTER or will be otherwise published as provided in department or agency procedures.

(i) Unless otherwise required by law, department or agency heads may waive the applicability of some or all of the provisions of this policy to specific research activities or classes of research activities otherwise covered by this policy. Except when otherwise required by statute or Executive Order, the department or agency head shall forward advance notices of these actions to the Office for Human Research Protections, Department of Health and Human Services (HHS), or any successor office, and shall also publish them in the FEDERAL REGISTER or in such other manner as provided in department or agency procedures.[1]

[1]Institutions with HHS-approved assurances on file will abide by provisions of title 45 CFR part 46, subparts A-D. Some of the other Departments and Agencies have incorporated all provisions of title 45 CFR part 46 into their policies and procedures as well. However, the exemptions at 45 CFR 46.101(b) do not apply to research involving prisoners, subpart C. The exemption at 45 CFR 46.101(b)(2), for research involving survey or interview procedures or observation of public behavior, does not apply to research with children, subpart D, except for research involving observations of public behavior when the investigator(s) do not participate in the activities being observed.

[56 FR 28012, 28019, June 18, 1991; 56 FR 29756, June 28, 1991, as amended at 70 FR 36328, June 23, 2005]

Following the link in the e-CFR displays the revised regulation in text form. Use the link to the *Federal Register* to view the .pdf version of the revised regulation.

FIGURE 9.12 **e-CFR DISPLAY OF CHANGES TO 16 C.F.R. PART 1028 AND § 1028.101**

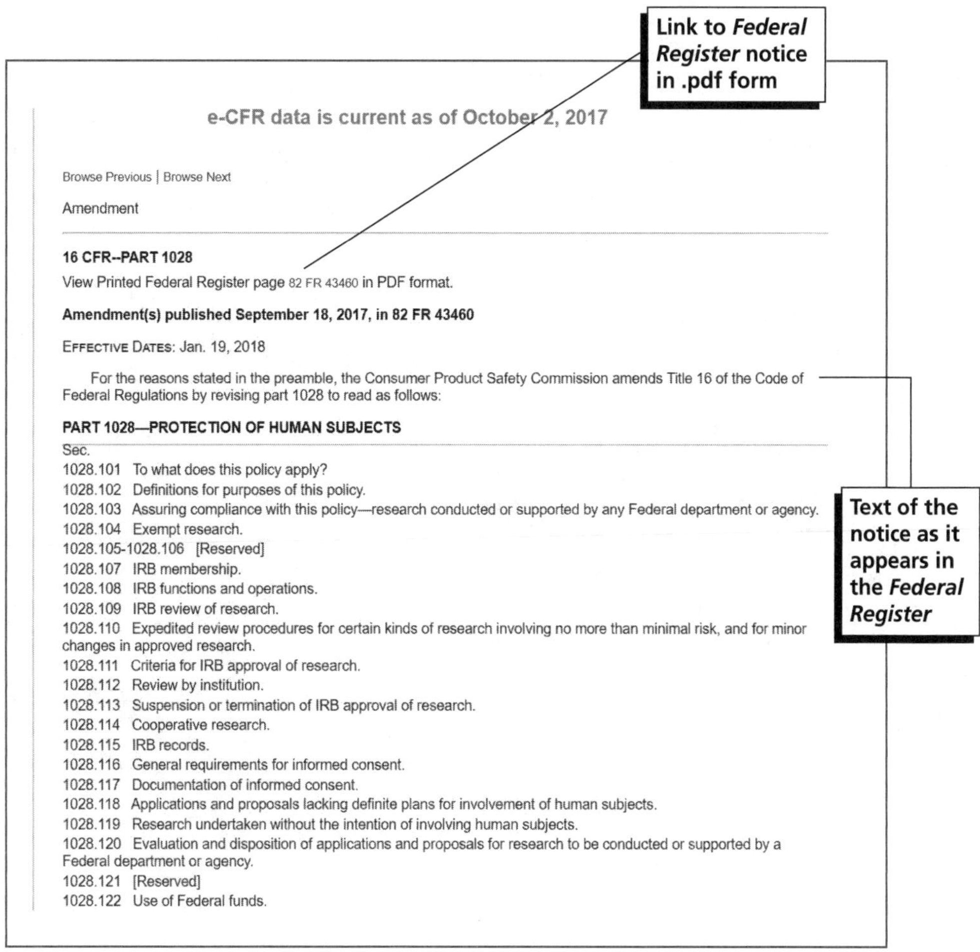
e-CFR data is current as of October 2, 2017

Browse Previous | Browse Next

Amendment

16 CFR--PART 1028

View Printed Federal Register page 82 FR 43460 in PDF format.

Amendment(s) published September 18, 2017, in 82 FR 43460

EFFECTIVE DATES: Jan. 19, 2018

For the reasons stated in the preamble, the Consumer Product Safety Commission amends Title 16 of the Code of Federal Regulations by revising part 1028 to read as follows:

PART 1028—PROTECTION OF HUMAN SUBJECTS

Sec.
1028.101 To what does this policy apply?
1028.102 Definitions for purposes of this policy.
1028.103 Assuring compliance with this policy—research conducted or supported by any Federal department or agency.
1028.104 Exempt research.
1028.105-1028.106 [Reserved]
1028.107 IRB membership.
1028.108 IRB functions and operations.
1028.109 IRB review of research.
1028.110 Expedited review procedures for certain kinds of research involving no more than minimal risk, and for minor changes in approved research.
1028.111 Criteria for IRB approval of research.
1028.112 Review by institution.
1028.113 Suspension or termination of IRB approval of research.
1028.114 Cooperative research.
1028.115 IRB records.
1028.116 General requirements for informed consent.
1028.117 Documentation of informed consent.
1028.118 Applications and proposals lacking definite plans for involvement of human subjects.
1028.119 Research undertaken without the intention of involving human subjects.
1028.120 Evaluation and disposition of applications and proposals for research to be conducted or supported by a Federal department or agency.
1028.121 [Reserved]
1028.122 Use of Federal funds.

FIGURE 9.12 **e-CFR DISPLAY OF CHANGES TO 16 C.F.R. PART 1028 AND § 1028.101 *(Continued)***

AUTHORITY: 5 U.S.C. 301; 42 U.S.C. 300v-1(b).

§1028.101 To what does this policy apply?

(a) Except as detailed in §1028.104, this policy applies to all research involving human subjects conducted, supported, or otherwise subject to regulation by any Federal department or agency that takes appropriate administrative action to make the policy applicable to such research. This includes research conducted by Federal civilian employees or military personnel, except that each department or agency head may adopt such procedural modifications as may be appropriate from an administrative standpoint. It also includes research conducted, supported, or otherwise subject to regulation by the Federal Government outside the United States. Institutions that are engaged in research described in this paragraph and institutional review boards (IRBs) reviewing research that is subject to this policy must comply with this policy.

(b) [Reserved]

(c) Department or agency heads retain final judgment as to whether a particular activity is covered by this policy and this judgment shall be exercised consistent with the ethical principles of the Belmont Report.[1]

[1]The National Commission for the Protection of Human Subjects of Biomedical and Behavioral Research—Belmont Report. Washington, DC: U.S. Department of Health and Human Services. 1979.

(d) Department or agency heads may require that specific research activities or classes of research activities conducted, supported, or otherwise subject to regulation by the Federal department or agency but not otherwise covered by this policy comply with some or all of the requirements of this policy.

(e) Compliance with this policy requires compliance with pertinent federal laws or regulations that provide additional protections for human subjects.

(f) This policy does not affect any state or local laws or regulations (including tribal law passed by the official governing body of an American Indian or Alaska Native tribe) that may otherwise be applicable and that provide additional protections for human subjects.

(g) This policy does not affect any foreign laws or regulations that may otherwise be applicable and that provide additional protections to human subjects of research.

(h) When research covered by this policy takes place in foreign countries, procedures normally followed in the foreign countries to protect human subjects may differ from those set forth in this policy. In these circumstances, if a department or agency head determines that the procedures prescribed by the institution afford protections that are at least equivalent to those provided in this policy, the department or agency head may approve the substitution of the foreign procedures in lieu of the procedural requirements provided in this policy. Except when otherwise required by statute, Executive Order, or the department or agency head, notices of these actions as they occur will be published in the FEDERAL REGISTER or will be otherwise published as provided in department or agency procedures.

(i) Unless otherwise required by law, department or agency heads may waive the applicability of some or all of the provisions of this policy to specific research activities or classes of research activities otherwise covered by this policy, provided the alternative procedures to be followed are consistent with the principles of the Belmont Report.[2] Except when otherwise required by statute or Executive Order, the department or agency head shall forward advance notices of these

F. CHECKLIST FOR FEDERAL ADMINISTRATIVE LAW RESEARCH

1. LOCATE PERTINENT REGULATIONS

☐ Use the cross-references to the C.F.R. in the annotations in U.S.C.S. and U.S.C.A.

☐ Use a subject index, such as the CFR Index and Finding Aids.

☐ In Lexis Advance
- In the **Explore Content** menu, select the C.F.R. under the **Federal** tab to execute a word search.
- Use the **Browse** menu to select the C.F.R. as a source; execute a word search or browse the table of contents.
- Execute a content-driven search that includes federal law; filter the results under **Administrative Codes & Regulations** to view federal regulations.
- Review regulatory annotations or use Shepard's for regulatory history and research references.

☐ In Westlaw
- Browse the CFR Index or table of contents.
- Select the **Code of Federal Regulations (CFR)** database and execute a word search.
- Execute a content-driven search that includes federal law; the search results will include a **Regulations** section.
- Review regulatory annotations or use KeyCite for regulatory history and research references.

☐ In Bloomberg Law
- Browse the C.F.R. table of contents.
- Select the C.F.R. as a source and execute a word search.
- Execute a content-driven search that includes federal law; the search results will include federal regulatory material.
- From a regulation, use the **Smart Code** link to locate citations to cases that have cited the regulation.

☐ In govinfo, search by word or citation or browse the table of contents.

2. UPDATE GOVINFO RESEARCH WITH THE e-CFR

☐ Compare the official C.F.R. text with the e-CFR version to determine whether the regulation has been amended; locate *Federal Register* notices as necessary for an official citation or additional information.

3. UPDATE C.F.R. RESEARCH USING OFFICIAL SOURCES

- ☐ Use the same process to update official sources in print or online.
- ☐ To update from the date of the C.F.R. volume through the end of the prior month, look up the regulation in the most recent **List of CFR Sections Affected** (**LSA**) to locate page numbers in the *Federal Register* reflecting changes to the regulation.
  - Look up the *Federal Register* page containing the change and read the information to see how it affects the regulation.
- ☐ To update from the end of the prior month to the present, use the most current issue of the *Federal Register.*
  - Use the cumulative table of **CFR Parts Affected** during the current month in the **Reader Aids** section in the back of the *Federal Register.*
  - If the Part in which the section appears is listed, look up each page number referenced in the table to see if the section has been affected.

4. CONTACT THE AGENCY FOR ADDITIONAL INFORMATION ON RECENT OR PROPOSED REGULATORY CHANGES

CHAPTER 10

Online Legal Research

A. Introduction to online legal research

B. Effective word searching

C. Additional online research resources

D. Citing authority obtained online

E. Checklist for online legal research

As Chapter 1 explains, legal research can be accomplished using both print and online research tools. Frequently, you will use some combination of these tools in completing a research project. Although print and online resources are often used together, this chapter introduces you to some search techniques unique to online research. Earlier chapters discussed both print and online research in the context of individual types of authority, such as cases or statutes. This chapter explains some of the basics of online searching that can be used effectively in a number of services, regardless of the type of authority you need to locate. In doing so, it focuses on research with the major commercial services. But these are not the only options for online research. You should be able to adapt the techniques described here to a wide range of services.

This chapter describes online search techniques in general terms and provides few specific commands for executing them. Research providers update their services regularly, thus making it impossible to describe commands with any accuracy. In fact, you will likely receive training through your law school on the use of at least Lexis Advance and Westlaw, if not other services, and those training sessions will cover the commands necessary to execute the functions in those services.

Legal research providers strive to make their services as user-friendly as possible. Because most of us search online regularly, legal research providers have tried to make their services feel as familiar as general Internet search engines. Legal research, however, is different from routine Google searching, and it is important to keep those differences in mind when you conduct legal research.

In daily life, you might go online to search for a specific item of information, such as an address or a phone number. You might use one of several largely interchangeable sources to locate generally available information, such as national news or sports scores. You might shop for something by comparing prices and shipping options from a universe of sellers that are largely already familiar to you, such as Amazon.com.

These types of searches are different from legal research. The searching you do on a daily basis is often intended to locate a single item of information that meets your needs. In legal research, by contrast, it is rare for a single piece of information to answer your research question. Usually your goal is to identify a relevant group of authorities that you use together to analyze a legal issue. Additionally, the sources of authority in legal research usually are not interchangeable; one case or statute will not be as good as another, and it may be difficult to tell at the beginning of your research process which sources you need to analyze your research issue accurately. You must continue the research process until you know enough to isolate the most relevant authorities, not just any authorities.

The experience you already have with online searching will inform your legal research, but it will not transfer completely to legal research. This chapter will explain search techniques and options that will help you build on the search skills you already have so that you can complete your legal research tasks thoroughly and accurately.

A. INTRODUCTION TO ONLINE LEGAL RESEARCH

1. OVERVIEW OF ONLINE LEGAL RESEARCH SERVICES

Online legal research services can be divided into three categories. Fee-based services charge individual users a fee every time the service is used. Subscription services charge the subscriber for access, but individual users ordinarily are not charged for researching with the service. Publicly available services are those available for free online. Appendix A contains the URLs for a number of publicly available research sites, including those discussed in this chapter and elsewhere in this text. A brief overview of some popular online legal research services follows.

a. Fee-Based Services

■ WESTLAW AND LEXIS ADVANCE

Westlaw and Lexis Advance are two of the most commonly available services for conducting legal research. Both of these services contain the full text of a broad range of primary and secondary authorities.

■ **BLOOMBERG LAW**

Bloomberg Law is an online service that provides access to the full text of a range of legal authorities. It can be a cost-effective alternative to Westlaw and Lexis Advance. Its coverage of legal information is comparable to but somewhat less comprehensive than the coverage of Westlaw and Lexis Advance. But its coverage of court dockets and business information is more comprehensive. It does not provide access to some traditional legal secondary sources, but its database includes BNA (Bureau of National Affairs) publications that are not available from other services.

■ **VERSUSLAW**

VersusLaw offers access to the full text of a range of legal authorities and can be a cost-effective alternative to other commercial services. Its coverage is less comprehensive than that of Westlaw and Lexis Advance.

■ **FASTCASE AND CASEMAKER**

These research services are made available through bar associations and provide access to the full text of a range of legal authorities. One or the other of them may be available through your state bar association.

b. Subscription Services

■ **INDEX TO LEGAL PERIODICALS AND LEGALTRAC**

These are index services, meaning that they will generate lists of citations to authorities. Although they primarily provide citations to legal periodicals, they also provide access to the full text of selected documents. These services are described in more detail in Chapter 4.

■ **HEINONLINE**

This service provides access to a wide range of authorities, including legal periodicals and other secondary sources; legislative documents, including compiled legislative histories; administrative materials, including the C.F.R. and *Federal Register*; and some international materials. HeinOnline's databases go back further in time than those of some other services. In addition, it provides access to documents in .pdf format. This service is described in more detail in Chapter 4, on secondary source research, and Chapter 8, on federal legislative history research.

■ **PROQUEST**

ProQuest is available at many law libraries. ProQuest Legislative Insight is an excellent resource for legislative history research. ProQuest Congressional also contains a wealth of legislative information, including federal statutes, congressional documents generated during the legislative process, administrative regulations, and news about activities taking place on Capitol Hill. ProQuest is described in more detail in Chapter 8, on federal legislative history research.

■ SUBJECT-MATTER SERVICES

Some specialty services are devoted to specific areas of the law such as employment law, tax, bankruptcy, and patent law. These providers include Bureau of National Affairs (BNA), CCH, Inc. (CCH), Clark Boardman Callaghan (CBC), Matthew Bender (MB), Pike & Fischer (P & F), and Research Institute of America (RIA). Most originated as print services that were published in three-ring binders and updated with new looseleaf pages, so they are still sometimes called looseleaf services. If you are researching or practicing in a specialized field of law, these services are invaluable resources because they integrate case law, statutes, regulations, and secondary material into a single source. Even as a student, you may be able to subscribe to their news services to obtain regular updates on developments in a field of law. If your law school subscribes to these services, you can access them through the library's portal.

c. Publicly Available Services

■ WEBSITES OPERATED BY GOVERNMENT OR PRIVATE ENTITIES

Government websites can provide access to local, state, and federal legal information. Some examples of useful sites for federal law include Congress.gov, which is maintained by the Library of Congress, and govinfo.gov, the Government Printing Office's official repository for federal government documents. These services are described in Chapters 8 and 9. Many courts also maintain websites where they publish the full text of opinions, local court rules, and other useful information. In addition, websites operated by trade, civic, educational, or other groups may provide useful information in their specialized fields.

■ LEGAL RESEARCH WEBSITES

A number of websites collect legal information, and these can be useful research sources. Examples of legal research websites include Google Scholar, FindLaw, and Casetext. In addition, several law schools have developed "virtual law library" sites, such as Cornell Law School's Legal Information Institute.

2. OVERVIEW OF THE ONLINE SEARCH PROCESS

When you research online, you need to follow an organized plan to research effectively. Effective online searching usually involves the following four steps.

a. Selecting a Service

You want to choose the service or services most likely to contain the information you need. You need to consider the type of information you need and the scope of coverage of the services available to you. In addition, although you may not be concerned with the cost of research while you are in law school, in practice, selecting a cost-effective service is also an important consideration.

b. Selecting a Search Technique

Once you have selected a service, you will probably have several options for searching for authority. As Chapter 1 explains, many online research services organize their content by jurisdiction and type of authority and require you to use a source-driven approach to your research. You may be able to search by subject or execute a word search to locate information within each database. Lexis Advance, Westlaw, and Bloomberg Law also offer the option of content-driven searching, which allows you to search for content before selecting a jurisdiction or type of authority. To search effectively, you must decide which approach is most likely to retrieve the information you need. Chapter 3 describes these two research approaches in more detail.

c. Planning and Executing a Search

After you select a search technique, you need to plan your search. If you use a source-driven approach, you must select a database to search or identify the subject headings you want to research. If you use a content-driven approach, you should determine any criteria by which you can pre-filter your choices (e.g., by jurisdiction). If you use word searching, you must draft a query to search for information. Chapter 2 discusses how to generate and prioritize your search terms. Word searching options are discussed below. Once you have completed the planning process, you are ready to sign on to a service and execute the search.

d. Reviewing and Filtering the Search Results

After you execute a search, you need to manipulate the results in a way that allows you to determine whether the search has been successful. You may need to view a list of documents retrieved, read the text of individual documents, find specific terms within a document, or use links to other documents. You may also need to filter the results to focus on the information most relevant to your research task. Content-driven searching in particular is likely to retrieve a large number of documents. Filtering the results according to the available criteria is critical to analyzing the effectiveness of your search.

In reviewing search results, it is important to pay attention to how the results are displayed. The default display may be by relevance, which means the documents with the best match to your search criteria appear first. "Relevance," however, is a relative concept. A document is likely to be deemed more relevant if the search terms appear frequently in the document or close to each other. The precise criteria for determining relevance varies by service, and the relevancy ranking of documents retrieved from the same search may vary depending on which service you use. You should treat the rankings as an approximation that cannot substitute for your own judgment about the relevance of the documents the search retrieves.

Depending on the service and search technique you use, your search results may not be ranked by relevance. It is common for cases to be listed in reverse date order, statutes in numerical order, and secondary sources in alphabetical order. Because most general search engines use relevancy rankings, most of us have been conditioned to review only the first few items in the results to assess the effectiveness of a search. If your results are displayed in a different way, however, the best information from your search could be in the middle or at the end of the results.

The most useful order for displaying search results will depend on your research task. Relevancy ranking is useful when the search retrieves a large number of documents. Reverse date order may be better if you are looking for the most recent authority on an issue. Often you will have the option to change the default order (from date to relevance or from relevance to alphabetical, depending on the source). Regardless of whether you can change the default setting, you must be aware of the order in which the results are listed to assess the effectiveness of the search.

Following these four steps is not always a linear process. You might decide first on your search technique, which could influence the service you select. Even if you follow the steps in order initially, you may repeat some of them based on the search results. For example, after reviewing your search results, you might go back to the second step and select a different search technique. A single search is unlikely to retrieve exactly the desired information, except when you are retrieving a document you need from its citation. One provider offers the following explanation of the search process in the context of word searching:

> Searching is a process, not an event. This should be your mantra when using [online research services]. Searching...is not about spending time and mental energy formulating the "golden query" that retrieves your desired information in a single stroke. In practice, good online searching involves formulating a succession of queries until you are satisfied with the results. As you view results from one search, you will come across additional leads that you did not identify in your original search. You can incorporate these new terms into your existing query or create a new one. After each query, evaluate its success by asking:
>
> - Did I find what I was looking for?
> - What better information could still be out there?

- How can I refine my query to find better information?

Issuing multiple queries can be frustrating or rewarding, depending on how long it takes you to identify the key material you need to answer your research problem.[1]

3. COST-EFFECTIVE SEARCHING

The cost of online research is something you might not notice as a law student because most, if not all, of the cost is subsidized. In practice, however, cost is an important consideration. You cannot use research services for which your client cannot or will not pay. Even if your client is willing and able to pay for some online research, you may not have unlimited ability to use fee-based services.

Of course, just because a service is fee-based does not mean it is a bad research option. It can be less expensive to locate authority through a fee-based service than it is to purchase books that would rarely be used, and some tasks can be accomplished more quickly online. In those situations, increased efficiency can justify the cost of using a fee-based service. You should not shy away from fee-based services simply because using them costs money. You should, however, be aware of cost issues and select the most cost-effective research options for your client, whether they are print or online, fee-based or free of charge.

It is difficult to generalize about the cost of fee-based services because many pricing options exist. Generally speaking, Westlaw and Lexis Advance are often the most expensive services to use. Some organizations negotiate flat rates for use of these services. But rates are based on the amount of usage, and the subscription package may not include all types of information available in the service. Charges can also be based on the amount of time spent online, the number of searches executed, or both. Premiums may be charged for accessing certain sources, especially those outside the user's subscription plan, and separate charges for printing or downloading information also may apply. You can view pricing information in Westlaw by reviewing the **Subscriber Pricing Guide** under the **Tools** tab. In Lexis Advance, pricing information is available from the **More** drop down menu at the top of the screen. Other fee-based services charge for use of their services as well, and you can view pricing information for these services on their websites.

Because pricing varies widely among fee-based services, it is important to investigate cost issues before you get online. When you work in a law office, you may be required to use a service such as Fastcase or

1. VersusLaw, Inc. Research Manual, Part 1, Electronic Searching Strategy, www.versuslaw.com; *select* FAQ/Help, Research Manual, Research Manual Part 1—Search Basics (accessed Nov. 14, 2017).

Casemaker before you are permitted to research with Westlaw or Lexis Advance. If the office has a large print collection, you may be required to use some material in print instead of accessing it from a fee-based service.

Subscription and publicly available services are economical choices for your client if they will give you the information you need. Although charges for access to subscription services are usually paid by the subscriber rather than the user, users can be charged for printing or downloading information. Publicly available services are the least expensive option because they involve only the cost of access to the Internet.

The following strategies can help you conduct cost-effective research:

a. Generate Search Terms and Plan Your Research Path in Advance

One of the best ways to cut costs is to draft your word searches and plan your research path before you get online. No matter how you are being billed, a thoughtful search strategy defined before you sign on is more likely to lead to useful results. This involves thinking about your search terms and deciding which sources to search or how to pre-filter your search.

This is especially true when you use an online service that requires you to select a source before you execute a search. Deciding in advance which sources you plan to search will allow you to search quickly and efficiently. Searching the narrowest source that meets your research needs makes evaluating your search results easier.

If you choose content-driven searching, you will still find it worthwhile to consider any appropriate pre-filtering criteria. Pre-filtering by jurisdiction, for example, will narrow the results of a content-driven search.

b. Use Research Assistance

Another way to cut costs is to use the research assistance provided by the service. For example, Westlaw and Lexis Advance employ research attorneys to provide assistance to users. You can obtain live help online or telephone assistance through their toll-free numbers. Bloomberg Law also offers online and telephone support. If you are unsure about whether your strategy is likely to be effective, you may want to contact the provider for assistance. The research attorneys will help you create searches to maximize the effectiveness of your research.

c. Execute Searches to Account for the Billing Structure

Once you have signed on to a research service, some search options may be more cost effective than others. If you are being charged by the amount of time you spend online, you want to work as quickly as possible to minimize your costs. In that situation, it is especially important that you plan your research before you sign on because you do not want to spend time thinking up your search once you have started accruing charges.

If you are being charged by the number of searches you execute, you may be able to modify your initial search at no additional cost. In that case, you may want to devise relatively broad searches, along with potential narrowing modifications. You can then execute the broad searches, browse the results, and execute modifications to narrow the results if necessary. This will be more cost effective than executing a series of new searches.

d. Determine Charges for Printing or Downloading Information

Separate charges may apply to downloading or printing documents. Even while you are in law school, there may be limits to the amount of printing you can do without charge. Therefore, whether you are at work or at school, be sure to investigate printing and downloading costs before you get online.

B. EFFECTIVE WORD SEARCHING

Most online research providers offer multiple ways to locate information. Citation and subject searching are discussed in more detail in the chapters devoted to individual types of authority. This section explains techniques for effective word searching that you can use to search for many kinds of authority.

Effective word searching requires an understanding of the types of word searches you can conduct. Understanding these options will help you select the type of word searching best suited to your research task, modify the default result display to highlight the most relevant information, and filter the results of the search effectively.

1. TYPES OF WORD SEARCHES

When you execute a word search, the search engine searches a database of documents and retrieves the documents that meet the criteria you set for the search. To do this, the search engine uses an algorithm, or set of rules, to evaluate the search criteria and the documents in the database. Search algorithms must balance two competing factors in retrieving results: recall and precision. Recall refers to identifying the universe of documents that meet the search criteria. Precision refers to the relevance of the results. An algorithm that emphasizes recall will retrieve many documents, not all of which may be relevant. An algorithm that emphasizes precision will focus on retrieving the most relevant results, to the exclusion of some documents that do not align as closely with the search criteria. There is no perfect relationship between these factors; each involves trade-offs. The algorithms in various search engines strike the balance differently. This is one reason why you can get different search results from the same search executed in multiple services.

A literal search algorithm searches for documents that contain the specific terms in your word search. A non-literal search algorithm also searches for documents that contain the search terms, but it does not limit the result to those documents. It uses the search terms to search background information or meta-data and includes in the results documents that appear relevant to the search terms even though they do not contain those terms. Legal research services use three types of search algorithms: terms and connectors (also called Boolean), natural language, and plain language.

A terms and connectors search is a literal search and emphasizes precision over recall. It identifies documents containing the precise terms you identify, in the precise relationships you request. For example, you could search for documents that contain both the phrase *"ice cream"* and the term *sundae.* Alternatively, you could search for documents that contain either the phrase *"ice cream"* or the term *sundae,* but not necessarily both. AND and OR are examples of connectors, which are the commands that define the relationships among the search terms. A list of the most commonly used commands appears in **Figure 10.1**.

Because you use commands to steer the search logic, you can control the search results more precisely than you can with other search algorithms. If you search for *"ice cream" /s sundae,* the search will retrieve only documents that contain the phrase "ice cream" in the same sentence as sundae; if a document contains "ice cream" and sundae but not within the same sentence, that document will not appear in the search results. The search may retrieve any number of documents, or no documents at all, depending on the number of documents that meet the search criteria. Lexis Advance, Westlaw, Bloomberg Law, and most other legal research providers offer the option of terms and connectors searching. More information on specific terms and connectors commands appears below.

A natural language search is also a literal search, but natural language search algorithms use embedded rules to balance recall and precision. Unlike a terms and connectors search, a natural language search does not require you to specify the relationships among the terms in the documents to be retrieved. Instead, the natural language algorithm evaluates the relationships among the search terms, which it then uses to determine which documents meet the search criteria. A natural language search for *ice cream sundae* will retrieve documents that contain all or

FIGURE 10.1 **COMMON TERMS AND CONNECTORS COMMANDS**

Exact Phrase	"Place terms in Quotation marks"
Alternative terms	Term1 **or** Term2
All terms	Term1 **and** Term2
Terms with grammatical proximity	Term1 **/p** Term2 (Term1 appears within the same paragraph as Term2) Term1 **/s** Term2 (Term1 appears within the same sentence as Term2)
Terms with numerical proximity	Term1 **/n** Term2 (Term1 appears within a certain number of words of Term2; n = a specific number)
Exclude terms	*Westlaw, Bloomberg Law*: Term1 **but not** Term2 *Lexis Advance, Bloomberg Law*: Term1 **and not** Term2
Expand terms	*Westlaw, Bloomberg Law:* Exclamation point (!) for variable word endings (Term! retrieves Term, Terms, Termed, Terming, Terminal, Terminable, and all other variations of the word) *Westlaw:* Asterisk (*) to substitute for variable individual letters (Te*m retrieves Term, Team, and Teem) *Lexis Advance:* Asterisk (*) or exclamation point (!) for variable word endings (Term* and Term! retrieve Term, Terms, Termed, Terming, Terminal, Terminable, and all other variations of the word) *Lexis Advance:* Asterisk (*) to substitute for variable multiple letters (S*holder retrieves Shareholder and Stockholder) *Lexis Advance:* Asterisk (*) or question mark (?) to substitute for variable individual letters (Te*m and Te?m retrieve Term, Team, and Teem)

some of those terms and will rank the results by relevance. Documents in which the terms appear frequently or close together will be ranked higher than documents that contain only one of the search terms. But because a natural language search is a literal search, recall is limited to documents that contain at least one of the search terms. Lexis Advance and Bloomberg Law offer natural language searching.

A plain language search, as that term is used in this text, refers to a variation of natural language searching that is non-literal. A plain language search also balances recall and precision, albeit using different tools than a literal natural language search. Like a natural language algorithm, a plain language algorithm uses embedded rules to evaluate which documents meet the search criteria, but it searches both the text of the documents in the database and meta-data associated with the documents. In addition to retrieving documents that contain the search terms, therefore, it can also retrieve documents that appear relevant according to the embedded search rules even though they do not contain the search terms. Westlaw and Google Scholar have plain language search engines.

2. COMPARING WORD SEARCH OPTIONS

Your search results can vary substantially depending on whether you use terms and connectors, natural language, or plain language searching. Understanding the results each type of search produces will help you choose the search method best suited to your research task. The research scenario introduced in Chapter 2 provides an example to illustrate the differences among the search methods:

> Your client recently ended a long-term relationship with her partner. She and her partner never participated in a formal marriage ceremony, but they had always planned to get married "someday." They lived together for five years and referred to each other as husband and wife. Your client and her former partner orally agreed to provide support for each other, and your client's former partner repeatedly made statements like, "What's mine is yours." Your client wants to know if she is entitled to part of the value of the assets her former partner acquired during their relationship or to any support payments.

One legal theory you might want to investigate in connection with this scenario is palimony, which is a claim for support made by an unmarried partner after the dissolution of a romantic relationship. It is similar to alimony granted after a divorce. If you execute a search for the term *palimony* in Florida appellate cases, the results will vary depending on the type of word search you conduct. The results of the searches are summarized in **Figure 10.2.**[2]

A terms and connectors search for *palimony* retrieves virtually the same results in Westlaw, Lexis Advance, and Bloomberg Law. All of the searches retrieve the same five cases that contain the term *palimony;* Lexis Advance retrieves one unpublished opinion that the other services did not, and Westlaw retrieves one case that contains the term *palimony* in a West headnote rather than the case itself. Natural language searches in Lexis Advance and Bloomberg Law produce the same results. This

2. The search results described in this section are current as of November 14, 2017. The results you get if you execute these searches may vary somewhat over time as new Florida cases are decided or as the meta-data associated with the cases changes.

FIGURE 10.2 ***PALIMONY* SEARCH RESULTS COMPARISON**

Service	Lexis Advance	Bloomberg Law	Westlaw	Westlaw	Google Scholar
Search Type	terms and connectors and natural language	terms and connectors and natural language	terms and connectors	plain language	plain language
Results (listed by relevance according to the search service's criteria)	1. *Lowry v. Lowry* 2. *Crossen v. Feldman* 3. *Posik v. Layton* 4. *Evans v. Wall* 5. *Gilvary v. Gilvary* 6. *Evans v. Wall* (unpublished opinion)	1. *Crossen v. Feldman* 2. *Evans v. Wall* 3. *Gilvary v. Gilvary* 4. *Lowry v. Lowry* 5. *Posik v. Layton*	1. *Posik v. Layton* 2. *Evans v. Wall* 3. *Crossen v. Feldman* 4. *Jarrell v. Jarrell* (term appears only in a headnote) 5. *Gilvary v. Gilvary* 6. *Lowry v. Lowry*	1. *Posik v. Layton* 2. *Evans v. Wall* 3. *Crossen v. Feldman* 4. *Jarrell v. Jarrell* (term appears only in a headnote) 5. *Gilvary v. Gilvary* 6. *Dietrich v. Winters** 7. *Bashaway v. Cheney Bros., Inc.** 8. *Stevens v. Muse** 9. *Kindle v. Kindle** 10. *Forrest v. Ron** 11. *Lowry v. Lowry* 12. *Poe v. Levy's Estate** 13. *Burger v. Burger** 14. *Addison v. Brown** 15. *Newberger v. Newberger** 16. *Metro Building Materials Corp. v. Republic National Bank of Miami** 17. *Hays v. Johnson** 18. *Castetter v. Henderson** 19. *Wright v. Wright** 20. *Garcia v. Manning**	1. *Posik v. Layton* 2. *Crossen v. Feldman* 3. *Evans v. Wall* 4. *Stevens v. Muse** 5. *Poe v. Estate of Levy** 6. *Gilvary v. Gilvary* 7. *Lowry v. Lowry* 8. *Eberhardt v. Eberhardt** 9. *Wakeman v. Dixon**
Marked cases (*) do not contain the search term *palimony*.					

is because the search consists of only one term, and the literal searches retrieved only documents that contain the search term.

Compare these results with the results of a plain language search. A plain language search for the term *palimony* in Westlaw retrieves 20 cases: 6 that contain the term *palimony* (and were in the Westlaw terms and connectors search results) plus 14 more that do not contain the term *palimony*. The cases are listed in **Figure 10.2.**

The plain language search retrieved the additional 14 cases because the meta-data they contain indicated that they met the embedded rules for relevance to the search term. Westlaw expanded the search beyond the document text to include West topics and key numbers (described in Chapter 5), KeyCite data (described in Chapter 6), and retrieval data from other users who have executed similar searches. A review of the cases in the *palimony* search results reveals that several of them share a common topic heading on informal or invalid marriage, and several of them cite or are cited by the cases that contain the term *palimony*. Westlaw used these and other criteria to connect the cases to the search term, and most of the additional 14 cases are, in fact, indirectly related to palimony. Several of them concern parties seeking property or support from a former partner or discuss doctrines that have some overlap with palimony, such as constructive trust. A few simply are not relevant.

When only a few documents contain your search terms, documents that do not contain the search terms but that nevertheless meet certain relevancy criteria appear in the Westlaw plain language search results. The relevance of documents that do not contain any of your search terms may be low, however, so Westlaw limits these search results to 20 documents. If more than 20 documents had contained the term *palimony*, Westlaw would not have limited the results to 20 documents. Westlaw also places some limits on the results even for documents that contain the search terms, based primarily on the documents' relevance. The Westlaw search algorithm uses these limits to balance recall and precision.

Once the relevance of the documents containing the search terms gets too low, Westlaw eliminates them from the search results. Westlaw also places an outer limit on the number of documents in the search results. It will not retrieve more than 10,000 documents in any single category of authority (e.g., cases, statutes, secondary sources).

A plain language search in Google Scholar retrieves the nine cases listed in **Figure 10.2**. The results include the same five cases containing the term *palimony* that the literal searches retrieved, as well as four additional cases that do not contain the search term but that contain meta-data connecting them to the search term. Google Scholar does not search the same meta-data that Westlaw does, and its coverage of state cases does not go back as far in time. This is why it retrieves fewer cases than Westlaw even though it uses a non-literal search algorithm. Google Scholar does not appear to limit the search results for cases that meet the relevancy criteria based only on meta-data.

Which results are best? The answer depends on your research task. If you only want to retrieve cases that specifically discuss palimony, the literal search results are better suited to your task because you will not have to sort through cases that do not specifically discuss palimony. If you are interested in learning about any claims the client might bring, the non-literal search results may suit your needs better because they may point you toward other legal theories that you had not considered. In a sense, the non-literal search results mimic the results you might get if you looked up a term in a print index and used cross-references to direct you to related topics.

The results in **Figure 10.2** are listed by relevance. You can see that different services ranked the relevance of the documents differently. If the results that include the term *palimony* in the court's opinions were listed in reverse date order, they would appear as follows: *Posik v. Layton*; *Crossen v. Feldman*; *Gilvary v. Gilvary*; *Evans v. Wall*; *Lowry v. Lowry*. These differences do not matter much in a search that retrieves only a few documents, but they can matter a lot in a search that retrieves 50, 100, or 1,000 documents. This simply serves to emphasize the importance of being aware of the way the results are ordered and of treating the relevancy rankings as approximate, rather than definitive.

3. EXECUTING, NARROWING, AND REVIEWING WORD SEARCHES IN LEXIS ADVANCE AND WESTLAW

Bloomberg Law and most other services allow you to execute a word search both as your initial search for documents and as a narrowing search within your initial search results. Although most services offer these options, this section discusses specific features of word searches in Lexis Advance and Westlaw.

a. Lexis Advance

Lexis Advance treats a search typed into the search box as a natural language search unless it includes terms and connectors commands. The Lexis Advance search algorithm errs on the side of recall over precision, which means it can return large numbers of documents.

With natural language searching, Lexis Advance automatically interprets many common legal phrases as phrases. The search results will include both documents that contain the phrase as well as those that contain each individual term, but documents that contain the phrase will have higher relevancy rankings. For words that Lexis Advance does not recognize as a phrase, the search algorithm searches each term separately as an individual word. Thus, it treats a search for *summary judgment* as a phrase, while terms it does not recognize as a phrase are connected with either AND or OR, depending on how commonly the terms appear within Lexis Advance (e.g., *ice AND cream* or *ice OR cream*). You can create a search phrase by putting the search terms in quotation marks.

Although natural language searching is the default option in Lexis Advance, terms and connectors searching is also an option. Entering a search that incorporates terms and connectors search commands (such as the /P or /S connectors) will cause Lexis Advance to execute the search as a terms and connectors search. The **Advanced Search** link above the search box opens a template you can use to create a terms and connectors search.

The default display for the search results is by relevance. You can change the default display setting using the **Sort by** options.

Once you execute your initial search, the **Actions** menu gives you choices for revising the search. You can re-run the search as either a natural language or terms and connectors search. You can also expand a natural language search to include all terms in your search, effectively applying OR as the default connector. When you expand the search this way, there is no outer limit on the number of documents retrieved, so the results may include thousands of documents, depending on your search terms.

To narrow the search results, use the options in the left-hand menu. If you use **Search within results**, the search will be a terms and connectors search even if your initial search was a natural language search.

Under the **More** dropdown menu at the top of the screen, the **Settings** option will allow you to change some of the default settings for searching and displaying the results.

b. Westlaw

Westlaw will ordinarily treat a search typed into the search box as a plain language search. The search algorithm recognizes many common legal phrases. If you search for a common legal phrase, the results should automatically be limited to documents containing the phrase (as opposed to documents that contain one or more of the terms separately).

Placing a search phrase in quotation marks can change the way Westlaw executes the search. A search that consists of a single phrase in quotation marks (*"ice cream sundae"*) will be executed as a terms and connectors search and will retrieve only documents that contain the precise phrase.

If the search contains a quoted phrase with additional terms, however, Westlaw will treat the search as a plain language search and will look for the quoted terms within three words of each other. Thus, a search for *"ice cream sundae" and chocolate* will retrieve documents that contain the phrase *ice cream sundae,* as well as those that contain *sundae with ice cream*, *ice cream cone or sundae*, and so on, as long as the quoted terms are within three words of each other. Additionally, if the results include documents that do not contain the quoted phrase, you will see a message indicating that and giving you the option to limit the results to documents that contain the precise phrase.

If your search does not include a quoted phrase, you still have the option to use terms and connectors searching. Entering a search that incorporates a grammatical, numerical, or exclusion connector or a term expander (see **Figure 10.1**) will automatically cause Westlaw to execute the search as a terms and connectors search. The **Advanced** link to the right of the search box brings up a template you can use to create a terms and connectors search, or you can type *adv:* followed by a search to execute it as a terms and connectors search.

Search results are ranked by relevance. Once you execute your initial search, you can narrow the search results using the filtering options in the **View** menu. If you use **Search within results**, the search will be a terms and connectors search even if your initial search was a plain language search.

You can change some of these default options. After you execute a search, use the **Sort by** options to vary the display order. The **Preferences** link at the bottom of the screen has a **Search** tab with additional options. You can change some of the plain language and terms and connectors search defaults, as well as the default display order of your search results.

4. TERMS AND CONNECTORS SEARCH COMMANDS

Terms and connectors searching is useful as an initial search strategy when you want to control the relationships among the search terms. It is also the form of searching you must use when you execute a narrowing search within the initial search results. Therefore, you need to understand how to use terms and connectors searching.

a. Terms and Connectors Search Logic

In terms and connectors searching, you define the relationships among the terms in the search using connectors and other commands. **Figure 10.1** lists the most commonly used commands.

Most searches contain several terms and may contain multiple connectors. When the search is executed, Boolean logic will process the connectors in a specific sequence. In Westlaw and Lexis Advance, the OR connector is processed first, followed by the numerical and grammatical proximity connectors (/N, /P, /S), and then the AND connector. Westlaw and Lexis Advance process an exclusion connector (AND NOT, BUT NOT) last. Bloomberg Law processes connectors from left to right, in the order they appear in the search. It is important to understand this hierarchy of connectors to create an effective search.

If you executed a search for *ice AND cream OR sundae* in Westlaw or Lexis Advance, the search for the terms *cream or sundae* would be processed first. After documents with one or the other of those terms were identified, the search for the term *ice* would begin. In effect, the query would be processed as a search for *ice and cream or ice and sundae.* If this was not the intended search, it could miss documents containing the terms you want or retrieve irrelevant documents.

There are two ways to modify this search so that it searches for the phrase "*ice cream*" or the individual term *sundae.* One is by searching for "*ice cream*" as a phrase instead of connecting the words with AND.

Another way to vary the search would be to segregate the *ice AND cream* portion of the search. In Westlaw, Lexis Advance, and Bloomberg Law, you can accomplish this by placing a portion of the search in parentheses: *(ice AND cream) OR sundae.* The terms within parentheses would be treated as a separate unit. Thus, the AND connector would apply only to the terms within the parentheses. In this example, adding parentheses would result in a search for the terms *ice AND cream* as a unit, and then in the alternative, for the individual term *sundae.*

b. Using Terms and Connectors for an Initial Search

When you use terms and connectors searching for your initial search, you will want to follow three steps:

- developing the initial search terms;
- expanding the breadth and depth of the search;
- adding connectors to clarify the relationships among the search terms.

In developing the initial search terms, you should use the process described in Chapter 2. Think about the problem in terms of the parties, any places or things, potential claims and defenses, and the relief sought.

Having identified the relevant terms, your next step is expanding the search. Recall that a terms and connectors search is a literal search. If an object, idea, concept, or action is expressed in a document using terms different from your search terms, a terms and connectors search will not locate the document. Unless you are searching for terms of art that need to appear precisely for a document to be useful, you need to expand the breadth and depth of the search, as explained in Chapter 2.

Expanding the breadth of the search involves generating synonyms and terms related to the initial search terms. You can also expand the breadth of an individual term by using a term expander, such as the asterisk (*) to substitute for individual letters and the exclamation point (!) to substitute for variable word endings. (Although many services use term expander characters, the functions of the characters are not standard. For example, the asterisk (*) in some services is used for variable word endings, not the exclamation point (!). You should review the search commands in any service with which you are unfamiliar.) Expanding the depth involves expressing the terms with varying degrees of abstraction.

Once you have developed and expanded the search terms, the next step is identifying the appropriate relationships among the terms using connectors. The closer the connections you require among the terms, the more restrictive the search will be, and the broader the connections, the more open the search will be. For example, the AND connector, which requires only that both words appear somewhere within the same document, will retrieve more documents than a proximity connector such as /P, which requires the words to appear within the same paragraph. Be sure to take the hierarchy of connectors into account as you consider the relationships among the search terms. If necessary, use parentheses to group categories of terms that you want to search together.

In addition to allowing you to search for terms within the body of a document, many services will allow you to limit your search to individual components of the document, such as words in the title or the name of the author. Although you will not always use this search option, it is an important feature to understand.

In Westlaw, the document components are called "fields"; in Lexis Advance they are called "segments." In either service, you can limit your search to a particular field or segment by typing specific commands in the search box. In Westlaw and Lexis Advance, field and segment searching options also appear in the **Advanced** search template. If you open the template without selecting a source, it will display limited field and segment searching options. If you select a source to search before opening the **Advanced** template, you will see the complete list of field and segment searching options available for the source you selected.

Although you can make a terms and connectors search very specific by using multiple search commands, an effective terms and connectors search does not have to use all or even most of the available commands. The structure and complexity of any search will depend on the nature of the information you need. The important thing is to know what the commands are so you can use them to steer the search engine to retrieve information relevant to your research task.

c. Using Terms and Connectors in a Narrowing Search

Regardless of the type of search you execute initially, a search within the search results in Westlaw and Lexis Advance will be a terms and connectors search. The way you draft the narrowing search will depend on how you want to filter the search results. Three ways you may want to narrow the search results include:

- adding terms that were not part of the initial search;
- focusing on terms that were part of the initial search;
- changing the relationships among terms that were part of the initial search.

The results of your initial search will depend in part on the level of abstraction of your search terms. If you execute a broad search for a general concept, you will likely retrieve many documents. You may want to narrow the results by adding more specific terms. For example, the doctrine of assumption of risk is a defense to a negligence claim. If you were researching assumption of risk in the context of rock climbing accidents, you might begin your research by looking more abstractly for material related to assumption of risk in sports or recreation. If that search retrieved too many documents to be useful, you could then execute a narrowing search for authority that specifically discusses rock climbing.

To use terms and connectors commands effectively in this context, the narrowing search could include *"rock climbing"* as a search phrase. You could also search for the terms in proximity to one another with a term expander to capture variations on the word *climb.* Thus, the narrowing search might look like this: *rock /5 climb!* This search would retrieve documents in which the term *rock* appears within five words before or after any variation of the word *climb* (climb, climbs, climber, climbed, climbing).

Another way to narrow the search results is by focusing on terms that were part of your initial search. If you execute a search for several alternative terms and retrieve too many documents, narrowing the search to focus on one or two specific terms will limit the search results.

A third way to narrow the search results is to use terms and connectors commands to change the relationships among the words in the search. The AND connector will limit the results by identifying documents that contain all of the specific terms instead of only one. Using the grammatical or numerical connectors (/P, /S, /N) to target documents that contain the terms close together is another good strategy. The exclusion connectors (AND NOT, BUT NOT) are useful when you have a term that is relevant when used in one context but not relevant in others. By excluding documents that contain terms associated with the irrelevant context, you can target more relevant documents.

C. ADDITIONAL ONLINE RESEARCH RESOURCES

1. ALERT OR CLIPPING SERVICES

Sometimes your work on a research project will be done in a few days, but other times it will extend over a longer period of time. In law school, you might work on a moot court brief or scholarly paper for several weeks or even an entire semester. In legal practice, work on individual cases often extends over months or years. When you are working on an issue over a period of time, one resource that may be useful to you is an alert or clipping service. These services automatically run searches and notify you when relevant new information is added to a database. They allow you to stay up to date on developments affecting your research while you are working on a project.

Many news services offer automatic updates on general news topics and current events. Providers of legal information also frequently offer alert or clipping services. Free services, such as Law.com, offer free daily updates on top legal stories. Fee-based services will often allow you to draft specific queries to update your research on a schedule you specify. You can specify the database(s) in which to run the search, the frequency with which the search is to be run, and the manner in which the search results will be delivered to you. Once you access the service, a menu of options will set out the choices available to you.

Westlaw offers several alert services. The two that are most likely to be of use to you in law school are KeyCite Alert and WestClip. KeyCite Alert, which is described in Chapter 6 on citators, notifies you when new information is added to the KeyCite entries for cases, statutes, federal regulations, or certain federal administrative agency decisions. WestClip allows you to draft a word search to be run periodically in the database(s) you specify and delivers the search results to you. The **Alerts** link at the top of the screen will open the menu of options for creating the search. Note, however, that WestClip works only with terms and connectors searches, not plain language searches.

Lexis Advance also allows you to create alerts. Shepard's Alert® is similar to KeyCite Alert and is also described in Chapter 6. It notifies you when new information is added to the Shepard's entries for cases, statutes, or federal regulations. You can also create an alert to run a word search at specified intervals and have the results delivered to you. After you Shepardize a document or run a search, click on the bell icon and follow the menu options to create the alert.

To create a search alert in Bloomberg Law, follow the **Create Search Alert** link in the search results.

Other services also offer clipping services. You should look for alert or clipping services in any online resource you use.

2. PUBLICLY AVAILABLE SOURCES

Legal research used to be accomplished primarily, if not exclusively, in a limited universe of research sources produced by legal publishers. As more and more information becomes available online, however, the range of sources available for researching legal issues continues to grow. Government, educational, non-profit, trade, and civic organizations that are engaged in public education efforts make useful information on many areas of the law available on their websites. In addition, blogs are becoming an increasingly important source of information both in our culture as a whole and in legal research. Law-related blogs are sometimes called blawgs.

Publicly available information is most likely to be useful to you when you are looking for information on a specific topic. If you find a relevant website or blog, it may provide you with background information on the topic, references to significant legal authorities, news about legislative initiatives pending at the local, state, or federal level, and links to other sites with useful information.

Publicly available sources are simply new types of secondary sources. When viewed this way, their role in legal research becomes clear. The caveats described in Chapter 4, on secondary source research in more traditional legal sources, also apply to publicly available websites: Use them to obtain background information on an area of law and to obtain citations to primary authority. Do not rely on them as authoritative sources of legal rules or as official sources of primary authority.

To make sure you use publicly available sources appropriately, you should follow four steps: (1) locate useful information; (2) assess the credibility of the source of the information; (3) save or print a copy of the information you are using; and (4) verify and update any legal authorities you locate through the source. In the following discussion of these four steps, you will find references to websites that may be useful to you. The URLs for all these sites appear in Appendix A at the end of this text.

To locate useful information, you could use a general search engine, such as Google, or a specialized search engine, such as Google Scholar for scholarly publications. You can also use a directory such as Blawg, a directory of law-related blogs.

Once you have located useful information, you must assess the credibility of the source. Anyone can post information online. Much information available online is inaccurate or out of date. Many individuals and groups post information to advance their social or policy agendas. Therefore, you need to make a separate assessment of how much weight to give to information posted on an individual's or organization's website. The sites you visit should contain information you can use to assess the sources' credibility. Most sites sponsored by organizations or entities include information about the group, such as its history and mission. The authors of many blogs will provide biographical information to help you assess their expertise.

If you find useful information online, be sure to save or print a copy of the page. Sites can change at any moment; the information most helpful to you could change or disappear altogether at any time. If you find that information you accessed earlier is no longer available, you can try to find it in an Internet archive, such as the Internet Archive Wayback Machine, which stores copies of sites for future reference. The University of North Texas library system also hosts the Cybercemetery of Former Federal Web Sites. Although these sites provide limited historical records of websites, you cannot count on finding an archived version of a web page that has been changed, moved, or deleted. The better practice, therefore, is to save or print useful information as you locate it.

If you find references to legal authorities through publicly available websites, the last step is verifying and updating your research. You should not assume that the authorities you have located are correct, complete, or up to date. Use the information you have found as a springboard into more traditional avenues of legal research to make sure that you have located all pertinent information and that the legal authority you cite is authoritative.

D. CITING AUTHORITY OBTAINED ONLINE

Much of the information you locate through online services will also be available in print format. Both the *ALWD Guide* (6th ed.) and the *Bluebook* (20th ed.) require that you cite the print format if possible.

This is not as difficult as it might seem. Many services provide all the information you need for a print citation, including page numbers. For cases, statutes, and other materials available only online, the following rules apply. This chapter does not contain complete explanations about citing cases, statutes, and other authorities. More information about citing each of these types of authority is included in the chapters devoted to those sources.

1. CASES

Citations to cases available only online are governed by *ALWD Guide* Rule 12.12-12.14 and *Bluebook* Bluepages B10.1.4. The citation must contain the following four components: (1) the case name; (2) the docket number for the case; (3) the database identifier, which often includes the year, the name of the database, and the unique document number; and (4) a parenthetical containing the jurisdiction and court abbreviations and the full date. A pinpoint reference can be provided with "at *" and the page number. Here is an example:

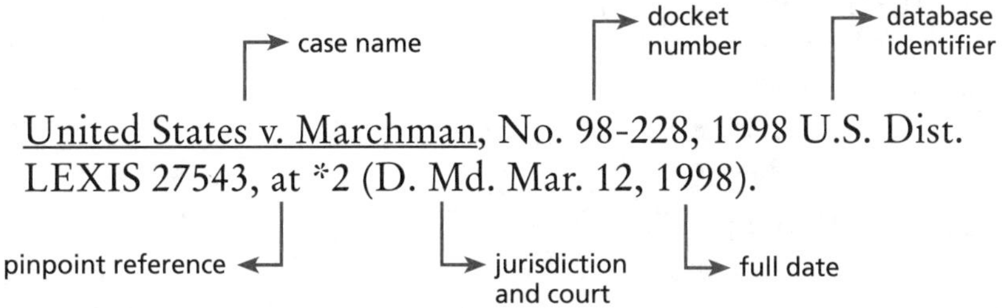

2. STATUTES

Statutory provisions retrieved online should be cited the same way print materials are cited, with additional information in the parenthetical indicating which service was accessed and the date through which the service was updated. Online statutory citations are covered in *ALWD Guide* Rule 14.2 and *Bluebook* Rule 12.5. Here is an example:

18 U.S.C. § 915 (Bloomberg Law through Pub. L. No. 115-82).

3. PUBLICLY AVAILABLE MATERIALS

Citations to online sources are discouraged if the document is available in print form because of the transient nature of many websites. If you are citing something you obtained online but that is available in print, you will generally be required to provide the print citation, supplemented with additional information indicating the online source.

In the *ALWD Guide*, Rule 30 provides general guidance on citing online sources, and Rule 31 covers citations to information available only online. In the *Bluebook*, information on online citations appears in Bluepages B18 and Rule 18. Rule 18.2 provides general guidance on citing online sources.

The components of a citation to an online source vary according to the nature of the source. In general, the citation should include the author's name (if available), the title of the item, a URL or other identifying information to guide the reader to the source, and the date. Examples of specific citation formats—including blogs, news reports, articles, and other sources—appear in the *ALWD Guide* and the *Bluebook*, but neither citation guide provides rules for citing every type of information available on the Internet.

Here is an example of a citation to an online news report:

Ciara Bri'd Frisbie, Kentucky Sues Maker of Controversial Opioid, CNN.com (Nov. 6, 2017, 9:37 PM), http://www.cnn.com/2017/11/06/health/opana-er-lawsuit-kentucky/index.html.

E. CHECKLIST FOR ONLINE LEGAL RESEARCH

1. SELECT A RESEARCH SERVICE

☐ Consider the scope of coverage of the service.
☐ Consider the cost of the service.

2. SELECT A SEARCH TECHNIQUE

☐ Retrieve a document from its citation.
☐ Execute a source-driven search by selecting a database and executing a word search or searching by subject.
☐ Execute a content-driven search by pre-filtering by jurisdiction (if possible), executing a word search, and filtering the results.

3. PLAN AND EXECUTE A SEARCH

☐ For word searches, consider the search options:
- Terms and connectors (Boolean) searching is literal and uses specific commands to define the relationships among search terms.
- Natural language searching is literal and uses embedded rules to define the relationships among search terms.
- Plain language searching is non-literal and uses embedded rules both to define the relationships among search terms and to search document meta-data.

☐ Be aware of the different word search options and tailor your search approach accordingly. Use terms and connectors searching effectively in an initial search:
- Develop the initial search terms.
- Expand the breadth and depth of the search.
- Specify the relationships among the terms using connectors.
- Use a field or segment restriction to target useful authorities.

4. REVIEW AND FILTER SEARCH RESULTS

☐ Relevance, date, or other result ranking choices affect which documents appear at the top of the search results.
☐ Narrowing searches will be terms and connectors searches even if the initial search is not; use terms and connectors commands to:
- Add search terms.
- Focus on terms in the initial search.
- Change the relationships among terms in the initial search.

5. USE ADDITIONAL TOOLS FOR EFFECTIVE ONLINE RESEARCH

☐ Use an alert or clipping service to keep research up to date.
- In Westlaw, use a KeyCite Alert and WestClip search.
- In Lexis Advance, use a Shepard's Alert® and search alerts.
- In Bloomberg Law, use a Search Alert.

- ☐ Use publicly available sources.
  - Locate useful sites to obtain background information on a topic or citations to primary authority.
  - Assess the credibility of the source.
  - Save or print copies of useful pages.
  - Verify and update any legal authorities you locate.

CHAPTER 11

Developing a Research Plan

A. INTRODUCTION TO RESEARCH PLANNING

When you get a research assignment, you might be tempted to begin the project by jumping directly into your research to see what authority you can find. In fact, searching for authority right away is not the best way to start. Thought and planning before you begin researching will help you in several ways. You will research more efficiently if you have a coherent research plan to follow. You will also research more accurately. Searching haphazardly can cause you to miss important authorities, and nothing is more disconcerting than feeling as though you came across relevant authority by accident. Following an organized plan will help ensure that you check all the appropriate places for authority on your issue and will give you confidence that your research is correct and complete.

B. CREATING A RESEARCH PLAN

Creating a research plan requires three steps: (1) obtaining preliminary information about the problem; (2) planning the steps in your research; and (3) working effectively as you execute your research plan. Each of these steps is discussed in turn.

1. OBTAINING PRELIMINARY INFORMATION

When you first receive a research assignment, you might feel like you do not know enough to ask very many questions about it. While this might be true as far as the substance of the problem is concerned, you need to determine the scope of your project by obtaining some preliminary information from the person making the assignment. Specifically:

■ HOW MUCH TIME DO I HAVE FOR THIS ASSIGNMENT?
The amount of time you have affects your overall approach, as well as your time management with other projects you have been assigned.

■ WHAT FINAL WORK PRODUCT SHOULD I PRODUCE?
You should determine whether you are expected to produce a memorandum, pleading, brief, or informal report of your research results. To a certain extent, this also will be a function of the amount of time you have for the project.

■ ARE THERE ANY LIMITS ON THE RESEARCH MATERIALS I AM PERMITTED TO USE?
As a matter of academic integrity, you want to make sure you use only authorized research tools in a law school assignment. In practice, some clients might be unable or unwilling to pay for research completed with tools requiring additional fees, such as Lexis Advance or Westlaw.

■ WHICH JURISDICTION'S LAW APPLIES?
This is a question the person giving you the assignment might not be able to answer. There will be times when the controlling jurisdiction will be known. In other cases, it will be up to you to determine whether an issue is controlled by federal or state law, and if it is a question of state law, which state's law applies.

■ SHOULD I RESEARCH NONBINDING AUTHORITY?
Again, the person making the assignment might not be able to answer this question. You could be asked to focus exclusively on the law of the controlling jurisdiction to answer your research question, or you could be asked specifically to research multiple jurisdictions. If either of those requirements applies to your research, you certainly want to know that before you begin your research. What is more likely, however, is that you will simply be asked to find the answer to a question. If the law of the controlling jurisdiction answers the question, you might not need to go further. If not, you will need to research nonbinding authority. Understanding the scope of the assignment will help you focus your efforts appropriately.

In your research class, there will be many parts of the assignment that your professor will expect you to figure out on your own as part of learning about the process of research. In a practice setting, however, you might also ask the following questions:

■ **DO YOU KNOW OF ANY SOURCES THAT ARE PARTICULARLY GOOD FOR RESEARCHING THIS AREA OF LAW?**

Practitioners who are experienced in a particular field might know of research sources that are especially helpful for the type of research you are doing, including services or sources devoted to specific subject areas.

■ **WHAT BACKGROUND ON THE LAW OR TERMS OF ART SHOULD I KNOW AS I BEGIN MY RESEARCH?**

In a law school assignment, you might be expected to identify terms of art on your own. In practice, however, the person giving you the research assignment might be able to give you some background on the area of law and important terms of art to help you get started on your research.

■ **SHOULD I CONSULT ANY WRITTEN MATERIALS OR INDIVIDUALS WITHIN THE OFFICE BEFORE BEGINNING MY RESEARCH?**

Again, in law school, it would be inappropriate to use another person's research instead of completing the assignment on your own. In practice, however, reviewing briefs or memoranda on the same or a similar issue can give you a leg up on your research. In addition, another person within the office might be considered the "resident expert" on the subject and might be willing to act as a resource for you.

2. PLANNING THE STEPS IN YOUR RESEARCH

Once you have preliminary information on your research project, you are ready to start planning the steps in your research process. The plan should have the following components:

- an initial issue statement
- a list of potential search terms
- an outline of your search strategy

a. Developing an Initial Issue Statement and Generating Search Terms

The starting points for your plan are developing an initial issue statement and generating possible search terms. The issue statement does not need to be a formal statement like one that would appear at the beginning of a brief or memorandum. Rather, it should be a preliminary assessment of the problem that helps define the scope of your research. For example, an initial issue statement might say something like, "Can the plaintiff recover from the defendant for destroying her garden?" This issue statement would be incomplete in a brief or memorandum because it does not identify a specific legal question and might not contain enough information about the facts. At this point, however, you do not know which legal theory or theories might be successful, nor do you know for certain which facts are most important. What this question tells you is that you will need to research all possible claims that would support recovery.

Alternatively, you might be asked to research a narrower question such as, "Can the plaintiff recover from the defendant *in negligence* for destroying her garden?" This issue statement again might be insufficient in a brief or memorandum, but for purposes of your research plan, it gives you valuable information. Your research should be limited to liability in negligence; intentional torts or contract claims are beyond the scope of this project.

Although this might seem like an exercise in the obvious, the discipline of writing a preliminary issue statement can help you focus your efforts in the right direction. If you are unable to write a preliminary issue statement, that is an indication that you are not sure about the scope of the assignment and may need to ask more questions about what you should be trying to accomplish.

Once you have written your initial issue statement, you are ready to generate a list of possible search terms. Chapter 2 discusses how to do this, and the techniques described in that chapter should be employed to develop search terms in your research plan.

b. Outlining Your Search Strategy

Once you have a preliminary view of the problem, the next step in creating an effective research plan is mapping out your search strategy. If you have access to a service that allows both source-driven and content-driven searching, you must decide which approach is best for your project. Considerations affecting this assessment are discussed in Chapter 3. If you use a content-driven approach, you must decide how to pre-filter a search for multiple types of authority. If you use a source-driven approach, you need to determine which research sources are likely to have relevant information. Then, you must determine the order in which you want to research those sources.

The best way to approach these tasks is to begin with what you know, identify what you do not yet know, and determine the best ways to fill in the blanks. Your goal should be to use the information you already have to begin narrowing the field of all legal information before you begin looking for authority. This will determine the level of generality at which to begin your research and set the framework for the research steps you need to follow. By answering a series of questions about your knowledge of the research issue, you can determine the best starting point for your research. **Figures 11.1** and **11.2** are flowcharts you can use to guide your inquiry and plan your research steps.

For many research projects, your ultimate goal will be to produce a written document, such as a brief or memorandum, describing and applying binding primary authority relevant to the issue. If this type of authority does not exist or does not fully resolve the question, then you will probably also need to discuss nonbinding primary authority, secondary authority, or both. Although this is not what you will be asked to do in every research project, this section will illustrate the process of outlining your research path based on this goal. As you will see, this process can be adapted for other types of research projects that you might be asked to complete.

The process of identifying what you know, identifying what you do not yet know, and determining how best to fill in the blanks can be applied to two components of the project: the search for binding primary authority, and the search for nonbinding authority. You might not be able to map out a complete research plan for both components of the project before beginning your research. At a minimum, however, you should try to plan your search for binding primary authority. If a search for nonbinding authority becomes necessary, you can then rework your plan to include those sources.

(1) Searching for binding primary authority

Beginning with the search for binding primary authority, the flowchart in **Figure 11.1** illustrates the process you might undertake.

As you can see from the flowchart, the more you can narrow the field of legal information at the start, the further down the process you can begin. If you know nothing about the subject, you will probably need to begin by reading secondary sources, either by choosing a particular secondary source or by reviewing the secondary sources retrieved from a content-driven search. If you already have a citation to an authority on point, you can use that as a starting point.

Once you have a sense of the applicable legal doctrine, you may also have a sense of whether the issue is a common-law issue governed by case law or an issue to which statutes, regulations, or other types of authority might apply. You can use this information to determine the best starting point for researching individual primary authorities or filtering the results of a content-driven search.

Once you have identified some binding primary authority on the issue, whether through secondary sources or some other avenue, you can use the information within individual authorities as a springboard to other primary authorities. As noted in the flowchart, for example, a case may contain headnotes that can lead you to other cases. The cases should also cite relevant statutory and regulatory provisions. Statutory annotations can lead you to legislative history, regulations, secondary sources,

FIGURE 11.1 **FLOWCHART FOR DETERMINING YOUR RESEARCH PATH**

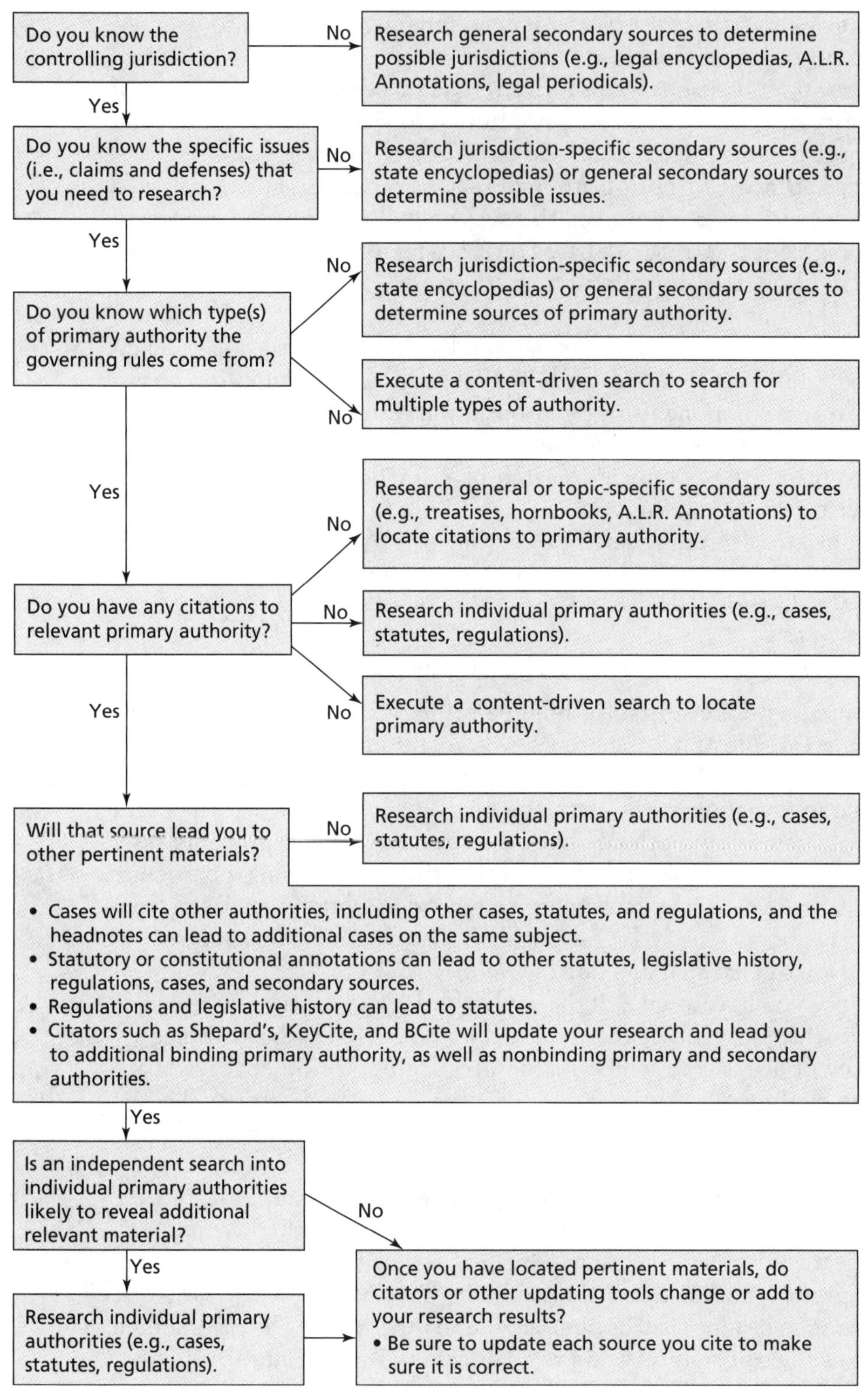

and cases. Of course, it is possible that the sources you consult initially will not lead you to other primary authorities. In that case, you might want to research individual primary sources independently to make sure you have located all of the relevant authority.

(2) Searching for nonbinding authority

As you conduct your research, you might determine that you need to search for nonbinding authority to analyze your research issue thoroughly. As in your search for binding primary authority, in your search for nonbinding authority, you should begin with what you know, identify what you do not yet know, and determine the best ways to fill in the blanks.

The first thing you need to know is why you are searching for nonbinding authority. Nonbinding authority can serve a variety of purposes in your analysis of a research question. Here are four common reasons why you would want to research nonbinding authority:

- When you want to buttress an analysis largely resolved by binding primary authority.
- When the applicable legal rules are clearly defined by binding primary authority, but the specific factual situation has not arisen in the controlling jurisdiction. You might want to try to locate factually analogous cases from other jurisdictions.
- When the applicable rule is unclear and you want to make an analogy to another area of law to support your analysis.
- When the issue is one of first impression in the controlling jurisdiction for which no governing rule exists. In this case, you might want to find out how other jurisdictions have addressed the issue, or if no jurisdiction has faced the question, whether any commentators have analyzed the issue.

In each of these situations, you might want to research nonbinding authority consisting of nonbinding primary authority from within the controlling jurisdiction, such as cases or statutes in an analogous area of law, primary authority from other jurisdictions, or secondary authority analyzing the law.

Once you have determined why you need to research nonbinding authority, you should review the material you have already located. In your search for binding primary authority, you might already have identified some useful nonbinding authority. Secondary sources consulted at the beginning of your research could contain persuasive analysis or useful citations to nonbinding primary authority. Secondary sources often identify key or leading authorities in an area of law, and that might be enough to meet your needs. A citator might also have identified useful nonbinding authority. If the authorities you have already located prove sufficient, you should update your research to make sure everything you cite remains authoritative and, if appropriate, end your search for nonbinding authority.

On the other hand, you might review the results of your research and determine that you need to undertake a separate search for nonbinding authority. When you first reviewed secondary sources and used citators, it might not have been with an eye toward locating nonbinding authority. Therefore, you might want to take a second pass at these sources. In addition, the nonbinding authority you ran across early in your research might not be the best material for you to cite; a more focused research effort could yield more pertinent material.

If you determine that you need to conduct a separate search for nonbinding authority, your next step will be deciding the best research path to follow. The flowchart in **Figure 11.2** illustrates several research avenues for locating nonbinding authority. Your research path will vary according to a number of factors, including the amount of time you have, the resources available to you, and the type of work product you are expected to produce. Therefore, the flowchart is intended simply to illustrate options that would be available to you, not to establish a definitive path for locating each type of authority.

One thing you might notice as you review the flowchart is that secondary sources play an important role in locating nonbinding authority. Unless you know the precise jurisdiction from which you plan to cite nonbinding authority, beginning your search for nonbinding authority in primary sources is not likely to be efficient in most cases. Secondary sources are key to determining which jurisdictions are likely to have relevant authority and which types of authority are likely to be helpful to you.

c. Incorporating Print Sources

One additional decision you will need to make in formulating a research plan is whether to incorporate print research into your research plan. Most researchers gravitate toward online sources, and some libraries no longer maintain extensive print collections. For certain tasks, however, you should consider print research. Libraries continue to hold secondary sources and statutes in print because those are sources lawyers continue to find useful.

Although many secondary sources are available online, many others are not. In particular, a number of treatises are only available in print, especially those in specialized areas of law or those devoted to the law of an individual jurisdiction. If you limit yourself to the treatises available online, you may miss important sources. A trip to the library to investigate treatises will often be a good use of your research time.

Print can also offer advantages in statutory research. Although some online services provide access to statutory indexes, most do not, which

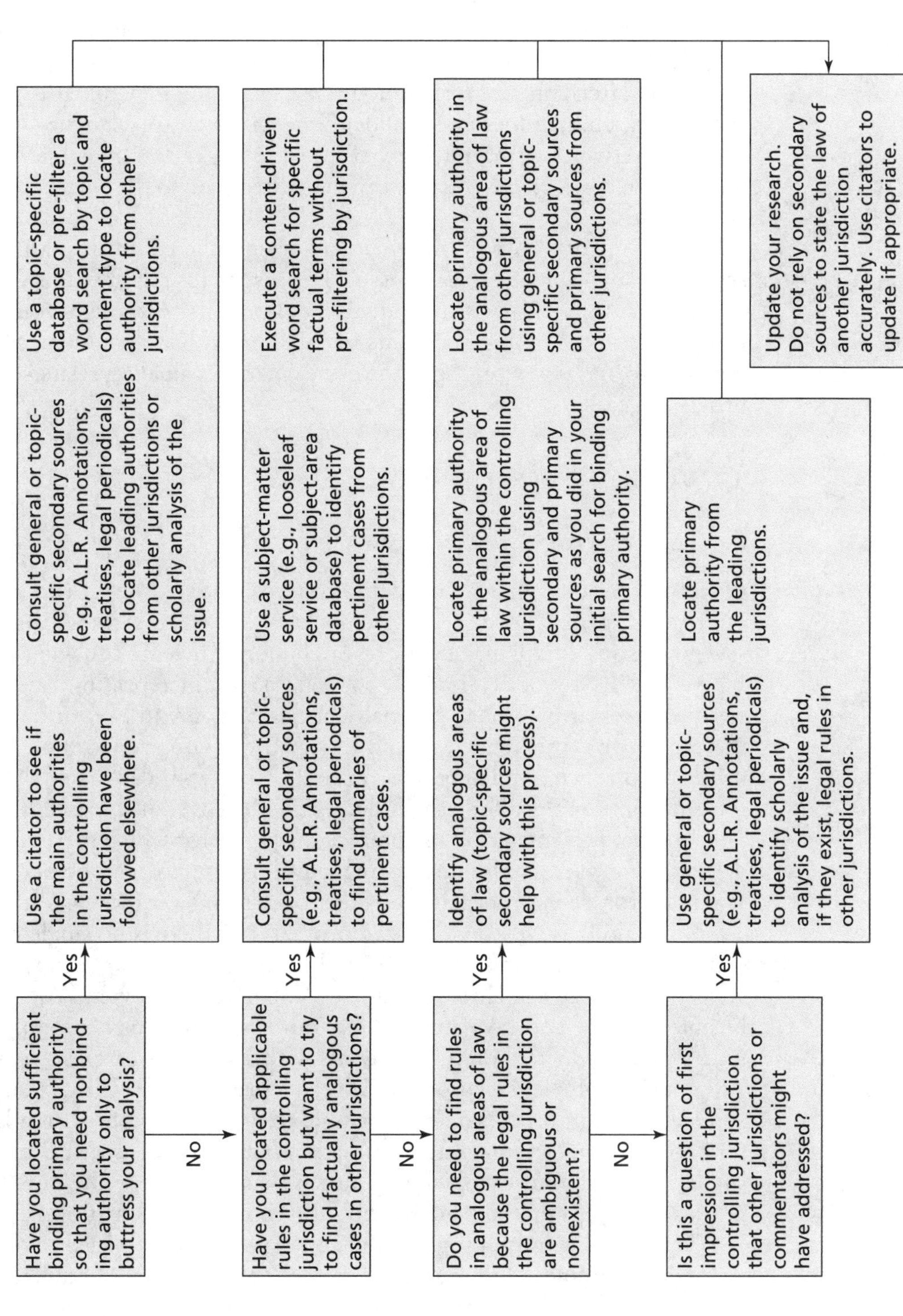

FIGURE 11.2 FLOWCHART FOR RESEARCHING NONBINDING AUTHORITY

means you must browse the table of contents or execute a word search to locate statutes online. The table of contents can be a cumbersome way to search unless you already know which titles or subject areas to search. Legislation is not always organized in an intuitive fashion. Further, legislation often contains terminology that might not be familiar to you. A word search that does not include the precise statutory language may not be effective. A print index, by contrast, is organized by subject and will contain cross-references that can help direct you to the correct terms or concepts.

Additionally, you will often need to review the complete statutory scheme to analyze your research issue. It is easy to lose sight of this when an online search retrieves individual code sections. Although you can usually access the table of contents from an individual document, some researchers find that working in the books makes evaluating related code provisions easier.

3. WORKING EFFECTIVELY

a. Keeping Track: Effective Note Taking

Once you have outlined your path, you are ready to begin executing your search plan. Keeping effective notes as you work is important for several reasons. It will make your research more efficient. You will know where you have already looked, so you can avoid repeating research steps unnecessarily. This is especially critical if you will be working on the project for an extended period of time or if you are working with other people in completing the research. You will also have all the information you need for proper citations. Moreover, if it happens that your project presents novel or complex questions for which there are no definitive answers, careful note taking will allow you to demonstrate that you undertook comprehensive research to try to answer those questions.

Note taking is an individualized process, and there is no single right way to do it. Some online services will keep track of your research by collecting a list of searches you run and documents you view. You may be able to name and save a record of your searches. This is useful, but unless you conduct all of your research with a single research service, it will not be a complete record of your search process, especially if you do some research in print. You may be able to download your search history so that you can integrate information from multiple services into a single record of your own, which you can then annotate with your own notes about steps that did and did not lead to useful information.

Once you begin locating specific authorities, you will need to organize what you find. Online services may allow you to create folders for research projects. You can also create your own folders outside of any research service to collect information on your project.

When you save or download documents, you may want to add notes to them. Online services may have functions that allow you to add sticky notes with notes about the document as a whole. You may also be able to highlight or mark text and append notes at particular locations within a document. You can also do these things without using a research service's tools. Free and inexpensive sticky note software is available, and many programs have commenting functions you can use to add notes to documents.

When you find useful information, you must decide how to organize your research, which documents or snippets to save, and what notes to add to what you have saved. You will probably want to begin by making a folder for all material related to the project as a whole. Sub-folders for research materials, your notes, and any factual documents related to the project may be useful. With respect to research materials, you may want to segregate content by issue if you are researching multiple issues or by type of authority if you are researching a single issue.

When it comes to saving documents, there is a constant tension between stopping to read what you find and saving the document for later. Most people save more than they need, and many students use collecting and saving documents as a procrastination technique, promising themselves that they will read the information later. Excessive downloading or printing will not improve your research. Certainly, having access to key authorities is important for accurate analysis, quotation, and citation. Facing a huge, disorganized collection of information, however, can be demoralizing, especially because most of the information will probably prove to be irrelevant in the end if you have not made thoughtful choices about what to save.

The fact is that you will not know for certain at the beginning of your research which authorities you should save and which you should not. Only as you begin to understand the contours of the legal issue will the relevance (or irrelevance) of individual legal authorities become apparent to you. Therefore, you should conduct some research before you begin saving material. As you delve into the research, you may find that you need to go back to materials you bypassed originally. You may also find it helpful to have a "maybe" folder for your research where you can collect authorities that you are not sure will be helpful. If you do this, however, it is important to return to that information periodically to assess its usefulness.

When you find information you want to save, you may be able to choose between saving the entire document or just a snippet. The benefit of saving a snippet is that you have the precise content that appears relevant.

Saving snippets also presents several potential pitfalls. The passage that seemed most relevant to you at one time may not turn out to be the best part of the document upon later reflection. You also run the risk of taking a passage out of context and representing it inaccurately in your analysis. If you save only snippets, you may be tempted to use a collection of snippets pasted into a document as a substitute for synthesis of the authorities. This can also lead to inadvertent plagiarism if each snippet is not properly cited.

There are times when just a snippet will do, such as when only a few pages out of a lengthy document are relevant to your research. You should be cautious, however, when choosing to save only snippets of documents. Often the better practice is saving the entire document even if you do not plan to use the entire document to analyze your research question.

The next step in documenting your research is deciding which notes to add to the item you save. For most items you will want to note the following information:

Citation	You need this information for two reasons: First, it will force you to pay attention to the status and weight of the authority so you can determine whether it is binding or nonbinding. Even if you use an online service that includes this information automatically when you save the document, you should note it yourself anyway so that you take account of the document's authoritative value. Second, if you use your research in a written document, you will need this information to cite your work properly. The information you put in your research notes does not need to be in proper citation form, but enough information for a proper citation should be included here. Note that citations provided by publishers are often not in the proper format for inclusion in a legal document.
Method of locating the document	This could include references to a secondary source that led you to the authority or the search terms you used in an index or database. Noting this information will help you assess which search approaches are most effective. A sticky note or comment at the beginning of the document is a good place to record this information.
The database or source for the document	If you use a folder in an online service, you may not need to note this. If you create your own folder, you should note where you located the item.
Summary of relevant information	This might be a few sentences or a few paragraphs depending on the document and its relevance. Making a note about why you saved the item may jog your memory about its relevance when you go back to

review it later, especially if you put the document into a "maybe" file.

Updating information Note whether the document has been updated and the method of updating. If you are researching in print, you should note the date of any pocket part or supplement.

This might not be the only information you need to note. If you search by subject, you might want to note the most useful subject categories you used. You also might want to make notes or highlight text within the body of a document to make the relevant portions easy for you to find. At a minimum, however, you should keep track of the pieces of information listed above.

Although many people keep notes in digital form and download most of their research material, some people still do better with hard copy. The physical acts of printing important sources, organizing them under tabs in a binder or stacking them in piles on the floor, and marking key portions with a highlighter and sticky notes can give you a different perspective on what you have found. If you have trouble visualizing the big picture of your project with a digital filing system, consider working with at least some of your research in hard copy as an alternative.

b. Deciding When to Stop

Deciding when your research is complete can be difficult. The more research you do, the more comfortable you will be with the process, and the more you will develop an internal sense of when a project is complete. In your first few research assignments in law school, however, you will probably feel uncertain about when to stop because you will have little prior experience to draw upon in making that decision.

One issue that affects a person's sense of when to stop is personal work style. Some people are anxious to begin writing and therefore stop researching after they locate a few sources that seem relevant. Others put off writing by continuing to research, thinking that the answer will become apparent if they just keep looking a little bit more. Being aware of your work style will help you determine whether you have stopped too soon or are continuing your research beyond what is necessary for the assignment.

Of course, the amount of time you have and the work product you are expected to produce will affect the ending point for your research. If you are instructed to report back in half an hour with your research results, you know when you will need to stop. In general, however, you will know that you have come full circle in your research when, after following a comprehensive research path through a variety of sources, the authorities you locate start to refer back to each other and the new sources you consult fail to reveal significant new information.

The fact that a few of the sources you have located appear relevant does not mean it is time to stop researching. Until you have explored other potential research avenues, you should continue your work. It might be that the authorities you initially locate will turn out to be the most relevant, but you cannot have confidence in that result until you research additional authorities. On the other hand, you can always keep looking for one more case or one more article to support your analysis, but at some point the benefit of continuing to research will be too small to justify the additional effort. It is unlikely that one magical source exists that is going to resolve your research issue. If the issue were clear, you probably would not have been asked to research it. If you developed a comprehensive research strategy and followed it until you came full circle in your research, it is probably time to stop.

C. FINDING HELP

Even if you follow all of the steps outlined in this chapter, from time to time, you will not be able to find what you need. The two most common situations that arise are not being able to find any authority on an issue and finding an overwhelming amount of information.

1. WHAT TO DO IF YOU ARE UNABLE TO FIND ANYTHING

If you have researched several different sources and are unable to find anything, it is time to take a different approach. You should not expect the material you need to appear effortlessly, and blind alleys are inevitable if you approach a problem creatively. Nevertheless, if you find that you really cannot locate any information on an issue, consider the following possibilities:

■ MAKE SURE YOU UNDERSTAND THE PROBLEM

One possibility is that you have misunderstood a critical aspect of the problem. If diligent research truly yields nothing, you might want to go back to the person who gave you the assignment to make sure you correctly noted all of the factual information you need and have understood the assignment correctly.

■ RETHINK YOUR SEARCH TERMS

Have you expanded the breadth and depth of your search terms? You might be researching the right concepts but not have expressed them in a way that yields useful information. Expanding your search terms will allow you to look not only more widely for information, but also more narrowly. For example, if you have searched unsuccessfully using *moving vehicle* as a search term for authority involving transportation equipment, you might need to move to more concrete terms, such as *automobile* or *car.*

In addition, you might need to rethink search terms directed to applicable legal theories. If you have focused on a theory of recovery for which you have not been able to locate authority, you might need to think about other ways to approach the problem. Try not to become so wedded to a legal theory that you pursue it to the exclusion of other viable claims or defenses.

■ USE SECONDARY SOURCES

If you did not consult secondary sources originally, you might want to take that route to find the information you need. The material on the issue might be scattered through many subject areas or statutory sections so that it is difficult to compile the relevant subset of information without secondary sources that tie disparate threads of authority together. In addition, the search terms that seemed applicable when you started your research might, in fact, not be helpful. Secondary sources can help point you in the right direction.

Another possibility is that you might be looking for the wrong type of authority or in the wrong jurisdiction. Although a content-driven search will retrieve multiple types of authority, pre-filtering by the wrong jurisdiction will take you in the wrong direction. If you are using source-driven searching, you may need to look in other sources if, for example, statutes as well as cases apply to the situation. Secondary sources can help you determine what type of primary authority is likely to be relevant to the situation.

Finally, secondary sources can help you determine whether you are facing a question of first impression. If the controlling jurisdiction simply has not faced this question yet, secondary sources should direct you to jurisdictions that have. If no jurisdiction has resolved the issue, secondary sources that analyse the law might identify arguments you can make for resolving the question.

2. WHAT TO DO IF YOU FIND AN OVERWHELMING AMOUNT OF MATERIAL

The same strategies that will help you if you are unable to find any material will also help if you find an overwhelming amount of material. Making sure you understand the problem, of course, is critical. Rethinking your search terms to narrow your approach can also help. If you located information primarily using word searches, you might want to try searching by subject, and vice versa. Consulting secondary sources, however, is probably the most useful strategy. Synthesizing large amounts of authority is difficult. Secondary sources can help you identify the key authorities and otherwise limit the scope of the information on the issue.

Another consideration here is the scope of your research. If much of the authority you have located is secondary authority or nonbinding primary authority, you might need to refocus on binding primary authority from the controlling jurisdiction. If the controlling jurisdiction has a sufficient amount of authority for thorough analysis of the issue, you might not need to cite nonbinding authority. You might also need to narrow the scope of your research by limiting the legal theories you are considering. If some are clearly more viable than others and you already have an overwhelming amount of authority, you might want to focus on the theories that seem to provide your client with the best chances of prevailing.

Even when you take these steps, finding an overwhelming amount of material is not uncommon with content-driven searching. Because the results include many types of authority and because of the way the search algorithms work, it is not unusual for a content-driven search to return thousands or tens of thousands of documents. This is obviously too much information to be useful.

With content-driven searching, using the relevancy rankings and filtering the search results are critical. Although you should not assume that the very best authority will be the first item in the search results, you must rely to some extent on the relevancy rankings when a search retrieves 10,000 documents. Those at the bottom of the list are not likely to be very relevant. Post-search filtering is also important. Even when you pre-filter by jurisdiction, you may retrieve both state and related federal information or cases from all levels of court within the state. Limiting the results to the controlling tribunal or a specific publication, using a date restriction, and searching for terms within the initial results are all good strategies for focusing on the most relevant information.

D. SAMPLE RESEARCH PLANS

The research plans in **Figures 11.3** through **11.6** are intended to help you develop a coherent research strategy for four common types of research: state common-law research, state statutory research, federal statutory research, and federal and state procedural research. These plans are representative samples of how you could approach the research process and may provide a useful starting point for your own research planning.

1. STATE COMMON-LAW RESEARCH

FIGURE 11.3 **FLOWCHART FOR STATE COMMON-LAW RESEARCH**

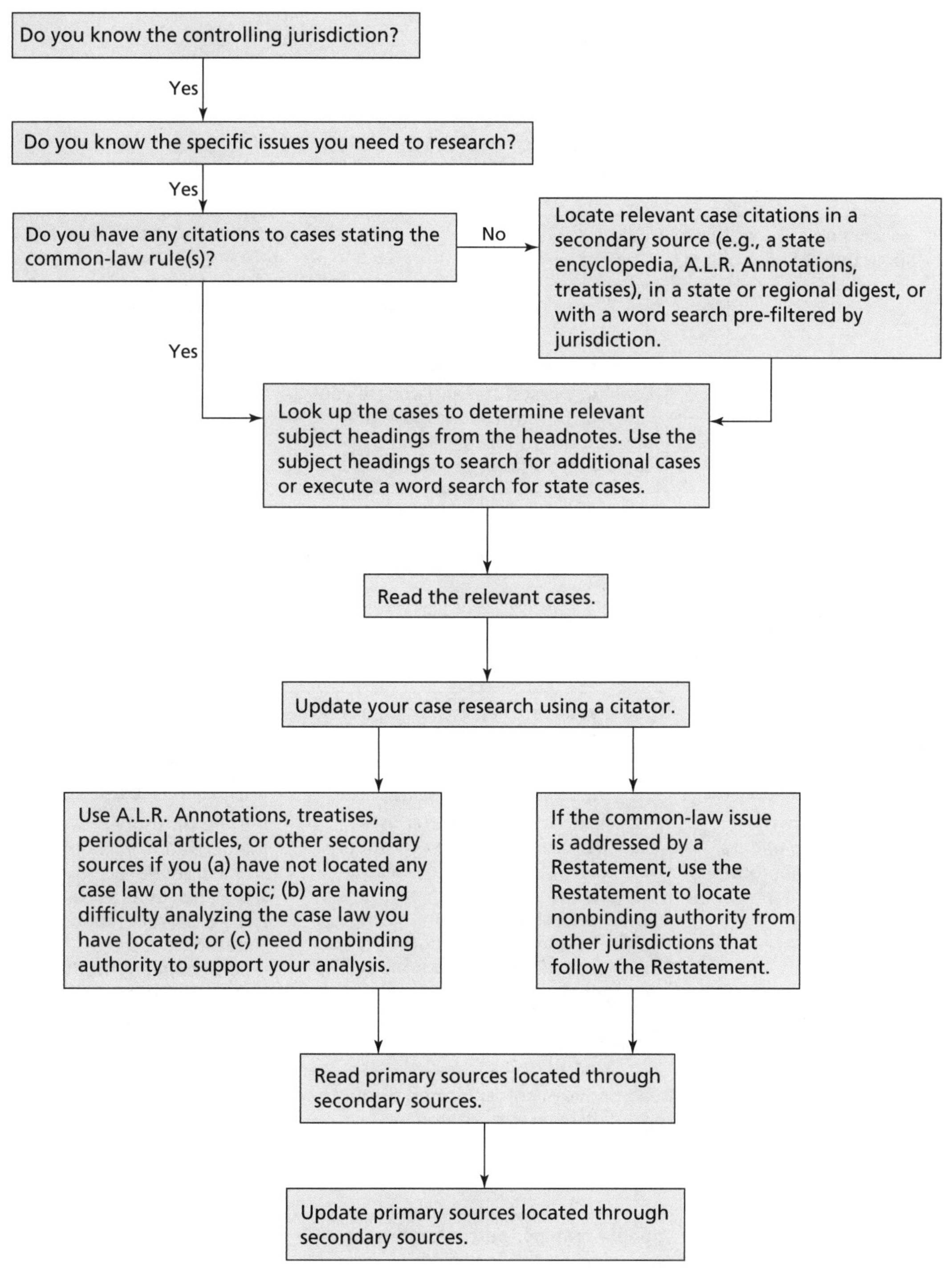

2. STATE STATUTORY RESEARCH

FIGURE 11.4 **FLOWCHART FOR STATE STATUTORY RESEARCH**

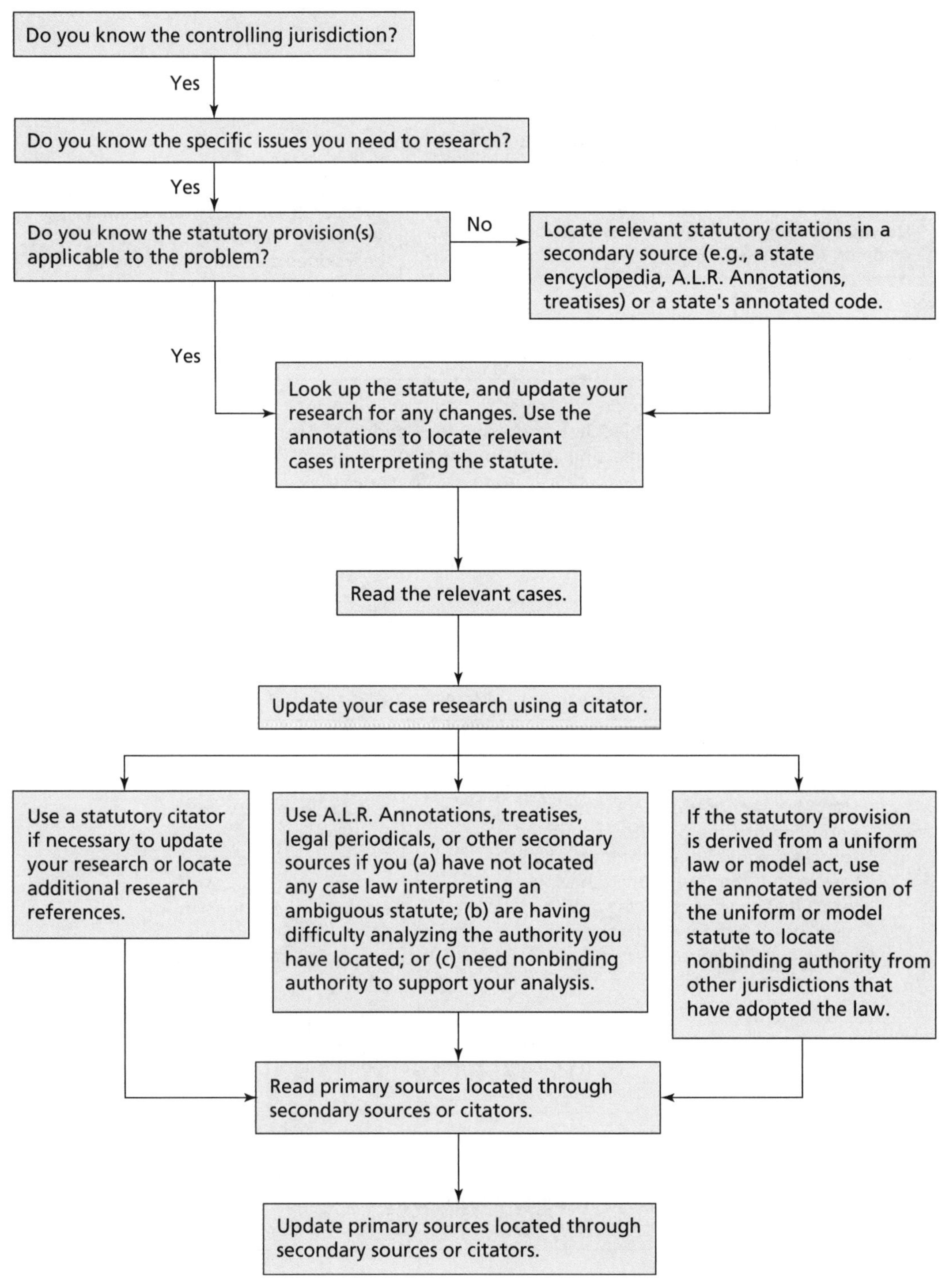

3. FEDERAL STATUTORY RESEARCH

FIGURE 11.5 **FLOWCHART FOR FEDERAL STATUTORY RESEARCH**

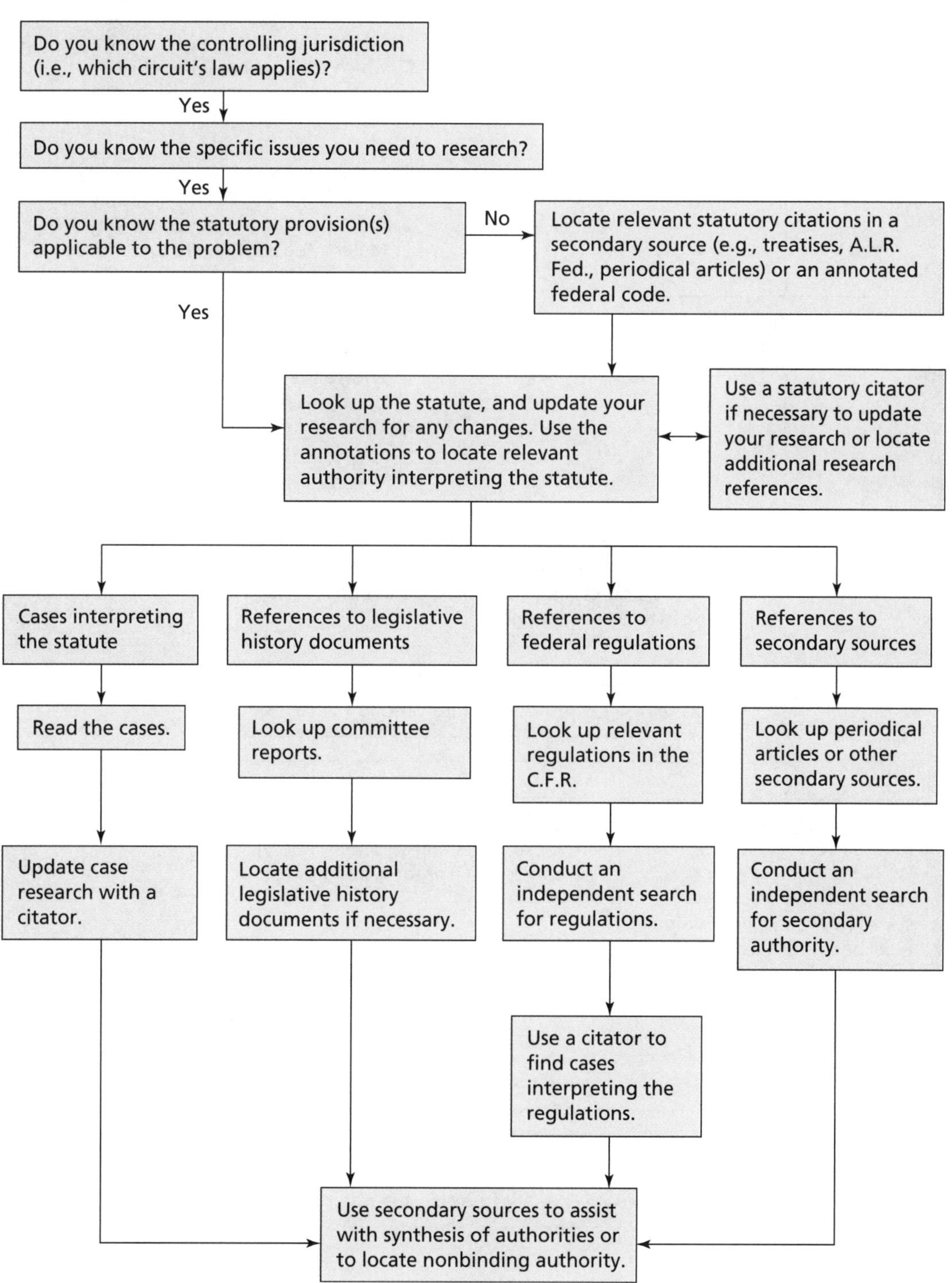

4. FEDERAL OR STATE PROCEDURAL RESEARCH

FIGURE 11.6 **FLOWCHART FOR RESEARCHING RULES OF PROCEDURE**

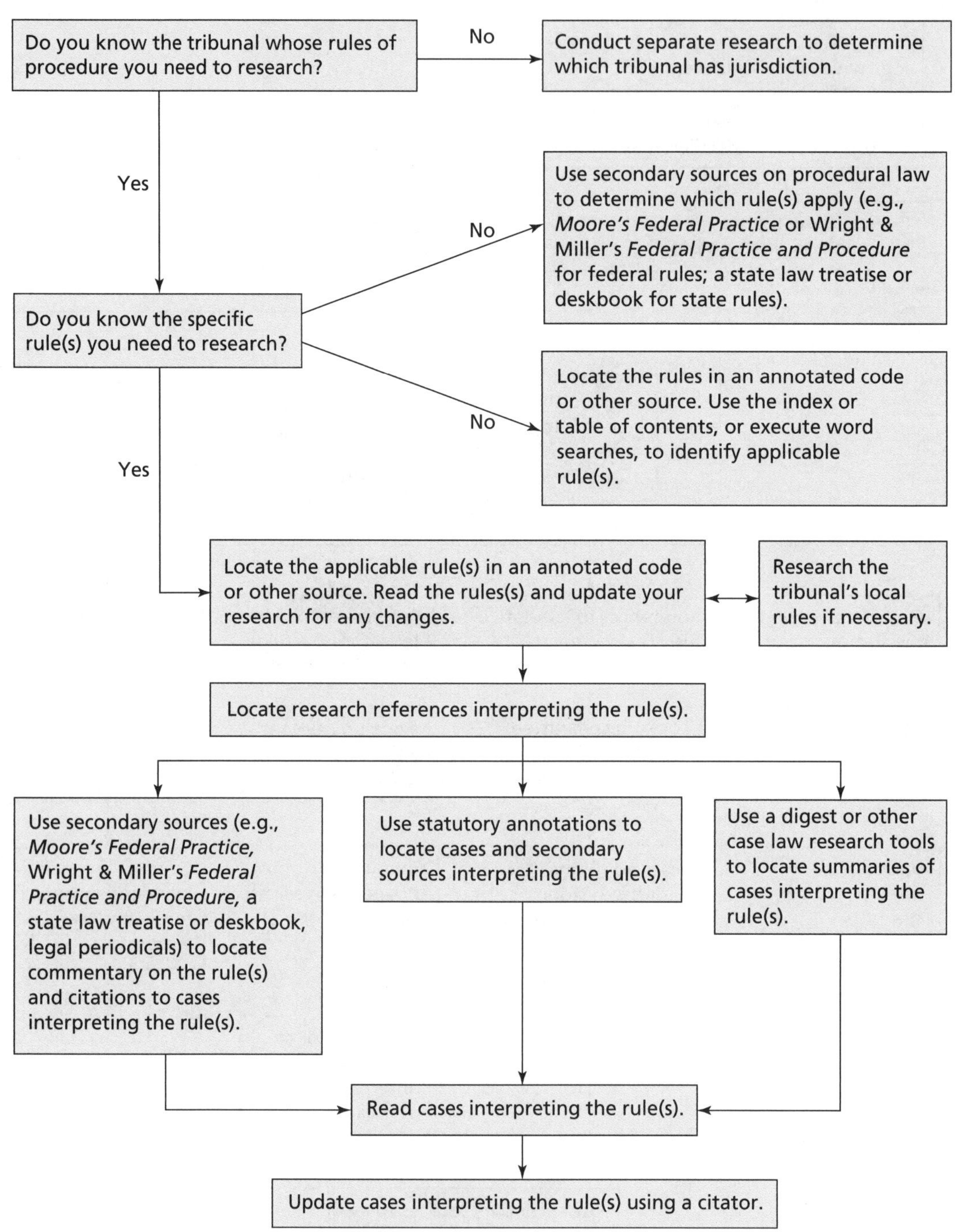

E. RESEARCH CHECKLISTS

1. CHECKLIST FOR DEVELOPING AN EFFECTIVE RESEARCH PLAN

1. OBTAIN PRELIMINARY INFORMATION ON THE PROBLEM

- ☐ Determine the due date, work product expected, limits on research tools to be used, controlling jurisdiction (if known), and whether nonbinding authority should be located (if known).
- ☐ If permitted, find out useful research tools, background on the law or terms of art, and whether other written materials or individuals with special expertise should be consulted.

2. PLAN THE STEPS IN YOUR RESEARCH

- ☐ Develop a preliminary issue statement.
- ☐ Generate a list of search terms.
- ☐ Identify the type and sequence of research tasks by identifying what you know, what you do not yet know, and how best to fill in the blanks.
  - Use what you already know about the research issue (e.g., jurisdiction) to narrow the field of legal information before you begin searching.
  - Use the information you already know to determine whether source- or content-driven searching is most efficient for your task.
  - Use secondary sources to narrow the field further. When you are ready to review primary authority, focus on binding authority first.
  - Locate nonbinding authority later, if necessary:
    - to buttress an analysis largely resolved by binding primary authority;
    - to locate factually analogous cases from other jurisdictions;
    - to make an analogy to another area of law when the applicable rule is unclear;
    - to locate commentary or applicable rules from other jurisdictions on an issue of first impression.
  - Determine the best mix of print and online research tools for your research project.

3. WORK EFFECTIVELY

- ☐ Keep effective notes.
- ☐ Stop researching when your research has come full circle.
- ☐ Find help if you need it.

- If you are unable to find anything or find too much material, make sure you understand the problem, rethink your search terms, consult secondary sources, and reevaluate the legal theories you are pursuing.

2. MASTER CHECKLIST OF RESEARCH SOURCES

The following is an abbreviated collection of the research checklists that appear at the end of the preceding chapters in this text. This master checklist may help you develop your research plan. It may also be useful to you as you conduct research.

Secondary Source Research

1. LEGAL ENCYCLOPEDIAS

- ☐ Use for very general background information and limited citations to primary authority, but not for in-depth analysis of a topic.
- ☐ Locate information in print by using the subject index or table of contents, locating relevant sections in the main volumes, and updating with the pocket part.
- ☐ Use source-driven word or table of contents searches in a legal encyclopedia in Westlaw and Lexis Advance.
- ☐ Use content-driven word searches in Westlaw and Lexis Advance by executing a search, reviewing results for secondary sources, and filtering the content by source or other appropriate criteria.

2. TREATISES

- ☐ Use for an in-depth discussion and some analysis of an area of law and for citations to primary authority.
- ☐ Locate treatises in print through the online catalog; locate information within a treatise by using the subject index or table of contents, locating material in the main volumes, and updating with the pocket part.
- ☐ Use source-driven word or table of contents searches in Westlaw, Lexis Advance, and Bloomberg Law to access selected treatises.
- ☐ Use content-driven word searches in Westlaw, Lexis Advance, and Bloomberg Law by executing a search, reviewing results for secondary sources, and filtering the content by source or other appropriate criteria.

3. LEGAL PERIODICALS

- ☐ Use for background information, citations to primary authority, in-depth analysis of a narrow topic, or information on a conflict in the law or an undeveloped area of the law.
- ☐ Use the LegalTrac and ILP indexes online to locate citations to legal periodicals and full text of selected articles.

☐ Use Westlaw and Lexis Advance to access most legal periodicals; use Bloomberg Law to access selected legal periodicals.
☐ Use HeinOnline, SSRN, and the Digital Commons Network to locate legal periodicals in .pdf format.
☐ Locate selected legal periodicals using a law-related website or general Internet search engine.

4. *AMERICAN LAW REPORTS*
☐ Use A.L.R. Annotations for an overview of an area of law and citations to primary authority.
☐ Locate material in a print A.L.R. by using the A.L.R. Index, locating material in the main volumes, and updating with the pocket part.
☐ Use source-driven word or table of contents searches in Westlaw and Lexis Advance to access A.L.R. Annotations; use Westlaw for the first series of A.L.R.
☐ Use content-driven word searches in Westlaw and Lexis Advance by executing a search, reviewing results for secondary sources, and filtering the content by source or other appropriate criteria.

5. RESTATEMENTS
☐ Use for research into common-law subjects and to locate binding and nonbinding authority from jurisdictions that have adopted a Restatement.
☐ Locate information within a print Restatement by using the subject index or table of contents to find Restatement sections in the Restatement Rules volumes, locating case summaries in the noncumulative Appendix volumes, and updating the Appendix volumes with the pocket part.
☐ Use Westlaw, Lexis Advance, and Bloomberg Law to access Restatement rules and case annotations.

6. UNIFORM LAWS AND MODEL ACTS
☐ Use to interpret a law adopted by a legislature and to locate nonbinding authority from other jurisdictions that have adopted the law.
☐ Locate in print using *Uniform Laws Annotated, Master Edition* (ULA) by using the *Directory of Uniform Acts and Codes: Tables and Index,* locating relevant provisions in the main volumes, and updating with the pocket part.
☐ Use Westlaw, Lexis Advance, and Bloomberg Law to access selected uniform laws and model acts.

Case Research

1. RESEARCH CASES WITH A PRINT DIGEST
☐ Select an appropriate digest.

- ☐ Locate topics and key numbers from the headnotes in case on point, the Descriptive-Word Index, or a topic entry.
- ☐ Read the case summaries, using the court and date abbreviations to target appropriate cases.
- ☐ Update with the pocket part for the subject volume and any cumulative or noncumulative interim pamphlets.

2. ONLINE CASE RESEARCH—SEARCHING BY SUBJECT

- ☐ In Westlaw, search for cases by subject using the **Key Numbers** function or from the headnote links in a case on point.
- ☐ In Lexis Advance, search for cases by subject using the **Practice Area or Industry** filter or from the headnote links in a case on point.
- ☐ In Bloomberg Law, search for cases by subject using **Points of Law** or from the headnote links in a case on point that has BNA Headnotes.

3. ONLINE CASE RESEARCH—WORD SEARCHING

- ☐ Execute source-driven word searches in Westlaw, Lexis Advance, and Bloomberg Law by selecting a case law database.
- ☐ Execute content-driven word searches in Westlaw, Lexis Advance, and Bloomberg Law and filter the results to target appropriate cases; pre-filter by jurisdiction if possible to limit search results.
- ☐ In Google Scholar, execute word searches for published cases.
- ☐ In Fastcase, execute word searches; use the Interactive Timeline, tag cloud, and Forecite to refine search results.
- ☐ In Casetext, use CARA to generate search results from an uploaded document instead of a search query.

Research with Citators

1. USE SHEPARD'S IN LEXIS ADVANCE

- ☐ Access Shepard's using the ***Shepardize*® this document** link from a relevant case.
- ☐ Interpret the entry.
  - Use the Shepard's Signal as a qualified indicator of case status.
  - View **Appellate History**, **Citing Decisions**, and **Other Citing Sources** for case history and sources that have cited the original case.
  - Use case history and treatment descriptions and headnote references to identify the most relevant citing cases.
  - Filter the display to focus on the most relevant information.
  - Use the **Map** view for a snapshot of case history in chart form and the **Grid** view for a snapshot of treatment by later citing cases in chart form.

2. USE KEYCITE IN WESTLAW

- ☐ Access KeyCite information under the tabs accompanying a relevant case.
- ☐ Interpret the entry.
  - Use the KeyCite status flag as a qualified indicator of case status.
  - View the **Negative Treatment, History**, and **Citing References** tabs for case history and sources that have cited the original case.
  - Use case history and treatment descriptions and headnote references to identify the most relevant cases.
  - Filter the display to focus on the most relevant information.

3. USE BCITE IN BLOOMBERG LAW

- ☐ Access BCite from a relevant case using the **BCite Analysis** link.
- ☐ Interpret the entry.
  - Use the BCite indicator as a qualified indicator of case status.
  - View **Direct History, Case Analysis**, and **Citing Documents** for case history and sources within Bloomberg Law that have cited the original case.
  - Use case history and treatment descriptions to identify the most relevant citing cases.
- ☐ Filter the display to focus on the most relevant information.

Statutory Research

1. LOCATE A STATUTE

- ☐ Use a subject index or popular name table in print.
- ☐ Use Westlaw, Lexis Advance, and Bloomberg Law to access state and federal statutes online using word, table of contents, or popular name searches; in Westlaw, use the statutory index.
- ☐ In Westlaw, Lexis Advance, and Bloomberg Law, pre-filter by jurisdiction and execute a content-driven search to retrieve statutes and other authorities; filter the results to target appropriate statutes.
- ☐ For free online research, locate statutes on government or general legal research websites.

2. READ THE STATUTE AND ANY ACCOMPANYING RESEARCH REFERENCES

- ☐ In an annotated code, use the annotations to locate authorities interpreting the statute.
- ☐ In Bloomberg Law, use the **SmartCode** function to retrieve citations to cases that have cited a statute.

3. UPDATE YOUR RESEARCH

- ☐ With print research, check the pocket part accompanying the main volume and any cumulative or noncumulative supplements accompanying the code.

- ☐ With state or federal statutory research, update your research or find additional research references using a statutory citator such as Shepard's in Lexis Advance or KeyCite in Westlaw.
- ☐ With free online sources, check the date of the statute and update your research accordingly; consider using a statutory citator to update your research and find additional research references.

Federal Legislative History Research

1. IDENTIFY THE SCOPE OF YOUR RESEARCH

- ☐ Determine whether you need to find the history of a particular statute or material on a general subject.

2. LOCATE A COMPILED LEGISLATIVE HISTORY

- ☐ Use the library's online catalog; Johnson, *Sources of Compiled Legislative Histories;* Reams, *Federal Legislative Histories;* HeinOnline's U.S. Federal Legislative History Title Collection; or compiled legislative histories in Westlaw.

3. LOCATE COMMITTEE REPORTS, FLOOR DEBATES, AND OTHER LEGISLATIVE HISTORY DOCUMENTS FOR A SPECIFIC STATUTE

- ☐ Use annotations in U.S.C.A. to locate cross-references to U.S.C.C.A.N.
- ☐ In Westlaw, retrieve the statute and locate legislative history references under the **History** tab; retrieve a statute by public law number and use links to legislative history documents.
- ☐ In Lexis Advance, use the public law number as a search term and use the link in the search results to **View References** to the bill; view the public law and use the link to **Bill Tracking**.
- ☐ In Bloomberg Law, use the popular name of the act as a search term in **U.S. Legislative**.
- ☐ In Congress.gov and govinfo, search by bill number or public law number to retrieve legislative history documents.
- ☐ In ProQuest Congressional, use Legislative Insight to search by bill number, public law number, or *Statutes at Large* citation to locate legislative history documents.

Federal Administrative Law Research

1. LOCATE PERTINENT REGULATIONS

- ☐ Use statutory cross-references or a subject index to locate federal regulations in the C.F.R. in print.
- ☐ Use Lexis Advance to locate an annotated, unofficial version of the C.F.R.; use Shepard's to locate citations to cases and other sources that cite a regulation.
- ☐ Use Westlaw to locate an annotated, unofficial version of the C.F.R.; use KeyCite to locate citations to cases and other sources that cite a regulation.

- ☐ Use Bloomberg Law to locate an unannotated, unofficial version of the C.F.R.; use the **SmartCode** function to locate citations to cases that cite a regulation.
- ☐ Use govinfo or other government websites to locate unannotated C.F.R. provisions; use govinfo for an official version of a regulation.

2. UPDATE GOVINFO RESEARCH WITH THE e-CFR

3. UPDATE C.F.R. RESEARCH WITH OFFICIAL SOURCES

- ☐ Update from the date of the C.F.R. volume through the end of the prior month by using the most recent LSA to find *Federal Register* references affecting the regulation.
- ☐ Update from the end of the prior month to the present by using the cumulative table of CFR Parts Affected for the current month in the Reader Aids section in the back of the most recent issue of the *Federal Register.*

4. CONTACT THE AGENCY FOR ADDITIONAL INFORMATION ON RECENT OR PROPOSED REGULATORY CHANGES

Online Legal Research

1. SELECT AN ONLINE RESEARCH SERVICE

- ☐ Consider the scope of coverage and cost.

2. SELECT A SEARCH TECHNIQUE

- ☐ Retrieve a document from its citation.
- ☐ Execute a source-driven search by selecting a database before executing a search.
- ☐ Execute a content-driven search by pre-filtering by jurisdiction, executing a word search, and filtering the results.

3. PLAN AND EXECUTE A SEARCH

- ☐ For word searches, consider the search options: terms and connectors, natural language, and plain language.
- ☐ Be aware of the different word search options and tailor your search approach accordingly.
- ☐ Use terms and connectors searching effectively in an initial search by developing the initial search terms, expanding the breadth and depth of the search, specifying the relationships among the terms, and using a field or segment search if appropriate.

4. REVIEW AND FILTER SEARCH RESULTS

- ☐ Relevance, date, or other result ranking choices affect which documents appear at the top of the search results.
- ☐ Narrowing searches will be terms and connectors searches even if the initial search is not; use terms and connectors commands to add search terms, focus on terms in the initial search, or change the relationships among terms in the initial search.

5. USE ADDITIONAL TOOLS FOR EFFECTIVE ONLINE RESEARCH

- ☐ Use an alert or clipping service to keep research up to date.
- ☐ Use publicly available sources.
  - Locate useful sites to obtain background information on a topic or citations to primary authority.
  - Assess the credibility of the source.
  - Save or print copies of useful pages.
  - Verify and update any legal authorities you locate.

APPENDIX A

Selected Online Research Resources

FEDERAL GOVERNMENT WEBSITES

Congress.gov
http://congress.gov
The official website for U.S. federal legislative information. This site contains committee reports, the *Congressional Record,* and other legislative history documents.

govinfo
http://www.govinfo.gov
The federal government's official online source for many government publications, including the *Code of Federal Regulations* and the *Federal Register.* Provides access to a wide range of legislative history documents. Links to the e-CFR for updating federal regulatory research and the CyberCemetery of Former Federal Web Sites for locating archived versions of federal websites. The govinfo website is the successor to the Federal Digital System (FDSys).

Library of Congress
http://www.loc.gov
Search the online catalog of the Library of Congress and locate a wealth of legal and general information.

United States House of Representatives Office of the Law Revision Counsel
http://uscode.house.gov
This site contains an online version of the *United States Code.* It is not an official source, but it is regularly updated, making it more useful than other free online sources of the federal code.

United States Supreme Court
http://www.supremecourtus.gov
The site for the U.S. Supreme Court.

USA.gov
http://www.usa.gov
The U.S. government's official portal to a wide range of governmental resources.

United States Courts of Appeals
http://www.[identifier].uscourts.gov
Each federal circuit court of appeals has its own website; insert *ca* and the number of the circuit as the identifier in the URL above to access a numbered circuit's site, e.g., *ca1* for the First Circuit; *ca2* for the Second Circuit, etc. The Federal Circuit is identified as *cafc*, and the District of Columbia Circuit is identified as *cadc*.

STATE GOVERNMENT WEBSITES

National Center for State Courts
http://www.ncsc.org
Provides links to court websites for each state.

National Conference of State Legislatures
http://www.ncsl.org
Provides links to legislative websites for each state.

Every state government has a portal that provides access to legal information for the state. You can locate a state's website using a search engine or through the library websites listed below.

LIBRARY WEBSITES

Law library websites can be used to search for a wide range of legal authorities, including state and federal cases and statutes, administrative materials, secondary sources, and legal news. Those listed here are good starting points for research, but many other library websites are also useful for legal research.

Cornell Law School's Legal Information Institute
http://www.law.cornell.edu

Georgetown Law Library
http://www.law.georgetown.edu/library

Washburn University School of Law WashLaw Legal Research on the Web
http://www.washlaw.edu

LEGAL RESEARCH WEBSITES

Some of these websites provide access to a wide range of legal materials, while others are more specialized. Some can be accessed free of charge; others are fee-based services.

Free Services

All Law
http://www.alllaw.com

American Bar Association: The Lawlink Legal Research Jumpstation
http://www.americanbar.org
Search for *lawlink jumpstation* on the ABA website.

FindLaw
http://lp.findlaw.com

Google Scholar
http://scholar.google.com
Searches case law and scholarly literature.

HG.org
http://www.hg.org

LLRX.com
http://www.llrx.com

Fee-based Services (with free access provided to students)

Bloomberg Law
http://www.bloomberglaw.com

Casetext (including CARA)
http://casetext.com

Lexis Advance for students
http://www.lexis.com/lawschool (follow the link to Lexis Advance to access full search functionality, or use *http://advance.lexis.com*)

VersusLaw
http://www.versuslaw.com

Westlaw for law students
http://www.westlaw.com (follow the link to Westlaw to access full search functionality, or use *http://lawschool.westlaw.com*)

OTHER WEBSITES OF INTEREST

ABA Journal Blawg Directory
http://www.abajournal.com/blawgs
Contains a directory of law-related blogs.

ALWD Guide to Legal Citation
http://www.alwdonline.com
Online companion to the *ALWD Guide to Legal Citation.*

http://wklegaledu.com
Search by author name (Barger) or title and follow the appropriate link to locate updates and information on the *ALWD Guide.*

The Bluebook
http://www.legalbluebook.com
Contains the online version of the *Bluebook,* along with tips and updates available without a subscription.

The Digital Commons Network
http://network.bepress.com/law
Provides full-text access to law journals in .pdf format.

Introduction to Basic Legal Citation
http://www.law.cornell.edu/citation
Provides tips on using the *Bluebook* and *ALWD Guide.*

Internet Archive Wayback Machine
http://www.archive.org
Contains archived web pages. To see what a website displayed on a date in the past, enter the URL for the site, and select the date.

Martindale-Hubbell
http://www.martindale.com
Search for individual lawyers, firms, or government agencies employing attorneys.

SCOTUS Mapper
http://law.ubalt.edu/faculty/scotus-mapping/index.cfm (SCOTUS Mapping Project, including library of maps)

https://www.courtlistener.com/visualizations/scotus-mapper (online tool for creating maps via Court Listener)
View or create maps tracing U.S. Supreme Court doctrines.

Social Science Research Network (SSRN), Legal Scholarship Network (LSN)
http://www.ssrn.com
Provides full-text access to published and forthcoming legal periodical articles.

SUBSCRIPTION SERVICES

This list of subscription services does not include their URLs because individual users cannot access these services' search features directly from their websites. Your library may subscribe to the services listed below. If so, you may be able to access them through the library's portal.

Casemaker
: A full-text research service providing access to a range of primary authorities that is available through some state bar associations.

Fastcase
: A full-text research service providing access to a range of primary authorities that is available through some state bar associations. Some libraries subscribe to Fastcase through HeinOnline.

HeinOnline
: A service providing access to legal periodicals, legislative history documents, the *Code of Federal Regulations*, and other publications.

Index to Legal Periodicals (ILP)
: A periodical index that also provides full text of selected articles.

LegalTrac
: A periodical index that also provides full text of selected articles.

ProQuest Congressional/Legislative Insight
: A service that provides full-text access to federal legislative history documents.

Index

Bold page numbers indicate reprinted examples.